WORDS AND WORKS:
STUDIES IN MEDIEVAL ENGLISH LANGUAGE AND LITERATURE
IN HONOUR OF FRED C. ROBINSON

Fred C. Robinson

Words and Works:
Studies in Medieval English
Language and Literature
in Honour of Fred C. Robinson

EDITED BY PETER S. BAKER and NICHOLAS HOWE

UNIVERSITY OF TORONTO PRESS
TORONTO   BUFFALO   LONDON

© University of Toronto Press Incorporated 1998
Toronto   Buffalo   London
Printed in Canada

ISBN 0-8020-4153-1

Printed on acid-free paper

Canadian Cataloguing in Publication Data

Main entry under title:
  Words and works : studies in medieval English language and literature in honour
  of Fred C. Robinson

  (Toronto Old English series)
  ISBN 0-8020-4153-1

  1. English philology – Old English, ca. 450–1100 – History and criticism.
  I. Baker, Peter S. (Peter Stuart), 1952–   .   II. Howe, Nicholas.   III. Robinson,
  Fred C. (Fred Colson), 1930–   .   IV. Series.

  PE26.R62W67 1998   429   C97-932010-0

University of Toronto Press acknowledges the financial assistance to its publishing
program of the Canada Council for the Arts and the Ontario Arts Council.

Contents

Preface

ægwæþres sceal

scearp scyldwiga   gescad witan,

worda ond worca,   se þe wel þenceð

The title for this volume of essays echoes the speech of the Danish coastguard as he explains to young Beowulf the need to judge a man by his words and works. The coastguard's phrase *worda ond worca*, rendered into Modern English, evokes wonderfully the reasons the students, friends, and colleagues of Fred C. Robinson have joined together on his sixty-fifth birthday to celebrate his achievements as a medievalist: he has left his mark on the field through his words and his works.

His scholarship on Old English – his works in words – includes essays ranging in subject from the establishment of texts to their interpretation, from the study of semantics to the study of names. He is also the author of major books, equally wide-ranging in scope, whose names we cite here: *Old English Literature: A Select Bibliography* (1970), *A Bibliography of Publications on Old English Literature to the End of 1972* (with Stanley B. Greenfield, 1980), *A Guide to Old English* (with Bruce Mitchell, third through fifth editions, 1982–94), *'Beowulf' and the Appositive Style* (1985), *Old English Verse Texts from Many Sources* (with E.G. Stanley, 1991), *The Tomb of Beowulf* (1993), and *The Editing of Old English* (1994). The words of these works, their governing ideas, have entered the working vocabulary of Anglo-Saxonists. To speak of 'appositive style' or the 'most immediate context of Old English literature', of 'artful ambiguities' or the 'afterlife of Old English', is to acknowledge the influence of Fred Robinson's work and also to signal a particular form of scholarly inquiry in early medieval studies.

In ways no one of us alone can fully know, he has worked with tireless energy and personal modesty for the common good of Old English studies and, on a larger scale, for the good of medieval studies. Most visibly, he served the Medieval Academy of America as its president in 1984. He has also worked actively as an advisory editor of the *Dictionary of Old English* since its inception in 1970, and he has served on the editorial boards of such distinguished series and journals as Anglistica, Early English Manuscripts in Facsimile, the *Journal of English Linguistics*, and *Anglo-Saxon England*. He has trained generations of students at Stanford, Cornell, and Yale since he received his PhD from the University of North Carolina under the tutelage of Norman E. Eliason. And, as many of us have reason to recall with gratitude, he has, over the years, aided numerous Anglo-Saxonists – veterans and beginners, students and strangers – with generous letters of recommendation, valuable references to obscure but relevant works, and postcards of encouragement.

The title of this volume honours Fred Robinson in another way, for it reminds us that his achievements as a scholar emanate from his love of words as the resonant constituents of language and his love of works as the larger forms into which words cohere. A philologist gifted at tracing the dynamic shape of texts and a critic gifted at giving voice to mute Old English words and names – only as we evoke these two styles of inquiry can we do justice to the achievements of Fred Robinson. It is thus appropriate that this volume should contain both philological and critical essays. Further, since both the life and the afterlife of Old English must be celebrated in any festschrift that lays claim to doing fair honour to Fred Robinson, these essays deal both with Anglo-Saxon language and culture itself and with later historical moments, as Anglo-Saxon texts and themes reappeared to shape the words and works of later writers.

It is in his own spirit of generous rigour and quiet passion that we dedicate these essays to Fred Robinson. He has been friend as well as teacher to us, whether we studied with him in the classroom or met him in the wider scholarly world. In ways that we hope will please him, we think the essays in this book will inspire others to enter the world of medieval studies. In that faith in scholarly continuity, that welcoming love for all things Old English, we can best locate the words and works of Fred C. Robinson.

PETER S. BAKER
NICHOLAS HOWE

Acknowledgments

We wish to thank Professor Linda Peterson and the Yale University Department of English for supporting this publication with a generous subvention.

The photographs of Cotton Tiberius A. vi (pp. 109–11), Cotton Tiberius B. i (pp. 112–14), and Cotton Tiberius B. iv (pp. 115–17) are published by permission of the British Library.

The photograph of the painting by Zeshin Shibata (p. 61) is published by permission of the Sensoji Temple, Asakusa, Tokyo.

The poetry in 'Praise and Lament' (pp. 293–310) has been quoted by permission, as follows:

Excerpts from *W.H. Auden: Collected Poems* by W.H. Auden, edited by Edward Mendelson. Copyright © 1976 by Edward Mendelson. Reprinted by permission of Random House, Inc. Reprinted by permission of Faber and Faber, Ltd. Publishers.

Excerpts from *Thom Gunn: Collected Poems*. Copyright © 1994 by Thom Gunn. Reprinted by permission of Farrar, Straus & Giroux, Inc. Reprinted by permission of Faber and Faber, Ltd. Publishers.

Excerpts from *Geoffrey Hill: New and Collected Poems 1952–1992*. Copyright © by Geoffrey Hill. Reprinted by permission of Houghton Mifflin Co. All rights reserved. Reproduced by permission of Penguin Books Ltd.

Abbreviations

ASE	*Anglo-Saxon England*
ASPR	Anglo-Saxon Poetic Records
BaP	Bibliothek der angelsächsischen Prosa
BAR	British Archaeological Reports
BAV	Bibliotheca apostolica vaticana
BL	British Library
CCCC	Cambridge, Corpus Christi College
CCSL	Corpus Christianorum, Series Latina
CCCM	Corpus Christianorum, Continuatio Medievalis
CUL	Cambridge University Library
DOE	*Dictionary of Old English*
EEMF	Early English Manuscripts in Facsimile
EETS	Early English Text Society
	e.s. Extra Series
	s.s. Supplementary Series
MED	*Middle English Dictionary*, ed. Hans Kurath, Sherman M. Kuhn, et al. (Ann Arbor 1952–)
MGH AA	Monumenta Germaniae Historica, Auctores Antiquissimi
MGH PL	Monumenta Germaniae Historica, Poetae Latini
OE	Old English
OED	*Oxford English Dictionary*, ed. J.A.H. Murray et al., 2nd ed. (Oxford 1989)

WORDS AND WORKS

Who Read the Gospels in Old English?

ROY MICHAEL LIUZZA

Every book ever made was made to some purpose, though reading is not always one of them; it is sometimes difficult, however, to reconstruct these purposes from the scanty evidence that has survived. The problem of intention and audience is particularly acute in Old English studies; a corpus of mostly undated and anonymous works offers only the sketchiest indications of context, and allows the modern reader to forget at times that meaning (at least as we must look at it, historically) is a conspiracy between intention and reception. One may be tempted to imagine a homogeneous and relatively static audience – in the aristocratic hall or the monastic refectory – for a given work; it is easy to overlook the possibility that the same text may be differently understood by different groups of people and at different times in its history. Sometimes the evidence for the early context and readership of a work is disguised, or jettisoned altogether, in modern printed editions; the story of Beowulf, to give only one striking example, is situated in its manuscript among stories of Judith and St Christopher, and tales of oriental marvels; the same scribes who copied these odd works, eloquent testimony to the pervasive influence of Christian Latin culture on Old English literary taste, also copied the most important survival of old Germanic legend in Anglo-Saxon England. This 'most immediate context'[1] ought to complicate, though it too seldom has, discussions of the audience of *Beowulf*. Moreover, while the intended audience of a work can sometimes be inferred from its language and style, and the format and history of its publication, this intended audience forms only one part of the equation that makes up the meaning of a text; the actual reception and use of the work by a real audience may be quite different from what its author intended. To further complicate the matter, the number of people who experience a text or are influenced by it has little to do with the number of people who actually read it. Brian

Stock's idea of 'textual communities' has supplied a persuasive model for the use of texts which depends only partly on literacy and access to books.[2] Even if the textual community must have a focus, a literate interpreter whose place in the centre depends on his or her use of a text and whose responses to this text are mirrored and multiplied in the actions of the members of the group, the group's mediated experience is far different from any modern notion of readership, and of course leaves little trace in the codicological record. So the purpose and audience of an Old English work is often hard to discern, much less describe.

VERTICAL AND HORIZONTAL CONTEXTS

The first editors of the Old English version of the Gospels[3] placed the work firmly in the context of the religious controversies of their own age. The printer John Daye had produced Archbishop Matthew Parker's *Testimonie of Antiquitie* in 1566–67,[4] and like that work, the first edition of the Old English Gospels in 1571[5] had a polemical function: it offered a historical precedent for the English church. The Preface to this edition, signed by the martyrologist John Foxe[6] and addressed to Queen Elizabeth, argues that the Old English Gospels teach us the following lesson: 'the religion presently taught & professed in the Church at thys present, is no new reformation of thinges lately begonne, which were not before, but rather a reduction of the Church to the Pristine state of olde conformitie, which once it had, and almost lost by discontinuance of a fewe later yeares.'[7] Parker and his circle sought an ideological warrant for their own endeavours from Anglo-Saxon antiquity, a vernacular tradition giving authority to their innovations. In the margins of this first edition of the Old English Gospels is printed Parker's English translation, the 'Bishops' Bible', and one may say that the old version explicates the new as much as the new version explicates the old.

Such a juxtaposition creates a 'vertical' context: the Old English Gospels are part of the history of Bible translation. Viewed from the vertical perspective, they are indeed similar to later productions such as the 'Bishops' Bible' or the Authorized Version – freestanding works of English prose, idiomatic but more or less literal renderings, parallel to but independent from versions in more ancient languages, in effect a replacement for the older text, all of which suggests a history of democratic access to the words of Scripture. Subsequent editions of the Old English Gospels subtly reinforce the assumption that the work is similar in function as well as form to a modern translation of the Bible. Bright's pocket editions at the beginning of the century,[8] for example, followed Skeat's practice[9] of breaking the text up into chapters and verses like a modern Bible, each verse numbered and on a separate line, rather than preserving the original paragraphs and continuous prose of the Old English manuscripts. Though on the surface a fairly innocent editorial decision, this is in effect a visual argument for the use of the Old English Gospels;[10] it implies what Foxe asserted: there is a continuity, or at least a similarity of purpose, between the Old English version and a modern translation. This essay addresses that assumption, offers a re-examination of the relation between the form and the function of the Old English Gospels, and tries to view them in the 'horizontal' context of later Old English literature and Anglo-Saxon ecclesiastical practice.

There is unfortunately no explicit testimony regarding either the intention of the author or the reception of the Old English Gospels – in fact, little evidence that they were widely known. The Gospels are not excerpted anywhere in any other manuscript,[11] a circumstance which might offer some idea of what sort of texts were read alongside them. In size, format, and quality, the manuscripts containing the Old English Gospels are fairly ordinary books. They lack the decorated initials and evangelist portraits of most Latin Gospels produced at this time, their scripts are not elaborate or calligraphic, their design is not visually powerful, their size is neither big enough for a lectern nor small enough for a cowl. They were apparently never objects of veneration like the breathtaking Gospels of Kells or Lindisfarne, nor masterpieces of artistic accomplishment like the Trinity Gospels or the Winchester Bible, nor tokens of private devotion like the pocket gospel-books of the Irish monks. In terms of cost, effort, and achievement, the Old English Gospels fall squarely in the middle of the spectrum of Anglo-Saxon book production – to the extent that we can perceive such things across these centuries, they seem workaday, practical, like nothing special.

The manuscripts do suggest, however, that there was a certain amount of interest in their production. The translation exists in a fair number of copies:[12] four more or less complete manuscripts and two fragments from the eleventh century, and two complete twelfth-century manuscripts, not so many as Ælfric's *Homilies* or the glossed psalters, but more than the various pieces of the Old English Old Testament. All the manuscripts in their original states appear to have contained all four Gospels. Three of the earlier manuscripts – B, C, and Cp – are closely similar,[13] down to their orthography and punctuation, suggesting a program of publication, the production of several copies from closely related exemplars at roughly the same time. The work was obviously the object of study and use; though the translation is not without some outlandish errors, there are glosses and corrections and additions in every surviving copy, and signs that the text was revised in the interest of readability and accuracy on at least two occasions in the course of its history, once in A (s. xi med., Exeter) and separately in the twelfth-century R and its copy H, both from Canterbury, where the Old English version was apparently still regarded as worth the parchment it was written on, more than a century after the Conquest. So the lack of external evidence for the audience of the Old English Gospels stands in strange contrast to the apparent interest in its publication and dissemination – the textual evidence suggests that the work was read, and copied, and used.

Yet there is no evidence that the Old English version was regarded as an authoritative translation. Its influence on the better-known works of Old English prose is negligible. It does not seem to have been used as the basis for any other biblical translations in Old English; the gospel passages translated in the course of homilies such as those in the Blickling and Vercelli collections differ in important ways from the Old English version.[14] Ælfric, who translated substantial parts of the Gospels piecemeal in his homilies,[15] seems not to have known of this version; in the preface to the first series of *Catholic Homilies,* written around 990,[16] he says, 'Me ofhreow þæt hi ne cuþon ne næfdon þa godspellican lare on heora gewritum, butan þam mannum anum ðe þæt leden cuðon, and buton þam bocum ðe Ælfred cyning snoterlice awende of ledene on Englisc, þa synd to hæbbene'.[17] Because he seems to have known most of the Alfredian translations,[18] this statement raises the possibility that the Old English version is not older than Ælfric; on the other hand, it should be remembered that he did not know of the existence of a translation of parts of the Old Testament either. The manuscript evidence, however, offers some support for the supposition that the translation is from Ælfric's time; none of the surviving manuscripts is earlier than the year 1000 and there is nothing about their language or the Latin text from which the translation was made[19] to suggest that they are late survivals of an early tradition.[20]

Whether the Old English Gospels belong to the tenth or eleventh century, they should be viewed in the context of the revival of monastic learning brought about by Dunstan and Athelwold and Oswald[21] and, more broadly, in the tradition of vernacular education fostered by Alfred the Great and his successors, in which the efforts of a century of scholars were directed to the translation of 'those books most necessary for all men to know' and the instruction of free-born children in English literacy.[22] It is, perhaps, easy to overrate this movement. Many modern readers, coming from a background in English literature and the study of Old English poetry, find the outpouring of post-Alfredian vernacular prose texts – laws, letters, lives, grammars, histories, chronicles, sermons, science books – impressive, and familiar in a way that is both surprising and comforting, but the fact is, these were made because hardly a soul in the whole country, even those whose business required it, could adequately understand Latin.[23] Men wrote books in English out of necessity, and only secondarily, if at all, as a matter of national pride or literary ambition; translations, particularly of the major liturgical or monastic texts, are concessions, not accomplishments. But the promotion of English as a literary language had collateral benefits. The reformers' drive to impose order on the life of monks and nuns was matched by a need for instruction of the secular clergy, whose latinity was apparently always doubtful;[24] Ælfric's first English letter to Wulfstan sets out this pastoral duty plainly: 'Us bisceopum gedafenæð, þæt we þa boclican lare þe ure canon us tæcð and eac seo Cristes boc, eow preostum geopenigen on Engliscum gereorde; forþam þe ge ealle ne cunnon þæt leden understandan.'[25]

As well as providing clerical education, the monastic revival fostered lay patronage and lay devotion; the need for English books among the clergy was paralleled by a demand for religious works from pious ealdormen and women.[26] Æthelwold translated the Benedictine Rule at the request of King Edgar and his wife;[27] Wulfstan wrote for two kings, Æthelred and Cnut; Ælfric's *Lives of the Saints* was composed at the request of Æthelweard and his son Æthelmær so that laymen might have the same readings as monks.[28] Sigeweard entreated Ælfric for copies of his works in English;[29] Æthelweard requested a copy of the first series of *Catholic Homilies*.[30] An illustrated copy of the Old English Hexateuch was apparently made for a lay reader, 'though hardly' its editors say, 'on the evidence of [its] quite moderate standards of workmanship . . . a royal or similarly high-ranking patron.'[31] Ælfric's preface to the translation of Genesis begins famously as follows: 'Ælfric munuc gret Æðelweard ealdormann eadmodlice. Þu bæde me, leof, þæt ic sceolde ðe awendan of Lydene on Englisc þa boc Genesis: ða þuhte me hefigtime þe to tiþienne þæs, and þu cwæde þa þæt ic ne þorfte na mare awendan þære bec buton to Isaace, Abrahames suna, for þam þe sum oðer man hæfde awend fram Isaace þa boc oþ ende.'[32] What is remarkable here is not that a lay patron is commissioning a book, but that he is offering bibliographical advice to a monk. Whatever Ælfric's share in this work,[33] its existence reveals a significant lay interest in the vernacular Bible at the beginning of the eleventh century and suggests that the readership for a translation of the Gospels might include educated laymen as well as monks and parish priests. One can thus imagine three possible intended uses for an Old English Gospel, ranging from relatively private to relatively public: devotional reading (whether lay or clerical); pastoral instruction; and liturgical recitation, that is, as a formal part of a public church service. These are not, of course, mutually exclusive categories, any more than they are for the Gospels today; they may be explored not only through the manuscript evidence, but also through comparison with other scriptural and homiletic works in Old English, a comparison which may offer a commentary on the ways in which the Anglo-Saxons experienced and imagined the Bible.

VARIETIES OF THE BIBLE IN OLD ENGLISH

The Anglo-Saxons seem to have felt, perhaps more strongly than other early medieval cultures, a vivid sense of continuity between the events of the Bible and their own history.³⁴ Alfred's law code begins with a version of Exodus xx–xxiii. The West-Saxon kings traced their lineage back through Woden to Noah and Adam. Patriarchs were portrayed as Germanic lords with retainers and halls; Christ was a young hero doing single battle against Satan. The Bible forms the background for most Old English poetry, from *Genesis* and *Exodus* to *Beowulf.* The Junius Manuscript was made at about the same time as the illustrated version of the Hexateuch,³⁵ suggesting a continuing audience for biblical poetry at the same time as the prose translations of the Bible were being made. Though the Anglo-Saxon church, unlike the church of later ages, had no prohibitions against Scripture in the vernacular, these poetic paraphrases were apparently the closest thing to a translation of the Bible available to most lay people before Ælfric's time; no trace has survived of Bede's alleged translation of John, or of any other early prose version of the Bible, except for parts of the Paris Psalter. These poetic versions are, of course, very different from translations; they are epic reimaginings of the history of the Israelites in terms of the legendary history of the Anglo-Saxons, inflected in the expansive solemnity of Germanic verse.³⁶ New Testament poems such as *Christ* or *The Dream of the Rood,* on the other hand, are scarcely narratives at all, but fantastical, surreal, and finally doctrinal works; as Barbara Raw has recently noted, 'they are not stories of Christ's life, but meditations on salvation history'.³⁷ They have little to do with the homely details of the gospel story which were so popular in the later Middle Ages; instead, they reflect an experience of the Gospels which is essentially liturgical, that is, symbolic, interpretive, cyclical, and static. They are the poetic equivalent of a homily, not a translation; as Beryl Smalley said of biblical exegesis, we are invited to look not at the text but through it.

A poetic paraphrase is quite a different thing from a prose translation, for reasons which go beyond merely formal considerations. In both Old and New Testament poetry in Old English the biblical text is mediated not only by the voice of the poet and the style of the poem but also by the logic of interpretation – the work is no substitute for the original, but an aesthetic response to it, a form of commentary. One is nowhere allowed to believe that this is the *ipsissima verba* of Scripture in English. A prose translation, on the other hand, has at least pretensions to being a replacement for the original, as the Septuagint was for the Hebrew and the Vulgate for the Hebrew and Greek. The absence of a mediating voice inherent in pure translation is apparently a situation of considerable anxiety for Ælfric. On at least two occasions he refuses to translate any more Scripture. At the end of the second series of *Catholic Homilies*, he says, 'Ic cweðe nu þæt ic næfre heononforð ne awende godspel oþþe godspeltrahtas of ledene on englisc; gif hwa ma awendan wille, ðonne bidde ic hine for godes lufan þæt he gesette his boc onsundron fram ðam twam bocum ðe we awend habbað we truwiað þurh godes diht',[38] and he says much the same thing at the end of his preface to Genesis: 'Ic cweðe nu ðæt ic ne dearr ne ic nelle boc æfter ðisse of Ledene on Englisc awendan; and ic bidde ðe, leof ealdormann, ðæt ðu me ðæs na leng ne bidde, ði læs ic beo ðe ungehyrsum, oððe leas gyf ic do'.[39] These protests are somewhat disingenuous, one suspects,[40] but they are in any case a public acknowledgment of the air of impropriety or scandal surrounding his task. Ælfric's anxiety is also evident in his language at the end of the preface to Genesis: 'We sceolon awendan urne willan to his gesetnyssum, and we ne magon gebigean his gesetnyssa on urum lustum'.[41] The relationship between our degenerate will and God's immutable commandments is expressed here, as often in Ælfric's writings, by the word *awendan* – which also means 'translate'.[42] *Awendan* has an interesting semantic range: it is elsewhere used commonly in charters for the illicit erasure or alteration of a decree set down in writing.[43] Its connotations express precisely the devolution of textual Latin into the mutable babel of English which constitutes, for Ælfric, the act of translation.

The anxiety about English Scripture is mitigated in the most common form of Bible translation in Anglo-Saxon culture, the glossed Latin text.[44] The large number of Old English interlinear psalters that have survived, compared with the one partial translation into prose and one into verse, indicates that though the Latin text may not always have been comprehensible, it was always considered necessary. Many of the glossed psalters were written and glossed by the same hand, and in the Cambridge Psalter the English gloss is 'given parity with the text',[45] suggesting that a gloss was by no means an afterthought or a 'crib' for the uneducated, but a deliberate compromise between the sanctity of the Latin and the necessity of the English. Even the Lindisfarne Gospels, certainly one of the most magnificent displays of the idea of a text ever constructed, are served by a gloss. This gloss must have been seen at some point in the manuscript's history as a useful and appropriate part of the book; Henry Hargreaves pointedly observed that 'in no well-regulated scriptorium would a scribe be allowed to insert *casually* into so precious a manuscript his own translation, like a schoolboy "glossing" his Caesar'.[46] The gloss is required for understanding, for study and teaching, but is not available for independent consultation or public reading; it serves as a point of entry into the Latin text but does not abrogate textual authority to itself. A gloss expresses the right relation between man's need and the word of God.[47]

Importantly, a gloss also preserves the word-order of the Latin text. Jerome's *Letter LVII to Pammachius,* the *locus classicus* for medieval theories of translation, states that translation ought to proceed, not word for word, but sense for sense, except in the case of the Bible, where 'et verborum ordo mysterium est'.[48] Ælfric echoes Jerome's 'sense for sense' dictum in the Latin preface to the first series of *Catholic Homilies,*[49] admitting a degree of latitude in his homiletic translations; but in the preface to Genesis he sets scrupulous literal fidelity as a goal and then admits the impossibility of preserving the word order of the original.[50] Though his actual practice is, quite sensibly, far more flexible than this intention would lead one to expect[51] (and in this he is not unlike Jerome),[52] the theory of translation available to Ælfric makes a successful vernacular Bible, which cannot be both idiomatic and faithful, inherently impossible. If the *mysterium* of the syntax is preserved, the version will be garbled, useless for pastoral or devotional purposes, and will need yet another text to interpret it; if the requirements of English are followed, the text will lose some layers of its truth. The close attention Ælfric pays to the grammatical forms of the biblical text is well known from the preface to Genesis: 'Eft is se halga ðrynysse geswutelode on ðisre bec, swa swa is on ðam worde, ðe god cwæð, Uton wyrcean mannan to ure anlicnisse. Mid ðam ðe he cwæð, "Uton wyrcean", is seo ðrynysse gebicnod; mid ðam ðe he cwæð, "to ure anlicnysse", is seo soðe annys geswutelod. He ne cwæð na manigfealdlice "to ure anlycnyssum" ac anfealdlice "to ure anlicnysse"'.[53] This attention to the textual surface, discerning the spiritual significance of singulars and plurals, is as much true *lectio* as the weaving of typological parallels between the Old and New Testaments; it is a process very similar to a grammatical explication in the schoolroom, the lectures of a teacher to a group of students. Similarly, many of Ælfric's homilies take the form of a 'continuous gloss' to a gospel text,[54] essentially a pedagogical device, and evidently a far more comfortable form of translation for Ælfric than a literal prose narrative.

Such practices, as with early medieval biblical reading generally, combined a strong belief in the power of the Latin text as an object with the certainty that the literal sense of the text is only part, and often not the important part, of its meaning.[55] The business of turning Latin words into English words was only the bare beginning of a complex process of reading, as Ælfric points out to Æthelweard: the danger of a translation, he notes, is that 'þonne þincþ þam ungelæredum þæt eall þæt andgit beo belocen on þære anfealdan gerecednisse, ac hit ys swiþe feor þam'.[56] Time and again in his homilies Ælfric moves from translation to interpretation with the phrase 'Þis godspell is nu anfealdlice gesæd'[57] and proceeds to unfold the *gastlice andgyt* (spiritual significance). In a homily for the second Thursday of Lent he follows his fairly literal translation with this comment: 'We habbað anfealdlice gesæd eow nu þis godspell, and we willað geopnian eow þæt andgyt nu, for ðam þe ge ne cunnon ealle tocnawan þa digelnysse, buton man eow secge þæra snotera lareowa trahtunge be þam, swa swa hit on bocum stent.'[58] The text of the Bible requires another text to explain it; it can only be glossed, never adequately translated, only explicated, never replicated. In the paraphrase, the exposition, or the sermon, the words of Scripture are an elaborate quotation by a narrator, the translation is a supplement rather than a substitute, and the encounter between the reader and the word of God is mediated by an authoritative interpreter.

This belief in the mysterious, inexhaustible and untranslatable depth of the text necessarily involves a concept of reading as a form of preaching or teaching, unfolding and pointing and directing; as in Augustine's *De doctrina Christiana*, Ælfric moves quite naturally from *lectio* to *praedicatio* as inseparable parts of the same process.[59] The Bible itself is only the means to an end, a good life; a homily is better than a translation because it is a performance to an audience, not a text – not just a speech, but a speech act.[60] Ælfric's homiletic work is thus a reaction to, and a movement away from, the possibility of an English Bible. If Ælfric's attitude may be taken as at all typical or influential, his deep and apparently long-standing anxiety on the subject makes it unlikely that a bare, unchaperoned translation of the Gospels into English would have had a large lay audience.

EVIDENCE FOR USE AND OWNERSHIP

The codicological evidence supports this assumption; the manuscripts whose provenance can be established do not seem to have been in the hands of laymen but were part of monastic or cathedral libraries, and their treatment there suggests that the translation existed in fairly close proximity to the authority of the Latin text. The Bodley copy was made to be a plain vernacular version, but not long after the manuscript was written a number of Latin headings were added in the margins, not systematically, to introduce some paragraphs. The Royal and Hatton manuscripts have the same Latin headings as the Bodley manuscript, but copied on separate lines as part of their textual design.[61] The Corpus manuscript has a dozen Latin headings as well, apparently independent of those in the Bodley copy, all in Matthew, consecutively over the first twelve paragraphs of the text; then they stop completely as if the annotator had run out of interest in the project.[62] These Latin headings are reference points to allow the Old English to be read in parallel to the Latin.[63] The surviving scraps of the Yale fragments show two Latin paragraph headings, both by the main scribe, and an added English rubric in a different hand between two lines at Mk 1:40, containing directions for the reading of the gospel pericope at Mass: 'This gospel belongs on Wednesday of the fifteenth week after Pentecost'.[64] In A, from Exeter, such Latin headings and English rubrics are systematically elaborated over the whole manuscript. Nearly all paragraphs are marked, and the system of readings covers the entire year – Sundays, Wednesdays and Fridays, major feasts and saints' days, and a number of full weeks in Lent. This manuscript is a later copy than Cp, B, C, and Y; its text seems to have been revised, and the liturgical directions were probably added then as well, first, perhaps, in the margins of its exemplar – as we may infer from the Yale fragments – and later incorporated into the page design itself.[65] The Cambridge copy also contains the apocryphal *Gospel of Nicodemus* and the *Vindicta Salvatoris*, written by the main scribe after the canonical Gospels, suggesting an impulse towards encyclopedic completeness on the part of its compilers. The book was assembled from different sources, like the later copies of Ælfric's homilies which, despite his warnings and fears, were quickly compiled and excerpted with other works, sometimes of questionable orthodoxy.

In these additions and alterations one can see the Latin text exerting a kind of gravitational pull on the English versions, keeping them in the role of gloss rather than text, supplement rather than substitute. In the Paris Psalter,[66] which has been described as a 'scissors and paste book',[67] the apparently independent prose and verse expositions of the Psalms were eventually copied into one codex in narrow columns alongside a Latin text from which they are not derived. The manuscripts of the Old English Gospels suggest a similar impulse, though less dramatically executed. The text began as an independent vernacular version, a state found in Cp, C, and B in their original forms; to some of these first copies Latin headings were added which allow a kind of cross-reference between the Latin and English;[68] a next generation of copies corrected the text, apparently from comparison to the Latin rather than reference back to some English exemplar, and added liturgical directions (such as are found in Y and, more systematically, in A) to further allow consultation between the Latin text and the English. The translation, originally free-standing, was drawn back into the orbit of the Latin text of the Gospels and the official occasions of its reading.

There are signs, however, that the manuscripts of the Old English Gospels were treated as if they were the equivalents of Latin gospel-books. The blank front leaves of Cp (from Bath Abbey), for example, are covered with manumissions;[69] the book was used like a Latin gospel-book as a place of record, a depository for important information, a fit container for facts which could not be altered or erased – *awende*.[70] The manuscript attracted relic inventories, a list of bishops and popes, an agreement of confraternity between the members of surrounding monasteries; it was a registry as well as a text, which makes it precisely like a Latin Gospel book in use, if not in language. Max Förster has noted that 'it seems to have been customary in Anglo-Saxon times to enter manumissions in liturgical manuscripts, because the holiness of the book was considered to guarantee the sacredness of the legal instrument. In fact all Anglo-Saxon manumissions – with only two exceptions in the *Liber Vitae Dunelmensis . . .* and the Rochester *Chartulary . . .* have come down to us in liturgical books'.[71] Like Cp, A originally contained added lists, records and notices, and manumissions, mostly from the first half of the twelfth century, and a list of the land, furniture, vestments, and books procured by Leofric for Exeter Cathedral.[72] These are now part of Exeter Cathedral Library MS 3501, the 'Exeter Book' of Old English poetry, but originally stood in the Old English Gospel manuscript in a position analogous to the list in Oxford, Bodleian Library Bodley Auct. D. 2.16, a Latin Gospel-book and another of Leofric's donations to Exeter. In other words, copies of the translation were sometimes treated like Latin gospel-books – immutable, authoritative, public, and sacral – whose power extended protection to the documents entered into them.[73]

The English liturgical rubrics in A have raised the possibility that the translation had some public life as a sort of Mass-lectionary.[74] The evidence, however, must be heavily qualified against anachronistic assumptions about the shape of the liturgy – or indeed the form of the spiritual life – in Anglo-Saxon times.[75] Liturgical headings do not necessarily imply liturgical recitation, just as a homiliary organized around the calendar need not have been preached publicly. Milton McC. Gatch has argued that Ælfric's homilies are more 'allied to the reform of monastic life or even to the pious practices of individuals than to the development of the secular or public liturgy';[76] similarly, the editor of the so-called *Benedictine Office* has cautioned against the supposition that 'the text is any kind of devotional book to be used in Church'.[77] Even the *capitularia* in Latin Gospel-books are often so badly copied that it is difficult to imagine they were ever used.[78] The evidence is tantalizingly ambiguous. The relative scarcity of surviving copies of the Old English Gospels, and the fact that only one copy contains fully integrated liturgical directions, argues against any widespread custom of reading the Gospel in English at Mass; moreover, if A is a Mass-book rather than a reference book it is hard to explain why the *Gospel of Nicodemus* was copied in it. But it is a provocative fact that the only copy that was systematically outfitted with liturgical references is from Exeter, a secular church rather than a monastery. To explore the possibility of the use of the Old English Gospels in the liturgy, the evidence from Ælfric's work is again illuminating.

Gatch has argued that it was Ælfric who promoted the explication of the Gospel in English as a regular part of secular liturgy.[79] Vernacular instruction in the Gospel was by no means an automatic part of public liturgical celebration; neither Amalarius of Metz nor the *Regularis Concordia* mentions homilies as a regular feature of the Mass.[80] Wulfstan seems to have been more concerned that the parish clergy teach by example and exhortation than by gospel homily; where the *Excerptiones pseudo-Ecgberti* specify that 'Ut omnibus festis et diebus Dominicis unusquisque sacerdos Evangelium Christi praedicet populo', Wulfstan's *Canons of Edgar*, derived in part from this collection, states merely that 'preostas ælce sunnandæge folce bodigan and aa wel bisnian'.[81] Ælfric's pastoral letter to Wulfsige, however, enjoins that 'se mæssepreost sceal secgan sunnandagum and mæssedagum þæs godspelles angyt on englisc þam folce'.[82] If this command were ever realistically to be fulfilled, one imagines, a translation of the Gospels would be a prerequisite – or a set or two of vernacular homilies on the Gospels.

Gatch sees Ælfric's *Catholic Homilies* as a movement towards the development of the Prone, a vernacular catechetical office after the gospel reading, as a regular occasion for gospel translation and exegesis during the Mass.[83] Though Gatch's use of the term may be somewhat anachronistic,[84] Ælfric's language in his homilies implies exactly this function; a few of the many examples include: 'Ic wolde eow trahtnian þis godspell þe man nu beforan eow rædde';[85] 'We wyllað nu þis godspel eow gereccan þe her nu gerad wæs';[86] '. . . ðæt halige godspel þe nu lytle ær ætforan eow geræd wæs'.[87] The evidence is inconclusive, but does not preclude the hypothesis that the Old English Gospels in a manuscript such as Y or A were used as a reading-book after the recitation of the Gospels in Latin on occasions when full homilies were not preached, or preliminary to an extemporaneous homily on the Gospel. It is possible, then, that in addition to its use as a devotional book for monastic or clerical reading, the Old English version may have been adapted to meet the same need as that which drove Ælfric to publish his homilies, to aid the secular priests' explication of the gospel pericope.

To the question posed in the title of this essay one must return an admittedly disappointing and predictable answer: in all probability the Old English Gospels reached the general lay audience, if at all, in the voice of a narrator, as a gloss on a recited Latin liturgical reading rather than as an independent text. There were many different ways in which the Bible was offered to the lay public – prose translation was only one of them, and in many respects the most unusual. The prohibitive cost of books and widespread non-literacy necessarily compelled, of course, a close relation between reading and teaching; the sermon rather than the text was the main source of knowledge of the Bible for most of society, and the words of Scripture reached the broader public in the Middle Ages in glosses, commentaries, and quotations, not texts. Given the fear of misinterpretation expressed by Bible translators, this was probably regarded as just as well. The anxiety expressed by Ælfric over the 'naked narrative' of the Bible can be seen throughout the Middle Ages in such productions as the *Ormulum* – where anxiety is clear in the style, the handwriting, even the neurotically precise spelling – and in the pages of the glossed books of the Bible used in the universities, where a tiny patch of Scripture is protected by an elaborate hedge of commentary. The vast number of copies of the Wyclif Bible testify to a great hunger for Scripture in English at the end of the fourteenth century, among pious lay people of unquestioned orthodoxy as well as among the promoters of Lollardry. The few copies of the Old English Gospels tell a different story. The fact that the Gospels were put into Old English at all says much about the state of learning and language in later Anglo-Saxon times, but it does not imply anything like the unmediated individual access to the word of God that was assumed in the arguments of Foxe's preface. Like Bede's translation of John, the Old English Gospels were made *ad utilitatem ecclesiae*; whatever their intended audience, their history is firmly within the walls of the Church.[88]

NOTES

1 The phrase is Fred C. Robinson's; see 'Old English Literature in its Most Immediate Context', in *Old English Literature in Context: Ten Essays*, ed. John D. Niles (Cambridge 1980), 11–29.
2 Brian Stock, *The Implications of Literacy* (Princeton 1983).
3 Referred to throughout this essay as the 'Old English Gospels' in preference to the usual title 'West-Saxon Gospels'.
4 For a general statement of the role of the *Testimonie* in Parker's advocacy of the English church, see Michael A. Murphy, 'Religious Polemics in the Genesis of Old English Studies', *Huntington Library Quarterly* 32 (1969) 241–48.
5 *The Gospel of the fower Euangelistes translated in the olde Saxons tyme out of Latin into the vulgare toung of the Saxons, newly collected out of auncient Monumentes of the sayd Saxons, and now published for testimonie of the same.*

6 The actual editing of the Old English text was almost certainly done by Parker and his secretary John Joscelyn. See Eleanor Adams, *OE Scholarship in England from 1566–1800*, Yale Studies in English, 55 (1917; repr. Hamden 1971), 31; for Foxe's limited knowledge of Old English, see Michael A. Murphy, 'John Foxe, Martyrologist and "Editor" of Old English', *English Studies* 49 (1968) 516–23.

7 *The Gospel of the fower Euangelistes*, 9.

8 Boston, 1904–06.

9 W.W. Skeat, ed., *The Holy Gospels in Anglo-Saxon, Northumbrian, and Old Mercian Versions* (Cambridge 1871–87).

10 Grünberg's 1967 edition of Matthew, *The West-Saxon Gospels: A Study of the Gospel of St Matthew with Text of the Four Gospels* (Amsterdam 1967), eschews biblical reference altogether, making the text rather more difficult of access than it should be. The page design adopted by the present author in *The Old English Version of the Gospels*, EETS 304 (Oxford 1994) aims at a compromise between the format of the manuscripts and the requirements of modern biblical reference.

11 A possible exception is Ker 112, from the collection of Albert Ehrman no. 888 (on deposit in the Bodleian Library, Oxford); a binding strip, now missing, contained fragments of Mt 27:45–66, which, according to Ker, 'appears to correspond in general with and is sometimes verbally the same as the OE version'. Ker made a transcript (see 'A Supplement to *Catalogue of Manuscripts Containing Anglo-Saxon*', *ASE* 5 [1977] 121–31, art. 112), but I have not seen this. The excerpt of Jn 14:1–13 in London, BL Cotton Vespasian D. xiv, fol. 87rv, printed by Ruby D.-N. Warner, *Early English Homilies from the Twelfth Century MS. Vespasian D. xiv*, EETS 152 (Oxford 1917), art. 77, is not related to the Old English version.

12 The surviving manuscripts include (reference numbers are from N.R. Ker, *A Catalogue of Manuscripts Containing Anglo-Saxon* [1957; repr. with supplement., Oxford 1990]):

A   Cambridge, University Library, Ii. 2. 11 (Ker 20)
Cp   Cambridge, Corpus Christi College, 140 (Ker 35)
C   London, British Library, Cotton Otho C. i vol. I (Ker 181)
R   London, British Library, Royal I A. xiv (Ker 245)
B   Oxford, Bodleian Library, Bodley 441 (Ker 312)
L   Oxford, Bodleian Library, English Bib. C. 2 (Ker 322)
H   Oxford, Bodleian Library, Hatton 38 (Ker 325)
Y   New Haven, Beinecke Library, 578 endleaf (Ker 1)

13 B and C are more closely related to each other than either is to Cp.

14 The corpus of vernacular homilies is surveyed by D.G. Scragg, 'The Corpus of Vernacular Homilies and Prose Saints' Lives before Ælfric', *ASE* 8 (1979) 223–77. A.S. Cook, *Biblical Quotations in Old English Prose Writers* (New York 1898) and *Second Series* (New Haven 1903), brings together many of the relevant quotations.

15 Most of the translations in the First Series of Ælfric's *Catholic Homilies* are not included in Benjamin Thorpe, ed., *The Homilies of the Anglo-Saxon Church: The First Part, Containing the Sermones Catholici, or Homilies of Ælfric*, 2 vols. (London 1844–46) (hereinafter cited as Thorpe), and are not in Cook's *Biblical Quotations*; they can be found in Arthur S. Napier, 'Nachträge zu Cook's *Biblical Quotations in Old English Prose Writers*', *Archiv* 101 (1898) 309–24, 102 (1899) 29–42, 107 (1901) 105–06.

16 Norman Eliason and Peter Clemoes say of Royal 7. C. xii, which does not contain the preface, that they 'would assign its production to the first half of 990 and its revision to the immediately succeeding months'; see *Ælfric's First Series of Catholic Homilies, British Museum Royal 7. C. xii, fols 4–218*, EEMF 13 (Copenhagen 1966), 35. For the dates of Ælfric's

works Peter Clemoes, 'The Chronology of Ælfric's Works', in *The Anglo-Saxons: Studies in some Aspects of their History and Culture Presented to Bruce Dickins*, ed. P.A.M. Clemoes (London 1959), 212–47, is still standard, though it may be supplemented by the introduction to John C. Pope, ed., *Homilies of Ælfric: A Supplementary Collection*, 2 vols, EETS 259–60 (Oxford 1967–68) (hereinafter cited as Pope).

17 Thorpe, 1:2, 'I regretted that they [i.e., the English] did not know and did not have the Gospel teachings among their writings, except for those who knew Latin, and except for the books which King Alfred wisely translated from Latin to English, which are available' (all translations from Old English and Latin are my own).

18 Malcolm Godden, 'Ælfric and the Vernacular Prose Tradition', in *The Old English Homily and Its Backgrounds*, ed. Paul E. Szarmach and Bernard F. Huppé (Albany, N.Y., 1978), 99–117; cf. 102–05.

19 The origin of the translation is not known. The Latin text on which it is based is occasionally archaic, containing a number of Old Latin and Irish readings, but this in itself is not an argument for an early date, and the translation has a number of readings which cannot be found in English manuscripts before the middle of the tenth century. Pending a thorough study of the manuscripts of the Latin Gospels in Anglo-Saxon England – earlier studies, including Hans Glunz, *Die lateinische Vorlage der westsächsischen Evangelienversion*, Beiträge zur englischen Philologie 9 (Leipzig 1928) and *History of the Vulgate in England from Alcuin to Roger Bacon* (Cambridge 1933), and Lancelot Minor Harris, 'Studies in the Anglo-Saxon Version of the Gospels. I: The Form of the Latin Original, and Mistaken Readings', (PhD diss., Johns Hopkins University 1901), are helpful but not always complete or accurate – the most one can say is that, on the whole, the Old English text seems most closely related to the sort of Latin gospel-text that had been brought to the continent by Insular missionaries, mixed there with the versions circulated by Alcuin and his successors, and was then brought back to England by the diplomatic activity of Athelstan in relation to Brittany and the monastic reformers of the later tenth century. (Representative manuscripts in this tradition include London, BL, Royal 1. A. xviii and Add. 9381.) It is a thoroughly mixed text, and as such it is a typical Anglo-Saxon one and difficult to date or localize precisely.

20 Grünberg, *West-Saxon Gospels*, argues that the translation was made in the ninth century using a Mercian gloss (her conclusions are summarized on pp. 366–68), but this is probably not the case: the orthographic evidence cited as early can also be explained as late; the reconstruction of the transmission of the text is unnecessarily elaborate; the understanding of the Latin original of the translation is based on misleading printed sources only and not on the considerably more complex manuscript evidence; and the lexical evidence adduced is almost entirely derived from R. Vleeskruyer, *The Life of St Chad* (Amsterdam 1953), a work whose problems have been ably analysed by Janet M. Bately, 'Old English Prose Before and During the Reign of Alfred', *ASE* 17 (1988) 93–138.

21 On the general subject of the monastic reform see David Knowles, *The Monastic Order in England: A History of Its Development from the Times of St Dunstan to the Fourth Lateran Council: 940–1216*, 2nd ed. (Cambridge 1963), 36–42. See also J. Armitage Robinson, *The Times of St Dunstan* (Oxford 1923), Margaret Deanesly, *Sidelights on the Anglo-Saxon Church* (London 1962) and the essays in David Parsons, ed., *Tenth-Century Studies: Essays in Commemoration of the Millennium of the Council of Winchester and Regularis Concordia* (Chichester 1975). A recent study is Veronica Ortenberg, *The English Church and the Continent in the Tenth and Eleventh Centuries* (Oxford 1992), and see also E. John, 'The Sources of the English Monastic Reformation: A Comment', *Revue Bénédictine* 70 (1960) 197–203.

Palaeographical evidence is in T.A.M. Bishop, *English Caroline Minuscule* (Oxford 1971), and see David N. Dumville, *English Caroline Script and Monastic History: Studies in Benedictinism, A.D. 950–1030* (Woodbridge 1993). For vernacular literary matters see H. Gneuss, 'The Origin of Standard Old English and Æthelwold's School at Winchester', *ASE* 1 (1972) 63–83, and Walter Hofstetter, 'Winchester and the Standardization of Old English Vocabulary', *ASE* 17 (1988) 139–61. See also the comments of R. Marsden, 'The Old Testament in Late Anglo-Saxon England', in *The Early Medieval Bible: Its Production, Decoration and Use*, ed. Richard Gameson (Cambridge 1994), 106–09.

22 Both are goals expressed in Alfred's preface to the translation of Gregory's *Pastoral Care* (ed. Henry Sweet, *King Alfred's West-Saxon Version of Gregory's Pastoral Care*, EETS, 45 and 50 [Oxford 1871]); a convenient modern edition of the preface is Bruce Mitchell and Fred C. Robinson, *A Guide to Old English*, 5th ed. (Oxford 1992), 204–07. The Alfredian achievement is astutely assessed by Janet Bately, 'Old English Prose before and during the Reign of Alfred'. More general works on lay literacy in Anglo-Saxon England include D.A. Bullough, 'The Educational Tradition in England from Alfred to Ælfric: Teaching *utriusque linguae*', *Settimane di studio del Centro Italiano de studi sull'alto medioevo* 19 (1972) 2: 453–94; Patrick Wormald, 'The Uses of Literacy in Anglo-Saxon England and Its Neighbours', *Transactions of the Royal Historical Society* 5th ser. 27 (1977) 95–114; and Susan Kelly, 'Anglo-Saxon Lay Society and the Written Word', in *The Uses of Literacy in Early Mediaeval Europe*, ed. Rosamond McKitterick (Cambridge 1990), 36–62.

23 An exceptionally critical opinion is offered by C.E. Hohler, 'Some Service-Books of the Later Saxon Church', in *Tenth-Century Studies*, ed. Parsons 60–83, at 74: '[E]verything conspires to suggest that the knowledge of Latin among the clergy was almost universally low, and that, except in so far as an insignificant minority of scholars was prepared, as well as able, to provide translations, the Church was cut off from the general cultural heritage of the West.' Ælfric, who was probably in a position to know, notes in his preface to his *Grammar* the decline of learning – specifically the ability to translate between Latin and English: 'Is nu forði godes þeowum and mynstermannum georne to wornigenne, þæt seo halige lar on urum dagum ne acolige oððe ateorige, swaswa hit wæs gedon on Angelcynne nu for anum feawum gearum; swa þæt nan englisc preost ne cuðe dihtan oððe asmeagean anne pistol on leden, oðþæt Dunstan arcebisceop and Aðelwold bisceop eft þa lare on munuclifum arærdon' ('Now therefore the servants of God and monks ought zealously to be on guard, so that the holy teaching in our day should not cool or decay, as it happened in England a few years ago, so that no English priest knew how to compose or interpret a letter in Latin, until Archbishop Dunstan and Bishop Æthelwold restored learning to the monastic life'). Julius Zupitza, ed., *Ælfrics Grammatik und Glossar, pt I: Text und Varianten* (Berlin 1880), 3. Though we should take Ælfric's assertions with as much caution as we take Alfred's similar assertions in the preface to the *Pastoral Care* (see, e.g., J. Morrish, 'King Alfred's Letter as a Source on Learning in England in the Ninth Century', in *Studies in Earlier Old English Prose*, ed. P.E. Szarmach [Albany, N.Y., 1986], 87–107), it is probably safe to believe that there is some degree of truth in them, and it is incredible to think that the situation could have been remedied in only one generation.

24 Education of the parish clergy is discussed by Frank Barlow, *The English Church, 1000–1066* (London 1963), 277–88. Milton McC. Gatch, 'The Office in Late Anglo-Saxon Monasticism', in *Learning and Literature in Anglo-Saxon England: Studies Presented to Peter Clemoes on the Occasion of His Sixty-Fifth Birthday*, ed. Michael Lapidge and Helmut Gneuss (Cambridge 1985), 341–62, sees 'the ordering of the liturgical life of monks and nuns' as 'a central objective (indeed, the primary purpose) of the late Anglo-Saxon monastic reform'

(341) but notes that many of the works of Ælfric are 'an adaptation of materials from the monastic devotional life to the devotional life of laymen and non-monastic clergy' (362).

25 'It behooves us bishops that we should open in the English language the bookish lore which our canon and the Gospel teaches us for you priests, because you do not all know how to understand Latin.' B. Fehr, *Die Hirtenbriefe Ælfrics*, BaP 9; repr. with supplement by Peter Clemoes (Darmstadt 1966), letter ii, 2. See also Dorothy Whitelock, M. Brett, and C.N.L. Brooke, *Councils and Synods with Other Documents Relating to the English Church* (Oxford 1981), 1:260–61.

26 A brief but interesting survey of relations between aristocratic patronage and the monastic movement is P.A. Stafford, 'Church and State in the Age of Ælfric', in *The Old English Homily and Its Backgrounds*, ed. Szarmach and Huppé, 11–42.

27 H. Gneuss, 'Die Benediktinerregel in England und ihre altenglische Übersetzung', in *Die angelsächsischen Prosabearbeitungen der Benediktinerregel*, ed. A. Schröer, BaP 2, 2nd ed. (Darmstadt 1964); see also Mechthild Gretsch, 'Æthelwold's Translation of the *Regula Sancti Benedicti* and Its Latin Exemplar', *ASE* 3 (1974) 125–51.

28 'Nu gewearð us þæt we þas boc be þæra halgena ðrowungum and life. gedihton þe mynstermenn mid heora þenungum betwux him wurðiað. Ne secge we nan þincg niwes on þissere gesetnysse. forþan ðe hit stod gefyrn awriten on ledenbocum þeah þe þa læwedan men þæt nyston' ('Now it occurs to us that we should compose this book concerning the passions and lives of the saints whom the monks honour among themselves in their services. We say nothing new in this composition, because it has long been written in Latin, although laymen did not know it'). In W.W. Skeat, ed., *Ælfric's Lives of Saints*, EETS 76, 82, 94, 114 (1881–1900; repr. in 2 vols Oxford 1966), Preface, 43–48.

29 S.J. Crawford, ed., *The Old English Version of the Hexateuch, Ælfric's Treatise on the Old and New Testament and His Preface to Genesis*, EETS 160 (1922; repr. with additions by N.R. Ker, London 1969), 16 (hereinafter cited as Crawford).

30 Kenneth Sisam, *Studies in the History of Old English Literature* (Oxford 1953), 160–61; noted in Milton McC. Gatch, *Preaching and Theology in Anglo-Saxon England: Ælfric and Wulfstan* (Toronto 1977), 48.

31 C.R. Dodwell and Peter Clemoes, eds, *The Old English Illustrated Hexateuch, British Museum Cotton Claudius B. IV*, EEMF 18 (Copenhagen 1974), 58.

32 Crawford, 76, 'Ælfric monk humbly greets Æthelweard ealdorman. You told me, lord, to translate the book of Genesis for you from Latin into English. It seemed burdensome to me to undertake that, and you said that I need only translate the book to "Isaac, Abraham's son", because some other man had translated the book from "Isaac" to the end'.

33 Evidence for authorship is presented in Dodwell and Clemoes, *The Old English Illustrated Hexateuch*, 43–53; see also Karl Jost, 'Unechte Ælfrictexte', *Anglia* 51 (1927) 81–103 and 177–219; J. Raith, 'Ælfric's Share in the Old English Pentateuch', *Review of English Studies* n.s. 3 (1952) 305–14; and Peter S. Baker, 'The Old English Canon of Byrhtferth of Ramsey', *Speculum* 55 (1980) 22–37.

34 A recent exploration of this theme is Nicholas Howe, *Migration and Mythmaking in Anglo-Saxon England* (New Haven 1989).

35 A.N. Doane, *Genesis A: A New Edition* (Madison, Wis., 1978), 13, proposes that the manuscript is first quarter of s. xi from St Augustine's, Canterbury; Peter Lucas, *Exodus* (London 1977) and 'MS Junius 11 and Malmesbury', *Scriptorium* 34 (1980) 197–220 and 35 (1981) 3–22, proposes a date of ca. 1000. Lucas's arguments for Malmesbury are evaluated and dismissed by Rodney Thomson, 'Identifiable Books from the Pre-Conquest Library of Malmesbury Abbey', *ASE* 10 (1981) 1–19, and Lucas's other arguments on the subject of the

manuscript's purpose and audience must be read against the views of Barbara Raw, 'The Construction of Oxford, Bodleian Library, Junius 11', *ASE* 13 (1984) 187–207.

36 Geoffrey Shepherd, 'Scriptural Poetry', in *Continuations and Beginnings: Studies in Old English Literature*, ed. E.G. Stanley (London 1966), 1–36, remains an excellent survey of this body of literature; more recent is Malcolm Godden, 'Biblical Literature: The Old Testament', in *The Cambridge Companion to Old English Literature*, ed. Malcolm Godden and Michael Lapidge (Cambridge 1991), 206–26.

37 In 'Biblical Literature: The New Testament', in *Cambridge Companion*, ed. Godden and Lapidge 227–42, at 242.

38 'I say now that henceforth I will never translate gospels or expositions of the gospel from Latin into English; if anyone wishes to translate more, then I ask him for the love of God to set his book apart from the two books which we have translated, we trust, with God's help.' Malcolm Godden, ed., *Ælfric's Catholic Homilies: The Second Series*, EETS s.s. 5 (Oxford 1979), 345 (hereinafter cited as Godden).

39 Crawford, 80, 'I say now that I dare not and will not translate a book from Latin into English after this, and I beg you, dear ealdorman, that you no longer ask me to do it, lest I be disobedient to you, or false if I do.'

40 A.E. Nichols, 'Ælfric's Prefaces: Rhetoric and Genre', *English Studies* 49 (1968) 215–23, discusses the formal rhetorical elements of these disclaimers.

41 Crawford, 80, 'We ought to turn our will to His [i.e., God's] decrees, and we must not bend His decrees to our desires.'

42 See A.E. Nichols, '*Awendan*: A Note on Ælfric's Vocabulary', *JEGP* 63 (1964) 7–13.

43 One such formula, found in the manumissions added to Cp, is in rhyme: 'Crist hine ablende þe þis æfre awende.'

44 'Of some 25 extant Psalters produced in England in Anglo-Saxon times, the Psalms were wholly or partly glossed in 15, and the Paris Psalter has a partial translation. If this is anything like the proportion in contemporary use, we must reckon the English glossed Psalters of the 10th and 11th centuries in hundreds.' Celia and Kenneth Sisam, eds., *The Salisbury Psalter*, EETS 242 (Oxford 1959), 75.

45 CUL Ff. I. 23 (s. xi med); the quotation is from Ker, *Catalogue*, 11.

46 Henry Hargreaves, 'From Bede to Wyclif: Medieval English Bible Translations', *Bulletin of the John Rylands University Library of Manchester* 48 (1965) 118–40, at 121 (emphasis added).

47 Provocative reflections on the act and process of glossing and annotation are found in *Annotation and Its Texts*, ed. Stephen A. Barney (Oxford 1991).

48 Jerome, Epist. LVII, in *Jerome: Lettres*, ed. Jérome Labourt (Paris 1953) 3:59: 'Ego enim non solum fateor, sed libera voce profiteor me in interpretationem Graecorum absque scripturis sanctis, ubi et verborum ordo mysterium est, non verbum e verbo sed sensum exprimere de sensu.' *Ordo* is taken as 'order' as argued by Harvey Minkoff, 'Some Stylistic Consequences of Ælfric's Theory of Translation', *Studies in Philology* 74 (1976) 29–41. For the pervasiveness of this idea see Flora Ross Amos, *Early Theories of Translation* (New York 1920, repr. 1973), and *The Medieval Translator: The Theory and Practice of Translation in the Middle Ages*, ed. R. Ellis (Cambridge 1989); a recent study is Rita Copeland, *Rhetoric, Hermeneutics, and Translation in the Middle Ages* (Cambridge 1991).

49 Thorpe, 1: 1, 'Nec ubique transtulimus verbum ex verbo, sed sensum ex sensu.' A similar statement is found in the Latin preface to the *Lives of the Saints* (Skeat, *Ælfric's Lives of Saints*, 4).

50 Crawford, 79–80, 'We durron na mare awritan on Englisc þonne þæt Læden hæfð, ne þa endebirdnisse awendan buton þam anum þæt þæt Læden and þæt English nabbað na ane

wisan on þære spræce fadunge. Æfre se þe awent oðđe se þe tæcð of Lædene on Englisc, æfre he sceal gefadian hit swa þæt English hæbbe his agen wisan, elles hit bið swiðe gedwolsum to rædenne þam þe þæs Lædenes wisan ne can' ('We dare not write more in English than the Latin has, nor change the arrangement, with the one exception that Latin and English do not have one manner of word-order in their speech. Whoever translates or teaches from Latin to English must arrange it so that the English has its own manner, or else it will be very misleading to read for anyone who does not know Latin'). Crawford reads the variant *fadunge* for printed *fandunge*.

51 See the excellent recent discussions by Frederick M. Biggs, 'Biblical Glosses in Ælfric's Translation of Genesis', *Notes & Queries* n.s. 38 (1991) 286–92, and Richard Marsden, 'Ælfric as Translator: The Old English Prose *Genesis*', *Anglia* 109 (1991) 319–58, who point out exceptions to the literality noted in Minkoff, 'Some Stylistic Consequences of Ælfric's Theory of Translation', and 'An Example of Lating [sic] Influence on Translation', *Neophilologus* 61 (1977) 127–42.

52 See, e.g., W.H. Semple, 'St Jerome as a Biblical Translator', *Bulletin of the John Rylands University Library of Manchester* 48 (1965) 227–43; E.F. Sutcliffe, 'Jerome', in *The Cambridge History of the Bible II: The West from the Fathers to the Reformation*, ed. G.W.H. Lampe (Cambridge 1969), 80–101; W. Schwarz, *Principles and Problems of Biblical Translation* (Cambridge 1955), 27–37.

53 Crawford, 77–78, 'The holy Trinity is revealed in this book in the words which God said: "Let us make man in our own image." When He said "Let us make", the Trinity is signified; when He said, "in our image", the true unity is signified. He did not say in the plural "to our likenesses", but in the singular "to our likeness".'

54 Peter Clemoes, 'Ælfric', in *Continuations and Beginnings*, ed. Stanley, 176–209, at 191–92. Ælfric's exegetical methods are briefly outlined by Paul Szarmach in 'Ælfric as Exegete: Approaches and Examples in the Study of the *Sermones Catholici*', in *Hermeneutics and Medieval Culture*, ed. Patrick J. Gallacher and Helen Damico (Albany, N.Y., 1989), 237–47.

55 Classic studies include Beryl Smalley, *The Study of the Bible in the Middle Ages*, 2nd ed. (Notre Dame 1964), and *The Cambridge History of the Bible II*, ed. Lampe, 155–279.

56 Crawford, 77, 'it will seem to the unlearned that all the sense is locked in the simple narrative, but it is very far from that.'

57 ÆCHom I, 21 (Thorpe, 1:300), 'This Gospel is now simply said', but cf. also ÆCHom I, 23 (Thorpe, 1:328); ÆCHom II, 30 (Godden, 235); ÆCHom II, 34 (Godden, 327); Pope, Homily 2.59, etc.

58 Pope, Homily 3.46. 'We have now said this gospel to you simply, and we will now unfold the significance, because you cannot wholly understand the mystery unless someone tells you the exposition of wise teachers regarding it, as it stands in books.'

59 Nicholas Howe discusses the semantic range of Old English *rædan* in 'The Cultural Construction of Reading in Anglo-Saxon England', in *The Enthography of Reading*, ed. Jonathan Boyarin (Berkeley 1993), 58–79. He notes that the word's various meanings – 'spoken discourse, the giving of counsel, and the interpreting of obscurity' (66) – suggest 'a textual community in which God's book is heard because it is read aloud and then interpreted' (67). Reading in Anglo-Saxon England, he argues, is almost inevitably a communal, interpretive, and didactic activity.

60 Ælfric makes this distinction in several places: see, e.g., his homily for the fifth Sunday after Easter: 'Nu sceole we gehyran þæt halige godspell mid onbryrdnysse, us to beterunge, and eac we sceolon witan hwæt ða word mænan, þæt we magon hi awendan to weorcum

þe eað; forðan þe se bið wis þe mid weorcum geswutelað þa halgan Godes lage and his
halgan lare, and se bið unrihtwis þe heorcnað þæra worda, and nele hi awendan to weorcum,
him to þearfe' (Pope, Homily 8.12, 'Now we ought to hear the holy Gospel with zeal, for
our betterment, and we also ought to know what the words mean, so that we may more
easily turn them to works; because he is wise who reveals God's holy laws and His holy
teaching with works, and he is unrighteous who hears the words, and will not turn them
to works to his own need'), and the *Treatise on the Old and New Testaments*: 'We magon
gehiran þæt se Hælend lufað swiþor þa dæde þonne þa smeðan word: þa word gewitað and
þa weorc standað. . . . Nu miht þu wel witan, þæt weorc sprecað swiþor þonne þa nacodan
word, þe nabbað nane fremminge. Is swa þeah god weorc on þam godan wordum, þonne
man oðerne lærð and to geleafan getrimð mid þære soþan lare, and þonne mann wisdom
sprecð manegum to þearfe and to rihtinge, þæt God si geherod, se þe a rixað' (Crawford,
57, 74, 'We should understand that the Saviour loves deeds better than smooth words:
words vanish and works remain . . . Now you might well know that works speak louder
than naked words, which have no effect. Nevertheless there are good works in good words,
when one teaches another and edifies him with true doctrine, and when a man speaks
wisdom for the need and direction of many, so that God might be praised, Who rules
forever').

61 Plate VII of Ker, *Catalogue*, reproduces fol. 80r of the Hatton manuscript, showing two of
these Latin headings.

62 Two headings, possibly in a different hand from that of the annotator of Matthew, are
added to consecutive paragraphs at Jn 10: 1 and 10: 11.

63 In contrast C is almost bare, though it was badly damaged in 1731 and has lost whatever
prefatory material it may have contained. Today only a translation of a letter from Pope
Sergius to Aldhelm of Malmesbury survives, which helps to localize the manuscript but
does not really offer evidence for how it was used.

64 See R.M. Liuzza, 'The Yale Fragments of the West-Saxon Gospels', *ASE* 17 (1988) 67–82.
Pl. VI in this volume reproduces the verso of these fragments, showing one of the Latin
headings in the hand of the main scribe and the added rubric in a different hand.

65 They are not original to the translation; this is seen in, among other things, the fact that
readings for some days are written at the wrong place – e.g., the reading for Sexagesima is
given as Mk 4: 3 rather than the standard (and parallel) Lk 8: 4; similarly Quinquagesima
is given as Mk 10: 46 rather than the standard (and parallel) Lk 18: 31. For the first Sunday
of Advent three readings are given, all parallel: Mt 21: 1, Mk 11: 1, and Lk 19: 29; only the
first was normally read at the Mass for the day. Most of the readings in A are common, but
I have found no surviving lectionary or capitulary which precisely parallels these unusual
headings in A; relevant manuscripts are catalogued in H. Gneuss, 'Liturgical Books in
Anglo-Saxon England and Their Old English Terminology', in *Learning and Literature*,
ed. Lapidge and Gneuss 91–141, at 106–09, and see also T. Klauser, *Das römische Capitulare
Evangeliorum*, Liturgiegeschichtliche Quellen und Forschungen 28 (Münster 1935), and
W.H. Frere, *Studies in the Early Roman Liturgy II: the Roman Gospel-Lectionary* (Oxford
1934). The liturgical headings in A may have been incorporated into a copy of the translation from a capitulary list or missal that included *incipits* but not Eusebian canon-num-
bers for reference (e.g., a missal such as Oxford, Bodleian Library, Bodley 579 [Ker 315],
which was among the donations of Leofric to Exeter). This would account for unusual
misattributions.

66 Paris, Bibliothèque Nationale, lat. 8824; see the facsimile ed. John Bromwich et al., *The
Paris Psalter (MS Bibliothèque Nationale Fonds Latin 8824)*, EEMF 8 (Copenhagen 1958).

67 By G.P. Krapp, *The Paris Psalter and the Meters of Boethius*, ASPR 5 (New York 1932), xviii.

68 A number of Latin headings in B were erased, probably in the sixteenth century (most likely in preparation for the 1571 edition), when the dependent relation of the translation to the Latin was no longer viewed with favour. At the same time the liturgical directions from A were added to the Bodley text, probably to suggest that the translation was widely used as a Mass-lectionary.

69 They are printed in John Earle, *A Handbook to the Land-Charters, and Other Saxonic Documents* (Oxford 1888), 269–71; additional manumissions from this manuscript, now part of CCCC 111, are printed in W. Hunt, *Two Chartularies of the Priory of St Peter at Bath*, Somerset Record Society 7 (1893). Some are catalogued in David A.E. Pelteret, *Catalogue of English Post-Conquest Vernacular Documents* (Woodbridge, Suffolk, 1990), nos 70–86; all are found in the introduction to *The Old English Version of the Gospels*.

70 Though, inexplicably, several manumissions have in fact been erased from Cp.

71 In R.W. Chambers, M. Förster, and R. Flower, eds, *The Exeter Book of Old English Poetry* (London 1933), 13.

72 The contents are catalogued in detail by Förster, *The Exeter Book of Old English Poetry*, 44–54; the Leofric list has been recently discussed by M. Lapidge, 'Surviving Booklists', 64–69.

73 See further M.T. Clanchy, *From Memory to Written Record, England, 1066–1307* (Cambridge, Mass., 1979), 126.

74 Grünberg, *West-Saxon Gospels*, 369.

75 For general background on this exceedingly complex question see S.J.P. van Dijk, 'The Bible in Liturgical Use', in *The Cambridge History of the Bible II*, ed. Lampe, 220–52; Josef Jungmann, *The Mass of the Roman Rite*, 2 vols (New York 1951–55); A. Hughes, *Medieval Manuscripts for Mass and Office: A Guide to Their Organization and Terminology* (Toronto 1982), 53–66; A.-G. Martimort, ed., *L'église en prière: Introduction à la liturgie*, 3rd ed. (Paris 1965); K. Young, *The Drama of the Medieval Church*, 2 vols (Oxford 1933), 1:15–75; Geoffrey G. Willis, 'Early English Liturgy from Augustine to Alcuin', in *Further Studies in Early Roman Liturgy* (1968), 189–243. For bibliography see R.W. Pfaff, *Medieval Latin Liturgy: a Select Bibliography*, Toronto Medieval Bibliographies 9 (Toronto 1982). On the question of gospel reading at Mass, Frere, *Studies in the Early Roman Liturgy*, and Klauser, *Das römische Capitulare evangeliorum*, are of central importance. On the difficulty of working with Old English liturgical history see Milton McC. Gatch, 'Old English Literature and the Liturgy: Problems and Potential', *ASE* 6 (1977) 237–47, though much fundamentally important work has been done since this was written.

76 Gatch, *Preaching and Theology*, 26.

77 James M. Ure, *The Benedictine Office* (Edinburgh 1957), 63.

78 Most have inaccurate numbers, and a group of otherwise fine manuscripts (Cambridge, Trinity College, B.10.4; Cambridge, St John's College, 73; BL Royal I D. ix; BL Harley 76) all fail to include the readings for most of August and September, apparently because a common ancestor had lost a few leaves at this point. This is noted by Frere, *Studies in the Early Roman Liturgy*, 158.

79 Gatch repeats and elaborates the arguments of *Preaching and Theology* in 'The Achievement of Ælfric and his Colleagues in European Perspective', in *The OE Homily and Its Backgrounds*, ed. Szarmach and Huppé, 43–73. See also Mary Clayton, 'Homiliaries and Preaching in Anglo-Saxon England', *Peritia* 4 (1985) 207–42, who qualifies Gatch's arguments for Ælfric's uniqueness.

80 Gatch, *Preaching and Theology*, 36; see 195, n. 64, for further references.

81 'On all feast-days and Sundays every priest should preach the Gospel of Christ to the people'; 'priests should preach to the people every Sunday and always teach by a good example.' Roger Fowler, ed., *Wulfstan's Canons of Edgar*, EETS, 266 (Oxford 1972), 12 (Wulfstan), 37 (*Exc. ps-Ecg.*). Wulfstan's emphasis on sermons rather than exegetical homilies is noted by Gatch, *Preaching and Theology*, 44–45.

82 Fehr, *Die Hirtenbriefe Ælfrics*, letter 1.61, 'On Sundays and mass-days the priest should relate the meaning of the Gospel to the people in English'; cited in Gatch, *Preaching and Theology*, 42. See also Whitelock et al., *Councils and Synods*, 1:208.

83 Gatch, *Preaching and Theology*, 51. He describes this office as follows: 'In its fully developed form, it was separable from the Mass, but usually it occurred after the Gospels and consisted of a translation and brief explanation of the pericope, announcement of forthcoming liturgical events, catechetical intstruction based on the Creed and the Lord's Prayer, and biddings or prayers and other devotions' (37).

84 Thomas L. Amos, 'Preaching and the Sermon in the Carolingian World', in *De Ore Domini: Preaching and the Word in the Middle Ages*, ed. Thomas Amos, E.A. Green, and B.M. Kienzle, Studies in Medieval Culture 27 (Kalamazoo 1989), 41–60, questions whether the Prone was a part of Carolingian liturgical renovation, as Gatch has argued.

85 ÆCHom I, 11 (Thorpe, 1:166), 'I will explicate to you this Gospel which has just been read before you.'

86 ÆCHom I, 18 (Thorpe, 1:246), 'We will now explain the Gospel which was just read here.'

87 ÆCHom I, 36 (Thorpe, 1:548), '. . . the holy Gospel which was read before you a little while ago.'

88 A version of this essay was read at the Second G.L. Brook Symposium at the University of Manchester; I am grateful to the organizers and participants for their comments and support, and to a number of readers who offered helpful suggestions, including Ursula Lenker, Richard Marsden, and Richard W. Pfaff.

Byrhtferth at Work

MICHAEL LAPIDGE

In recent decades, scholarly attention has increasingly been devoted to glossed manuscripts of the Anglo-Saxon period. The harbinger of this attention was a pioneering article by Fred C. Robinson, first published in 1973, on the syntactical markings which are often found in Anglo-Saxon manuscripts.[1] Before this time, scholarly interest in glosses and glossing had been primarily lexicographical,[2] characterized, say, by the publications of A.S. Napier[3] and H.D. Meritt;[4] but Robinson's article opened up a new scholarly perspective on how manuscripts were studied and annotated by the Anglo-Saxons themselves, and his initiative was followed by research not only on syntactical markings,[5] but on wider questions bearing on the function of glossing (both ink and dry-point)[6] and the purposes for which glossed manuscripts were intended, that is, whether manuscripts carrying glosses were intended primarily for use in the classroom or for private study in the library.[7] As a contribution to the study of how glossed manuscripts were used in Anglo-Saxon England, I should like to consider the uses made of them by one identifiable Anglo-Saxon scholar, namely Byrhtferth, who was schoolmaster at the Benedictine monastery of Ramsey from some time in the 980s until the second decade of the eleventh century.[8] Byrhtferth has left a large corpus of writing, in Latin and Old English, and from these works it is possible to see that he was exceptionally widely read in patristic and Carolingian literature.[9] Furthermore, it was characteristic of Byrhtferth's method of composition that he quoted from these earlier authorities, both *in extenso* and verbatim. The nature of his quotation raises the possibility of identifying the very manuscripts he used from among the thousand or so manuscripts which have survived from Anglo-Saxon England.[10] This possibility is especially challenging in the case of Ramsey, because although we know from Byrhtferth's quotations that Ramsey must have possessed a very substantial library, thus far only a tiny handful of manuscripts has been identified as having probably been written or owned at Ramsey. Of a scriptorium at Ramsey we know nothing: Ramsey is not so much as mentioned in T.A.M. Bishop's study of Anglo-Caroline script,[11] and, in his more recent treatment of the same subject, David Dumville could find only three manuscripts for which there are convincing grounds for supposing a Ramsey origin (a psalter and two pontificals, books which will, in any case, not have formed part of the monastic library).[12] It is unlikely that so substantial a library should have perished entirely without trace, and the possibility must remain that, among the thousand or so surviving manuscripts which were written or owned in Anglo-Saxon England, some may have belonged to the Ramsey library to which Byrhtferth had access. I should like to explore this possibility by considering Byrhtferth's quotations from Bede's *De arte metrica* and *De schematibus et tropis*, Boethius's *De consolatione Philosophiae*, and Aldhelm's prose and verse versions of his *De virginitate*. These quotations throw interesting light on Byrhtferth's scholarly methods and on his use of glossed manuscripts in particular.

BEDE, *DE ARTE METRICA* AND *DE SCHEMATIBUS ET TROPIS*

Byrhtferth begins his *Vita S. Oswaldi* with a characteristically flamboyant passage in which he asks why, since the *Iliad* and *Odyssey* and Vergil's *Aeneid* have been composed by learned men, he should be silent about the outstanding deeds of St Oswald: 'Cum sollerter Ylias et Odissia atque Eneidos Virgilii sint exarata et a plerisque uiris miro ingenio inuestigata, cur nos, fideles piissimi saluatoris seruuli, desidia opprimit, ut sui dignissimi sacerdotis taceamus insignia gesta . . .?'[13] In spite of appearances here, however, Byrhtferth had no firsthand experience of the *Iliad* or *Odyssey*; rather, he has lifted this impressive-sounding sentence almost verbatim from a passage of Bede's treatise *De arte metrica*, where Bede is discussing 'common' or 'mixed' style: 'Coenon est uel micton in quo poeta ipse loquitur et personae loquentes introducuntur ut sunt scripta Ilias et Odyssia Homeri et Aeneidos Virgilii . . .'[14] As schoolmaster at Ramsey, Byrhtferth had responsibility *inter alia* for teaching his young charges the intricacies of quantitative verse composition; and, like all schoolmasters, from the eighth century to the fifteenth, he based this teaching on Bede's *De arte metrica*. In his *Enchiridion*, Byrhtferth includes frequent excurses on various pedagogical subjects, including grammar and metre. One such excursus consists of a long discussion of the various figures of speech, and this discussion is prefaced with a brief statement concerning the three kinds of poetry, drawn directly from Bede's *De arte metrica*. Once again the reader is treated to the learned-sounding reference to Homer and Vergil: 'Þonne se sceop in gebringð oðre hadas þe wið hine wurdlion swylce hig him andswarion, þonne byð seo gesettnys coenon uel micton geciged. Swa þas þing synd gesette þe man nemð *Ylias* and *Odissia* Omeri and *Eneidos* Virgilii. (*Ilias*, þæt beoð gewyn, and *Odissia* beoð gedwyld, swa Omerus on þære bec recð.) Se ðe wyle ymbe þæs gerimes deopnyssa spyrian, þonne mæg he gemetan þisra þreora cynna rake on þam gewefe.'[15]

Immediately following this quotation from *De arte metrica*, Byrhtferth goes on to treat various figures of speech, and these are drawn from Bede's *De schematibus et tropis* (a work which was frequently combined in manuscript with *De arte metrica*, and to which it forms a sort of appendix). Since Byrhtferth here as elsewhere quotes his source verbatim, it is possible to form some opinion of the nature of the manuscript he was using. In discussing *anadiplosis*, for example, he writes as follows: 'Anadiplosis ys on þære fiftan stowe amearcod; þæt ys on Lyden iterata dupplicatio and on Englisc geedlæcend twyfealdnyss, þonne þæt uers geendað on þam naman þe hit eft onfeð.'[16] This account of *anadiplosis* is derived directly from Bede: 'Anadiplosis est congeminatio dictionis in ultima parte praecedentis uersus et prima sequentis.'[17] All the manuscripts collated by the most recent editor of Bede's treatise read *congeminatio dictionis*, not *iterata dupplicatio*, as in Byrhtferth, with one exception, a manuscript now Cambridge, Trinity College, O. 2.24 (1128)(Rochester, s. xii[i]). The Trinity manuscript at this point reads *iterata duplicatio*, exactly as in Byrhtferth. Of course the Trinity manuscript is too late to have been used by Byrhtferth; but there are reasons to suspect that some at least of its contents (particularly the 'Metrical Calendar of York' and Bede's metrical *Vita S. Cuthberhti*) were copied from an earlier Anglo-Saxon exemplar, perhaps of Northumbrian origin.[18] Byrhtferth, in theory, might have been using this lost Northumbrian exemplar.

The matter is complicated by another consideration, however. The texts of Bede's *De arte metrica* and *De schematibus et tropis* in the Trinity manuscript carry no glosses. Byrhtferth, on the other hand, seems to have been using a manuscript in which the text of Bede was accompanied by the commentary of Remigius of Auxerre (d. 908), the great Carolingian scholar whose commentaries shaped the ways in which curriculum texts were studied in medieval schools for several centuries.[19] The matter may be illustrated from Byrhtferth's discussion of *paranomasia*. Bede had simply written (in *De schematibus et tropis*), 'Paranomasia, id est, denominatio, dicitur, quoties dictio pene similis ponitur in significatione diuersa',[20] whereupon Remigius glossed Bede's adjective *diuersa* as follows: 'DIVERSA id est uaria ut amans et amens, semen sementis seminarium. Tria sunt in uaria significatione: hoc semen, huius seminis dicitur de omnibus annonis et animalibus; haec sementis, huius sementis de frugibus; hoc seminarium uero cuiuscumque rei origo est et initium.'[21] In treating the same figure, Byrhtferth wholly incorporated Remigius's gloss into his own explanation: 'Paronomasia, id est denominatio on Lyden. Þis hiw byð gesett on myslicum andgite, swylce ic þis do to bisne: amans and amens, and semens and sementis and seminarium. Amans homo byð lufwende man, and amens byð awoffod, and semens byð sawende, and sementis byð sawendis, and seminarium byð ⟨sædhus⟩.'[22] There are several other examples of verbatim dependence on Remigius's commentary in this section of the *Enchiridion*,[23] enough to suggest that Byrhtferth's two treatises carried the Remigius commentary in the form of marginal or interlinear gloss.

It may also have carried a certain amount of glossing in Old English. As we shall see when discussing Byrhtferth's indebtedness to Aldhelm, Byrhtferth was capable of copying a Latin lemma, *together with* its accompanying gloss, into a work of his own. He may have done the same thing in the case of Bede. Consider the passage quoted earlier, where Byrhtferth, after his pretentious allusion to the *Iliad* and *Odyssey*, explained the meaning of the Homeric titles: '*Ilias*, þæt beoð gewyn, and *Odissia* beoð gedwyld'. It is likely that these Old English equivalents are glosses to explanations offered by Remigius (commenting in turn on the passage of Bede):

ILIAS. subuersiones Troiae
ODYSSIA. id est errores Vlixis.[24]

Byrhtferth may simply have rendered *subuersiones* as *gewyn* and *errores* as *gedwyld*, but he may equally have copied the Old English equivalents intact from his exemplar, which, on this evidence, contained Bede's *De arte metrica* and *De schematibus et tropis*, together with Remigius's commentaries to these two texts, accompanied perhaps by Old English glosses. Unfortunately, no surviving Anglo-Saxon manuscript fits this description: only one manuscript of Bede's *De arte metrica* contains any Old English glossing (Worcester, Cathedral Library, Q. 5: two glosses, neither corresponding to those quoted above),[25] and there is no surviving Anglo-Saxon manuscript which contains the Remigian commentaries to *De arte metrica* and *De schematibus et tropis*. Interestingly, several of the very few surviving manuscripts of these works of Bede which do preserve the Remigian commentaries are from Fleury,[26] and there were very close links between Ramsey and Fleury during Byrhtferth's lifetime.[27] This may suggest, in turn, that Byrhtferth acquired his (now lost) exemplar through the agency of his master Abbo. So our search for a

Byrhtferthian manuscript of Bede's two works ends in frustration. Let us see if we have more luck with Boethius.

BOETHIUS, *DE CONSOLATIONE PHILOSOPHIAE*

There is no doubt that Byrhtferth was thoroughly familiar with the *De consolatione Philosophiae*, which by the tenth century had become a staple feature of the scientific curriculum, and had attracted the attention of numerous Carolingian commentators, from the ninth century onwards.[28] By my own count, Byrhtferth quotes this work of Boethius (often *in extenso*) twelve times in his *Historia regum*,[29] seven times in his *Vita S. Oswaldi*, once in his *Vita S. Ecgwini*, and once in his *Enchiridion*. His knowledge of the text is undoubted, therefore; but it is equally clear that Byrhtferth studied it by means of the extensive commentary by Remigius of Auxerre.[30] Proof that Byrhtferth knew this commentary of Remigius is provided by the fact that, in his Latin *Computus*, Byrhtferth included a short excerpt of Remigius concerning the regions of the heavens (inc. 'Iginus et alii astrologi ferunt quod quinque sunt zone celi');[31] by the same token, one of the twelfth-century manuscripts of Byrhtferth's *Computus* contains as a short marginal scholion an excerpt from Remigius's commentary concerning the nature of the north wind (London, British Library, Cotton Tiberius C. i, 111r):[32] 'Boreus frigidissimus est uentus dissipans nubes. Ipse est Aquilo. Aquilo dicitur eo quod aquas stringit, nubes dissipet. Flat enim ab yperboreis montibus, inde est origo eius.' Byrhtferth had clearly internalized Remigius's explanation of Boreas (the north wind), because it crops up again in his *Vita S. Oswaldi*, where he is describing the miraculous moral fibre of St Oswald, and adds that the might of the north wind could not deflect him from his purpose: 'Boreus namque frigidissimus uentus (qui et Aquilo dicitur) non illum a suo cepto opere prohiberi ⟨potuit⟩, licet suos emitteret diros flatus ab Threicio antro, ex quo procedere solet ⟨ad Angliam⟩ que est in Aquilonari parte posita.'[33] Here the point of reference is Boethius, *De consolatione Philosophiae* I Metre 3, where Boethius metaphorically implies that, just as the north wind (Boreas) blowing from Thrace disperses the clouds, so does Philosophy dispel the clouds of the mind:

Hanc si Threicio Boreas emissus ab antro
    Verberet et clausam reseret diem . . .[34]

Remigius explains Boethius's metaphor by explaining the nature of the north wind, and how, blowing from the Hyperborean mountains, it is able to check the rain and dispel the clouds: 'HANC SI THREICIO. Boreus uentus septentrionalis frigidissimus est dissipans nubes. Ipse est Aquilo. Aquilo dicitur quod aquas stringat nubes dissipet. Est enim gelidus et siccus ab hiperboreis montibus flat. Inde enim origo eius est unde naturam eius designat de quo procedit dicens . . .'[35] This passage, in other words, is that which Byrhtferth copied as a scholion into the manuscript of his *Computus*, which served as an exemplar (at however many removes) for Tiberius C. i, and which he remodelled in his *Vita S. Oswaldi*, where the poem of Boethius and the commentary of Remigius are woven together into one fabric.

Byrhtferth clearly knew Remigius's commentary on Boethius intimately. At another point in his *Vita S. Oswaldi*, in discussing miracles performed by St Oswald, Byrhtferth reflects that he has already told two miracles; but since there are three kinds of musical form – he specifies them as chromatic, diatonic and enharmonic – so it is appropriate to relate three miracles concerning St Oswald: 'Sicut enim sunt tria genera musice artis – chromaticum, diatonicum atque enarmonicum: quod primum sonat (.i. chromaticum) mellifluum est, secundum (⟨.i.⟩ diatonicum) durissimum est, tertium (.i. enharmonicum) dulcissimum ⟨est⟩ – sic sit et tertium miraculum, quod hic inserere breuiter placet.'[36] It is clear that the source of this pedantic aside is a passage in Remigius's commentary on Boethius pertaining to Book II Pr. 1, where Philosophia explains the *grauiores modos* or 'sadder notes' which music sometimes chants: 'GRAVIORES MODOS. Tria enim sunt genera musicae artis chromaticum diatonicum et enarmonicum; quorum diatonicum durissimum est, enarmonicum dulcissimum.'[37] Although there are some minor, perhaps significant, discrepancies (such as the fact that Byrhtferth explains *chromaticum* as *mellifluum*, whereas no such explanation is found in Remigius), it is clear once again that Byrhtferth drew his pedantic aside from Remigius.

One final example may be given to illustrate Byrhtferth's familiarity with Remigius's commentary on Boethius, namely his discussion of the concord among the four elements, their qualities, the four seasons, and the four ages of man, as expounded in part I of the *Enchiridion*:

Ver humidum et calidum, aer humidus et calidus; pueritia humida et calida. Sanguis, qui in pueris pollet, humidus et calidus est. Aestas calida et sicca; ignis calidus et siccus; adolescentia calida et sicca.   Colera rubea crescunt in ⟨adolescentibus⟩; calida et sicca ⟨sunt⟩. Autumnus siccus et frigidus; terra sicca et frigida; iuuentus sicca et frigida. Colera nigra in autumno crescunt; sicca et frigida sunt. Hiemps frigida et humida; aqua frigida et humida; flegmata dominantur in senibus. Colera nigra (id est melancolia) in transgressoribus uiget (id est qui ⟨in⟩ iuuentute sunt).[38]

This passage is clearly indebted to a gloss by Remigius on Boethius, *De consolatione Philosophiae* III Metre 9 (the famous cosmological poem in which Boethius explains how God bound up the four elements in celestial harmony):

ELEMENTA. Quatuor sunt elementa aer ignis aqua terra. Aer calidus et humidus est, uer calidum et humidum. Similiter et sanguis est humidus in puero et calidus. Pueritia enim calida et humida est. Ignis calidus est et siccus; aestas calida et sicca. Cholera rubea quae abundat in adulescente calida et sicca est. Adulescentia etiam calida et sicca est. Terra frigida et sicca; autumnus frigidus et siccus. Melancholia id est cholera nigra quae est in iuuenibus frigida et sicca. Iuuentus frigida et sicca. Aqua frigida et humida est, hiems frigida et humida. Flegma quae abundat in senibus frigida et humida, senectus frigida et humida.[39]

Although the sense of the two passages is identical in detail, there are some minor discrepancies in wording which are explicable on the assumption that Byrhtferth here was also drawing on Bede, *De temporum ratione* ch. xxxv (which was also an important source for Remigius).[40] In sum, these three passages of Byrhtferth – on *Boreas* the *uentus frigidissimus*, on the three kinds of music, and on the harmony of the cosmic fours – demonstrate beyond question that Byrhtferth studied Boethius by means of the commentary of Remigius of Auxerre.

So the question arises: did Byrhtferth study Boethius in a glossed manuscript which carried the Remigius commentary as marginal and interlinear gloss? From the late ninth century onwards, it became conventional – given the important place which Boethius occupied in the Carolingian curriculum – for manuscripts of the *De consolatione Philosophiae* to be laid out so as to incorporate marginal and interlinear glossing. Of the many Boethian commentaries in existence, that by Remigius enjoyed the widest circulation: some fifty manuscripts of the Remigian commentary have been identified.[41] Furthermore, unlike the case of Remigius's commentaries on Bede's *De arte metrica* and *De schematibus et tropis* (which often circulated *separately* from Bede's texts), the commentary on Boethius almost invariably circulated in the form of marginal and interlinear gloss. The presumption must be, therefore, that Byrhtferth studied Boethius in a glossed manuscript which carried the Remigius commentary.

It is interesting to note, therefore, that some eleven Anglo-Saxon manuscripts of the *De consolatione Philosophiae* carry Remigius's commentary (as marginal and interlinear gloss) on the text:[42]

Antwerp, Plantin-Moretus Museum, M. 16.18 (190)(Abingdon, s. x/xi)
Cambridge, University Library, Gg. 5.35 (CaA, s. xi^{med})
Cambridge, University Library, Kk. 3.21 (Abingdon, s. x/xi)
Cambridge, Trinity College, O. 3.7 (1179)(CaA, s. x²)
El Escorial, Real Biblioteca, e. II. 1 (s. x/xi)
Geneva, Bibliotheca Bodmeriana, Bodmer 175 (Canterbury, s. x²)
Oxford, Bodleian Library, Auct. F. 1.15, fols. 1–77 (CaA, s. x²)
Oxford, Corpus Christi College 74 (s. xi²)
Paris, Bibliothèque Nationale, lat. 6401A (CaCC, s. x^{ex})
Paris, Bibliothèque Nationale, lat. 14380 (CaCC, s. x^{ex})
Paris, Bibliothèque Nationale, lat. 17814 (? Canterbury, s. x^{ex})

The evidence shows, at the least, that there was a huge explosion of scholarly interest in the text of Boethius in the later tenth century, particularly in Canterbury and Abingdon, and that this interest resulted in the production of a number of beautifully written and attractively decorated manuscripts carrying the commentary of Remigius as ancillary to study of the text of the *De consolatione*. In spite of the supposed origins of the manuscripts listed above in Canterbury and Abingdon (and elsewhere), all but two of these manuscripts (CUL, Gg. 5.35, which was written a generation or so after his death, and Oxford, Corpus Christi College 74, written in the later eleventh century) could in theory have been used by Byrhtferth.

Unfortunately, identification is not a simple process in this case. In the first place, there is no adequate (or even minimally usable) edition of Remigius's commentary on the *De consolatione Philosophiae*: H.F. Stewart in 1916 published a few excerpts of (what he deemed to be) philosophical interest,[43] and in 1935 E.T. Silk published a few more excerpts (again, mainly of philosophical interest, and largely overlapping with those printed by Stewart).[44] Since then, nothing further has been published. In 1977 J.S. Wittig and D.K. Bolton announced an edition of the Remigius commentary; but, to my knowledge, this edition has not yet appeared. In other words, the situation as I write is that there is no complete edition of Remigius's commentary against which variant readings could be collated; with the result that anyone wishing to consult the commentary of Remigius at any point other than the few excerpts printed by Stewart and Silk, must resort to manuscripts.[45] Furthermore, commentaries to school texts such as Boethius were notoriously subject to revision: to addition, deletion, alteration. It is not surprising, therefore, that D.K. Bolton was able to identify a number of 'revisions' among the surviving Anglo-Saxon manuscripts of Remigius's commentary.[46]

These considerations need to be borne in mind in the attempt to identify the manuscript of Boethius used by Byrhtferth. The manuscript in question must be deemed to contain the following three passages of Remigius commentary (discussed above), which for sake of convenience may be labelled as follows:

A = the passage on Boreas, the *uentus frigidissimus*;
B = the passage on the three kinds of music (chromatic, diatonic, enharmonic);
C = the passage on the concord among the four elements, their qualities, the four seasons, and the four ages of man.

I have collated these excerpts in the surviving Anglo-Saxon manuscripts of Boethius, *De consolatione Philosophiae*, with the following results. The text of Remigius's commentary in CUL, Kk. 3.21, is a redaction (referred to by Bolton as K); of the three passages in question, it includes A and B, but has an entirely different account of the cosmic harmonies (C) from that in Remigius and Byrhtferth. Paris, BN, lat. 6401A similarly contains a redaction of Remigius (Bolton's redaction BN): of the passages in question, it contains A and B, but (as in the case of CUL, Kk. 3.21) contains a generalized account of cosmic *concordia* quite unlike that in Remigius and Byrhtferth (C). Cambridge, Trinity College, O. 3.7 also contains a redaction of Remigius: it contains passages A and B, but lacks altogether the account of the concord among the cosmic fours (C) preserved in Remigius and Byrhtferth. Escorial e. II. 1 contains a much-abbreviated version of Remigius's commentary; of the three passages in question, it contains only a fragment of A, a fragment of C, and lacks B altogether. Of the two Oxford manuscripts, Bodl. Auct. F. 1.15 has passage A, but not passage B and only a drastically abbreviated version of passage C (like that in the Escorial manuscript). Oxford, Corpus Christi College 74 is only lightly glossed: it lacks all three passages, A, B, and C, and is in any event – on my dating – too late to have been used by Byrhtferth. Two Paris manuscripts (BN lat. 14380 and 17814) contain passages A and B, but have only an abridged version of passage C. All these manuscripts may therefore be eliminated from our enquiries. This leaves only two manuscripts which contain the three passages of Remigius drawn on by Byrhtferth: Antwerp, Plantin-Moretus M. 16. 8 and (presumably) Geneva, Bodmer 175.[47] At this point, unfortunately, our enquiry comes to an end: our criteria (namely the three designated passages) are too crude to allow more precise verbal criticism. Because (as we have seen) Byrhtferth combined passage C with borrowings from Bede, *De temporum ratione*, no direct verbal links can be established between his paraphrase in the *Enchiridion* and the Remigian commentary as preserved in the two manuscripts; and, in the case of passage B, no manuscript of Remigius appears to contain Byrhtferth's observation that 'chromatic' music is *mellifluum*, which implies either that the observation is Byrhtferth's own, or else that he derived it from a copy of Remigius's commentary unlike any which have been printed or collated. In the present state of our knowledge it is impossible to proceed farther, owing to the inadequacy of our present criteria (passages A, B, and C).

ALDHELM, *DE VIRGINITATE*

Whereas it is possible to count the number of Byrhtferth's verbal debts to Boethius, the number of his debts to Aldhelm are literally uncountable. There is scarcely a sentence of his Latin prose that does not bear the imprint of Aldhelm's distinctive verbosity, and in many passages of his English prose as well, the influence of Aldhelm's style is unmistakable. An example will illustrate the nature of the debt. In his *Vita S. Ecgwini*, Byrhtferth has occasion to describe the glory of King Edgar, who 'Habuit pariter secum Cerethi et Phelethi, sicut Dauid manu fortis; qui habebat et sapientiam Salomonis et prudentiam Danielis.'[48] The Cerethi and Phelethi are biblical tribes that accompanied Joab on an expedition against Seba (2 Kgs [= 2 Sam] 20: 7). Of all the obscure tribes mentioned in the Old Testament, why should Byrhtferth have seized on the Cerethi and Phelethi? The answer is that Byrhtferth had in mind a passage of Aldhelm's prose *De virginitate* which contains a description of the accomplices of Satan, and these accomplices include (strangely) the Cerethi and Phelethi: 'primitus, ut dixi, principalium bis quaternos vitiorum duces, quibus Cerethi criminum et Felethi facinorum cum horrendo belli apparatu.'[49] That Byrhtferth *was* thinking of Aldhelm's mention of the two tribes, rather than the Old Testament, is confirmed by a passage in the *Vita S. Oswaldi*, where Byrhtferth is describing the insurgency of Danish vikings in the reign of Æthelred the Unready: 'surrexit contra eum [*scil.* King Æthelred] princeps Beemoth, cum omni apparatu suo, et satellitibus suis, habens secum Cerethi (id est mortificantes).'[50] Where did Byrhtferth derive the notion that the word *Cerethi* meant *mortificantes*, 'bearers of death'? Surprisingly, the gloss *mortificantes* on *Cerethi* is not found in Jerome's treatises on Hebrew names, which constituted the principal source for such information in the early Middle Ages.[51] It is therefore striking that the following gloss is found in a well-known manuscript of Aldhelm (now Brussels, Bibliothèque Royale, 1650), where it occurs as a marginal comment to the passage quoted above: 'Celethi et felethi due legiones erant que semper cum rege morabantur et quos uellent uiuificabant, quos uellent mortificabant; inde cerethi mortificantes, phelethi uiuificantes interpretantur.'[52] Byrhtferth, then, apparently took the explanation in his *Vita S. Oswaldi* (quoted above), of *Cerethi id est mortificantes*, from a glossed manuscript of Aldhelm. Before we jump to the conclusion that the manuscript in question was Brussels 1650, other evidence needs to be considered. But the example shows, at the least, that Byrhtferth was using a manuscript of Aldhelm which carried some form of glossing.

We can acquire a more accurate notion of what form this glossing took by examining two passages in Byrhtferth's *Vita S. Ecgwini*. First, a passage from the very beginning of the work, where Byrhtferth has adapted a sentence of Aldhelm in order to praise the life of dedication to God. Aldhelm had compared the nuns of Barking, to whom he addressed his prose *De virginitate*, to 'talented athletes under some experienced instructor training in the gymnasium' ('ac uelut sagaces gimnosofistas sub peritissimo quodam agonitheta . . . in gimnasio exerceri');[53] Byrhtferth applied Aldhelm's metaphor to the Three Boys in the Furnace, as described in the biblical book of Daniel. In the unique manuscript which preserves the *Vita S. Ecgwini*, the passage is glossed in Old English as follows:

> .i. plegmen
> Tum gymnosophiste sagaci mente ludebant et, uelut in gymnasio constituti, ludibus plaudebant . . .[54]

Similarly, in a later passage in the *Vita S. Ecgwini*, Byrhtferth adapted an extended metaphor from Aldhelm's prose *De virginitate* in order to describe the beauty of St Ecgwine's soul. In an allusion to the beauty of the curtains which hung in the Temple, Aldhelm had described them as having 'blazed with gold, blue, purple, twice-dyed scarlet or vermilion with twisted cotton of diverse tints' ('nam et curtinae veteris delubri . . . ex auro, iacintho, purpura, bis tincto cocco sive vermiculo cum bisso retorto dispari murice fulsisse describuntur').[55] Byrhtferth adapted the Aldhelmian passage as follows (note how it is particularly the words borrowed from Aldhelm which are provided with glosses in Old English):

> hæwen   weol⟨c⟩read
> Sic ex auro, hiacincto purpuraque, bis tincto cocco
>   wealhbasu uel mædre   mid hwitum twinum
> siue   uermiculo   cum bisso retorto fulgescere fecit acta bona sue castissime anime, ut digna fieret esse allecta in celesti curia.[56]

In each of these cases it seems clear that, in copying and adapting phrases from Aldhelm, Byrhtferth also copied the accompanying Old English glosses contained in his exemplar of Aldhelm's work.

A final passage from Byrhtferth throws light on the nature of this exemplar. In his *Enchiridion*, Byrhtferth at one point prepares himself for describing the complexities of Easter reckoning by invoking the inspiration of the Cherubim; as part of this invocation, he banishes from him the classical pagan gods of poetic inspiration, such as the Castalian nymphs and Latona, the mother of Phoebus Apollo: 'Ic hate gewitan from me þa m⟨e⟩remen þe synt si⟨ren⟩e geciged, and eac þa Castalidas nymphas (þæt synt dunylfa), þa þe wunedon on Elicona þære dune; and ic wylle þæt Latona (þære sunnan moder and Apollonis and Diane) fram me gewite, þe Delo akende, þæs ðe ealde swæmas gecyddon.'[57] In fact Byrhtferth's poetic inspiration here was Aldhelm, who at the opening of his *Carmen de virginatate* uttered a similar prayer to be free from the inspiration of the pagan gods and goddesses – the Castalian nymphas who dwell on Mt Helicon, and Phoebus Apollo himself – and instead to receive the inspiration of Christ:

> Non rogo ruricolas versus et commata Musas
> Nec peto Castalidas metrorum cantica nimphas,
> Quas dicunt Elicona iugum servare supernum,
> Nec precor, ut Phoebus linguam sermone loquacem
> Dedat, quem Delo peperit Latona creatrix . . .[58]

Byrhtferth combined this passage from the *Carmen de virginitate* with another passage in Aldhelm's prose *De virginitate* concerning the Sirens;[59] in any case it is clear that, in so doing, Byrhtferth incorporated from these same sources a number of Old English glosses:

sirene: meremen
Castalidas nymphas: dunylfa
Elicona: þære dune
Latona: þære sunnan moder and Apollonis and Diane

A large number of glossed manuscripts of Aldhelm – both of the prose *De virginitate* and of the *Carmen de virginitate* – survives from Anglo-Saxon England. However, on the assumption that Byrhtferth drew all the Old English glosses from the one manuscript, none of the surviving manuscripts can have been his exemplar, since none of them contains *all* the glosses listed above. There is, however, one source which contains all the glosses in virtually the forms cited by Byrhtferth, namely the so-called Third Cleopatra Glossary (London, BL, Cotton Cleopatra A. iii, fols 92–117).[60] The relevant glosses from that glossary are as follows:

Gimnosophistas. plegmen
Iacintho. hewen
Cocco. weolocread
Vermiculo. wealhbaso
Bisso retorto. hwite twine geþrawen
Sirenarum. meremennena
Castalidas nymphas. dunælfa
Elicona. swa hatte sio dun
Latamina [*sic for* Latona]. mater solis.[61]

Cotton Cleopatra A. iii is of mid-tenth-century date and probable Canterbury origin;[62] it could in theory have been consulted by Byrhtferth a half-century later. However, given Byrhtferth's comprehensive knowledge of Aldhelm's writings, it seems more likely that he had at his disposal a glossed manuscript (containing all the Old English glosses listed above, as well as the marginal gloss on *Cerethi* quoted earlier) than that he picked out a few isolated words from a glossary such as that in Cleopatra A. iii; and his (correct) spelling of *Latona* would, in any case, argue against his use of that glossary. The best explanation is that the Aldhelm manuscript drawn on by the compiler of the 'Third Cleopatra Glossary' was subsequently used by Byrhtferth, but since that time has unfortunately perished.

CONCLUSIONS

Our search among surviving Anglo-Saxon manuscripts for evidence of use by Byrhtferth has ended in (temporary) failure. Yet there is reason for mild optimism that such manuscripts may yet come to light. As we come to a better understanding of Byrhtferth's working methods, we may develop more precise criteria for identifying his manuscript sources, so that, for example, it may ultimately be possible to establish a firmer link between Byrhtferth and the surviving Boethius manuscripts than I have been able to do in this essay. An aspect of Byrhtferth's work which may yield such results is the study of his language. He obviously loved the sound of learned, glossary-derived words, in both Latin and Old English, and it is striking that there is considerable overlap between Byrhtferth's ornate, 'hermeneutic' vocabulary and the glosses in a small number of Anglo-Saxon manuscripts. Two glossed manuscripts in particular may be mentioned: London, British Library, Royal 7. C. IV (s. xi^med), which contains Defensor's *Liber scintillarum*, Isidore's *Sententiae* and a number of extracts from Ecclesiasticus; and Copenhagen, Det Kongelige Bibliotek, G.K.S. 2034 (s. xi^i), which contains Bede's metrical *Vita S. Cuth-*

berhti.[63] In the case of the first manuscript, Byrhtferth was certainly familiar with Ecclesiasticus (he quotes frequently from the wisdom books throughout his writings) as well as with Isidore's *Sententiae*, from which he quotes and translates in the postscript to his *Enchiridion*; but no evidence has yet come to light of Byrhtferth's familiarity with Defensor's *Liber scintillarum*. In the case of the Copenhagen manuscript, no quotation of Bede's poem has yet been identified in Byrhtferth's writings, though there need be no difficulty in assuming that he had read it. It is possible, therefore, that we may yet succeed in identifying a manuscript which passed through the hands of Byrhtferth and belonged to the library of Ramsey.[64] In the meantime, it needs hardly be stressed that much more work – of the sort initiated by Fred Robinson in 1973 – is needed on the glossed manuscripts which have survived from the pre-Conquest period.

NOTES

1 'Syntactical Glosses in Latin Manuscripts of Anglo-Saxon Provenance', *Speculum* 48 (1973) 443–75.

2 See my remarks in 'Old English Glossography: the Latin Context', in *Anglo-Saxon Glossography*, ed. R. Derolez (Brussels 1992), 45–57, esp. 45–47.

3 A.S. Napier, *Old English Glosses, Chiefly Unpublished* (Oxford 1900).

4 Illustrated in several of his publications: *Old English Glosses (A Collection)* (New York 1945); *The Old English Prudentius Glosses at Boulogne-sur-Mer* (Stanford 1959); and *Some of the Hardest Glosses in Old English* (Stanford 1968).

5 M. Korhammer, 'Mittelalterliche Konstruktionshilfen und altenglische Wortstellung', *Scriptorium* 34 (1980) 18–58.

6 See the important articles by R.I. Page, 'More Old English Scratched Glosses', *Anglia* 97 (1979) 27–45, and 'The Study of Latin Texts in Late Anglo-Saxon England [2]: The Evidence of English Glosses', in *Latin and the Vernacular Languages in Early Medieval Britain*, ed. N. Brooks (Leicester 1982), 141–65.

7 See M. Lapidge, 'The Study of Latin Texts in late Anglo-Saxon England [1]: The Evidence of Latin Glosses', in *Latin and the Vernacular Languages*, ed. Brooks, 99–140, together with the reply by G.R. Wieland, 'The Glossed Manuscript: Classbook or Library Book?', *ASE* 14 (1985) 153–73, and the qualifications to Wieland's reply suggested by R.I. Page, 'On the Feasibility of a Corpus of Anglo-Saxon Glosses: the View from the Library', in *Anglo-Saxon Glossography*, ed. Derolez, 77–95.

8 See the account of Byrhtferth's life and writings in Peter S. Baker and Michael Lapidge, eds, *Byrhtferth's Enchiridion*, EETS s.s. 15 (Oxford 1995), xxv–xxxiv.

9 Five major works are in question: a Latin *Computus*; an introduction to the use of that *Computus*, containing much ancillary material of pedagogical and arithmological interest, entitled the *Enchiridion*; a historical compilation called the *Historia regum*, and two saints' lives, the *Vita S. Oswaldi* and *Vita S. Ecgwini*. The *Computus* and the *Enchiridion* are quoted from Baker and Lapidge, ed., *Byrhtferth's Enchiridion*; the *Historia regum* from T. Arnold, ed., *Symeonis Monachi Opera Omnia*, 2 vols (London 1882–85), 2:3–91; and the

two saints' lives from my forthcoming edition, *Byrhtferth of Ramsey: The Lives of Oswald and Ecgwine*, but for these reference is also given the nineteenth-century editions of the *Vita S. Oswaldi* by J. Raine, *Historians of the Church of York*, 3 vols (London 1879–94), 1:399–475, and of the *Vita S. Ecgwini* by J.A. Giles, *Vita Quorundum Anglo-Saxonum* (London 1854), 349–96. On Byrhtferth's reading in patristic and Carolingian literature as witnessed by the *Enchiridion*, see Baker and Lapidge, ibid., pp. lxxiv–xciv. The sources of his other writings await detailed examination; see, for now, M. Lapidge, 'Byrhtferth of Ramsey and the Early Sections of the *Historia Regum* Attributed to Symeon of Durham', *ASE* 10 (1982) 97–122.

10 See Helmut Gneuss, 'A Preliminary List of Manuscripts written or owned in England up to 1100', *ASE* 9 (1981) 1–60, where 947 manuscripts are listed; but at least fifty more Anglo-Saxon manuscripts have come to light since 1981, and these will be included in a revised version of the 'Preliminary List' which Helmut Gneuss has in preparation, and which will form part of *A History of the Book in Britain, I: From the Romans to the Normans*, ed. M. Lapidge (Cambridge, forthcoming).

11 *English Caroline Minuscule* (Oxford 1971).

12 D.N. Dumville, *Liturgy and the Ecclesiastical History of late Anglo-Saxon England* (Woodbridge 1992), 79 (London, BL, Cotton Vitellius A. vii, fols 1–112), and *English Caroline Script and Monastic History: Studies in Benedictinism, A.D. 950–1030* (Woodbridge 1993), 58–65 (London, BL, Harley 2904 and Cambridge, Sidney Sussex College 100). It is also possible that a single leaf of a manuscript of Cassiodorus, *Expositio psalmorum*, now Cambridge, St John's College, H. 6 (209) (? Northumbria, s. viii), is a fragment of a manuscript once owned at Ramsey: see M. Lapidge, *Anglo-Latin Literature, 600–899* (London 1996), 432.

13 'Given that the *Iliad* and *Odyssey* and the *Aeneid* of Vergil were skilfully written and studied by many men of marvellous intelligence, why does idleness overcome us, O faithful servants of the holy Saviour, so that we are silent concerning the outstanding deeds of his bishop [Oswald]'? *Vita S. Oswaldi*, prol. (ed. Raine, 399).

14 'The "common" or "mixed" style is that in which the poet speaks in his own person and speaking characters are introduced, as in the *Iliad* and *Odyssey* of Homer and the *Aeneid* of Vergil . . .' C.B. Kendall, ed., *De arte metrica et De schematibus et tropis*, CCSL 123A (Turnhout 1975), 140.

15 'When the poet brings in other personae who speak with him as if to answer him, then the composition is called *koenon* or *micton*. The things that one calls *The Iliad* and *The Odyssey* of Homer and *The Aeneid* of Virgil are composed in this way. (*Ilias* means strife, and *Odyssey* means wandering, as Homer tells us in that book.) He who wishes to investigate the profundity of the computus may find these three kinds of discourse in the text.' *Enchiridion* iii. 3. 14–20 (ed. Baker and Lapidge, 162).

16 '*Anadiplosis* is written in the fifth position; in Latin it is called *iterata duplicatio* and in English repeating duplication. It occurs when a verse ends with the noun that the next one begins with.' Ibid. iii. 3. 48–52 (ed. Baker and Lapidge, 164).

17 CCSL 123A, 146.

18 See M. Lapidge, 'A Tenth-Century Metrical Calendar from Ramsey', *Revue Bénédictine* 94 (1984) 326–69, at 371–3, and 'Prolegomena to an Edition of Bede's Metrical *Vita S. Cuthberti*', *Filologia mediolatina* 2 (1995) 127–63, at 160–62.

19 On Remigius, see C. Jeudy, 'L'oeuvre de Remi d'Auxerre', in *L'école carolingienne d'Auxerre de Murethach à Remi, 830–908*, ed. D. Iogna-Prat, C. Jeudy, and G. Lobrichon (Paris 1991), 373–96. Remigius's commentary on Bede's *De schematibus et tropis* was first identified in

Vatican City, BAV, Reg. lat. 1560 (Fleury, s. ix/x) by J.P. Elder, 'Did Remigius of Auxerre comment on Bede's *De schematibus et tropis?*', *Mediaeval Studies* 9 (1947) 141–50; the commentary is edited and printed alongside Bede's text by M.H. King, CCSL 123A, 142–71.

20 'It is called *paranomasia*, that is, *denominatio* [metonymy], when a closely similar word is used with a different meaning.'

21 'DIVERSA, that is, distinct, such as *amans* [loving] and *amens* [mindless], *semen* [seed], *sementis* [sowing], *seminarium* [seed-plot]. The last three have distinct meanings: *hoc semen, huius seminis* [in the genitive] is used of all produce and animals; *haec sementis, huius sementis* [in the genitive] is used of crops; but *hoc seminarium* refers to the origin or beginning of anything.' CCSL 123A, 147.

22 '*Paronomasia* is called *denominatio* [metonymy] in Latin. This figure is written in differing sense, as I show in this example: *amans* and *amens*, and *semens* and *sementis* and *seminarium*. An *amans homo* is a lovable man, and *amens* means mad, and a *semens* is a sowing, and *semens* is a sowing, and *sementis* means of a sowing, and a *seminarium* is a seed-house.' *Enchiridion* iii. 3. 70–74 (ed. Baker and Lapidge, 166).

23 See the commentary in Baker and Lapidge, eds, *Byrhtferth's Enchiridion*, 330–31.

24 'ILIAS. the overthrow of Troy.' 'ODYSSIA. that is the wanderings of Ulysses.' CCSL 123A, 140.

25 Napier, *Old English Glosses*, no. 30.

26 Vatican City, BAV, Reg. lat. 1560 and Orléans, Bibliothèque Municipale 296 (249); on these, see M. Mostert, *The Library of Fleury: A Provisional List of Manuscripts* (Hilversum 1989), nos BF 778 and 1507 respectively.

27 See M. Lapidge, 'Abbot Germanus, Winchcombe, Ramsey and the Cambridge Psalter', in *Words, Texts, and Manuscripts. Studies in Anglo-Saxon Culture Presented to Helmut Gneuss on the Occasion of His Sixty-Fifth Birthday*, ed. M. Korhammer (Cambridge 1992), 99–129.

28 See P. Courcelle, *La 'Consolation de Philosophie' dans la tradition littéraire* (Paris 1967); E. Jeauneau, 'L'héritage de la philosophie antique durant le haut moyen âge', *Settimane di studio del Centro italiano di studi sull'alto medioevo* 22 (1975) 17–54, esp. 25–27; and M. Gibson, 'Boethius in the Tenth Century', *Mittellateinisches Jahrbuch* 24–25 (1991) 117–24.

29 Lapidge, 'Byrhtferth of Ramsey and the Early Sections', 114–15.

30 On this commentary of Remigius, see D.K. Bolton, 'Remigian Commentaries on the "Consolation of Philosophy" and Their Sources', *Traditio* 33 (1977) 381–94, and Jeudy, 'L'oeuvre de Remi', 388.

31 Baker and Lapidge, eds, *Byrhtferth's Enchiridion*, 426.

32 'Boreas is an extremely cold wind, dispersing the clouds. It is Aquilo. It is called Aquilo because it constrains the *aquas* [rain], disperses the clouds. It blows from the Hyperborean mountains, whence its origin.' On this manuscript, see ibid., lv–lvii.

33 'For Boreas, the icy north wind, which is called Aquilo, could not keep him from the task he had begun, even though it sent its terrible blasts from the Thracian cave, whence it normally sets out for England, which is located in the north.' *Vita S. Oswaldi* iv. 1 (ed. Raine, 433).

34 'But if fierce Boreas, sent from the Thracian cave, were to strike, and restore the darkened day . . .'

35 'HANC SI THREICIO. Boreas the north wind is extremely cold, dispersing the clouds. It is Aquilo. It is called Aquilo because it constrains the *aquas* [rain], dispels the clouds. It is icy and dry, and blows from the Hyperborean mountains. That is its origin and where it gets its character, concerning which [Boethius] says . . .' For editions of Remigius's com-

mentary, see below, nn. 41–42; the quotation is taken from Cambridge, Gonville and Caius College, 309/707 (not foliated: see below, n. 43), collated with several other Anglo-Saxon manuscripts.

36 'Just as there are three kinds of music – chromatic, diatonic and enharmonic: the first (i.e. chromatic) is mellifluous, the second (i.e. diatonic) is most unpleasant, the third (i.e. enharmonic) is the sweetest – so let there be a third miracle, which it is fitting to insert here briefly.' *Vita S. Oswaldi* iv. 10 (ed. Raine, 442).

37 'GRAVIORES MODOS. For there are three kinds of music, chromatic, diatonic, and enharmonic: of these, diatonic is the harshest, enharmonic the sweetest.' Ed. Silk (as cited below, n. 44), 323.

38 'Spring is moist and hot, air is moist and hot, childhood is moist and hot. The blood, which prevails in children, is moist and hot. Summer is hot and dry; fire is hot and dry; adolescence is hot and dry. Red choler flourishes in adolescence; it is hot and dry. Autumn is dry and cold; earth is dry and cold; manhood is dry and cold. Black choler flourishes in autumn; it is dry and cold. Winter is cold and moist; water is cold and moist; phlegm prevails amongst the aged. Black choler (that is, melancholy) flourishes in those in a state of transition (that is, those in their manhood).' *Enchiridion* i. 1. 105–13 (ed. Baker and Lapidge, 10–12).

39 'There are four elements: air, fire, water, earth. Air is hot and moist, spring hot and moist. By the same token the blood is moist in a child, and hot. For childhood is hot and moist. Fire is hot and dry; summer is hot and dry. Red choler, which abounds in adolescence, is hot and dry. For adolescence is hot and dry. Earth is cold and dry; autumn is cold and dry. Melancholy, that is the black choler which is in young men, is cold and dry. Manhood is cold and dry. Water is cold and moist, winter cold and moist. The phlegm which abounds in old men is cold and moist, old age is cold and moist.' Ed. Stewart (as cited below, n. 43), 33; ed. Silk (as cited below, n. 44), 336–37.

40 See the commentary in Baker and Lapidge, eds, *Byrhtferth's Enchiridion*, 255.

41 See the list compiled by Colette Jeudy in *L'école carolingienne*, 485–88.

42 Cf. the list (and valuable discussion) by J.S. Wittig, 'King Alfred's *Boethius* and Its Latin Sources: A Reconsideration', *ASE* 11 (1983) 157–98, at 187–88. The abbreviations CaA and CaCC refer to St Augustine's and Christ Church, Canterbury, respectively; for the manuscripts in Cambridge and Oxford, see M.T. Gibson and L. Smith, *Codices Boethiani: A Conspectus of Manuscripts of Boethius. I, Great Britain and the Republic of Ireland* (London 1996). In the case of Oxford, Corpus Christi College, 74, I dissent from earlier authorities: in my view, the manuscript was principally written by a Norman scribe in the later eleventh century, although this Norman scribe was collaborating with an Anglo-Saxon scribe, whose script is seen (e.g.) on 57v.

43 H.F. Stewart, 'A Commentary by Remigius Autissiodorensis on the *De Consolatione Philosophiae* of Boethius', *Journal of Theological Studies* 17 (1916) 22–42.

44 E.T. Silk, ed., *Saeculi Noni Auctoris in Boetii Consolationem Philosophiae Commentarius* (Rome 1935), 305–43.

45 Of the manuscripts containing the 'pure' Remigian commentary (R), I have used Cambridge, Gonville and Caius College 309/707 (English, s. xii²) for sake of convenience; but this manuscript is exceedingly carelessly written, and omits many glosses (such as those on *Cons.* III Metre 9, where the scribe was apparently too lazy to copy them all); furthermore, the manuscript is unfoliated. It would appear that the most reliable manuscript of the Boethian commentary is Trier, Stadtbibliothek, 1093 (s. x), but I have not seen this. I have collated the remaining manuscripts either in the flesh or from microfilm. I should like to

express my thanks to David Dumville for the loan of microfilms of manuscripts otherwise difficult of access, including that in El Escorial.

46 D.K. Bolton, 'The Study of the *Consolation of Philosophy* in Anglo-Saxon England', *Archives d'histoire doctrinale et littéraire du moyen âge* 43 (1977) 33–78. Bolton distinguishes the 'pure' Remigian version (R) from the following redactions (pp. 39–47): T (Cambridge, Trinity College, O. 3. 7); BN (Paris, BN, lat. 6401A); and K (CUL, Kk. 3. 21).

47 Bolton points out ('The Study', 53) that the Remigian gloss in Auct. F. 1. 15 was 'almost certainly copied' from Antwerp M. 16.8. I have not collated Geneva, Bodmer 175, but have relied on the collations printed by Stewart for passage C (Stewart did not print passages A and B).

48 'He had the Cerethi and Phelethi with him always, like David strong-of-hand; he also had both the wisdom of Solomon and the foresight of Daniel.' *Vita S. Ecgwini* iv.11 (ed. Giles, 395).

49 'First of all, as I said, [he had] the eight leaders of the principal vices, among which were the Cerethi of crimes and the Felethi of sins, with their terrifying apparatus of war.' Prose *De virginitate*, ch. 12; R. Ehwald, ed., *Aldhelmi Opera*, MGH AA 15 (Berlin 1919), 240.

50 'and prince Beemoth arose against him [King Æthelred], with all his apparatus [of war] and all his attendants, having with him the Cerethi, that is, bearers of death.' *Vita S. Oswaldi* v. 4 (ed. Raine, 455). See discussion of this passage by M. Lapidge, 'The Life of St Oswald', in D. Scragg, ed., *The Battle of Maldon AD 991* (Oxford 1991), 51–58, at 56–57, n. 7.

51 Nor is it listed by M. Thiel, *Grundlagen und Gestalt der Hebräischkenntnisse des frühen Mittelalters* (Spoleto 1973), 277.

52 'The *celethi* and the *felethi* were two legions which always accompanied the king, and gave life to those whom they wished, and brought death to those whom they wished; whence *cerethi* means "death-bringers" and *phelethi* means "life-bringers".' G. van Langenhove, ed., *Aldhelm's De Laudibus Virginitatis with Latin and Old English Glosses: Manuscript 1650 of the Royal Library in Brussels* (Bruges 1941), 7v.

53 Prose *De virginitate*, ch. 2 (ed. Ehwald, 230).

54 'At that moment the ascetics were, with shrewd perception, making sport of it, and as if placed in a gymnasium, were cheering in jest . . .' *Vita S. Ecgwini*, epil. (ed. Giles, 349).

55 Prose *De virginitate*, ch. 15 (ed. Ehwald, 244).

56 'thus he made the good deeds of his pure soul shine out, as of gold, hyacinth and purple, twice-dyed scarlet or vermilion with twisted linen, so that it would be worthy to be led into the heavenly court.' *Vita S. Ecgwini* ii.1 (ed. Giles, 361).

57 'I command to depart from me the mermaids who are called Sirens, and also the Castalian nymphs (mountain elves) who dwelled on Mount Helicon; and I desire to depart from me Latona (the mother of the sun, Apollo and Diana) whom Delos brought forth, as ancient idlers made known.' *Enchiridion* iii. 1. 205–14 (ed. Baker and Lapidge, 134).

58 'I do not seek verses and poetic measures from the rustic Muses, nor do I seek metrical songs from the Castalian nymphs who, they say, guard the lofty summit of Helicon, nor do I ask that Phoebus grant me an eloquent tongue – Phoebus, whom his mother Latona bore on Delos . . .' *Carmen de virginitate* 23–27 (ed. Ehwald, 353).

59 Prose *De virginitate*, ch. 40 (ed. Ehwald, 292).

60 T. Wright, *Anglo-Saxon and Old English Vocabularies*, 2nd ed. rev. R.P. Wülcker, 2 vols (London 1884), 1: cols 485 (line 21)–535 (line 11). The link between the 'Third Cleopatra Glossary' and the glosses to the *Vita S. Ecgwini* was first pointed out by Peter Baker, 'The Old English Canon of Byrhtferth of Ramsey', *Speculum* 55 (1980) 22–37, at 29–30.

61 Wright and Wülcker, ed., *Anglo-Saxon and Old English Vocabularies*, I, cols 485, line 23; 491, lines 7–10; 506, line 5; and 516, lines 28–31.

62 N.R. Ker, *Catalogue of Manuscripts Containing Anglo-Saxon* (Oxford 1957), 180–82; D.N. Dumville, 'English Square Minuscule Script: The Mid-Century Phases', *ASE* 23 (1994) 133–64, at 137.

63 See Baker and Lapidge, eds, *Byrhtferth's Enchiridion*, cviii–cix.

64 There is always the possibility that more writings by Byrhtferth will come to light, now that we are beginning to understand his working methods. One tantalizing example may be cited. Students of Byrhtferth will know that, among the works of Bede printed by Johannes Herwagen at Basel in 1563 were extensive glosses to Bede's *De natura rerum* and *De temporum ratione*, taken from a now-lost manuscript, and described by Herwagen as *Glossae Brideferti Ramesiensis*. These 'Byrhtferth Glosses' consist of extensive quotations from patristic and Carolingian sources intended to illustrate and amplify Bede's discussion. In 1938 the great student of medieval computus, Charles W. Jones ('The Byrhtferth Glosses', *Medium Ævum* 7 [1938] 81–97) demonstrated that these 'Byrhtferth Glosses' contained long quotations from Remigius and Heiric of Auxerre, and suggested that they were the product of ninth-century Auxerre, not of eleventh-century Ramsey. Jones's demonstration has been accepted uncritically by Byrhtferth scholars for the past fifty years (the 'Byrhtferth Glosses', for example, are not treated consistently as a source or analogue in the recent EETS edition of the *Enchiridion*, even though the first sentence of that work derives unmistakably from them). Recently, however, Michael Gorman ('The Glosses on Bede's *De temporum ratione* attributed to Byrhtferth of Ramsey', *ASE* 25 [1996] 209–32) has shown that Jones's arguments will not bear close examination – after all, there is no difficulty in accepting that Byrhtferth knew the works of Heiric and Remigius, for we have seen him quoting Remigius's commentaries on Bede and Boethius – and hence that the 'Byrhtferth Glosses' are indeed by Byrhtferth. My own recent re-examination of these 'Byrhtferth Glosses' in Herwagen's edition has convinced me that Gorman's assessment is correct. If so, we have some further hundred pages of verbatim quotation from patristic and Carolingian authors compiled by Byrhtferth, and demanding source-identification and republication. I mention this possibility simply to show that, in the field of Anglo-Saxon source-studies, there is an enormous amount still to be learned.

An *Anser* for Exeter Book Riddle 74

DANIEL DONOGHUE

To just about any other scholar I would feel obliged to apologize for the pun in the title, but Fred C. Robinson has done as much as anyone to direct attention to paronomasia as a respectable and effective rhetorical device used by Anglo-Saxon poets. His close reading of the Book Moth riddle, for example, persuasively demonstrates how 'a concatenation of puns' makes 'the poem self-referential in a complex and sophisticated way, forcing the words themselves to display the simultaneous reality and insubstantiality of language'.[1] The riddle that is the subject of this essay cannot lay claim to such lofty ambitions. It is a more familiar kind of trick question, which describes a common object in oblique anthropomorphic and metaphoric terms, forcing the reader to suspend his or her customary way of perceiving things. What sets Exeter Riddle 74 apart from most other riddles is the unusual legend behind its solution: an *anser* with a unique history.

My apologies should go instead to users of the *Guide to Old English*, who are invited by Professor Robinson and his co-editor Bruce Mitchell to try their hand at Exeter Riddle 74, which stands enticingly unsolved at the end of a selection of riddles.[2] It has been my experience in teaching from the *Guide* that students are eager to match wits with the riddle and propose solutions. So it is with some misgivings I propose one of my own: if it is accepted, either the *Guide*-users will be deprived of an enjoyable challenge or the editors will have to find another to take its place.

Exeter Riddle 74 reads in the *Guide to Old English*:

Ic wæs fæmne geong, feaxhār cwene,
ond ænlic rinc on āne tīd;
flēah mid fuglum ond on flōde swom,
dēaf under ȳþe dēad mid fiscum,
ond on foldan stōp; hæfde ferð cwicu.[3]

The text poses few difficulties for translation: 'I was a young maiden, a greyhaired woman, and a peerless man at the same time; [I] flew among the birds and swam on the water, dove under the waves dead among the fish, and stepped on the earth; I had a living soul.' The poem divides neatly in half, setting up two sets of paradoxes that seemingly defy resolution: on the one hand, the creature was simultaneously a young woman, an old woman, and a man (lines 1 and 2), and on the other it flew in the air, swam on and under the water, stepped on the land, was dead underwater yet alive (lines 3–5).

Over the years since 1859 the riddle has elicited at least eleven solutions: 'cuttlefish', 'siren', 'water', 'swan', 'soul', 'rain', 'writing', 'sea eagle', 'ship's figurehead', 'reflection', and 'swan-' or 'goose-quill'. The scholarly consensus that has developed around most riddles, including the other fourteen in the *Guide*, is missing here. Following Bruce Mitchell and Fred Robinson, I consider it unsolved and will discuss other proposed solutions only when they touch on the argument.[4]

One reason Riddle 74 has proven so intractable is its length: five lines do not give much evidence to go on. Another is that, according to my reading, it manipulates one of the main conventions of riddling, indirect description. By 'indirect description' I mean the way riddles avoid stating categories or terms closely associated with the solution. For example, none of the Old English riddles for sword explicitly mentions 'weapon' or 'iron'. It would be giving away too much. Similarly the riddles for cuckoo and swan never mention birds for the simple reason that they *are* birds.[5] When a riddle extensively draws on avian imagery, as in Exeter 31, the reader can expect the solution to be something else – in this case a bagpipe. What the riddle literally describes is what the solution cannot be. Or, as Jorge Luis Borges put it, '"In a riddle whose answer is chess, what is the only prohibited word?" I thought a moment and replied, "The word chess."'[6] But indirect description is part of the charm of riddles: in relying on figurative language they encourage a kind of mental agility in avoiding well-worn conceptual categories.

Because Riddle 74 explicitly mentions birds and fish in the phrases *mid fuglum* and *mid fiscum* we should, according to this logic, eliminate 'cuttlefish', 'swan', 'sea eagle', and perhaps even 'swan-' and 'goose-quill'. The solution should be neither fish nor fowl. Yet there is something too convenient in the categorical exclusion of these two kinds of creatures – not to mention women (*fæmne*, *cwene*) and men (*rinc*) – in such a short riddle, especially since more than a few of the earlier proposed solutions concern a creature that flies or swims. But is the convention of indirect description applied in a straightforward way in Riddle 74? Could its subversion be one of the riddle's clues, so that indirection becomes misdirection?[7] What if Riddle 74 doubles back on the explicit reference to point to a creature that could claim to be both fish *and* fowl?

For centuries such a creature was thought to exist, and it provoked a stream of commentary from learned authorities who struggled with the zoological and theological consequences of its dual nature. The creature is the barnacle goose, which, according to legend, began life underwater as a shellfish and matured into a waterfowl. My reading of Riddle 74, in short, is that the third, fourth, and fifth lines accurately describe different stages in the life cycle of the barnacle goose, and that the first two lines allude to the way the bird does not participate in the reproduction of its own species. If *mid fuglum* and *mid fiscum* individually direct us away from birds and fish, together they point straight to the barnacle goose. Who would expect a solution that combines both?

'Barnacle goose' is already the consensus solution to another riddle, Exeter Riddle 10, which complements Riddle 74 in interesting ways. But the solution for Riddle 10 has been so readily accepted since it was first proposed in 1892 that no one has reviewed the evidence (all of which is post-Conquest) for the existence of the legend in Anglo-Saxon England.[8] In the following pages I undertake such a review before turning my attention to Riddle 74.

The goose that now has the scientific name *branta leucopsis* has its nesting grounds on inaccessible cliffs in Greenland and Spitsbergen Island, where it spends the warmer months, before travelling south to winter over in northern Europe.[9] The mature bird is smaller than most geese, with black and white plumage. Its nesting grounds were not discovered until the early twentieth century.[10] For centuries it seemed to northern Europeans that the goose appeared from nowhere each winter and disappeared in the spring without nesting like other waterfowl. The other participant in this legendary life cycle is the familiar shellfish now called the barnacle, a blanket term for a variety of marine crustaceans of the order Cirripedia, such as *lepas anatifera,* a species commonly found on driftwood along the shores of England and Ireland. In all barnacles a calcified shell protects the main body, which is permanently attached to a firm object such as wood by a stalk, or peduncle. From the shell retractable feathery arms, or cirri, extend to comb the water for food. When the barnacle is fully extended under water, its three parts – peduncle, shell, and cirri – bear a remarkable resemblance (in profile) to a small goose-like bird.

The history of the word 'barnacle' is closely related to the legend. According to *The Oxford English Dictionary*, 'the name was originally applied to the *bird* which had the marvellous origin, not to the *shell* which, according to some, produced it'.[11] Only in relatively recent times has the noun 'barnacle' come to refer primarily to the shellfish and secondarily as a modifier for the bird, 'barnacle goose'. The *OED*, for this reason, rejects a Celtic etymology (citing as possible cognates Gaelic *bairneach*, Welsh *brenig*, 'limpets'), arguing that a word meaning 'goose' cannot derive from a word meaning 'shellfish'. But here I think the editor and amateur botanist James A.H. Murray was letting the distinctions of modern science obscure the word's early use, because for hundreds of years the barnacle and the goose were thought to be different stages of the same life cycle, comparable to the relation between a tadpole and a frog, but even closer in appearance. A closer examination of the earliest citations will show that the same word, *barnacle*, applied to the shellfish and the bird, at times together, at times separately. The Merriam-Webster *Third New International Dictionary*, in contrast to the *OED*, unreservedly – and I think correctly – gives a Celtic etymology.

However the legend first arose, it provided a convenient way to connect two natural phenomena: a goose with no known nesting ground, and a shellfish that looks like a goose. At some early date the shellfish was invoked to explain the origin of the bird. This improbable linking may sound strange, even bizarre today, but in my investigations I have been impressed with the reasonableness of the legend. It is not as though the Anglo-Saxons and other northern Europeans were unobservant about nature or ignorant about breeding habits. The Exeter Book riddles themselves are testimony that the Anglo-Saxons had a very detailed knowledge of the natural world and were not given to inventing far-fetched stories to patch up gaps in their knowledge. Moreover, the legend is not a fantastic story about an exotic beast, easily dismissed as the product of an overactive imagination, like the phoenix or amphisbaena from bestiaries. On the contrary it was eminently practical. Barnacles and geese were very much a part of the local landscape in northern Europe, and the legend of the life cycle gained widespread acceptance because it very plausibly explained the observed phenomena: on one hand a goose that was never known to lay eggs and on the other a shellfish that looks like a small goose. It might have remained a harmless and perhaps unrecorded curiosity if it had not had a practical but controversial application: to Christians it justified the eating of barnacle geese during Lent and other days of abstinence because, as the reasoning would go, any animal born as a fish could not be meat. To Jewish communities it posed a different problem relating to diet: whether this unusual bird should be ritually slaughtered or whether it should be eaten at all. Interestingly, both the Old English riddles and the theologians take as their starting-point the anomaly of the creature's dual nature, though where one makes a game out of the dilemma the other finds a threat to one's immortal soul and, at times, a figure of divine mysteries.

The three earliest references to the life cycle of the barnacle goose date from the second half of the twelfth century, but in each the author assumes a widespread knowledge of the legend. Alexander Neckam, for example, writes:

The bird which is commonly called *bernekke* takes its origin from pinewood which has been steeped for a long time in the sea. From the surface of the wood there exudes a certain viscous humour, which in course of time assumes the form of a little bird clothed in feathers, and it is seen to hang by its beak from the wood. This bird is eaten by the less discreet in times of fasting because it is not produced by maternal incubation from an egg. But what is this? It is certain that birds existed before eggs. Therefore should birds that do not emerge from eggs follow the dietary laws for fish any more than those birds which are begotten by the transmission of semen? Have not birds derived their origin from the waters according to the irrefutable pages of heavenly doctrine? Thus barnacles are not begotten except from wood submerged in the sea or from trees strewn along the shore's edge.[12]

Neckam's reference to the heavenly ordained origin of birds from water is most likely an allusion to Genesis 1: 21, where God makes creatures that swim in the water and the birds that fly in the air on the same day. But the important point is that Neckam is willing to grant the aquatic origin of the bird without conceding that it is therefore a fish. One might summarize his argument with a modification of the old adage: if it looks like a goose, waddles like a goose, honks like a goose, swims like a goose, and does everything but lay eggs like a goose – it must be a goose! As a bird, therefore, it cannot be eaten during Lent.

Writing at about the same time, Gerald of Wales recounts the legend in his *Topographia Hibernica* with extraordinary detail but with concerns similar to Neckam's:

There are in this place [Ireland] many birds which are called *Bernacæ;* against nature, nature produces them in a most extraordinary way. They are like marsh-geese, but somewhat smaller. They are produced from fir timber tossed along the sea, and come first into existence like gum. Afterwards they hang down by their beaks as if from a seaweed attached to the timber, enclosed by shells, in order to grow more freely. Having thus, in process of time, been clothed with a strong coat of feathers, they either fall into the water or fly freely away into the air. They derive their food and growth from the sap of the wood or the sea, by a secret and most wonderful process of alimentation. I have frequently, with my own eyes, seen more than a thousand of these small bodies of birds, hanging down from one piece of timber on the sea-shore, enclosed in shells, and already formed. They do not breed and lay eggs, like other birds; nor do they ever hatch any eggs; nor do they seem to build nests in any corner of the earth. Hence bishops and clergymen in some parts of Ireland do not scruple to dine of these birds at the time of fasting, because they are not flesh, nor born of flesh. But these are thus drawn into sin; for if a man during Lent had dined of a leg of our first parent [Adam], who was not born of flesh, surely we should not consider him innocent of having eaten what is flesh.[13]

Like Alexander Neckam, Gerald accepts the validity of the legend and adds to it a compelling eyewitness account: *Vidi multoties oculis meis plusquam mille minuta hujusmodi avium corpuscula.* He regards the eating of their meat during Lent as an Irish abomination (though other evidence indicates that the practice was widespread across much of Europe). The linking of this abuse with cannibalism (*ex primi parentis . . . femore comedisset*) is meant to shock the reader into condemning it, but on closer inspection Gerald's argument is weak. Eating a drumstick in Lent is hardly the same as eating Adam's leg. Moreover, other prohibitions forbid cannibalism whether or not it forms part of one's Lenten observance, and Adam's origin is certainly a unique case. Unlike Adam, every generation of barnacle geese started off as fish – hence the ingenious argument that they could be eaten as fish. In fact, Gerald appears to condone the reasoning of the Irish when he repeats their argument: *tanquam non carneis quia de carne non natis.* Still, even if the logic of his argument is weak, his verdict against eating the barnacle goose during Lent is quite clear.

If the Irish are guilty of one kind of abuse, the Jews are guilty of worse, because they refuse to accept the doctrine of the incarnation even in the face of its analogue from nature, the barnacle goose. In a survey of the four means of procreation Gerald inserts the barnacle's life cycle as a figure of the incarnation, which the Jews, he contends, are too stubborn to recognize:

Be wise at length, wretch, be wise even though late! In observance of your law you do not dare to deny the first generation of mankind from dust without male or female [Adam] and the second from the male without the female [Eve]. Reluctantly you approve and affirm only the third, from male and female, because it is common. But with obstinate malice you detest to your own destruction the fourth, in which alone is salvation, from female without male. Blush, wretch, blush, and at least turn to Nature! She is an argument for the faith, and for our instruction procreates and produces every day animals without either male or female.[14]

Nature's example of the last animal is, of course, the barnacle goose. Here again the force of Gerald's condemnation is clearer than his logic, because the miracle of the incarnation involved human conception in a virgin (known as parthenogenesis), whereas the barnacles reproduce by spontaneous generation from dead matter, without any assistance from a parent (a process known as abiogenesis). In fact the animal that reproduces *sine omni mare vel femina* by Gerald's own analysis ought to be parallel to Adam's generation *ex limo sine mare et femina* and not to Christ. It makes a poor analogue to the incarnation. But I doubt these logical quibbles would have detained Gerald, whose diatribe was most likely intended for domestic consumption and not for the purpose of converting Jews.

Medieval Jews were concerned about the unusual origin of the barnacle goose for their own reasons. Jewish communities in northern Europe had to decide whether the barnacle goose could be eaten with or without the ritualized slaughter, or whether it could be eaten at all. If it was judged to be a fowl like a duck or another species of goose, it had to be ritually slaughtered (*shehitah*). If, as the product of submerged wood, it came to life like fruit on a tree, then slaughter would be unnecessary. If it were considered a shellfish, then of course it could not be eaten at all. The records for the rabbinical discussions of this issue are sketchy but they seem to go back early, even before Alexander Neckam and Gerald of Wales, to Rabbi Jacob ben Meir Tam, who lived in Ramerupt on the Seine and died around 1171.

Rabbi Tam's opinion is preserved in the *responsa* of Rabbi Meir of Rothenberg, who lived about 1225 to 1293. In a passage discussing whether barnacle geese should be ritually slaughtered, Meir writes: 'My teacher, the Lion [Sir Leon of Paris] told me that he had heard from his father R. Isaac, that R. Tam directed that they should be slaughtered after the Jewish fashion, and sent this decision to the sons of Angleterre'.[15] If the genealogy of opinion given here is correct, then it locates the legend in England and antedates Gerald of Wales, because Jacob Tam died before the conquest of Ireland, and Gerald wrote his *Topographia Hibernica* for Henry II afterwards. For many years after Tam 'Jewish scholars in France and Germany discussed whether they were fish or fowl, and whether, according to the dietary laws, they were permissible as food. Some authorities answered in the affirmative; others declared them unlawful'.[16] The precise answers they gave these questions are less important than the fact that they were discussing them at all. Even if the evidence is indirect, it points to a widespread dissemination of the legend, outside of England and Ireland and beyond Christian communities.

The date of these early references is important because the Old English riddles were copied in the Exeter Book before the year 1000, so the earliest explicit mention of the legend postdates Riddle 74 by close to 200 years.[17] Yet

I think it still is safe to propose an early date for the origin of the legend, for two reasons. First, all three early references assume that the legend was already widely believed and address secondary concerns (dietary restrictions) that could only have arisen after the legend had been in circulation for some time. Second, the references locate the belief in Ireland, England, and continental Europe, in both Jewish and Christian communities. Surely an issue so widespread could not be recent. No one can tell exactly when the legend first arose, but I would put it well before the copying of the Exeter Book.

Alexander Neckam, Gerald of Wales, and Jacob Tam are only the earliest references. In later centuries there is abundant evidence that the legend was widely believed and (among Christians) repeatedly interpreted in the most favourable light for Lenten observances. The scandal of using the geese to circumvent the rules of abstinence reached such proportions that even the Pope may have been induced to act. According to Vincent of Beauvais's *Speculum naturale*, Pope Innocent III, during the fourth Lateran Council in 1215, prohibited the eating of barnacle geese in Lent.[18] Papal authority may have curbed but did not eliminate the practice. Many later sources mention it if only to condemn it, and it continued well into modern times. Max Müller in the mid-nineteenth century writes, 'I am informed that in Brittany Barnacles are still allowed to be eaten on Fridays, and that the Roman Catholic Bishop of Ferns may give permission to people out of his diocese to eat these birds at his table'.[19]

Despite the the widespread belief and apparent plausibility of the legend, it was never accepted by every authority. Among those who denied its validity were Frederick II (d. 1250), Albert the Great (d. 1280), and Roger Bacon (d. 1294). Aenius Sylvius Piccolomini (later Pope Pius II) on a visit to King James I of Scotland in 1435 inquired about the bird and, after learning he would have to go farther north to the Orkneys, complained that miracles always flee farther and farther.[20]

But the number of learned authorities who believed and perpetuated the myth outstrips the sceptics for many years. Heron-Allen's *Barnacles in Nature and in Myth* lists many of the foremost scholars well beyond the Middle Ages, including John Trevisa, Hector Boece, Julius Caesar Scaliger, William Turner, Raphael Holinshed, Thomas Campion, John Gerarde, Richard Hakluyt, and more.[21] It was not until the middle of the seventeenth century that the weight of scientific opinion began to turn against the legend. But even so, it did not disappear easily. Among those who perpetuated the belief was the first president of the Royal Society, John Morey, who delivered a paper in 1661 entitled 'A Relation concerning Barnacles', which describes how he pried open the little shells that still clung to some driftwood and found inside them 'little Birds, perfectly shaped, supposed to be Barnacles.

. . . The Shells hang at the Tree by a neck longer than the shell. . . . This Bird in every Shell that I opened, as well the least as the biggest, I found so curiously and compleatly formed, that there appeared nothing wanting as to internal parts for making up a perfect Sea-fowl'.[22] I find this reference particularly illuminating because the Royal Society was founded to promote the scientific method, to make pronouncements only after careful observation, not to perpetuate unfounded myths like that of the barnacle goose. Morey was following this process of direct observation, yet his description is strikingly similar to that of Gerald of Wales, who followed the same procedure of direct observation almost five hundred years earlier ('I have frequently, with my own eyes, seen more than a thousand of these small bodies of birds, hanging down on the sea-shore from one piece of timber, enclosed in shells, and already formed'). I mention this story not to ridicule Morey, but simply to illustrate the legend's plausibility, its reasonableness. Other references attesting to the veracity of the legend appear throughout the seventeenth and eighteenth centuries, and even into the nineteenth century, though by this time the supporters are fighting a rearguard action against modern science.

Perhaps this digression on the history of the barnacle seems like an excessive prelude to what is, after all, a five-line riddle. And it may seem even more excessive in light of the fact that another riddle, Exeter Book 10, has had 'barnacle goose' as the consensus solution for over 100 years (see n. 8):

> Neb wæs min on nearwe,   ond ic neoþan wætre,
> flode underflowen,   firgenstreamum
> swiþe besuncen,   ond on sunde awox
> ufan yþum þeaht,   anum getenge
> liþendum wuda   lice mine.
> Hæfde feorh cwico,   þa ic of fæðmum cwom
> brimes ond beames   on blacum hrægle;
> sume wæron hwite   hyrste mine,
> þa mec lifgende   lyft upp ahof,
> wind of wæge,   siþþan wide bær
> ofer seolhbaþo.   Saga hwæt ic hatte.[23]

The first five lines describe its earliest stage of life as a shellfish attached to a piece of wood, its *neb* constrained, under water (although 'mountain streams' seems out of place).[24] The sixth line contains what is the most striking similarity between the two poems, *Hæfde feorh cwico*, 'I had a living soul', versus Riddle 74's *hæfde ferð cwicu*, 'I had a living spirit', which are discussed below. Riddle 10 goes on to describe the bird's white and black plumage and ends

with references to flight over the ocean. Because the details of the riddle fit
the legend so well, it is easy to see why 'barnacle goose' has been universally
accepted as the solution.

The fit is harder to see with Riddle 74, which is more condensed and
allusive in its references. In manuscript the riddle has no punctuation except
for the end mark, and the clauses stand without any grammatical subordination in a stylistic construction known as parataxis.[25] In other words, the syntactic guides in the manuscript and the edited text are sparse, so the reader
must infer any causal, temporal, or other relations. The poem without modern punctuation (a syntactic intervention at the editorial level which in this
case obscures as much as it helps) reads:

> ic wæs fæmne geong   feaxhar cwene
> ond ænlic rinc   on ane tid
> fleah mid fuglum   ond on flode swom
> deaf under yþe   dead mid fiscum
> ond on foldan stop   hæfde ferð cwicu

While parataxis demands the reader's engagement and creates the possibility
of ambiguity (or, in extreme cases, misinterpretation), it also opens up interpretive possibilities by inducing the reader to unravel implicit meanings.
The parataxis of the last three lines of Riddle 74, I would argue, deliberately
generates ambiguity by listing various stages of the barnacle goose's life cycle
out of chronological order. This disruption creates a temporary confusion
that is an essential part of the riddle. By reanalysing the relations (a process
that parataxis invites), the following sequence can be constructed:

> deaf under yþe   dead mid fiscum
> hæfde ferð cwicu
> ond on foldan stop
> ond on flode swom
> fleah mid fuglum

In the simplest translation, this could be: 'First I sank under the wave dead
among fish; then I had a living spirit; and then I stepped on land; and then I
swam on water; then I flew among the birds'.[26] It first sinks as submerged
wood, comes to life as a shellfish, and emerges as a waterfowl. Given in this
order, the details of the last three lines fit the legend of the barnacle goose
quite closely.

The similar half-lines in each poem, Riddle 10's *Hæfde feorh cwico*, 'I had
a living soul', and Riddle 74's *hæfde ferð cwicu*, 'I had a living spirit', are
crucial clues in both riddles, because one of the things that makes the bar-

nacle unique (as Gerald of Wales and others attest) is that it comes to life from dead matter by spontaneous generation. It is not the offspring of a living parent, like a bird from an egg or an infant from a mother. The clear reference to death forces some strained figurative readings, even emendations, in other proposed solutions, but with the barnacle it can be taken literally. Only a barnacle can be dead under water, but later have a living spirit.

The first two lines of Riddle 74 have been a stumbling-block to every proposed solution. No matter how the lines are interpreted, they cannot literally mean that one object is a young woman, an old woman, and a man simultaneously. The contrast in gender (*fæmne, cwene, rinc*) and in age (*geong, feaxhar*) must be significant, but it is not immediately clear how. There is one feature, however, that all three figures have in common (*on ane tid*), but to see it depends on attributing a different meaning to *ænlic*. According to the *Dictionary of Old English*, the primary meaning of *ænlic* is 'single, one and only', hence the figurative extension 'peerless' seems appropriate applied to *rinc*. But another meaning of *ænlic* is 'solitary', glossing Latin *unicus*.[27] If 'solitary man' is taken as the equivalent of 'bachelor, man without a sexual partner', then what all three figures have in common is their non-participation in human sexual reproduction. A virgin, a woman after child-bearing years, and a man without a mate cannot make babies. As such they are fitting anthropomorphic figures for the barnacle goose, which, unlike other animals, does not participate in the reproduction of its own species. To Gerald of Wales, Vincent of Beauvais, and others,[28] it seemed that the barnacle goose lived a sexually inactive life, and new generations of geese were created without the agency of parents.

Riddle 74 strikes me as a riddler's riddle. In contrast with Riddle 10, which is relatively transparent in its full description, Riddle 74 is sparing in its details, plays with the conventions of the genre, and exploits the potential ambiguity of parataxis to raise the game of riddling to a higher level. Though we may never be sure whether 'barnacle goose' is the correct solution that the Anglo-Saxons had in mind, I offer it here in the hope that our honorand will find it an *anser,* not a *canard.*

NOTES

1 'Artful Ambiguities in the Old English "Book Moth" Riddle', in *The Tomb of Beowulf and other Essays* (Oxford and Cambridge, Mass., 1993), 104. Originally published in *Anglo-Saxon Poetry: Essays in Appreciation for John C. McGalliard,* ed. Lewis E. Nicholson and Dolores Warwick Frese (Notre Dame 1975), 355–62.

    I would like to thank the participants of Harvard's Medieval Doctoral Conference for their comments on an earlier version, and James Barton, Jacqueline Brown, Charles

Donahue, David Hillman, Margaret Kim, Linda Ehrsam Voigts, and Jan Ziolkowski for help with sources.

2 *A Guide to Old English*, 5th ed. (Oxford and Cambridge, Mass., 1992), 240. The standard edition of the Exeter Book Riddles is G.P. Krapp and E.V.K. Dobbie, eds, *The Exeter Book*, ASPR 3. (New York 1936), 234. All subsequent quotations are from this edition. The Krapp–Dobbie reading is the same as Mitchell–Robinson except for long vowel marks and different punctuation before the final half-line. The same riddle is number 72 in Craig Williamson, ed., *The Old English Riddles of the Exeter Book* (Chapel Hill 1977). The most recent edition is Hans Pinsker and Waltraud Ziegler, eds, *Die altenglischen Rätsel des Exeterbuchs*, Anglistische Forschungen 183 (Heidelberg 1985).

3 Line 5 ferð: MS forð.

4 Besides Williamson's 'ship's figurehead', two other solutions deserve mention. Frederick Tupper argues for the solution 'siren' in three publications ('Originals and Analogues of the *Exeter Book Riddles*', *Modern Language Notes* 18 [1903] 100; 'Solutions of the *Exeter Book Riddles*', *Modern Language Notes* 21 [1906] 98–99; and his edition *The Riddles of the Exeter Book* [Boston 1910]: 214–15). Kevin Kiernan, in 'The Mysteries of the Sea-Eagle in Exeter Riddle 74', *Philological Quarterly* 54 (1975) 518–22, rejects Tupper's solution and argues instead for 'sea eagle'. Interestingly, Kiernan and both of Tupper's articles draw attention to similarities between Riddle 74 and Riddle 10, which has the solution 'barnacle goose'. For a convenient summary of the solutions up to 1980 see Donald Fry, 'Exeter Book Riddle Solutions', *Old English Newsletter* 15/1 (1981) 22–33. Peter Kitson's 'Swans and Geese in Old English Riddles' (*Anglo-Saxon Studies in Archaeology and History* 7 [1994] 79–84), which came to my attention after I had finished the draft of this article, argues that the solution for Riddle 74 is *ylfetu* ('migrant swan') and comments briefly on the legend of the barnacle.

5 There are some revealing exceptions. Riddle 24, for example, in describing a jay refers to the sounds of the goose, the hawk, the eagle, and the mew, as well as the dog and the goat, where the extent of the list makes the guessing-game harder, not easier.

6 Quoted by Wim Tigges as an epigram to 'Signs and Solutions: A Semiotic Approach to the Exeter Book Riddles', in *This Noble Craft . . . Proceedings of the Xth Research Symposium of the Dutch and Belgian University Teachers of Old and Middle English and Historical Linguistics, Utrecht, 19–20 January 1989*, Costerus n.s. 80, ed. Erik Kooper (Amsterdam and Atlanta 1991), 59–82.

7 Compare the riddle 'Who was buried in Grant's tomb?' where the answer is so obvious (Grant) that the reader/listener casts about for something more devious.

8 Stopford Brooke first proposed the solution in *The History of Early English Literature, Being the History of English Poetry from Its Beginnings to the Accession of King Ælfred* (New York 1892), 179–80. The most thorough review has been Tupper's two articles and edition.

9 The most comprehensive account of barnacles and the barnacle goose is Edward Heron-Allen, *Barnacles in Nature and in Myth* (London 1928). Another influential source is Max Müller, *Lectures on the Science of Language*, 7th ed. (London 1873), 2: 583–605. The later editions of Müller have considerably more information. Both Müller and Heron-Allen detect two strands of the barnacle legend, not always clearly distinguished in later sources, the second of which concerns birds growing like leaves on a tree and falling into the water. Heron-Allen suggests that it has a Mediterranean origin.

10 The discovery is recounted by Francis C.R. Jourdain in the foreword to Heron-Allen, *Barnacles in Nature*, xiv–xv.

11 *OED*, s.v. barnacle n².

12 'Ex lignis abiegnis salo diuturno tempore madefactis originem sumit avis quæ vulgo dicitur bernekke. A superficie itaque ligni exit quædam viscositas humorosa, quæ tractu temporis lineamenta corporis aviculæ plumis vestitæ suscipit, ita quod a ligno dependere videtur avicula per rostrum. Hac quidam minus discreti etiam tempore jejunii vescuntur, eo quod ex ovo non prodierit beneficio maternæ incubationis. Sed quid? Constat quod prius fuerint aves quam ova. Numquid ergo aves quæ ex ovis non eruperunt potius legem piscium quoad esum sequuntur, quam illæ quæ ex sementina traductione ortæ sunt? Nonne item aves ex aquis originem sumpserunt, secundum cœlestis paginæ doctrinam irrefragabilem? Unde et bernekke non nascuntur nisi ex lignis salo obnoxiis, aut ex arboribus consitis in marginibus riparum.' *De Naturis Rerum, Libri Duo,* ed. Thomas Wright (London 1863), cap. xlviii. Translation adapted from Heron-Allen, *Barnacles in Nature,* 10–11. See also Neckam's poem *De Laudibus Divinae Sapientiae,* lines 481–84 (Wright, p. 384), where he seems to cast doubt on the veracity of the legend.

13 'Sunt et aves hic multæ, quæ bernacæ vocantur; quas mirum in modum, contra naturam, natura producit; aucis quidem palustribus similes, sed minores. Ex lignis namque abietinis, per æquora devolutis, primo quasi gummi nascuntur. Dehinc tanquam ab alga ligno cohærente, conchilibus testis ad liberiorem formationem inclusæ, per rostra dependent; et sic quousque processu temporis, firmam plumarum vestituram indutæ, vel in aquas decidunt, vel in aeris libertatem volatu se transferunt. Ex succo ligneo marinoque, occulta nimis admirandaque seminii ratione, alimenta simul incrementaque suscipiunt. Vidi multoties oculis meis plusquam mille minuta hujusmodi avium corpuscula, in litore maris ab uno ligno dependentia, testis inclusa, et jam formata. Non ex harum coitu, ut assolet, ova gignuntur; non avis in earum procreatione unquam ovis incubat; in nullis terrarum angulis vel libidini vacare, vel nidificare videntur. Unde et in quibusdam Hiberniæ partibus, avibus istis, tanquam non carneis quia de carne non natis, episcopi et viri religiosi jejuniorum tempore sine delectu vesci solent. Sed hi quidem scrupulose moventur ad delictum. Si quis enim ex primi parentis, carnei quidem licet de carne non nati, femore comedisset, eum a carnium esu non immunem arbitrarer.' *Giraldus Cambrensis, Topographia Hibernica, et Expugnatio Hibernica,* Rolls Series 21/5, ed. James F. Dimock (London 1867, Kraus Reprint 1964), cap. xv, pp. 47–48. Translation adapted from Müller, *Lectures on the Science of Language,* 597–98.

14 'Resipisce, infelix Judæe, resipisce vel sero. Primam hominis generationem ex limo sine mare et femina, secundamque ex mare sine femina, ob legis venerationem diffiteri non audes. Tertiam solam, ex mare scilicet et femina, quia usualis est, dura cervice approbas et affirmas. Quartam vero, in qua sola salus est, ex femina scilicet sine mare, obstinata malitia in propriam perniciem detestaris. Erubesce, miser, erubesce; et saltem ad naturam recurre. Quæ ad argumenta fidei, ad instructionem nostram, nova quotidie animalia sine omni mare vel femina procreat et producit.' Dimock, 48–49.

15 Translated in Joseph Jacobs, *The Jews of Angevin England: Documents and Records,* English History by Contemporary Writers (London 1893), 54. Jacobs identifies Sir Leon of Paris with Leo Blund, 1166–1224.

16 G.A. Kohut, 'barnacle goose', *The Jewish Encyclopedia* (New York and London 1903).

17 Patrick Conner argues for a date between 950 and 968 in his recent *Anglo-Saxon Exeter: A Tenth-century Cultural History,* Studies in Anglo-Saxon History 4 (Woodbridge and Rochester 1993), ch. 4, esp. p. 94.

18 *Vincentii Burgundi in ordine praedicatorum venerabilis episcopi Bellovacensis Speculum quadruplex* (Douai, 1624) vol. 1, bk 16, ch. 40. 'Vnde et carnibus earum in quadragesima nonnulli etiam Christiani in nostra ætate in locis, vbi auium huiusmodi copia est, vti

solebant. Sed Innoc. Papa III. in Lateranensi Concilio generali hoc vltra fieri vetuit.' I have not been able to find a record of the prohibition. Other early thirteenth-century discussions of the barnacle goose include Gervase of Tilbury and the French *Ymage du monde*.

19 Max Müller, *Lectures on the Science of Language*, 598. See also Kohut for later rabbinical references.

20 Recounted in Müller, *Lectures on the Science of Language*, 599–600. See also Heron-Allen, *Barnacles in Nature*, 20. For Frederick II see Ernst Kantorowicz, *Frederick the Second, 1194–1250*, trans. E.O. Lorimer (New York 1957), 361–62.

21 Heron-Allen, *Barnacles in Nature*, 72–105.

22 Quoted from Heron-Allen, *Barnacles in Nature*, 70.

23   My beak was bound and I was immersed,
        the current swept round me as I lay covered
        by mountain streams; I matured in the sea,
        above the milling waves, my body
        locked to a stray, floating spar.
        When, in black garments, I left the waves
        and the wood, I was full of life;
        some of my clothing was white
        when the tides of air lifted me,
        the wind from the wave, then carried me far
        over the seal's bath. Say what I am called.
    Trans. Kevin Crossley-Holland, *The Exeter Riddle Book* (London 1978), 30.

24 *Neb* is commonly translated 'beak', and for that reason may seem opposed to the convention of indirect description discussed above. But 'beak' is not the only meaning, nor the primary one. It can be used for a number of beak-shaped objects.

25 See Daniel Donoghue and Bruce Mitchell, 'Parataxis and Hypotaxis: A Review of Some Terms Used for Old English Syntax', *Neuphilologische Mitteilungen* 93 (1992) 163–83.

26 *DOE* gives 'to sink' as one of the senses for *dufan* used by Ælfric (s.v. *dufan* A.2). Carving up and rearranging the half-lines is not the only way to make the point. Keeping the clauses in order but specifying grammatical relations, one could translate, however inelegantly: 'Before I flew among the birds and swam on the water, I sank under the wave dead among the fish, after which I stepped on the land, but only after I had a living spirit.'

27 s.v. *ænlic*, sense 2.

28 Vincent of Beauvais writes, 'De his itaque certum est quod in orbe nostro circa Germaniam, nec per coitum generant, nec generantur', xvi, 40.

An Ogre's Arm:
Japanese Analogues of *Beowulf*

MICHIKO OGURA

PROLOGUE

There is no knowing whether the Vikings took a round-the-world trip to Japan, bringing their tales of ogres with them, or whether the Huns and the Mongolian nomads left traces of their primitive beliefs along the way as they rode across the Asian steppes to northern Europe, but the similarities between ancient Japanese and Icelandic or Germanic stories are seductive enough to cause us to speculate about mutual influences.

We cannot expect a direct connection between the Anglo-Saxons and the Japanese, but some scholars of Japanese literature suggest that the story of *Beowulf* was imported just as the story of Ulysses was brought sometime in the seventeenth century by a Christian mission to transform itself into the *Yuriwaka* [júriwàkə] story. We cannot deny the possibility on the whole, since most of the Japanese analogues are much later than *Beowulf*. One of these analogues, the story of Watanabe-no-Tsuna, was pointed out by Powell in 1901 and again by Chambers in 1932.[1] Two stories of this hero, *The Book of Swords* (thirteenth century) and *Taiheiki* (ca 1370) have been studied by several Japanese scholars, including Fujiwara and Oshitari.[2] But first of all we must make clear that these analogues were derived from various legends from the tenth to the eleventh century. These legends were handed down to be compiled in *The Book of Swords*, which consisted of two parts: (1) the hero takes the arm of an ogre, (2) then a woman, the ogre in disguise, comes back to restore the arm. Later, in the style of Noh songs, these two parts were established separately as *Rashohmon* and *Ibaragi*.

In this short paper I will present the complicated connections between the analogues and show that no matter how the arm-taking, the arm-restoring, the woman ogre, and the other themes resemble our legends, it is almost certain that our hero, Watanabe-no-Tsuna, is not Beowulf, owing to two crucial ways in which the Japanese stories differ from the story of *Beowulf*.

OTHER EPISODES OF THE EIGHTH CENTURY

Various elements and episodes which can be considered analogues to *Beowulf* are dated around the eighth century. The dragon fight resembles the fight between Prince Susanoh and Yamata-no-Orochi (the eight-headed snake) in *Kojiki* (literally 'ancient chronicle', dated 712). The main difference is the happy ending of the Japanese story: Prince Susanoh helps a beautiful young princess, kills the snake, and wins renown. Beowulf's death can be compared with Prince Yamato-Takeru's death, again in *Kojiki*. The prince, by his uncle's malicious command, is forced to cross Mt Ibuki in a blizzard, meets a monstrous wild boar, and dies a violent death. Manlike monsters appear not infrequently in our (real?) history. Soga-no-Iruka, a young rogue of the Soga clan who had political power in the early seventh century, was said to have the blood of both a deer and a human being and therefore could be killed only with difficulty.

OGRES IN EARLIER DAYS

Let us see where the ogre and the ogre's arm come from. The image of the 'ogre' itself must have been introduced with Buddhism; the ogre in human form, in particular, must have had its origin in an ogre of hell. In twelfth-century scroll paintings hungry ogres are found among the dying people.[3] Ogres which may be the prototypes of the ogre of *Rashohmon*, however, may show either a good or an evil nature in different episodes of the thirteenth-century literature.[4] In *Jikkinshoh* (collections of the legends of art and poems, compiled 1252),[5] a person who is unable to think of the second half-line (consisting of seven Chinese characters) of an assigned verse is said to hear a voice from above the tower-gate (Rajohmon, an older name for Rashohmon). It turns out to be an ogre (or a goblin, since Japanese has only one word, *oni*, for both) who teaches him the half-line. In an episode of *Konjaku Monogatari* (lit. 'the once-upon-a-time stories', compiled 1100), a goblin steals a famous *biwa* (lute) and plays it on the tower-gate (Rajohmon). In another story a goblin plays Parcheesi with a man of letters (Ki-no-Haseo) on the tower-gate (Suzakumon), and in a scroll painting a goblin sits on a cloud and flies with another man of letters (Kibi-no-Makibi).[6] The tower-gate must have been Rajohmon, the southern gate, but often it is written as Suzakumon, the northern gate of the main road.

It seems that our ogre became completely evil only after the fifteenth century. Social conditions after the War of Ohnin (1467–78), which was accurately described as a hell on earth, and the tales of evil spirits in Mt Ohe or Mt Togakushi, influenced the character of our wise, friendly ogre and turned it violent and malicious.

The Demon Ibaragi recovering its arm: a votive painting by Zeshin
Shibata (1845), donated to Sensoji Temple, Asakusa, Tokyo

THE ARM-TAKING THEME

How far could the arm-taking theme go back? In *Ohkagami* (a historical narrative, written 1060), a noble warrior almost cuts off the arm of an ogre who has seized his scabbard. In *Konjaku*, one of the brother hunters is caught by the hair from behind, finds his attacker to be an ogre, and skilfully shoots off its arm with an arrow. On returning home the brothers hear their old mother groaning and find that the arm was hers. The anonymous editor of the story explains that in ancient times people believed that all parents eventually turned into ogres in their old age and wished to devour their children. Here we have a prototype of the woman ogre and of the arm-taking.

Why an arm? In *Beowulf* the hero takes Grendel's arm in the fight at Heorot, but finally he brings back his head from the bottom of the mere. In *Grettis Saga*, Grettir cuts off Glámr's head after a long fight, and, while wandering as the outlaw Gestr, meets a woman ogre and cuts off her right arm. An arm can be proof of the occurrence of a fight that none or few have witnessed. Taking a head proves not only that a fight occurred, but also that a killing took place. In *Beowulf* and *Grettis Saga*, taking an arm wounds the enemy mortally. In *Konjaku* a woman ogre, the hunters' mother, dies after losing her arm, while the ogre in *Rashohmon*, though he flees from the spot, is never weakened by the defeat.

The ogre may lose either the right or the left arm. Shimazu tells that *Taiheiki* (a war chronicle written between 1368 and 1379) clearly describes the lost arm as the right one. In Noh and Kabuki *Ibaragi*, it is the left arm, because the actor has to use a fan with his right (literally right and legitimate) arm while dancing as a woman.[7]

An ogre's hand has three fingers, which represent covetousness, anger, and foolishness, and lacks two fingers, which represent mercy and wisdom. In the Noh play *Ibaragi*, however, the hand has four fingers, because the ogre needs wisdom to deceive Tsuna.

A WOMAN OGRE

A woman ogre is another element. Grendel's mother in *Beowulf* and a she-troll in *Grettis Saga* (chapter 65) remind us of a woman ogre in a Noh play, *Modoribashi*. We find a legend of Rajohmon (now widely known through Ryunosuke Akutagawa's novel of 1915) in *Konjaku*, volume 29, in which a man who wants to be a thief meets an old woman at the gate of Rajohmon. She picks up the hair of a young woman, her dead mistress, to make a wig of it. The would-be thief is at first terrified by the scene, taking her for an ogre.

As soon as he perceives that she is an ordinary human being, he robs her of the hair and the clothes of both women and runs away.

A woman ogre always appears at a bridge and/or a river. In *Konjaku*, volume 27, a beautiful woman at a bridge, an ogre in disguise, robs a warrior of his horse. Again in *Konjaku*, there is a story of *Ubume* (the spirit of a woman who was pregnant, probably died in labour, and became a bird), in which a female ghost appears at a riverside with her baby in her arms and asks a noble warrior to hold it. When the ghost tries to reclaim her baby, the warrior rides away, but later finds that the baby is in fact a leaf. A legend of (Uji-no-)Hashi-hime (lit. 'the princess at a bridge over the river Uji') seems to be closely related to the stories of a woman ogre. There is no telling whether they were mixed up by confusion or by intentional conflation, but the result is a remarkable metamorphosis: a sudden change from a young, beautiful princess to an ugly ogre. In *The Book of Swords*, there is a legend of a jealous young woman who for seven days prays to a god to make her into an ogre so that she can kill whatever women she feels jealous of. Following the god's advice, she alters her fashion and hairdo. She paints her face and body red, binds her long hair up into five parts and makes them stand up like five horns, puts an iron ring around her head, burns three candles on the three points of the ring and another two at her mouth, goes running to the river Uji, bathes in the water for three weeks and so becomes a living ogre. She skilfully changes herself into a woman to kill men and into a man to kill women.

The story of *Modoribashi* first appears in *The Book of Swords*. Our hero Watanabe-no-Tsuna is on an errand at night. When he passes Modoribashi (lit. 'the bridge of return'), a beautiful lady asks him to escort her. He places her on horseback and says, 'I will go wherever you like'. Then the lady changes into a horrible ogre and says, 'It's Mt Otagi[8] I'm heading for!' grabs his hair, and flies into the air. Tsuna draws his sword and cuts off the ogre's arm. He falls onto the roof of the cloister of Kitano-Shrine and the ogre flees to Mt Otagi. The latter part of the legend is a prototype of *Ibaragi*. Lord Yorimitsu sees the ogre's arm, consults Dr Abe-no-Seimei,[9] and commands Tsuna to confine himself for seven days in his house (Tsuna-yakata). On the evening of the sixth day an elderly woman, Tsuna's aunt who brought him up, visits him and asks him to show her the ogre's arm. As soon as she has identified the arm, she turns into the horrible ogre, seizes the arm, kicks the gable open, and vanishes in the air.

The story from Taiheiki (ca 1370), book 32, has been translated by Oshitari.[10] It differs from *Modoribashi* in that it is Tsuna who disguises himself as a woman, seduces an ox-ogre, and cuts off its arm. The ogre comes to Lord

Yorimitsu's house in the guise of Yorimitsu's elderly mother. This time it is Yorimitsu who cuts off the ogre's head.[11]

In a later Noh play called *Momijigari* (lit. 'a maple-hunting', written around the sixteenth century), a beautiful princess, the demon of Mt. Togakushi in disguise, tries to seduce Lord Taira-no-Koremochi but is killed by the power of his sword.

SUMMARY

I would sum up the relations of the stories as follows:

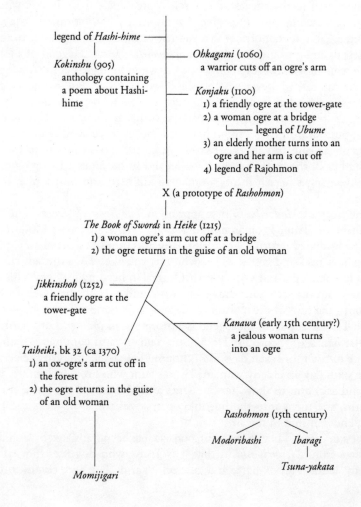

legend of *Hashi-hime* ———

Kokinshu (905)
   anthology containing
   a poem about Hashi-
   hime

Ohkagami (1060)
   a warrior cuts off an ogre's arm

Konjaku (1100)
   1) a friendly ogre at the tower-gate
   2) a woman ogre at a bridge
          └—— legend of *Ubume*
   3) an elderly mother turns into an
       ogre and her arm is cut off
   4) legend of Rajohmon

X (a prototype of *Rashohmon*)

The Book of Swords in *Heike* (1215)
   1) a woman ogre's arm cut off at a bridge
   2) the ogre returns in the guise of an old woman

Jikkinshoh (1252) ———
   a friendly ogre at the
   tower-gate

Kanawa (early 15th century?)
   a jealous woman turns
   into an ogre

Taiheiki, bk 32 (ca 1370)
   1) an ox-ogre's arm cut off in
       the forest
   2) the ogre returns in the guise
       of an old woman

Rashohmon (15th century)

Modoribashi   *Ibaragi*

Tsuna-yakata

Momijigari

The mysterious Hashi-hime is probably a prototype of a woman ogre. The arm-taking theme comes from *Ohkagami*, and all other plots are found in *Konjaku*. The most difficult part is that *Konjaku* includes various stories of India, ancient China, ancient Japan, and Buddhism, and it seems impossible to find the ultimate source of these stories. But as I mentioned earlier in this essay, *Beowulf* and *Rashohmon* differ at two crucial points: (1) an arm-taking is neither a killing nor a stage in the killing of the ogre but rather a proof of the fight and a foreshadowing of the plot of the latter half of the story (i.e., the return of the ogre); and (2) the main theme of the latter part is the metamorphosis of a woman into an ogre.

NOTES

1 Frederick York Powell, 'Béowulf and Watanabe-no-Tsuna', in *An English Miscellany: Presented to Dr Furnivall in Honour of his Seventy-Fifth Birthday* (Oxford 1901), 395–96; R.W. Chambers, 'Recent Work on *Beowulf* to 1930', in *'Beowulf: An Introduction to the Study of the Poem*, 3rd ed. with supplement by C.L. Wrenn (Cambridge 1959), 481 (the section appeared in the 2nd ed., 1932).

2 Hiroshi Fujiwara, 'Pagan Tradition and Christian Culture—in the Case of *Beowulf*', *Bulletin of the Language Institute of Gakushuin University* 10 (1987) 108–21 [In Japanese]; Kinshiro Oshitari, 'A Japanese Analogue of *Beowulf*', in *Philologia Anglica: Essays Presented to Professor Yoshio Terasawa on the Occasion of His Sixtieth Birthday*, ed. K. Oshitari et al. (Tokyo 1988), 259–69.

3 See *Gaki Zōshi* [Scrolls of Hungry Ghosts] in *Japanese Scroll Paintings*, vol. 6 (Tokyo 1960), 16–17, pl. 10.

4 Episodes are cited from Hisamoto Shimazu, *Rashohmon no Oni* [An Ogre at Rahohmon] (Tokyo 1929) [in Japanese]. The book was reprinted in 1975 under another title, but it was a tremendous loss that in the reprint all illustrations were cut out because the publisher found 'most of them insignificant and hard to reproduce'. I think the latter reason was the main one, for most of the visual images supplemented the explanations in significant ways.

5 The dates of each work are from Hideo Komatsu et al., *Supplement* to *The Illustrated Dictionary of Ancient Japanese*, 2nd ed. (Toyko 1985).

6 From *Kibi Daijin Nittō-e* [Kibi's Adventure in China] in *Japanese Scroll Paintings*, vol. 5 (Tokyo 1962), 25, pl. 15.

7 In the Kabuki dance *Modoribashi*, the story of which is based on *The Book of Swords*, it is the right arm, because the cutting off of the arm is set at the end of the dance.

8 Pronounced [ɔtági], later spelled Mt Atago and pronounced [ɔtágɔu]. The ogre in Mt Otagi would be more properly called a demon, owing to its supernatural power.

9 A famous philosopher-astrologist-diviner, who mastered a Chinese philosophy, the *Inyoh-Gogyo* theory (lit. 'the positive and negative forces of the five natural elements', i.e. fire, water, earth, wood, and metal). Oshitari, in 'A Japanese Analogue', 263, calls him 'the doctor of oneiromancy', but Abe seems to have had a profound knowledge of natural (and supernatural) phenomena in general.

10 'A Japanese Analogue', 262–64.

11 The sword is named *Hige-kiri* (lit. 'beard-cutter') in *Modoribashi*, later changes its name to *Oni-maru* after it cuts *oni*, an ogre; in *Taiheiki* it is called *Oni-kiri* (lit. 'ogre-slayer'). Lord Yorimitsu has an excellent band of warriors, among them Tsuna, one of the four distinguished retainers. In a later Noh play, *Tsuchigumo*, a lone retainer called Hirai-no-Yasumasa, who ranks higher than the four, kills a monster-spider who comes to Yorimitsu's house in the guise of a noble monk.

Courtliness and Courtesy in *Beowulf*
and Elsewhere in English Medieval Literature

ERIC GERALD STANLEY

I. LUCAS, THE ENGLISH MINOR FUNCTIONARY, INSPIRITS THE DANISH ARMY AS THEIR COURAGE FAILS

Saxo Grammaticus is much read for all manner of reasons that lie outside his *History of Danish Kings and Heroes*:[1] read by source-hunting Shakespearians who quarry Book III to see how Amlethus turns into Hamlet;[2] read by annotators of *Beowulf* in hot pursuit of Hugletus, Ingellus, Scioldus, Frotho, Haldanus, Roe and Helgo, Biarco and Rolvo, Roricus, Uffo, Iarmericus, several of them with variant spellings, and all of them discussed by many scholars of the poem;[3] and read by editors and annotators of *Widsith* and *Deor* for Ingellus, Uffo and Iarmericus again, and to give substance to the shadowy figures of Ealhhild and Hilda, to explain the geographical concept *eastan of Ongle*, and perhaps to elucidate Heorrenda by reference to Hiarnus, a poet and a king of the Danes.[4] All this legendary or historical, early material comes in the first nine books of Saxo's *History*, and other than historians of medieval Scandinavia, especially of the twelfth century, not many seem to have read and commented on books X to XVI; but those books are now available in an English translation,[5] and some details are of considerable interest to anyone concerned with the history of medieval English literature; thus:[6]

Tunc Lucas, Christifori scriba, nationis Britannicæ, litteris quidem tenuiter instructus, sed historiarum scientia apprime eruditus, cum infractos exercitus nostri animos videret, mæstum ac lugubre silentium clara voce perrumpens,[7] sollicitudinem alacritate mutavit. Siquidem memoratis veterum virtutibus nostros ad exigendam a sociorum interfectoribus ultionem tanta disserendi peritia concitavit, ut non solum mæstitiam discuteret, verum etiam cunctorum pectoribus fortitudinem ingeneraret, dictuque incredibile fuerit, quantum virium in nostrorum animos ab alienigenæ hominis sermone manaverit.

. . . Itaque cultius armatis in acie præire iussis, ignobilibus quibusque subsequendi locum attribuunt. At barbari non per acies, sed passim munitione delapsi, ingenti clamore edito, in pugnam prosilire cœperunt, existimantes Danos, strepitus viribus perterrefactos, primo congressionis impetu superandos. Tantus autem clamoris eorum horror increbruit, ut in postrema acie collocatis non solum metum, sed fugam incuteret. Verum a præcedentibus secus ac rebantur excepti, non minore impetu castra, quam reliquerant, repetebant. Complures ex eis cæsi, solus e nostris Olavus, guttur telo traiectus multoque sanguinis profluvio debilitatus, semianimis in littus refertur.

[Then Lucas, an Englishman, a clerk of Christophorus, educated pretty poorly in letters, but very expert in historical learning, perceiving the broken spirit of our army, overcame with clear voice the gloomy and mournful silence, and quickly changed the anxiety. Indeed, calling to mind the valour of their forebears, he roused our troops to vengeance on the slayers of their comrades by a speech of such skill that he not only dispelled the gloom, but also instilled courage in the hearts of all, and it is incredible to say how much strength was infused into our spirits by the speech of that foreigner.

. . . And so the more elegantly armed were ordered to make up the van, assigning the rear to the common soldiery. But the barbarian foe came down from the fortification not in battle-order, but helter-skelter; uttering a prodigious roar, they began to hurl themselves forward into battle, supposing that the Danes, frightened utterly by the din, would be overcome by the force of their first onslaught. So time and again such terror was caused by their uproar that not only fear but flight afflicted those stationed hindmost. But from those in the van they caught worse than they had expected, and they flung back to camp with no less of a rush than when they had left it. Many of them were slain; of our men only Olavus was struck in the throat, and, enfeebled by the effluxion of blood, was borne half-dead to the shore.]

Christophorus was Duke of Sleswig, the son of King Valdemar I, born 1131, king of Denmark from 1157, died 1182. This is recent: Saxo was born in about 1150 (or even a little earlier); the latest events recorded by him are of 1208, and he might have completed the work some years, at most ten years, later.[8] This part of the *Historia* is obviously not legendary but political, perhaps propagandist.[9]

The interest of the passage quoted is in several directions. Saxo marvels that an Englishman, *nationis Britannicæ* 'one of the British nation' (Saxo does not distinguish 'British' from 'English'), should have so inspirited the Danes. That need mean no more than that he thinks that the Danes, his fellow-countrymen, should be made aware that they no longer possess the warlike virtues of Danish antiquity: it took a foreigner to remind them of what was required of them at that time. It is an implicit rebuke, Tacitean in recalling the glory that was theirs, and leaving it to a foreigner to teach the lesson of vengeance. More important, especially in terms of literary history, is the distinction between the lack of clerical skill of the minor functionary of the Duke of Sleswig and the rhetorical expertise with which he urged on the Danes. The contrast is clear: Lucas, a *scriba* 'clerk, scribe, minor functionary, ecclesiastic' – the word does not occur in the *Historia* till the beginning of book xi,[10] where it is used of one Wilhelmus, according to Saxo,[11] another Englishman, *et scriba et sacerdote* at the court of Kanutus the Elder – Lucas seems to have been pretty incompetent in the profession of letters for which he was employed, and Saxo himself expert in that line, and also highly competent in skills, orally transmitted, that take us back from this period in the second half of the twelfth century to traditions of valour and glory, in short, to the Germanic Heroic Age of myth and legend.

2. THE MYTH OF THE HEROIC AGE

The myth of the Heroic Age goes back centuries further than our earliest knowledge of Germanic tribes, to Greece in Hesiod's *Works and Days*.[12] He gives the Five World-Ages, the fourth of which is that of the generation of heroes: warriors and founders of nations. Richmond Lattimore renders the passage (lines 157–73) thus, retaining the mystery in which Hesiod shrouded the age preceding his own:[13]

> Now when the earth had gathered over this generation
> also, Zeus, son of Kronos, created yet another
> fourth generation on the fertile earth,
>   and these were better and nobler,
> the wonderful generation of hero-men, who are also
> 160   called half-gods, the generation before our own
>   on this vast earth.
> But of these too, evil war and the terrible carnage
> took some; some by seven-gated Thebes
>   in the land of Kadmos
> as they fought together over the flocks of Oidipous;
>   others
> war had taken in ships over the great gulf
>   of the sea,
> 165   where they also fought for the sake

> of lovely-haired Helen.
> There, for these, the end of death was misted
>   about them.
> But on others Zeus, son of Kronos, settled a living
>   and a country
> of their own, apart from human kind,
>   at the end of the world.
> And there they have their dwelling place,
>   and hearts free of sorrow
> in the islands of the blessed
>   by the deep-swirling stream of the ocean,
> prospering heroes, on whom in every year
>   three times over
> the fruitful grainland bestows its sweet yield.
>   These live
> far from the immortals, and Kronos
>   is king among them.
> For Zeus, father of gods and mortals,
>   set him free from his bondage,
> although the position and the glory still belong
>   to the young gods.

Anglo-Saxonists may see their own heroes, Beowulf especially, reflected in this fourth generation of better, nobler men. That similarity has long been recognized, and it was given a significant turn in the direction of myth when Hector Munro Chadwick made it the pivot of his book, *The Heroic Age*, the influence of which is still felt.[14]

Yet textual scholars of *Works and Days* were not always inclined to see in the mention of 'lovely-haired Helen' an identification, authentically by Hesiod himself, of the men and women of Homer's Greece and Troy with the heroes of the Heroic Age, Hesiod's fourth generation. And so they disintegrated the poem, much as their contemporaries in Old English studies disintegrated *Beowulf*. The very neatness of Hesiod's mention rendered his Theban and Trojan allusions suspect to the disintegrationists; thus F.A. Paley:[15] 'It is not indeed improbable that the whole passage 161–69 was added by the rhapsodists in consequence of the celebrity of the Thebaid and the Iliad, which were alike attributed to Homer.' These lines of the myth of the Heroic Age, whether or not scholars of the last century or of ours attributed or attribute them to the rhapsodists, are reminiscent, not so much of *Beowulf*, as of the British foundation myth with which, for example, *Sir Gawain and the Green Knight* opens majestically:[16]

SIÞEN þe sege and þe assaut watz sesed at Troye,
Þe borȝ brittened and brent to brondez and askez,
etc.

We have created a division: Epic and Romance; and this is the world of romance. Of course, this opening goes back to no Heroic Age, only to Geoffrey of Monmouth, the great fabricator, who died in 1154 when Saxo was a boy. Whereas Saxo recalls for us a mythical Germanic Heroic Age, Homer and Hesiod together with the mythical Greek Heroic Age are out of sight and mind as we hear, in Geoffrey's creation, Diana addressing Brutus on his journey westwards; in Milton's rendering:[17]

> *Brutus* far to the West, in th'Ocean wide
> Beyond the Realm of *Gaul*, a Land there lies,
> Sea-girt it lies, where giants dwelt of old,
> Now void, it fitts thy people; thether bend
> Thy course, there shalt thou find a lasting seat,
> There to thy Sons another *Troy* shall rise,
> And *Kings* be born of thee, whose dredded might
> Shall aw the World, and Conquer Nations bold.

The tone is heroic, both of the first stanza (and more) of *Sir Gawain* and of Milton's eight lines giving us Diana's prophecy of the glory that shall come to the heirs of Brutus, Britain's Trojan founder – as the world believed till well into the eighteenth century.[18] The tone matters for our feel of the heroic.

3. EPIC OR ROMANCE?

Different traditions of literary history define *epic* and *romance* differently. *Epic* is, in some traditions, factually delimited by the metre used, as in Greek and as in the *chanson de geste*, the *épopée* of medieval France, though to ears attuned to English medieval poetry the *chanson de geste* seems a romance rather than an epic. Differing definitions of these poetic kinds lead to a different understanding in the various traditions of what is *epic*, what is *romance*.

In English literary history, an end in which all live happily ever after, our hero or his foe or foes in disguise, our hero unaware of his own princely or aristocratic rank, our hero in love, our hero in courteous, amorous converse with one or more ladies of quality, or in a more direct relationship with a low-born female, preferably young – in fact and in feminist language, the relationship is rape intended or achieved – all these are indicative of romance. The metre plays no great part in our perception: the Anglo-Saxons had only one alliterative verse form (with very minor differences in the handling by poets over many centuries, and with occasional use of longer, hypermetric lines),[19] and the Middle English poets, who had the choice between the metres of alternating stress and unstress – as Chaucer says, referring to a verse form, 'The note, I trow, imaked were in Fraunce'[20] – and alliterative metre, felt to be traditionally English by the *Gawain* poet,[21]

> I shal telle hit as tit as I in toun herde
>   with tonge,
>   As hit is stad and stoken
>   In stori stif and stronge,
>   With lel letteres loken
>   In londe so hatz ben longe.

[I shall relate it (the story) at once with my tongue as I heard it told, as it is recorded and set down in brave and mighty story, bound with correctly alliterating letters as has been the custom in the land for a long time.]

The poet uses phrases of pretended aural reception (*I . . . herde*) and oral delivery (*telle . . . with tonge*) when he refers to this particular poem, and combines them with an alliterative phrase of written record (*stad and stoken*) when he refers to the tradition of alliterative verse in England. Perhaps this sophisticated poet wishes to indicate by his choice of the alliterative metre that his poem opens as if, in medieval terms, *historial*: of the siege of Troy, the traitor Aeneas, and Brutus, founder of Britain; but there is no telling in English. *Sir Gawain and the Green Knight* has a complex stanza form which, as far as we can tell, does not go back a long way, and of which the bob and wheel are not native, whereas the body of the stanza (before the bob) is native.[22] The choice of metre in Middle English appears to be guided less by the subject-matter than it is influenced by what is customary in a particular part of the English-speaking British Isles. The choice appears not to affect at all the treatment of the subject, except that, perhaps for some kinds of depiction, of battle scenes, for example, alliterative metre does well. Even so, if the question is asked of any Middle English narrative poem, Is it heroic poetry or is it a romance?, not many critics would answer 'heroic poetry'.

The distinction – whether the figures of narrative verse typify heroic poetry or verse romances – applies to medieval creations only. A transference to more recent times does not work well. For example, Napoleon with his mistress of Polish origin is a modern, novelettish subject, perhaps of a kind to excite, in Johnsonian terms (probably bowdlerized),[23] the amorous propensities of a more innocent age than ours; Napoleon's dying words, *Tête d'armée*, are heroic, because, whether he said them or not, they are words designed to elevate the spirit. In medieval narrative, a mixture of the amorous with the heroic characterizes romance; English heroic poetry is unadulterated by moments or longer periods of amorous adventure.

The personages of heroic verse, engaged in warfare, or in voyaging undertaken to achieve glory in battle, must be princely or noble. The proper heroic attitude, a haughty spirit, is shown in the account in Saxo of the battle in which the Danes had the victory, made bold by the speech of Lucas, the English clerk. How many were lost of the common soldiery that bore the brunt of the first onslaught, who knows? Who cares? Of the enemy, many were slain, and we lost only Olavus of name. The exchange of question and answer between Leonato and the Messenger about the recent hostilities, in the opening scene of *Much Ado about Nothing*, shares that spirit, though the play as a whole is very far from heroic literature:

> *Leon.* How many Gentlemen haue you lost in this action?
> *Mess.* But few of any sort, and none of name.

Messengers themselves may be 'of any sort'; they have a function, and when they occur in heroic verse, as in *Beowulf* (lines 2892–3030a), they have no name. Heroic poems are interested only in persons of rank.[24]

4. TWO POPULAR ROMANCES

It is easier to sense what is heroic than to define it in words. It is easy to see when the heroic is not present in a work. Of the Middle English verse romances, *Havelok the Dane* and *The Tale of Gamelyn* are perhaps the clearest examples of what is not heroic. There may be fighting or other contests involving physical strength and other displays of strength in situations distinctly unheroic. Hrothgar's emphasis on Beowulf's physical strength is significant because that strength overcomes a superhuman foe, in Hrothgar's speech on hearing of Beowulf's arrival in Denmark (lines 377–81):

> Đonne sægdon þæt sæliþende,
> þa ðe gifsceattas Geata fyredon
> þyder to þance, þæt he þritiges
> 380 manna mægencræft on his mundgripe
> heaþorof hæbbe.

[The seafarers who transported there the rich gifts by way of thanks for the Geats said further that he, a man of martial fame, has in his hand-grip the strength of thirty men.]

The strength of Havelok and his foster-brothers manifests itself more crudely, in porterage, in wrestling matches, and in bashing up foes with whatever comes to hand. But, then, *Havelok the Dane* is far away from the courtly society of heroic poetry or, for that matter, Arthurian romance, of which, in Middle English, *Sir Gawain and the Green Knight* is the supreme example. That *Havelok* is socially lower, though its hero, Havelok, becomes, as the poem unfolds, king of two realms (confirmed by the damaged incipit, '[Incipit vita Hav]elok quondam Rex Anglie et Denemarchie') shows itself in several ways.[25]

First, *Havelok* is for delivery in a place, a market ale-booth or an ale-house, where ale is asked for at the outset by the person about to deliver the poem, so that the performance may be piously lubricated (lines 13–16):

> At the beginnig of vre tale
> Fil me a cuppe of ful god ale,
> And wile drinken her Y spelle
> Þat Crist vs shilde alle fro helle.

[At the outset of our story let me have a drinking vessel of very good ale, and, before I tell the tale, I will confirm with a drink my prayer that Christ may keep us all out of hell.]

Secondly, the work-ethos, admirable for the working man, would never do for the medieval aristocracy of England (lines 799–803):

> Swinken ich wolde for mi mete:
> It is no shame for to swinken.
> Þe man þat may wel eten and drinken
> Þat nouth ne haue but on swink long –
> To liggen at hom it is ful strong.

[I am willing to work for my food: there is nothing dishonourable in working. Let no one who is at all ready to eat and drink have anything unless it is because of work done – it's a bit much just to loaf around at home.]

The clothes worn by Havelok, the journey to his workplace, his dealings with competing workmen, and the first work undertaken by him are rough and hard (lines 858–79):

He tok þe sh[e]res of þe nayl
And made him a couel of þe sayl,
860 And Hauelok dide it sone on.
Hauede neyþer hosen ne shon,
Ne none kines oþe[r] wede:
To Lincolne barfot he yede.
Hwan he kam þe[r] he was ful wil,
865 Ne hauede he no frend to gangen til.
Two dayes þer fastinde he yede,
Þat non for his werk wolde him fede.
Þe þridde day herde he calle,
'Bermen, bermen, hider forth alle!'
. . .
872 Hauelok shof dun nyne or ten
Rith amideward þe fen,
And stirte forth to þe kok.
. . .
877 Þe bermen let he alle ligge,
And bar þe met to þe castel,
And gat him þere a ferþing wastel.

[He (Grim) took the scissors from the nail and made a hooded garment[26] from the sail for him. Havelok put it on at once. He possessed neither stockings nor shoes, nor any other kind of clothes: barefoot he went to Lincoln. When he got there he was at a loss what to do, not having any friend to go to. For two days he was continuously without food, because nobody was willing to give him food in exchange for his work. On the third day he heard a cry shouted: 'Porters, porters, come forward this way, all of you!' . . . Havelok pushed down nine or ten, into the mud right in the middle, and hurried on to the cook. . . . He left all the porters sprawling, and carried the food to the castle; and there he earned a farthing-cake for himself.]

Thirdly, the fights in which Havelok and his friends get involved are no knightly encounters, and the weapons used are unchivalrous. Havelok himself, handsomer, taller, and also more virtuous and gracious than anyone else (lines 980–1067, and cf. 1700–02), is soon the victor in English market sports, especially putting the stone. In Denmark, the assault of sixty-one thieves on the company including especially Bernard Brown and Havelok (who had by then achieved some grandeur) is beaten off, as we are told in a long description of which this is from the climax (lines 1791–1860):

He gripen sone a bulder-ston,
And let it fleye, ful god won,
Agen þe dore þat it torof.
Auelok it saw, and þider drof,
1795 And þe barre sone vt-drow
Þat was unride and gret ynow,
And caste þe dore open wide
And seide, 'Her shal Y now abide,
Comes swiþe vnto me:
1800 Daþeyt hwo you henne fle!'
'No,' quodh on, 'þat shaltou coupe!'
And bigan til him to loupe,
In his hond his swerd utdrawe;
Hauelok he wende þore haue slawe.
1805 And with [him] comen oþer two
Þat him wolde of liue haue do.
Hauelok lifte up þe dore-tre,
And at a dint he slow hem þre;
Was non of hem þat hise hernes
1810 Ne lay þer ute ageyn þe sternes.
Þe ferþe, þat he siþen mette,
Wit þe barre so he him grette
Bifor þe heued þat þe rith eye
Vt of þe hole made he fleye,
1815 And siþe clapte him on þe crune
So þat he stan-ded fel þor dune.
Þe fifte þat he ouertok
Gaf he a ful sor dint ok
Bitwen þe sholdres þer he stod,
1820 Þat he speu his herte blod.
Þe sixte wende for to fle,
And he clapte him with þe tre
Rith in þe fule necke so
Þat he smote his necke on to.
1825 Þane þe sixe weren doun feld
Þe seuenþe brayd ut his swerd,
And wolde Hauelok riht in þe eye.
And Haue[lok] le[t þe] barre fleye
And smot him sore ageyn þe brest,
1830 Þat hauede ne neuere sch[r]ifte of prest,

. . .

Alle þe oþere weren ful kene,

. . .

Þey drowen ut swerdes ful god won,
And shoten on him so don on bere
1840 Dogges þat wolden him totere
Þanne men doth þe bere beyte.
Þe laddes were kaske and teyte
And vnbiyeden him ilkon.
Sum smot with tre and sum wit ston,
1845 Summe putten with gleyue in bac and side
And yeuen wundes longe and wide
In twenti stedes and wel mo
Fro þe croune til þe to.
Hwan he saw þat, he was wod,
1850 And was it ferlik hw he stod.

. . .

But þanne bigan he for to mowe
With þe barre, and let hem shewe
1855 Hw he cowþe sore smite,
For was þer non, long ne lite,
Þat he mouthe ouertake
Þat he ne garte his croune krake,
So þat on a litel stund
1860 Felde he twenti to þe grund.

[They at once got hold of a large stone and hurled it with great force against the door so that it burst in pieces. Havelok saw it and ran there, and at once pulled out the door-bar which was sufficiently huge and big, and threw the door wide open, saying, 'I'll now wait here. Come on here to me, at once! [1800] God damn whichever of you flees from here!', 'No,' said one of them, 'you'll pay for that!' and proceeded to run towards him, his drawn sword in his hand; he expected to have slain Havelok there. And two others came with him who wanted to do him to death. Havelok lifted up the door-bar and at one stroke he felled three of them. There was not one of them but his brains [1810] lay there openly, facing the stars. The fourth, whom he encountered next, he assailed so with the bar in the front of his head that he made his right eye fly out of its socket, and next he struck him on the top of his head that he fell down stone-dead there. The fifth that he caught up with he also gave a very fierce blow between his shoulders as he was standing there [1820] so that he puked out his heart's blood. The sixth one thought to escape, and he banged him with the bar right on his filthy neck so that he struck his neck in two. When the six were felled to the ground the seventh drew out his sword, and wanted to hit Havelok right in the eye. And Havelok let fly the bar and struck him direct on his breast [1830] so that he never managed to be shriven by a priest . . . All the rest were very bold . . . They drew their swords mightily and rushed at him as do dogs [1840] at a bear which they want to tear in pieces whenever one baits bears. The fellows were lively and ready for the fray, and they all surrounded him. One struck out with a bar, another with a stone, still others thrust into back and side with their swords and inflicted long and wide wounds in twenty places, and even more, from head to foot. When he saw that he got angry, [1850] and how he stood up was a marvel . . . But then he began to mow them down with the bar and let them see how grievously he could strike, for there was not one of them, tall or little, when he caught up with him but he made his skull crack so that in a little space of time [1860] he felled twenty to the ground.]

And so on, till at last all sixty-one are killed by Havelok and his friends wielding different crude weapons as they came to hand, the dead left to rot without thought of decent burial (lines 1911–26):

> He maden here backes al so bloute
> Als he[re] wombes and made hem rowte
> Als he weren kradel-barnes,
> So dos þe child þat moder þarnes.
> 1915 Daþeit þe recke, for he it seruede!
> Hwat dide he þore? Weren he werewed.
> So longe haueden he but and bet,
> With neues under hernes set,
> Þat of þo sixti men and on
> 1920 Ne wente þer awey liues non.
> On þe morwen h[w]an it was day
> Ilc on oþer wirwed lay
> Als it were dogges þat weren henged,
> And summe leye in dikes slenget,
> 1925 And summe in gripes bi þe her
> Drawen ware and laten þer.

[They (Havelok and his friends) made their (the thieves') backs as soft as their bellies and caused them to howl as if they were babies in their cradles, as does a child that wants its mother. God damn him who cares, for they deserved it! What did he do there? They were snuffed out. So long had they (Havelok and his friends) thrust and beaten, with fists applied to under their ears, that of the sixty-one men not a single one went away from there alive. In the morning when it was light they were lying snuffed out on each other as if they were dogs that had been hanged, and some were lying flung into ditches, and others had been dragged by their hair into ditches, and left there.]

Fourthly, the evil Earl Godard receives too base a punishment for an earl to suffer at the hands of Havelok's men, as he is brought before Havelok, who is by now the rightful king (lines 2446–53):

> Wolden he nouht þerfore lette
> Þat he ne bounden hond and fet.
> Daþeit þat on þat þerfore let,
> But dunten him so man doth bere,
> 2450 And keste him on a scabbed mere:
> His nese went unto þe cri[c]e.
> So ledden he þat ful swike
> Til he was biforn Hauelok brouth.

[They would not on that account (on account of the earl's cries for mercy) leave off, but they bound him hand and foot. God damn anyone who desists for such a reason, but they beat him as one beats a bear, and they threw him on to a scabby mare: his nose went to the cleft between the buttocks. Thus they led that foul traitor till he was brought before Havelok.]

Next, Godard is flayed alive, a punishment in accordance with the sentence of the royal court of justice constituted for that purpose by the king (lines 2493–512):

> Þat he sholde þarne lif
> Sket cam a ladde with a knif
> 2495 And bigan rith at þe to
> For to ritte and for to flo;
> And he bigan for to rore,
> So it were grim or gore,
> Þat men mithe þeþen a mile
> 2500 Here him rore, þat fule file.
> Þe ladde ne let nowith forþi
> Þey he criede, merci! merci!'
> Þat ne flow eueril del

> With knif mad of grunden stel.
> 2505 Þei garte bringe þe mere sone.
> Skabbe*d* and ful iuele o bone,
> And bunden him rith at hire tayl
> With a rop of an old seyl,
> And drowen him unto þe galwes,
> 2510 Nouth bi þe gate, but ouer þe falwes,
> And henge þore bi þe hals:
> Daþeit hwo recke – he was fals.

[So that he should be deprived of life a fellow came quickly, knife in hand, and at the very toe began to make cuts and to flay; and he (Godard) started to roar as if it were a fit of frenzy or rage, so that he could be heard roaring a mile off, that filthy scum. The fellow did not at all leave off on that account, though he cried, 'Mercy!, Mercy!', except that he flayed him all over with his whetted steel knife. They had the mare brought at once, scabby and in very bad condition, and tied him right to her tail-end with a rope off an old sail, and dragged him to the gallows, not by the lane, but across the fallow fields, and hanged him there by the neck: God damn him who cares – he (Godard) was a traitor.]

These scenes are felt from below. The actions, the sentiments, the allusions, and the curses are low: the strength in porterage, the wrestling, and the fights; the rope off an old sail such as might be appreciated best by an audience of fishermen; the feelings of gutter joy as Godard is made to ride skimmington or worse; the crude violence of the flaying; and the dragging alive of the bloody body to the gallows – God damn all who feel pity – reminiscent of the joy of the *tricoteuses* as they watched the tumbrils roll to Dr Guillotine's merciful contraption and cheered as it fulfilled its function.

Havelok is not unique in its crudeness; *The Tale of Young Gamelyn* comes close to it, as J.E. Wells said long ago in an account which seems to use 'primitive and unsophisticated' as terms of approval:[27]

Connection with *Havelok* is suggested in Gamelyn's prowess as a wrestler, and in his beating of his opponents with the pestle and with a staff . . .

The poem has genuine merit. It is primitive and unsophisticated in all its details; in its attitude as well as in its matter and its manner, it is to be associated with the ruder Germanic romances – with *Havelok* and *Horn*, and with the ballads.

Gamelyn is preserved in no fewer than twenty-five of the manuscripts of the *Canterbury Tales*, spuriously given to the Cook[28] (by way of a second, more complete tale), a low fellow, if ever there was one,[29] whose genuine tale Chaucer broke off after no more than fifty-eight lines, and to which, it is usually thought, he never intended to devote any more than fifty-eight lines.[30] The aspirations and successes set forth in *Gamelyn* correspond to low hopes. If one were to talk in terms of wish-fulfilment within medieval narration, the wishes fulfilled in this tale are such as might be entertained by the lower orders. Who ever first thought it might fit, superficially at least, into the framework of Chaucer's tales, and gave it to the Cook judged the story matter and narrative line well, though – obviously, as it may seem to a twentieth-century reader – without any understanding of the high art displayed by Chaucer in the tales he wrote for the low pilgrims who perform in the first Fragment of the *Canterbury Tales*, and without any understanding of Chaucerian metres. The first modern editor of Chaucer, Thomas Tyrwhitt, understood that when he gave his twofold reasons for not including *Gamelyn* among the genuine tales.[31] First, he rejects a spurious conclusion to *The Cook's Tale*: 'It seems to have been an early, though very unsuccessful attempt to supply the deficiencies of that Tale, before any one had thought of tacking *Gamelyn* to it.' Secondly, Tyrwhitt rejects *Gamelyn* as a second *Cook's Tale*, whereas he had sound reasons for including what is still regarded as genuinely *The Cook's Prologue* and *The Cook's Tale*:[32]

There was not the same reason for inserting the story of GAMELYN, which in some Mss. is annexed to the *Cokes Tale*. It is not to be found in any of the Mss. of the first authority; and the manner, style, and versification, all prove it to have been the work of an author much inferior to Chaucer.

One quotation from *Gamelyn* will suffice to illustrate that its manner, style, and versification all are inferior in art to Chaucer, who burlesqued popular verse romances in both uncourtliness and lack of technical finesse when he gave *Sir Thopas* to Chaucer the Pilgrim.[33] A typical encounter in *Gamelyn* is that between the sheriff's men and Gamelyn and Adam, with characteristic dialogue and a merry piece of irony in which the knocking out of brains is expressed as an invitation to have a drink of wine, but with rather fewer oaths than usual in this romance (lines 589–98):[34]

     Atte posterne-gate · Gamelyn out wente,
590 And a good cart-staf · in his hand he hente.
     Adam hente sone · another gret staf
     For to helpe Gamelyn · and goode strokes 3af.
     Adam felde tweyne · and Gamelyn felde thre.

The other setten feet on erthe · and bygonne fle.
595   'What!' seyde Adam · 'so euer here I masse!
I haue a draught of good wyn · drynk er ye passe!'
'Nay, by God,' sayde thay · 'thy drynk is not good;
It wolde maken a mannes brayn · to lien in his hood.'

[Gamelyn went out by the back door, taking a good cart-staff in his hand. Adam immediately took another big staff in order to help Gamelyn, and he struck out well. Adam knocked down two, and Gamelyn three. The others took to their heels. 'What!' said Adam, 'by the mass I hope I may hear always, I have a draught of good wine: have a drink before you leave!' 'No, by God,' they said, 'your drink is no good; it would make a man's brains lie scattered in his cap.']

5. THE OLD ENGLISH *WALDERE* FRAGMENTS

In Old English poetry, the obvious choice for anyone wishing to illustrate what is courtly and heroic is *Beowulf*; yet the two *Waldere* fragments, each just over thirty lines long, serve that purpose well because their fragmentary state makes it essential to view them as they have come down to us, out of context. We have, as may be inferred but is not explicit in the fragments themselves, a pair of lovers of royal parentage, in a warlike situation away from court and courtly *entourage*. Contextual information is derived from the Latin *Waltharius*,³⁵ a poem of some length, 1456 hexameters, which has been characterized as a type of *Epos* (the German term *Epos* is wider than English *epic*) the hero of which is in flight, a *Fluchtdichtung*, thus designated in an abstraction of comparativist criticism that prefers the generic to the unique.³⁶ The woman's name is not preserved in the Old English fragments; she corresponds to Hiltgunt of *Waltharius*, for which the Old English name, known in Anglo-Saxon name-giving from the ninth century onwards, is Hildegyþ.³⁷ Commentators have stressed the leisurely style of the fragments, and that has led them to assure us, and reassure each other, of the length of the original; thus, in 1860, George Stephens (whose 'lines' are, of course, half-lines): 'It is evident from the Epical breadth of treatment which we find in these leaves, that the Lay has been on an extensive scale, some 6 or 8,000 lines';³⁸ and more recent critics: 'in a leisurely epic style that suggests that the poem in its complete form may have been as long as *Beowulf*',³⁹ and 'the complete poem must originally have been at least 1000 lines long'.⁴⁰ Arguments by analogy may persuade only to mislead; and yet would anyone who watches the race from only one point venture to guess the length of the course by the impression of pace alone, without assessing the skill of the jockey and the quality of the horse? However we view the length and epic nature of *Beowulf* and *Waldere*, however little faith we may have in them as genuine products of the Germanic Heroic Age, if we come to them from the rough-and-tumble world of *Havelok* and *Gamelyn*, we sense a higher courtliness, a greater nobility of purpose and achievement.

The order of the two manuscript leaves which form the fragments of *Waldere* is uncertain, and I follow the order now usually adopted. Of the three speeches in the fragments, the speech filling all of fragment I is, and is generally agreed to be, by Hildegyth. Commentators and editors usually give the second speech, fragment II lines 1–10, to Guthhere, but others have suggested that the speaker might be Waldere or Hagena; and the third speech, fragment II lines 14–31, is stated (II line 11) to be by Waldere. The relationship of the Old English fragments to the Latin *Waltharius* is not known, except that it is clear they share in the same story matter. The Old English fragments differ in some significant details from the Latin, so that it is unlikely that the Latin is its source, even if a date of composition is accepted for the Old English poem later than the date of composition of *Waltharius*, usually now considered to be of the ninth century.[41] *Waltharius* could be derived from a lost vernacular source, presumably a continental narrative if there was such a thing; and that lost work could perhaps be an analogue to the Old English poem of which so little survives. Hedged about with so many ifs and perhaps, the Latin is little help in determining some of the essential facts of the Old English fragments, their order especially, or who speaks the second speech.

Waldere and his beloved, Hildegyth, have taken to flight together, and in the fragments, as he faces the danger of combat, she 'encouraged him eagerly' *hyrde hine georne*. The interpretation of the opening word is uncertain, and *hyrde* could be from *hyran*, that is, 'she heard him eagerly'; since she does the talking rather than the listening to him, that seems the less likely interpretation. Her behaviour is not that of a little thing mincing by his side: she speaks her mind, in singleness of spirit and with directness of voice, perhaps reminding us of Wealhtheow's speeches in Hrothgar's court, and certainly conforming with that part of the Exeter Book *Maxims* that deals with a queen's noble duty in giving the king good counsel (lines 91b–92),[42] that she must 'him ræd witan || bold-agendum bæm ætsomne' [give good counsel for them, together the joint owners of their house[43]]. Wealhtheow in *Beowulf*, Ealhhild in *Widsith* (lines 5–9 and 88–111),[44] and the queen of the *Maxims* are royal ladies at court; Hildegyth is a royal lady in armed flight, during which she sees her duty in sharing courage with Waldere even as she shares danger with him.

It has been said that no other Old English heroic poem shows a woman in that situation with that fortifying spirit. That seems right to me, though the statement, Hermann Schneider's, seems wrong in several other directions. First, he reduces the roles of Wealhtheow and of Ealhhild in *Widsith* to something unimportant, ladylike ornaments at their husbands' court; secondly, a speculative genesis and classification of *Waldere* are implied as if they were undeniable facts, that *Waldere*, being no longer at the early stage of literary development of heroic lay, but already at the later epic stage, surprises in retaining features which Schneider thinks belong more properly to the stage of the heroic lay;[45] and, thirdly, a chronology of composition is implied, similarly as if factual, by which *Waldere* is early and the Latin *Waltharius* is later (and is to be securely ascribed to Ekkehard of St Gall):[46]

Der Waldere ist, wenngleich Epos, noch altertümlich in der Auffassung des Weibes, Hildgund die einzig heroisch gesehene Frau der englischen Heldendichtung. Schon Ekkehard nahm sie ganz anders. Dem Beowulf ist die Frau so bedeutungslos wie den alten Nordländern. Zu einem Hofhalt gehören Damen, vor allem die liebenswürdige Königin. Freigebig und freundlich vermittelnd erscheint auch die Ealhhild des Vidsið.

[*Waldere*, though an epic, is still antiquated in its conception of the woman: Hildegyth, the only lady who is seen heroically in English heroic poetry. Ekkehard perceived Hiltgund quite differently. As far as *Beowulf* is concerned, ladies are as insignificant as they were to the ancient Scandinavians. Ladies are part of a court, above all else the gracious queen. Ealhhild too, in *Widsith*, appears generous and mediates with kindness.]

Importance in heroic poetry is, so it seemed to Schneider, a quality of prowess in war. A lady's grandeur and wisdom in court and council are of the Christian Middle Ages. Assessed in terms of an idealized and hypothesized Heroic Age where the male is the measure, the lady is of no significance. The Old English poems themselves have no warrant for such an assessment.

As one praises Hildegyth for grandeur, and, applauding her address of Waldere as *wine min* (I line 12) – to be translated 'my friend', or perhaps 'my lord and friend' or 'my generous lord', but not 'O lover mine'[47] – a sneaking doubt creeps in: by what measure are we weighing *her* excellence? J. Grimm's seductive vagueness in his praise of Hiltgunt in *Waltharius* comes to mind:[48]

Hildgund, die überall im lied weder zu wenig noch zu viel auftritt, hinterlässt wunden bindend und weinbereitend am schlusse einen wolthuenden eindruck.

[Hiltgunt, appearing everywhere in the poem, neither too little nor too much, leaves us, as she binds up wounds and prepares wine, in the end with a comforting impression.]

Except in the binding of wounds and the preparing of wine, details absent from the English fragments, this means little more than that, first, Grimm had not had too much of her; secondly, that he had not wanted more of her; and, thirdly, that, willing to be won over by her to admiration, he did think her agreeable.

H. Althof, at the beginning of this century, was a less distinguished commentator, and less restrained, as he attached his comments to Grimm's comments on Hiltgunt; she, a royal, foreign captive at the court of the Huns, is able, *durch persönliche Vorzüge* [as a result of her personal advantages], to ameliorate her sad lot:[49]

Ihre Sittsamkeit und ihr rühriger Eifer in der Erfüllung weiblicher Obliegenheiten gewinnen ihr das Herz der Königin, und . . . so freut sie sich, in dem fremden alleinstehenden Mädchen eine zuverlässige Persönlichkeit gefunden zu haben, der man die selbständige Leitung der häuslichen Geschäfte und die Aufsicht über die Schätze des Königshauses übertragen kann.

[Her maidenly reserve and her busy diligence in fulfilling female duties gain for her the queen's heart, and so the queen rejoices that she has found a reliable character in the foreign, companionless girl, one to whom the unsupervised direction of the domestic affairs of the royal household and the control of its treasures could be transferred.]

Here indeed is the ideal ur-*au pair* from Germany: and that sense is heightened by a generalizing, glowingly enthusiastic footnote (too dependent on reducing Klärchen in Goethe's *Egmont* to a comfortable domesticity):

Aus dem wenigen, was von ihr, aber meisterhaft, gesagt wird, und aus dem vielen, was verschwiegen wird, läßt sich ein Bild zusammenstellen, das urdeutsch wird und – obschon sie eine Fürstentochter ist – Egmonts Klärchen außerordentlich gleicht: 'Velle tuum meum est' ist der Inbegriff ihres Lebens. Dienen, raten, helfen, heilen, lieben, so erscheinen die deutschen Weiber in Geschichten und Gedichten bei Tacitus – und bei Goethe.

[From the little that is said about her, but that in masterly fashion, and from the great deal left unsaid, we are able to put together the picture of a person who is German to the core, and who is – though she is a prince's daughter – extraordinarily like Egmont's Klärchen: 'Thy will is mine' is the essence of her life. To serve, to counsel, to help, to restore to health, and to love, that is how German women appear in histories and imaginative writings, in Tacitus – and in Goethe.]

Hiltgund is better described by George Stephens, the first editor of the Old English fragments:[50] 'The fidelity of HILTGUND, who acts as the page and guard and butler of her sore-prest lover is very touchingly dwelt upon.' Perhaps I exaggerate Althof's *petit bourgeois* view of Hiltgund in the Latin poem; in any case, other than the counselling and the helping, nothing much of the abidingly German picture of his reading of the Latin poem is to be seen in the Old English *Waldere* fragments: in the early Middle Ages princesses did not go satisfactorily into domestic service, and may not have excelled in the attitudes and actions pleasing to a German *Hausfrau* as understood by Althof at the turn of the century. Waltharius and Hiltgund, both of royal Germanic birth and held hostage in the land of the Huns, escaped together: and she stood by him, not as an ur-*au pair*, but as a companion in need, wise and resolute of counsel for them both. After all, the age of the Germanic world, if not genuinely a Heroic Age, is certainly not an age of middle-class domesticity, but of glorification of arms.

Hildegyth's speech to inspirit Waldere is nobly supportive (I lines 6–7):

> Ætlan ordwyga,   ne læt ðin ellen nu gyt
> gedreosan to dæge   dryhtscipe . . .

[Spear-warrior of Attila, let not your courage, your prowess, fail this day . . .]

Waldere must not be seen as a weakling, lacking courage, and considered by the more valiant Hildegyth to be about to fail. That view, advanced, in commenting on Hildegyth's words to Waldere (I line 24) *Ne murn ðu for ði mece* [Have no concern for the sword], by F. Dieter (among others) who suggested that the only unforced interpretation of these words was that Waldere had lost his sword in a previous encounter but should not let that worry him,[51] was well controverted by L.L. Schücking in a distinguished study:[52]

Eine Reihe von Auslegern wie Dieter, Anglia XI 165, verstehen überhaupt die Stelle falsch, indem sie glauben, Hildegund belebe den sinkenden Mut des Waldere wieder. Von Mutlosigkeit bei Waldere kann gar nicht die Rede sein. Es handelt sich hier vielmehr um den typischen Zuspruch im Kampf, bei dem Hildegund an die Stelle des jungen Gefolgsmannes tritt. Vgl. die auf uns Heutige überraschend väterlich wirkende Art, wie der junge Wiglaf zum greisen König Beowulf spricht: 'Lēofa Biowulf, læst eall tela, swā þū on geoguð-fēore geāra gecwæde' etc. 2663.

[A number of commentators, such as Dieter, *Anglia* 11: 165, misunderstand the passage altogether, in that they believe that Hildegyth is reviving Waldere's sinking courage. There can be no question of lack of courage as regards Waldere. Rather we are dealing with typical words of encouragement in battle, with Hildegyth taking the place of the young retainer. Cf. the manner, seeming to us moderns surprisingly paternalistic, in which young Wiglaf speaks to the aged King Beowulf (lines 2663 ff.):

Leofa Biowulf,   læst eall tela,
swa þu on geoguðfeore   geara gecwæde,
etc.

(Beloved Beowulf, perform everything well, as, long ago in the time of your youth, you said, etc.)]

Perhaps one might with justice go further than that. The relationship of the warrior to his sword, the famous named sword Mimming in this poem, is fundamental to Germanic heroism, and Hildegyth reinforces the strength of that relationship. We would do better to regard her as a sword-maiden (though that category is not prominent in the secondary writings on Germanic heroism), rather than as a shield-maiden (the category to which, as we shall see shortly, she is, or used to be, assigned). The importance of the sword emerges from the high frequency in the use of words for 'sword' in *Beowulf*, higher than of words for 'shield'; but that is merely an outward reflection of something greater, well discussed by Wilhelm Levison in connection with a wider antiquity than that of Germania alone:[53]

Das Schwert war schon sehr früh eines der vornehmsten Waffenstücke, eine 'adlige' Waffe, zu der der Inhaber – dank dem Zierwerk und der Art der Handhabung – eine stärkere persönliche Beziehung hatte. Bereits in alter Zeit galt es als Emblem weltlicher Macht, namentlich des Rechtes, über Leben und Tod zu entscheiden, die Todesstrafe zu verhängen; es ist ein Attribut der Könige und hohen Beamten.

[The sword was even at a very early period one of the most distinguished pieces of weaponry, a weapon noble in rank, to which its owner had, on account of its ornamental work and the manner of handling it, a very strong personal relationship. As early as classical antiquity it was regarded as emblematic of secular power, especially of the legal power to decide over life and death, to inflict capital punishment. It is an attribute of kings and of high dignitaries.]

Hildegyth strives to recall to Waldere the strength of that bond between him and Mimming. This is a grander courtesy than lies in the ancillary function of any shield-maiden: both she and he were of princely rank.

In the Latin poem, Hiltgund shows herself fearful as she with Waltharius seeks the cover of darkness (lines 348–53):

> Prima rubens terris ostendit lumina Phoebus,
> In siluis latitare student et opaca requirunt,
> 350 Sollicitatque metus uel per loca tuta fatigans.
> In tantumque timor muliebria pectora pulsat,
> Horreat ut cunctos aurae uentique susurros,
> Formidans uolucres collisos siue racemos.

[When glowing Phoebus sent forth his first radiance over the lands, they sought the cover of darkness, thinking to conceal themselves in the woods; and tormenting anxiety disturbed her even in secure places. And fear so struck her maidenly breast that she took fright at every rustling of air and wind, trembling at the flight of birds or the striking together of berry clusters.]

She is indeed a timid maiden, and nevertheless binds up the wounds of heroes (cf. line 1407–08). In her fearfulness, she even counsels Waltharius to flee Guntharius and Hagano (line 1213), 'Fuge, domne, propinquant!' [Flee, my lord, they come!].

In the Old English fragments, Hildegyth shows no fear. Though the syntax of Fragment I lines 12–19a is not entirely clear, her speech at that point appears to mean that his valour in battle is such that she will never have cause to chide him for yielding in battle or for fleeing to save his life when hard-pressed. She shows a warlike interest in the arms and armour her hero bears and wears. Waldere's sword is Mimming, forged by Weland, the Vulcan of Germanic antiquity.

The only fear she shows is fear of God, though the statement in which that is expressed used to be interpreted differently, and Germanic fatalism was at one time discerned by many scholars in the use of *metod* in Fragment I line 19: '*metod*, here, as originally, "fate," "destiny" (cf. O.N. *mjotuðr*); usually an epithet applied to the Creator.'[54] That interpretation is still accepted in editions of 1979 and 1994.[55] The word comes in a pious passage in Hildegyth's speech (I lines 19–23), and is probably better interpreted without advertence to fate or destiny, a pagan sense which the Old English word *metod* cannot be shown to have in any extant Old English text:

> Ðy ic ðe metod ondred,
> 20 þæt ðu to fyrenlice   feohtan sohtest

æt ðam ætstealle   oðres monnes
wigrædenne.   Weorða ðe selfne
godum dædum   ðenden ðin God recce.

[On your behalf I therefore feared the Lord,[56] that you strove to fight too fiercely
at that hostile place of battle in warfare against the other man. Achieve honour for
yourself in deeds of valour as long as God has you in his care.]

There is, in Hildegyth's speech, an element of piety including evidence
that she was God-fearing – and fearing no one else – and the God-fearing
part of her make-up cannot go back to a pre-Christian antiquity. In fearing
nothing in this world, she is unlike Hiltgund; and that part of her may have
its roots in the warlikeness of Germanic women more generally. A good example of that occurs in Saxo, in a passage to which attention was drawn long
ago in connection with *Schildmädchen*, 'shield-maidens', who appear to en-
joy affinity or even identity with Valkyries.[57] Saxo, in *Gesta Danorum*, after
relating the slaying at Walbrunna of Sigarus and how his son Siwaldus avenged
his father's death, continues:[58]

Adeo autem Sigari clades Sywaldique caritas promiscuos plebis animos incitabant,
ut uterque se bello sexus impenderet, nec certamen cerneres femineis caruisse præsidiis.

[To such an extent did the killing of Sigarus and the affection of Siwaldus incite the
spirit of the people every one, that both sexes applied themselves to war, and you
would not perceive that the battle lacked the help of women.]

The women gave help, but nothing more than help; help was all that
Hildegyth gave to Waldere (as far as the fragmentary state of the poem allows
us to assume): the concept of a *Schildmaid* does not go beyond an ancillary
role in battle. According to Saxo, however, not all noble women confined
themselves to mere ancillary roles in battle. Regnerus, Ragnar Lothbrok king
of the Danes, wooed and won a woman made of sterner stuff, Lathgertha,
who was of barbarian – probably Norwegian – noble birth:[59]

Quo tempore rex Suetiæ Frø, interfecto Norvagiensium rege Sywardo, coniuges
necessariorum eius prostibulo religatas[60] publice constuprandas exhibuit. Quo
Regnerus audito, avitæ ultionis studio Norvagiam petivit. Eo veniente, matronæ
complures, quæ corporum suorum ludibria aut nuper passæ fuerant aut in proximo
pudicitiæ periculum verebantur, viriliter cultæ cupide castris eius adproperare
cœperunt, profitentes se fatum contumeliæ prælaturas. Nec erubuit futurus muliebris

improperii vindex adversum auctorem turpitudinis, quarum ignominiam ulcisci venerat, auxilia mutuari.

Inter quas affuit et Lathgertha, perita bellandi femina, quæ virilem in virgine animum gerens, immisso humeris capillitio, prima inter promptissimos dimicabat. Cuius incomparabilem operam admirantibus cunctis – quippe cæsaries tergo involare conspecta feminam esse prodebat – Regnerus . . . de puella, quam in acie præviam prænotaverat, commilitiones plurimum percontatus est, unius feminæ viribus victoriam sibi constitisse professus. Quam cum illustri inter barbaros loco natam cognovisset, per internuntios procari perstitit.

Illa legatione tacite spreta, consensum simulat. Cumque datis fallaciter responsis anhelanti proco potiendi voti fiduciam attulisset, adiectum urso canem in ædis suæ vestibulo religari præcepit, contra omne amatoris studium per obiectas beluas proprium tutatura conclave. Regnerus vero favorabili nuntio recreatus navigium scandit, emensusque fretum, comitibus apud Gølerdal – id valli nomen est – subsistere iussis, solitarius puellæ penates accedit. Ubi exceptus a beluis, alteram telo traicit, alteram faucibus apprehensam obtorto gutture strangulavit, virginemque victi periculi præmium habuit.

[At this time, Fro, King of Sweden, having slain Siward, King of the Norwegians, displayed for public rape the wives of Siward's relations whom he had bound fast in a brothel. When Ragnar heard this he went to Norway to avenge his grandfather. When he arrived, not a few ladies, who had either recently suffered bodily abuse or feared immediate danger to their chastity, began to hasten eagerly to his camp dressed in male garb, declaring that they would prefer death to abuse. Nor did the future avenger of the women's dishonour blush to get help against the man who had abused them from those whose shame he wished to avenge.

Present among them was also Lathgertha, a woman skilled in waging war, a young woman displaying manly courage, who fought in front among the bravest, her hair loose over her shoulders. One and all marvelled at her matchless actions, for her hair flowing down to her back showed that she was a woman. Ragnar . . . repeatedly asked his fellow-soldiers concerning the girl whom he had noticed at the very front, declaring that he had gained the victory by one woman's strength. When he learnt that she was of illustrious birth among the barbarians he at once persistently wooed her by his messengers.

She secretly spurned his messages, but pretended agreement. By giving false replies she led her panting suitor to have confidence that he would have his will, but commanded that a bear and a dog should be tied up in the porch to her dwelling, safeguarding her chamber as her own against all the zeal of a lover by setting fierce beasts in his way. Ragnar, cheered by the favourable message, embarked, and when he had crossed the shallow sea, ordered his men to stay at Gølerdal – that is the name of the valley – and went alone to the dwelling of the girl. There, intercepted by the beasts, he transfixed one of the two with his spear, and seizing the other by its gullet, wrung its neck and strangled it. And he received the maiden as the prize for dangers overcome.]

These were wild carryings-on in the eyes of Saxo, a civilized Latin author, writing centuries later; and to him we are indebted for all we know about Lathgertha. It is easy to dismiss it all: Fro is the mythical founder of the Swedish royal dynasty, Ragnar Lothbrok is mythical too, and the fierce Lathgertha is described by Saxo as of barbarian stock. And yet she stands for a specimen of womanhood we do not meet in Old English literature: a *Schildmaid* perhaps, but one who goes beyond mere help in battle, to do battle. That is how she incites love in Ragnar, a Brynhild to be won through strength: in story-pattern, a shrew to be tamed, beyond the terms of ordinary courtesy when wooed, beyond the means of ordinary men to win.

6. BEOWULF

In story it is the women who set the tone. It is easy to speak with veneration and admiration of the widow Judith, about whom we have an Old English poem to celebrate her triumph in dealing with the rapist Holofernes. The biblical Book of Judith was regarded by Ælfric as valuable in teaching resistance to the English at a time of trouble:[61]

Iudith seo wuduwe, þe oferwann Holofernem þone Siriscan ealdormann, hæfð hire agene boc betwux þisum bocum be hire agenum sige; seo ys eac on Englisc on ure wisan gesett eow mannum to bysne, þæt ge eowerne eard mid wæpnum bewerian wið onwinnendne here.

[The widow Judith, who overcame Holofernes the Syrian leader, has her own book among these (Old Testament) books about her own triumph; it is also translated into English in our manner[62] for your example, that you too should with arms defend your country against a conquering enemy army.]

Judith – as shown by her own deeds and not, like Hildegyth, by words only, however inspiriting – is of a warlike disposition. That is unusual, though reminiscent of Alfred the Great's daughter Æthelflæd, the Lady of the Mercians, who at a time of danger, in the years 910 to her death in 918, built fortifications, or obtained them by some other means, to defend the land against the enemy.[63]

The women in *Beowulf* are not like that. Except for Grendel's mother, they are all royal ladies; and except for Grendel's mother they play no active part in fighting. They are mainly the victims of war, most emphatically so, Hildeburh in the Finnesburh Episode and Freawaru in the Heathobard Episode. Less dramatically, Wealhtheow expresses false hopes for her sons, with dramatic irony as it seems to audience or readers who know what will happen to them; while Hygd, widowed through warfare, disappears from view after she has made arrangements for her dead royal husband's succession. That too is the real world of story, but the flavour is more courtly and tamer. These ladies are unlike Modthrytho, though that contrast is expressed only in connection with Hygd; and both Hygd and Modthrytho are quite unlike Lathgertha.

We have been prepared for courtliness and gracious courtesy by the descriptions and speeches near the beginning. Hrothgar's success in battle leads not to glorious conquests, but to the architectural triumph of a royal hall to provide a suitable setting for royal liberality. Everything was to be distributed (line 73)

> buton folcscare   ond feorum gumena

[except for public (or common?) land and the lives of men].

Klaeber thought that line out of place in a footnote that seems strange now, nearly three-quarters of a century after it was written:[64] 'This line could be explained as a corrective addition. The legal allusion of 157 f. can also be spared.' Of course, a diligent commentator might gladly spare the difficulty of the 'folk-share', the explanation of which, whether the same as 'the rare term' *folcland*[65] and somehow to be reconciled with *folcriht*, must depend to some extent on one's view of the date of composition and how far the poet presents England at the poet's own time,[66] or presents England, or perhaps a country other than England, as it was thought by him to have been long ago. The king's court of Heorot may be the place where law is administered according to Danish custom. One wonders how the queen and the princess fit into that aspect of Hrothgar's hall.

The courteous tone of Wealhtheow's speeches accords with that of the speeches of such officials as the coastguard (lines 237–57, 287b–300, and 316–19), with the diplomatically couched threat that unless he is told who the disembarked heroes are they will be received as *leassceaweras* 'deceitful spies' (line 253). More prominent in them than the implicit threat are the several gracious, proverblike generalizations – platitudes to those modern readers who have no taste for courtly wisdom. Beowulf's part in this dialogue is equally courteous, as he reveals his identity by giving his father's name,[67] and bidding the coastguard: *wes þu us larena god!* ['be good to us by way of precepts!'] (line 269b). Wulfgar's tone on receiving Beowulf and his men at Heorot (lines 333–39) and the tone of Beowulf's reply (lines 342b–47) are courtly, including *Beowulf is min nama* [Beowulf is my name] (line 343b), and the many references to the kings of Denmark and his royal father and of Geatland. Courteous and courtly salutations are offered by Beowulf when he is presented to Hrothgar (lines 407–55). Hrothgar réplies (lines 457–90) with references to the Geats' honourable demeanour, as he extends to them the hospitality of his court.

7. DRINKING AND DRUNKENNESS AT COURT, AS DESCRIBED IN *BEOWULF*

Unferth's rudeness in adverting to Beowulf's contest with Breca (lines 506–28) contrasts with the prevailing suavity. Beowulf's reply is little better, especially at lines 530–32a and 587–89. Beowulf refers to Unferth's drunkenness (531a), *beore druncen* 'drunk with beer'.

Anglo-Saxonists minimize this aspect of Germanic courtly life, unlike Tacitus who, in *Germania*, makes more of it than seems ideal for warrior nations:[68]

sine apparatu, sine blandimentis expellunt famem. adversus sitim non eadem temperantia. si indulseris ebrietati suggerendo quantum concupiscunt, haud minus facile vitiis quam armis vincentur.

[They banish hunger without great preparation or appetizing sauces, but there is not the same temperance in facing thirst: if you humour their drunkenness by supplying as much as they crave, they will be vanquished through their vices as easily as on the battlefield.]

The minimization of Unferth's weakness in particular, and perhaps for this Germanic weakness more generally, proceeds by way of translation; and in this connection I recall with pleasure Fred C. Robinson's important and salutary paper on the dangers of translation.[69] Kemble translates 'drunken with beer', Ettmüller introduces a poeticizing genitive construction 'Bieres trunken' and that perhaps takes the reader away from the prosaic reality.[70] Moritz Heyne's excellent glossary[71] shows how the reader can be guided by glossarial manipulation; he distinguishes between uses of the past participle *druncen* with the instrumental of the beverage 'drunk with wine or beer', as were the

Danes as they boasted that they would take on Grendel in the beer-hall (lines 480–83), and as was Unferth in Beowulf's opinion (line 531a) and in the poet's reference to that incident for which he changes the beverage to *wine druncen* (line 1462a) perhaps because he needs the initial *w* for the alliteration. When the participle is used absolutely, that is, without the instrumental stating the beverage, however, Heyne sees no drunkenness, just drinking at line 1231 and, surprisingly, also at line 2179, two uses to be considered further. R.W. Chambers follows Heyne cautiously in his glossary:[72] '*pp.* "drunk, having drunk (not *necessarily* to intoxication)".' Klaeber's glossary has 'pp. druncen, *flushed with drink*', the translation by E.T. Donaldson[73] has 'the retainers cheered with drink' for *druncne dryhtguman*.

The reception of heroes on the shore, the royal hall built for feasting and for largesse within the limits permitted by the nation's laws, and gracious speeches by royal hosts and their guest, these are part of the ideal of courtesy and courtliness which the poet presents to audience and readership. That is how we idealize their present which is our past. Yet there is more to the reality of the hall than courtesy and courtliness. Quarrelling is more than a momentary verbal lapse; it probably arises commonly as manly pride or vanity is inflamed by drink. Quarrelling breaks out at Ingeld's wedding-feast when (line 2041) an old warrior speaks *æt beore* 'at the beer-drinking' or 'in beer'. Chambers, wisest of *Beowulf* scholars, is cleverly ambiguous in his use of 'not *necessarily* to intoxication': (1) truly, there was no need for them to get drunk; or, alternatively, (2) surely, we are not forced to interpret the poet's words as meaning that the men in the hall were drinking to intoxication.

And so we come to Wealhtheow's courteous speech to Beowulf as she bestows on him treasure, lines 1224b–31. She seems aware of the dangers to her sons, and bids him be kind to them in that Germanic world in which men, 'drunk, having drunk (not *necessarily* to intoxication)', seem to be true to one another, and, as they drink the drink she has offered them, seem willing to do her bidding:

> Wes þenden þu lifige,
> 1225 æþeling, eadig!   Ic þe an tela
> sincgestreona.   Beo þu suna minum
> dædum gedefe,   dreamhealdende!
> Her is æghwylc eorl   oþrum getrywe,
> modes milde,   mandrihtne hold:
> 1230 þegnas syndon geþwære,   þeod ealgearo,
> druncne dryhtguman   doð swa ic bidde.

[Be happy, Prince, as long as you live! I wish you well of (these) treasures. Be an active, joy-sustaining friend to my sons! Here every man is true to every other, kind in spirit, loyal to his liege-lord: the retainers are united, a body of men quite ready, noble warriors when they have drunk will do as I command.]

These are uneasy truths: her retainers seem loyal, and they have drunk, who knows how much? The ideal of queen and court crumbles before us, and reveals a reality whether of feuding kinsmen or of alcohol-based obedience.

Heyne saw no drunkenness at the court of Heremod, who is not named in lines 2177–83a though referred to implicitly, contrasting his tyrannous kingship with that of Beowulf, son of Ecgtheow:

> Swa bealdode   bearn Ecgðeowes,
> guma guðum cuð,   godum dædum,
> dreah æfter dome.   Nealles druncne slog
> 2180 heorðgeneatas.   Næs him hreoh sefa,
> ac he mancynnes   mæste cræfte,
> gimfæste gife   þe him God sealde,
> heold hildedeor.

[Thus the son of Ecgtheow bore himself bravely, a man renowned in battles, in deeds of valour, acted to achieve glory. Not at all did he slay his closest comrades in their drink. His heart was not cruel, but the man of warlike courage possessed the greatest strength of all mankind, a glorious, ample gift that God had given him.]

Praise by contrast is not uncommon in the poem. In the speech in which at the end of his life Beowulf surveys his achievements he includes among the good things he can say of himself two items negatively expressed (lines 2738–9a):

> ne sohte searoniðas,   ne me swor fela
> aða on unriht.

[I did not seek treacherous quarrels, nor did I much perjure myself.]

8. A CONCLUSION OF CONTRASTS

The crude hopes and cruel tyrannies of romances such as *Havelok the Dane* and *Gamelyn* are far removed from the royal and noble endeavours of *Beowulf.*

Brute strength leads the heroes of these romances out of discomfiture unbefitting their royal or noble rank. The comparable strength of Beowulf is *gimfæste gife þe him God sealde* [the glorious, ample gift that God had given him]. The villains of the romances are not only lacking in every virtue, but are in the end physically too weak in fighting to retain the position of power they have gained by usurpation.

In heroic verse, we are shown courtliness and courtesy, but also drunkenness and disloyalty. The speeches are elaborate, and redolent of what appears to be, for the poet and his contemporaries, a bygone politesse. The poets of heroic verse in any language, including the great epics of ancient times, look back to a warrior world of nobles long ago, and see that Heroic Age, nostalgically perhaps, as an ideal, as nearly perfect as anything human can be in human experience.

The contrast with 'popular romances', such as *Havelok the Dane* and *Gamelyn*, is that the romancers are describing the high world of nobles from below, presumably without having experienced courtliness and high courtesy in the real world. They describe the villain of the piece as bad through and through. The villain or villains must come from the higher reaches of society; except for that, royalty, the nobility, the gentry even, are set forth as flawless; flawless beyond the hope of any man or woman to attain to such perfection.

Beowulf, near his death, recalls guileful disloyalty and perjury among dangerous failings he has avoided. Courtliness and courtesy colour the fictive reality of the poem. But there are stains too: quarrelsome drunkenness is not the least of them. The ideal heroic world, as depicted by the poet, is not unsullied nor unbroken by human insufficiency. Yet the glory of the past outweighs the memory of failure, and, in ways undreamt of by the romancer of *Havelok the Dane*, Saxo, probably more or less contemporary with the composition of that romance, tells of how Lucas, the English minor clerical functionary, recalled that glorious past to inspirit the valour of a no longer heroic, Danish present:

Siquidem memoratis veterum virtutibus nostros ad exigendam a sociorum interfectoribus ultionem tanta disserendi peritia concitavit, ut non solum mæstitiam discuteret, verum etiam cunctorum pectoribus fortitudinem ingeneraret.

[Indeed, calling to mind the valour of their forebears, he roused our troops to vengeance on the slayers of their comrades by a speech of such skill that he not only dispelled the gloom, but also instilled courage in the hearts of all.][74]

NOTES

1 A.C. Knabe and P. Herrmann, eds, rev. J. Olrik ad H. Ræder, *Saxonis Gesta Danorum*, 2 vols (Copenhagen 1931 and 1957). This edition is cited throughout for the Latin text of Saxo.

2 Cf. O. Elton, trans., *The First Nine Books of the Danish History of Saxo Grammaticus*, Publications of the Folklore Society 33 (London 1894), 398–413 (appendix II, Saxo's Hamlet); I. Gollancz, *Hamlet in Iceland being the Icelandic Romantic Ambales Saga* (London 1898); P. Herrmann, *Die Heldensagen des Saxo Grammaticus* (Leipzig 1922), 248–96; K. Malone, *The Literary History of Hamlet*, I: The Early Tradition, Anglistische Forschungen, 59 (Heidelberg 1923). In J. Schick, *Corpus Hamleticum: Hamlet in Sage und Dichtung, Kunst und Musik* (Berlin, later Leipzig 1912–38), Shakespeare and Saxo, disappointingly in view of the title (and as acknowledged by Schick in the Vorwort to the last volume published, I, 5/2 [1938], p. vii), serve only as a point of departure (vol. I [1912], 1–14) for a survey (unindexed, alas) that, in the eyes of a non-comparativist, soon appears to have lost touch with Saxo's and Shakespeare's Denmark and its Prince.

3 Conveniently brought together in Oliver Elton's translation by G.N. Garmonsway and J. Simpson, trans., *Beowulf and its Analogues* (London 1968).

4 See R.W. Chambers, ed., *Widsith* (Cambridge 1912); K. Malone, ed., *Widsith*, 2nd ed., Anglistica 13 (Copenhagen 1962).

5 E. Christiansen, ed. and trans., Saxo Grammaticus, *Danorum Regum Heroumque Historia Books X–XVI*, 3 vols, British Archaeological Reports, International Series, 84, 118(1), and 118(2) (Oxford 1980–81). Books X–XVI of the first edition (Paris 1514) are reproduced in facsimile by Christiansen.

6 Saxo, XIV.xl.9–10, Copenhagen ed., 479–80; cf. E. Christiansen, 514–18, and 850–51 nn. 544 and 545.

7 The Copenhagen editors have emended to *perrumpens*, which is presumed in my translation; the Paris edition has *prorupens* 'bursting forth'.

8 For the dating, cf. I. Skovgaard-Petersen, 'Saxo', in *Kulturhistorisk Leksikon for Nordisk Middelalder* 15 (Copenhagen 1970), cols 49–57.

9 See Christiansen, 671.

10 Copenhagen ed., 304; Christiansen, 52–53.

11 See Christiansen, 221 n. 3, for doubts if William really was English, since before the Conquest the name was very rare indeed, and Saxo appears to be alone in describing him as an Englishman.

12 Cf. H.G. Evelyn-White, ed. and trans., *Hesiod*, The Loeb Classical Library (Cambridge, Mass., and London 1954), 12–15.

13 R. Lattimore, trans., *Hesiod* (Ann Arbor, Mich., 1959, repr. 1978), 37–39 (the line numbers are as in Lattimore's translation and refer to the line numbering of the Greek). At line 160, Lattimore records a significant variant (in translation): 'followed by the great age of Heroes'. Cf. H.G. Evelyn-White, *Hesiod*, 12–15, *Works and Days* lines 156–73 (and 169, 169a,b). For the best-known earlier translation into English, see Thomas Cooke, *The Works of Hesiod Translated from the Greek* (London 1728), I: 82–83, bk I lines 210–25:

> To these a fourth, a better, Race, succeeds,
> Of godlike Heros, fam'd for martial Deeds;
> Them Demigods, at first, their matchless Worth

Proclaim aloud all, thro the boundless Earth.
These, horrid Wars, their Love of Arms, destroy;
Some at the Gates of *Thebes*, and some at *Troy*.
These for the Brothers fell, detested Strife!
For Beauty those, the lovely *Greecian* Wife.
To these does *Jove* a second Life ordain,
Some happy Soil far in the distant Main,
Where live the Hero-shades in rich Repast,
Remote from Mortals of a vulgar Cast.
There in the Islands of the Bless'd they find,
Where *Saturn* reigns, an endless Calm of Mind;
And there the choicest Fruits adorn the Fields,
And thrice the fertile Year a Harvest yields.

The second edition of Cooke's translation [(London 1740), 23–25, bk I lines 218–33] has abandoned the capitalization of the initial letters of common nouns, and there are minor changes in punctuation at the end of lines: destroy,‖ wife!‖ cast.‖.

14 H.M. Chadwick, *The Heroic Age* (Cambridge 1912).

15 F.A. Paley, ed., *The Epics of Hesiod with an English Commentary* (London 1883), 27.

16 *Sir Gawain and the Green Knight*, lines 1–2. Cf. I. Gollancz, ed., *Pearl, Cleanness, Patience and Sir Gawain Reproduced in Facsimile from the Unique MS. Cotton Nero A.x in the British Museum*, EETS 162 (1923), fol. 91ʳ.

17 J. Milton, *The History of Britain, That Part especially now call'd England. From the first Traditional Beginning, continu'd to the Norman Conquest. Collected out of the Ancientest and Best Authors thereof* (London, 1677), 17. See E. Faral, ed., 'Geoffroy de Monmouth *Historia Regum Britanniae*', in E. Faral, *La légende arthurienne*, 3 vols, Bibliothèque de l'École des Hautes Études 255–57 (Paris 1929), 3:84 (ch. 16). Cf. A. Griscom, ed., *The Historia Regum Britanniæ of Geoffrey of Monmouth* (London, New York, and Toronto 1929), 239–40; N. Wright, ed. and trans., *The Historia Regum Britannie of Geoffrey of Monmouth*, I: *Bern, Burgerbibliothek MS. 568* (Cambridge 1984), 9, [and for these verses within a versified paraphrase] V: *Gesta Regum Britannie* (Cambridge 1991), 18.

18 Cf. G.[S.] Gordon, 'The Trojans in Britain', *Essays and Studies* 9 (1924) 9–30; reprinted in G.[S.] Gordon (ed. M. Gordon), *The Discipline of Letters* (Oxford 1946), 35–58; and T.D. Kendrick, *British Antiquity* (London 1950).

19 See A.J. Bliss, *The Metre of Beowulf*, rev. ed. (Oxford 1967), chs 14–16.

20 Chaucer, *The Parliament of Fowls*, line 677; see M.B. Parkes and R. Beadle (introduction), *Poetical Works Geoffrey Chaucer A Facsimile of Cambridge University Library MS Gg.4.27* (Cambridge 1979), fol. 481v line 12.

21 *Sir Gawain and the Green Knight*, lines 31–36, fol. 91v. The translation is interpretative rather than literal.

22 Cf. E.G. Stanley, 'The Use of Bob-Lines in *Sir Thopas*', *Neuphilologische Mitteilungen* 73 (1972) 417–26.

23 James Boswell, *Life of Johnson*, 1794; see G. Birkbeck Hill, ed., *Boswell's Life of Johnson*, rev. ed. by L.F. Powell, 2 vols (Oxford 1934–1950), I: 201, and appendix G, 538–39.

24 Cf. Chadwick, *Heroic Age*, ch. XVI.

25 See G.V. Smithers, ed., *Havelok* (Oxford 1987), 1. All quotations of the poem (including the incipit) are taken from that edition, which is, however, not followed in every detail. Use has, of course, been made of its valuable notes and the glossary.

26 Cf. H. Döll, *Mittelenglische Kleidernamen im Spiegel literarischer Denkmäler des 14. Jahrhunderts* (Giessen doctoral diss. 1932), 77.

27 J.E. Wells, *A Manual of the Writings in Middle English, 1050–1400* (New Haven and London 1916), 27.

28 See F.R. Rogers, 'The *Tale of Gamelyn* and the Editing of the *Canterbury Tales*', *Journal of English and Germanic Philology* 58 (1959) 49–59. R.H. Robbins and J.L. Cutler, *Supplement to the Index of Middle English Verse* (Lexington, Kentucky, 1965), 221 no. 1913, wrongly give John Stow's edition of *The Workes of Geffrey Chaucer* (1561) as the first printing of *Gamelyn*; credit for that must go to John Urry, ed., *The Works of Geoffrey Chaucer* (London 1721), 36–48. Urry, in his elegant edition, has a spurious conclusion to '*The COKE's TALE*' proper, and an introduction to the '*COKE's TALE of Gamelyn*' in which he expresses surprise that the previous editors of Chaucer did not edit *Gamelyn* (35–36):

> This is all of the COOKE's TALE as yet found.
> In some of the MSS is the History of Gamelyn under the Title of the Cooke's Tale; but it is not the Cooke's Tale that Lidgate saw, for that was, as he says, of Ribaldrie, as the abovesaid Tale savour of, and which in the MSS is joined to this by these Verses.

> But herof, Siris, I woll pass as now,
> And of yong Gamelyn I wol tell you.   Qð the Cook.

> So many of the MSS have this Tale, that I can hardly think it could be unknown to the former Editors of this Poet's Works. Nor can I think of a Reason why they neglected to publish it. Possibly they met only with those MSS that had not this Tale in them, and contented themselves with the Number of Tales they found in those MSS. If they had any of those MSS in which it is, I cannot give a Reason why they did not give it a Place amongst the rest, unless they doubted of its being genuine. But because I find it in so many MSS, I have no doubt of it, and therefore make it publick.

Urry's reference to 'the Cooke's Tale that Lidgate saw' is in the modern edition, *Lydgate's Siege of Thebes*, ed. A. Erdmann, EETS e.s. 108 (1911), 2 lines 25–28; Urry knew the poem from one of the following editions: John Stow's *The Workes of Geffrey Chaucer* (two issues, 1561), Thomas Speght *The Workes of Our Ancient and Learned English Poet, Geffrey Chaucer* (editions, 1598, 1602; and *The Works of Our Ancient, Learned, & Excellent English Poet, Jeffrey Chaucer*, 1687).

29 No single principle governs Chaucer's poetic art in the grand variety of the *Canterbury Tales*, but, in the *Prologue* especially, there is a depiction of estates, a range below the highest and above the lowest of his time, and for the lower half of that range the depiction often tends towards satire; cf. J. Mann, *Chaucer and Medieval Estates Satire: The Literature of Social Classes and the General Prologue to The Canterbury Tales* (London 1973).

30 Cf. E.G. Stanley, '"Of This Cokes Tale Maked Chaucer Na Moore"', *Poetica* 5 (Tokyo 1976) 36–59.

31 T. Tyrwhitt, ed., *The Canterbury Tales of Chaucer* 1 (London 1775), p. xix note (*m*) rejecting the spurious conclusion to *The Cook's Tale* in Bodleian MS Bodley 686, for which see J.M. Manly and E. Rickert, eds, *The Text of the Canterbury Tales* (Chicago 1940), 5:437.

32 Tyrwhitt, *The Canterbury Tales* 4 (London 1775), 144–45.

33 Cf. my article on the art of *Sir Thopas*, referred to in n. 22, above.

34 Cf. W.W. Skeat, ed., *The Tale of Gamelyn*, 2nd ed. (Oxford 1893), 22–23.

35 For the Latin poem, see K. Strecker, ed., *Waltharius*, MGH PL, 5/1 (1951), 1–85; and cf. K. Strecker, ed., and P. Vossen, trans., *Waltharius* (Berlin 1947); cf. H. Althof, trans., *Das Waltharilied – Ein Heldensang aus dem zehnten Jahrhundert* (Leipzig 1902). For an excellent, brief account of the Latin poem, see K.C. King and D.R. McLintock, rev. ed. of J.K. Bostock, *A Handbook of Old High German Literature* (Oxford 1976), 259–70.

Several of the editions of the Old English fragments have been used; among them: G. Stephens, ed., *Two Leaves of King Waldere's Lay* (Copenhagen 1860); F. Holthausen, ed., *Die altenglischen Waldere-Bruchstücke*, Göteborgs Högskolas Årsskrift 5 (Gothenburg 1899); B. Dickins, ed., *Runic and Heroic Poems of the Teutonic Peoples* (Cambridge 1915); F. Norman, ed., *Waldere* (London 1933); E.V.K. Dobbie, ed., *The Anglo-Saxon Minor Poems*, ASPR 6 (New York 1942); U. Schwab, ed., *Waldere: Testo e Commento* (Messina 1967); A. Zettersten, ed., *Waldere* (Manchester 1979); J. Hill, ed., *Old English Minor Heroic Poems*, Durham Medieval Texts 4, rev. ed. (Durham 1994).

36 F. von der Leyen, *Deutsches Sagenbuch*, 2: *Die deutschen Heldensagen*, 2nd ed. (Munich 1923), 193–96.

37 For occurrences of that name, cf. Dobbie, *The Anglo-Saxon Minor Poems*, p. xxiv and n. 2; and see: R.I. Page, *An Introduction to English Runes* (London 1973), 54; F.S. Scott, 'The Hildithryth Stone and the Other Hartlepool Name-Stones', *Archæologia Æliana* 4th ser. 34 (1956) 196–212; R.W.V. Elliott, *Runes: An Introduction*, 2nd ed. (Manchester and New York 1989), pl. XII fig. 30, and p. 107; H. Sweet, ed., *The Oldest English Texts*, EETS 83 (1885), 155 line 40, 166 line 445, and A. Hamilton Thompson, ed., *Liber Vitae Dunelmensis: A Collotype Facsimile*, Surtees Society Publication, 136 (1923), fols 14r and 40r. The use of the second ⟨i⟩ in Hildi- in the Hartlepool inscription is not so much a sign of an early date as of economy of effort since runic ⟨i⟩ is a single vertical stroke, whereas runic ⟨e⟩ is like a capital M. Economy of effort may have led to the confusion of ⟨i⟩ for final unstressed /e/ earlier /æ/ in the Ruthwell Cross inscription, as I have suggested elsewhere, 'The Ruthwell Cross Inscription: Some Linguistic and Literary Implications of Paul Meyvaert's Paper "An Apocalypse Panel on the Ruthwell Cross"', in E.G. Stanley, *A Collection of Papers with Emphasis on Old English Literature*, Publications of the Old English Dictionary 3 (Toronto 1987), esp. 392–95.

38 *King Waldere's Lay*, p. x.

39 H.B. Woolf, *The Old Germanic Principles of Name-Giving* (Baltimore 1939), 145.

40 J. Hill, *Old English Minor Heroic Poems*, 11.

41 For doubts about the date of composition in the first quarter of the tenth century, and the ascription to Ekkehard 1 of St Gall, while still a schoolboy, both at one time generally accepted, see A. Wolf, 'Der mittellateinische Waltharius und Ekkehard 1. von St Gallen', *Studia Neophilologica* 13 (1940–41) 80–102; O. Schumann, 'Waltharius-Probleme', *Studi Medievali* n.s. 17 (1951) 1. Zeit der Abfassung, 177–83; K. Hauck, 'Walthariusepos des Bruders Gerald von Eichstätt', *Germanisch-Romanische Monatsschrift* 4 (1954) 1–27; all three reprinted in E.E. Ploss, ed., *Waltharius und Walthersage* (Hildesheim 1969), 33–55, 109–15, and 135–61, respectively.

42 See G.P. Krapp and E.V.K. Dobbie, eds, *The Exeter Book*, ASPR 3 (New York 1936), 159–60.

43 The number of *him* is ambiguously either 'him' or 'them', and 'him' would go well with what precedes, the lord of the house; but *bold-agendum bæm ætsomne* is unambiguously plural. It would be possible to translate the short passage, she must 'give him good counsel, give good counsel for them both, joint owners of their house together'.

44 See R.W. Chambers, ed., *Widsith*, 21–28. R. Frank has noted, playfully, that 'the name "hild" ("battle") seems favoured by Old English poets for the sorrowful princesses of Ger-

manic legend' ('Germanic Legend in Old English Literature', in *The Cambridge Companion to Old English Literature*, ed. M. Godden and M. Lapidge [Cambridge 1991], 88–106, at 90), but that is perhaps due to the likelihood that several of the royal ladies so named are the same one or two persons (as suggested by Chambers), rather than that the sorrowful princess is a role-model for Germanic girls who are named accordingly by their parents or by the poets.

45 Cf. E.G. Stanley, 'The Germanic "Heroic Lay" of Finnesburg', in *A Collection of Papers* (see n. 37, above), 281–97.

46 H. Schneider, *Germanische Heldensage*, Grundriss der germanischen Philologie, ed. H. Paul 10/2.ii (Berlin and Leipzig 1934), 70.

47 Thus B. Dickins, *Runic and Heroic Poems*, 57; and cf. J. Hill, *Old English Minor Heroic Poems*, glossary, 59: 'WINE, m., friend; nom.sg. *Wald.* I, 12 (= beloved), II, 14 (= lord).'

48 J. Grimm and A. Schmeller, eds, *Lateinische Gedichte des X. und XI. Jh.* (Göttingen 1838), 98.

49 H. Althof, *Das Waltharilied*, 45.

50 G. Stephens, ed., *King Waldere's Lay*, ix.

51 F. Dieter, 'Die Walderefragmente und die ursprüngliche Gestalt der Walthersage', *Anglia* 11, Hefte 1 and 2 (1888) 165.

52 L.L. Schücking, 'Waldere und Waltharius', *Englische Studien* 60 (1925–26) 18 and n.; repr. in Ploss, *Waltharius und Walthersage* (see n. 41, above), 308 and n.

53 W. Levison, 'Die mittelalterliche Lehre von den beiden Schwertern', *Deutsches Archiv für Erforschung des Mittelalters* 9 (1951) 17.

54 B. Dickins, ed., *Runic and Heroic Poems*, 58. Cf. R. Jente, *Die mythologischen Ausdrücke im altenglischen Wortschatz*, Anglistische Forschungen 56 (Heidelberg 1921), 72, who gives this use first place in a list of occurrences of the word *metod*, all of which, he believes, appear to preserve the ancient pagan meaning 'fate'.

55 A. Zettersten, 38 s.v.; and J. Hill, *Old English Minor Heroic Poems*, glossary, 52 s.v.; nothing in the notes in either edition indicates the possibility of any other interpretation.

56 The interpretation goes back to S. Bugge, 'Spredte iagttagelser vedkommende oldengelske digte om Beowulf og Waldere', *Tidskrift for Philologi og Pædagogik* 8 (1868) 74. It is accepted by Dobbie, ASPR 6: 138; and G. Nickel, gen. ed., *Beowulf und die kleineren Denkmäler der altenglischen Heldensage Waldere und Finnsburg*, 1 (Heidelberg 1976), 207.

57 Cf. Karl Müllenhoff, *Deutsche Altertumskunde* 5 (ed. M. Roediger, Berlin 1891, and again 1908), 345 and n.; Müllenhoff shows a more general interest in Germanic warlike women in his commentary on Tacitus's *Germania*, ch. VIII, in *Deutsche Altertumskunde* 4 (ed. M. Roediger, Berlin 1898, and ed. A. Heusler, Berlin 1920), 207–12. Cf. J. de Vries, *Altgermanische Religionsgeschichte*, 2: *Religion der Nordgermanen*, Grundriss der germanischen Philologie, ed. H. Paul 12/2 (Berlin and Leipzig 1937), 384–85, § 315.

58 Saxo, 200 (VII.viii, 5).

59 Saxo, 251–52 (IX.iv.1–3). P. Herrmann, *Die Heldensagen des Saxo Grammaticus*, 632, rendering Saxo's *perita bellandi femina*, calls Lathgertha *eine kriegsgewohnte Schildmaid* [a shield-maiden accustomed to war], and compares the deeds of the valiant maiden with those of other women; the best-known among them is Brynhild.

60 The editors accept the emendation *relegatas* 'put away' for *religatas* 'bound, fettered'. Unemended *religatas* underlies the translation.

61 See S.J. Crawford, ed., *The Old English Version of the Heptateuch, Ælfric's Treatise on the Old and New Testament and his Preface to Genesis*, EETS 160 (1922), 48.

62 That is, I think, Ælfric's style of alliterative prose.

63 See D. Whitelock, trans., *The Anglo-Saxon Chronicle* (London 1961), 61–67; cf. S. Taylor, ed., *MS B*, vol. 4 of *The Anglo-Saxon Chronicle*, gen. ed. D. Dumville and S. Keynes (Cambridge 1983), 49–50; H.A. Rositzke, ed., *The C-Text of the Old English Chronicles*, Beiträge zur englischen Philologie 34 (Bochum-Langendreer 1940, repr. New York and London 1967), 45.

64 F. Klaeber, ed., *Beowulf and the Fight at Finnsburg* (Boston, New York, and Chicago 1922), p. cix n. 5; retained in the 3rd ed. (Boston 1936), p. cvii n. 1, with the parenthetical '(Similarly perhaps 3054^b ff.?)' introduced before 'The legal allusion . . .'

65 See F. Liebermann, ed., *Die Gesetze der Angelsachsen*, 2/1 (Halle 1906), 73 s.vv. Cf. D. Whitelock, *The Beginnings of English Society*, The Pelican History of England 2 (Harmondsworth 1952), 154:

> The king always retained the jurisdiction over those men who held bookland, which meant that if any of them committed a deed which involved forfeiture, the land came into the king's hands. Litigation about bookland is often brought before Church synods in the eighth and ninth centuries, and later before the king and his council. Land not so freed, land still subject to the king's farm and other charges, and bound by customary rules of descent, is probably what is meant by the rare term 'folkland'. Disputes concerning this were dealt with in the ordinary courts.

66 Cf. F. Liebermann, *The National Assembly in the Anglo-Saxon Period* (Halle 1913), 73–74:

> One notion comprised indissolubly king's folkland and national property administered by government; the witan, therefore, had to guard the disposition of crown domains against reckless squandering, which would deprive future governments of the possibility of rewarding out of public property warriors and officers, probably the descendants of the now dominating class. They controlled the giving away of crownland, not as a circle of personal associates and vassals of the king, but as a national representation. To be a good 'treasurer (hoardguardian) of the heroes', i.e. a conscientious administrator of the public means for national, chiefly military purposes, is in Beowulf [footnote: Verse 1851 sqq.] the ideal required by the Gauts from the king whom they elect.

> For his dating of *Beowulf*, see F. Liebermann, 'Ort und Zeit der Beowulfdichtung', *Nachrichten von der Königlichen Gesellschaft der Wissenschaften zu Göttingen*, Philologisch-historische Klasse 1920, no. 3, 255–76. Liebermann dates the poem as no later than 725 (p. 270): 'Sicher spricht kein historisches Kriterium für eine Abfassungszeit des Beowulf nách 725' [Certainly, no historical criterion supports a date for the composition of *Beowulf* even later than 725].

67 The father's name alone is enough to identify the speaker for anyone at home in the world of Germanic heroes, as is made clear in *Hildebrandslied* (lines 8b-13):

>   her fragen gistuont
> fohem uuortum,   wer sin fater wari
> 10 fireo in folche, 'eddo welihhes cnuosles du sis?
> Ibu du mi ęnan sages, ik mi de odre uuet,
> chind, in chunincriche: chud ist mir al irmindeot.'

[he began to ask in a few words who of the men in any nation his father was, 'or of what stock you are? If you, young man, tell me one of these facts I shall know the other and in what kingdom: all humankind is known to me.']

68 M. Hutton, ed. and trans., rev. E.H. Warmington, Tacitus, *Germania*, Loeb Classical Library (Cambridge, Mass., and London 1970), ch. 23, pp. 166–67.

69 Fred C. Robinson, 'Lexicography and Literary Criticism: A Caveat', in *Philological Essays: Studies in Old and Middle English Language and Literature in Honour of Herbert Dean Meritt, ed.* J.L. Rosier (The Hague 1970), 99–110; repr. in Fred C. Robinson, *The Tomb of Beowulf and Other Essays on Old English* (Oxford and Cambridge, Mass., 1993), 140–52. Fred C. Robinson's sensitive discussion of Germanic drinking, *'Beowulf' and the Appositive Style* (Knoxville 1985), 75–79, takes a less negative view than I suggest in this paper.

70 J.M. Kemble, *A Translation of the Anglo-Saxon Poem of Beowulf* (London 1837), 22; L. Ettmüller, *Beowulf: Heldengedicht des achten Jahrhunderts. Zum ersten Male . . . in das Neuhochdeutsche stabreimend übersetzt* (Zürich 1840), 87, his line 534.

71 M. Heyne, ed., *Beovulf – Mit ausführlichem Glossar*, 1st ed. (Paderborn 1863), 150–51, s.v. *drincan*. The later editions by Heyne and by A. Socin retain the distinction made in the first edition; the editions by L.L. Schücking amplify the distinction, which is abandoned only by E. von Schaubert when she takes over 'Heyne's *Beowulf*'; for bibliographical details of 'Heyne's *Beowulf*', see S.B. Greenfield and F.C. Robinson, eds, *A Bibliography of Publications on Old English Literature to the End of 1972* (Toronto 1980), 127 no. 1637.

72 R.W. Chambers, ed., *Beowulf with The Finnsburg Fragment Edited by A.J. Wyatt* (Cambridge 1914, repr. 1920), 191 s.v. *drincan*.

73 E.T. Donaldson, *Beowulf: A New Prose Translation* (New York 1966, London 1967), 22 (section XVIII).

74 J.H. Colin Leach (Pembroke College, Oxford) very kindly checked my translations from Latin for me. What errors and infelicities remain are mine.

Æðelflæd of Mercia: *Mise en page*

PAUL E. SZARMACH

My thesis is that when we read an Old English literary text we should take care to find out what precedes it in its manuscript state and what follows it. We should know whether it is an independent text or part of another, larger text. We should have some sense of the poem's *mise en page* and some conception of the manuscript as a whole.[1]

Fred C. Robinson's classic article, 'Old English Literature in Its Most Immediate Context' argues for the incorporation of information regarding the physical context of the manuscript to help establish 'the main course of a poem's thought' and to help determine 'the most relevant meanings of individual words within the text'.[2] Appearing in a collection citing 'a variety of interlocking contexts'[3] that underlie the earliest English literature, this article now, in retrospect, offers theoretical directions that may not have been so easy to discern as theoretical concerns per se in the period *ante theoriae aduentum*, whose watershed date for Old English studies may very well be 1983.[4] One may find in this article, for example, a rebuttal to old-style formalism, which argues that the text alone is all that is needful to know, and a gentle chiding of editorial practices that mask the immediate, meaningful context, which chiding carries within it the post-modern theme that scholarship obfuscates as much as it clarifies – if not more. In the long view of the total subject, the article plays a prominent role in the movement to return to the manuscripts, which is a general feature of study in the last two decades, and it has inspired many articles in turn. Roy Liuzza, for example, applies and extends Robinson's ideas to the Exeter Book, *Christ*, and *Guthlac*, concluding that 'the careful critic must always read manuscripts, not poems', which is a clear riposte to formalists. In a second study Liuzza shows how a close attention to the manuscript of the two texts of Riddle 30 has implica-

tions for the conception of transmission theory.[5] Sarah Larratt Keefer has
considered the contexts for Old English liturgical poems and, like Liuzza,
sees wider implications, particularly for editorial practices.[6] In this article I
would like to extend the discussion of meaningful physical manuscript characteristics to an important prose piece, the account of Æðelflæd in the *Anglo-
Saxon Chronicle*, along the lines cited from Robinson above. While it may
seem an artless or simple homage to apply to prose ideas that were originally
applied to poetry, I hope to sound some themes common *post theoriae
aduentum*, particularly those involving the reality and representation of women
and the idea of 'erasure'. The discerning reader will note the quiet move
herein to consider the *Chronicle* as a literary text. The proper beginning to
this discussion, however, is an introduction to Æðelflæd and her story in the
Chronicle, or as it is more commonly known, the *Mercian Register*.

The story of Æðelflæd appears in three of the *Chronicle* versions, viz.,

B = London, BL, Cotton Tiberius A. vi, art. 1, fols 1–35, and Cotton Tiberius
   A. iii fol. 178; Ker no. 188, Gneuss no. 364, which extends to 977;
C = London, BL, Cotton Tiberius B. i, art. 4, fols 115v–64; Ker no. 191, Gneuss
   no. 370, which extends to 1056 and for 1065 and 1066;
D = London, BL, Cotton Tiberius B. iv, only art., fols 3–86, 88–90; Ker no.
   192, Gneuss no. 372, which extends to 1079[7]

and within these three versions at the following, reproduced here in facsimile: B = fols 30r–31r, C = fols 140r–141r, D= fols 47v–48v (partial).

It was Plummer who offered the the the original description of this section of
the *Chronicle*: 'B and C after closing the year 915 (918Ⱥ) fetch back to 896
(the annals 896 to 901 being blank) and introduce the present episode, which
may be considered to close at 924 (925Ⱥ). Both are then barren to 934 (935Ⱥ)
where they fall in with the usual current of history. The episode forms therefore a little *Mercian Register* of about twenty years, and might be styled the
"Annals of Æthelflæd".'[8] The reference to Ⱥ is to the Parker Chronicle, which
often serves as Plummer's point of reference. Plummer's succinct description
links B and C together, as any reasonable textual editor might, but the precise relation of the two manuscripts has occupied scholars thereafter. Whether
C is a copy of B, or both descend from a common exemplar, are issues easily
clouded by the difficulty of comparison that is caused by varying scribes and
scribal practices over different sections and the apparent need, in certain
places, to postulate or hypothesize the existence of possible intermediate,
but non-extant, manuscripts. D has no part in the BC relationship of identity, but rather represents a different development in which the story of

Æðelflæd, admittedly with some difficulty, is the product of an attempt to 'level' it into the main narrative flow of the *Chronicle*. Effectively Plummer has identified a text by virtue of the chronological dislocation, which is apparent, and by the special focus on Æðelflæd and Mercian affairs. While it may be easy to say that Plummer has therefore discovered the obvious, one nevertheless has to celebrate the descriptive textual method whereby he retains the evidence of the manuscripts in front of him, making it possible to discern the military and political activities of a powerful woman of the House of Wessex. He does not, in other words, dismiss the the account of her deeds as an interpolation in some idealized view of what the *Chronicle* should contain, neither levelling nor erasing it. Here Plummer silently and implicitly accepts as well the now-reigning view of the *Chronicle* as a composite, open to all sorts of interventions from regional or dynastic interests to the merest scribal idiosyncrasy. The insertion of the *Battle of Brunanburh* as the 937 entry may be the most famous literary intervention, and indeed a more literary view of the whole *Chronicle* and its parts would be to consider *Brunanburh*, the story of Æðelflæd, and similar self-contained units as examples of intercalation.

There is, however, more evidence to adduce to the story of Æðelflæd from the BC telling, which makes Plummer's description even more certain and, as will be argued below, ultimately reveals more of Anglo-Saxon attitudes towards female agency. The layout and design of the *Mercian Register* as well as certain of its internal features mark it as a separate text.[9] The scribes of B and C may share the same core text, but they display this text differently (albeit with an ultimately similar result). The C scribe offers the easier point of reference (see figs 4–6). C's page and the rationale of its layout are immediately evident to the eye: the left hand of any page, recto or verso, offers the year entered in red 'flush left', in the form 'añ. + number', the numbers for the year tend to invade the text space, the entry proper begins with an initial in red, and the text continues to the right margin; should the text spill over the right margin onto the next line, the text does not continue 'flush left' under 'añ.' but is rather indented under the year entered, which then becomes rather like a header or subhead in its visual impact. While the logic of this layout seems transparent, there are minor variations. On recto pages, where the gutter is on the left, run-over text gets tucked in under the numbers for the year, not the century, at a horizontal, page-length ruling. On the verso page, where the gutter is on the right and the left margin is therefore more open, run-over text is indented under the first letter of the prose for the entry. This alternation has its contemporary analogue in word-processing programs that change margins, recto–verso, to account for binding [cf. the

Old English Newsletter]. The C scribe has no *horror vacui*, particularly evident in his allowing some eleven prose lines to remain unfilled, but he does feel obligated to list a year even when, so to speak, nothing happens. Six times, for 903, 906, 908, 920, 922, 923 – all presented in red – the scribe puts in an annal entry after the text of the previous year. In this way the C scribe can maintain the linear flow of dated entries, honouring his obligation to the genre of the annal, and keep to the logic of the layout by avoiding unsightly blank spaces at what would have to be the most important junction of the visual and the textual, the beginning of an entry. This self-consciousness about dates for entries offers the major, hitherto unnoticed, layout evidence for the coherence of the *Mercian Register*. For the years before this block of text, viz., 896–901, and for the years after it, 925–33, the scribe writes in the years only, filling in the line to the right margin until he begins the *Mercian Register* in the former case, and ends it in the latter. Thus, annal number entries, all in red, become a frame or a border marking the *Mercian Register* off from the main flow of the *Chronicle* and marking it off, for example, from the *Battle of Brunanburh*, which soon follows. The scribe acknowledges in visual terms the integrity of this narrative section, its separateness, and by implication its unique origin. Before the closing border of dates C, like B, offers an error in the incomplete sentence 'ꝺ he geaf his sweostor' ['and he gave his sister'], which D completes. This shared error (unless one wishes to argue *lectio difficilior* that the sentence is completely grammatical as 'he married his sister off') at the point of closure cements B and C together.

The B scribe offers his *Mercian Register* in a generally similar, if less elaborated fashion (see figs 1–3). A string of annal numbers for 896–901, in the usual form 'an. + date', precedes the text proper and a string for 925–33 closes it. The scribe seems a bit confused or inattentive in that he drops a 'c' from the dating for 896–99, i.e., 'dcccxui' for 'dcccxcui', thus actually writing 816–19. There is room for 'dccccii' on the same lines as 899–901, but there is no number. The *Mercian Register* begins simply as 'her ealhswið' at left margin. Annal numbers for 903, 905, and 908 fill up lines, while the number for 904 is crammed into the left margin and written in two decks, the top having .iiii, the bottom dcccc (d nearly lost); the annal number for 906 starts at the right margin and is written out towards the edge of the page. These two annal numbers seem to be an afterthought, as if the scribe realized that he was not following his exemplar here *or* realized that he had failed to exert any control over design. That the number 905 is embedded in the text and that there is no number 907 (C has it) further suggest a confusion at the start of the *Mercian Register*. There are no other annal numbers after 908 for any other entries in the body of the *Mercian Register*, an absence that

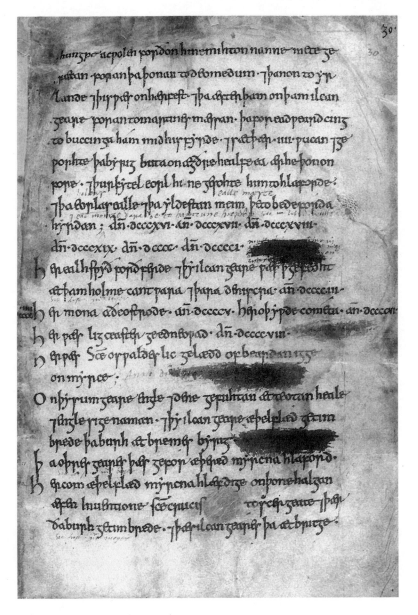

fig. 1. London, British Library, Cotton Tiberius A. vi, fol. 30r

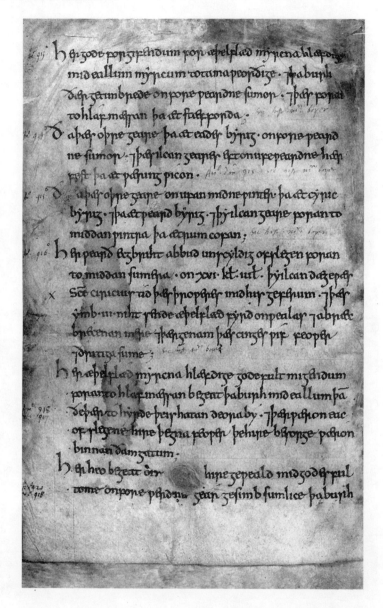

fig. 2. London, British Library, Cotton Tiberius A. vi, fol. 30v

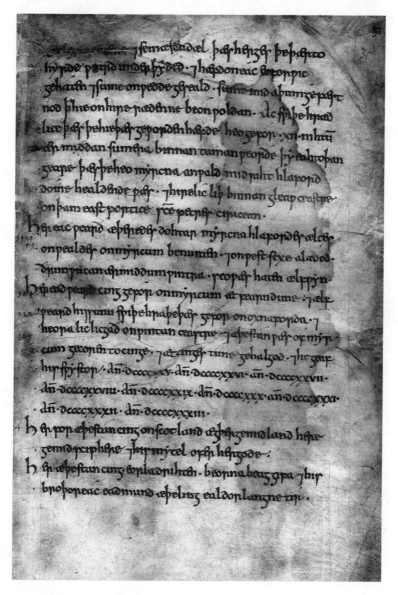

fig. 3. London, British Library, Cotton Tiberius A. vi, fol. 31r

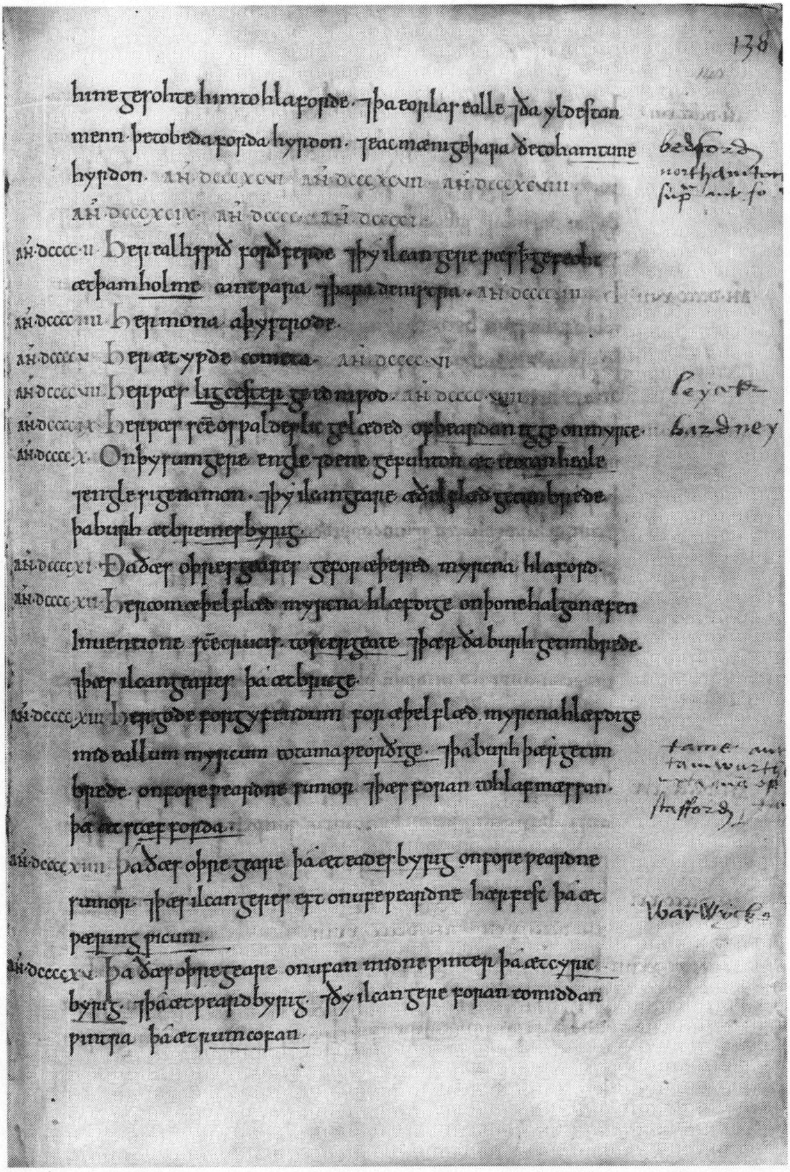

fig. 4. London, British Library, Cotton Tiberius B. i, fol. 140r

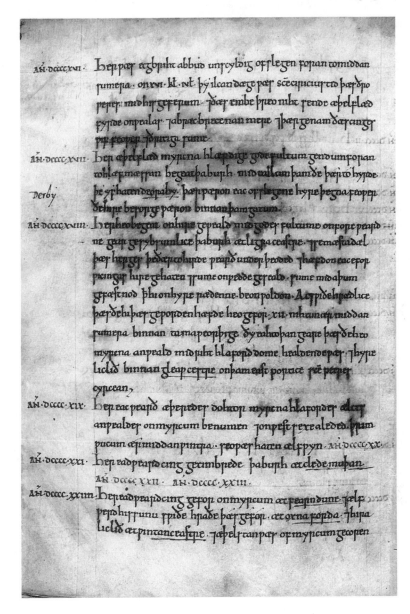

fig. 5. London, British Library, Cotton Tiberius B. i, fol. 140v

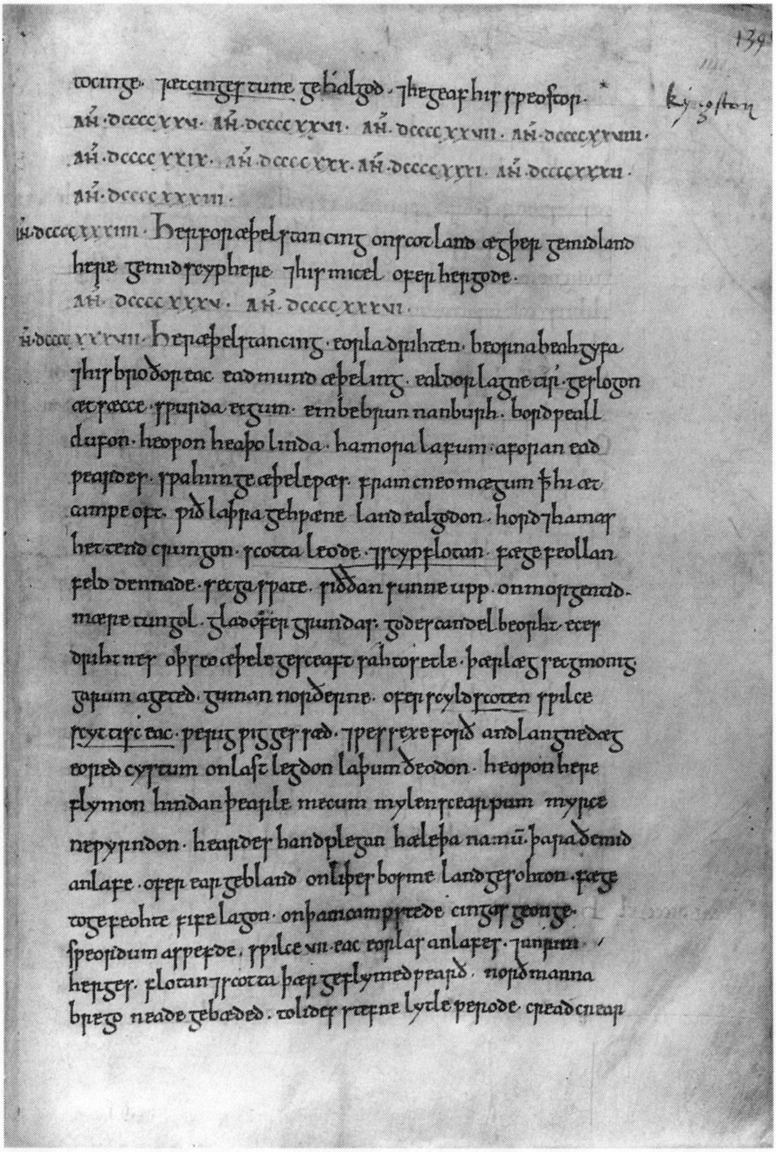

fig. 6. London, British Library, Cotton Tiberius B. i, fol. 141r

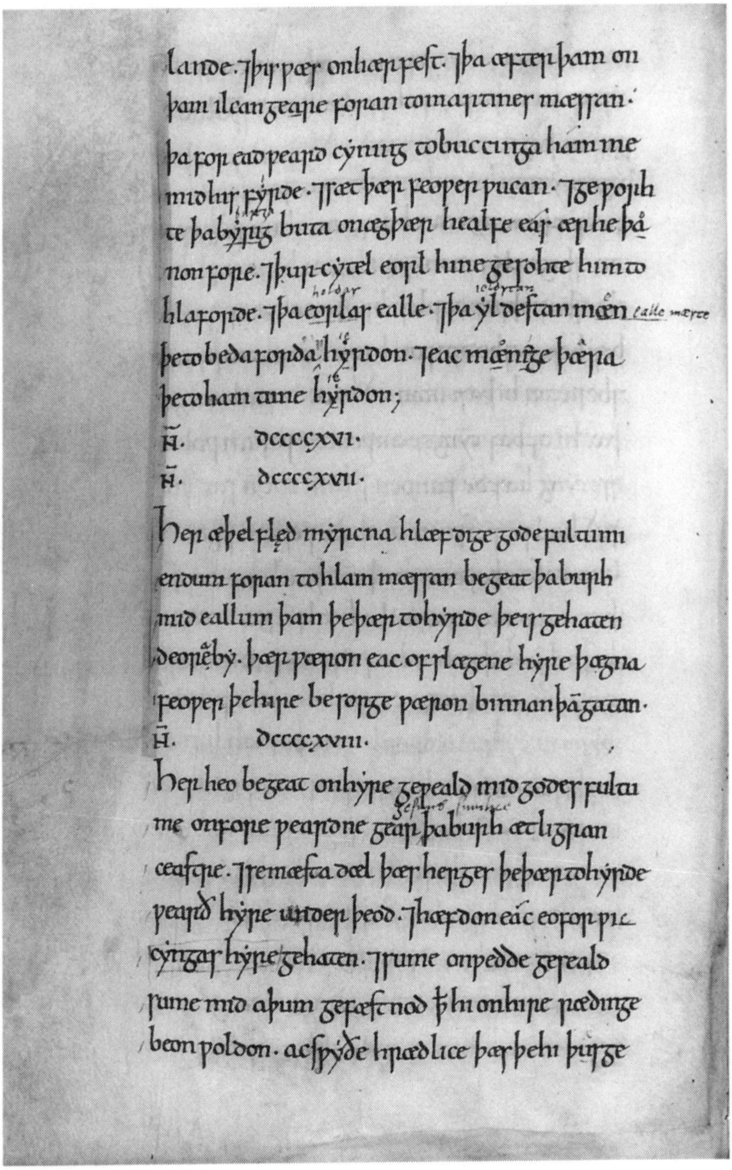

lanðe. ⁊hyr þær onhæp peſc. ⁊þa æptep þam on
þam ilcan geape popan toinapitineſ mæſſan·
þa pop eaðpeapð cýninᵹ tobuc cinᵹa ham me
miðluſ pýpðe· ⁊þæt þæp peopeſ pucan· ⁊ᵹepopþ
te þabýſiᵹ buta onæᵹþæſ healpe eaſ æphe þa
non pope. ⁊þuſ cýtel eopl hine ᵹepohte him to
hlapoſðe· ⁊þa coplaſ ealle· ⁊þa ýl ðeſtan mæn
þeto beða popða hýpðon· ⁊eac mænᵹe þæſ þa
þeto ham tine hýpðon;

Ħ·   ðcccċxvi·

Ħ·   ðcccċxvii·

Heſ æþel plæð mýrcna hlæpðiᵹe ᵹoðepultum
enðum popan tohlam mæſſan beᵹeat þabuſh
mið eallum þam þe þæp tohýpðe þeiſ ᵹehaten
ðeop̈ëbý· þæp pæpon eac opplæᵹene hýſe þæᵹna
ſpeopeſ þehſe beſopᵹe pæpon binnanþaᵹatan·
Ħ·   ðcccċxviii·

Heſ heo beᵹeat onhýſe ᵹepealð mið ᵹoðeſ pultu
me onpope peaſone ᵹæſ þabuſh æclisſan
ceaſſte· ⁊pemæſca ðæl þæſ heſᵹeſ þeþæp tohýpðe
peapð hýſe uttoeſ þeoð· ⁊hæpðon eac eoſoſ piſ
cýnᵹaſ hýſe ᵹehaten· ⁊ſume onpeððe ᵹepealð
ſume mið apum ᵹepæſcnoð þ hi onhſſe pæðinᵹe
beon poldon· ac ſpýðe hſæðlice þæſ þehi þiſ ᵹe

fig. 7. London, British Library, Cotton Tiberius B. iv, fol. 47v

,popðen hæpðe heoᵹepop .xii. nihtum ppiðie ið
,iunu. æþmiððan puinepa, binnan tam peopðe
·þý ealtoðan ᵹeape þæp þeheo mýpena anpeald
miðpultæ hlapopð dome healðenðe pæp. ᴣ þipe
lic lið binnan ᵹlepe ceapᵹie innan þam eaſt pop
ticæ ꝥcꝥ peᵹiep cýpicean·

ꜧ· dcccxviiii. Hep eac peapð æþelpe
·ðep ðohtep mýpena hlapopð ðep ælcep anpealðep
·onmýpcum benumen· ᴣonþeſt pᵹxe, alæded
,ppým pucum æþmiððan piitpe pepæp hatenælppýn·

ꜧ·   dccccxx.

ꜧ·   dccccxxi. Hep eadpeapð cýninᵹ
ᵹeumbpoðe þabuph æt cleðemuþan·

ꜧ·   dccccxxii·

ꜧ·   dccccxxiii· Hep pignolð cýninᵹ
ᵹe pan eopop pic·

ꜧ·   dccccxxiiii· Hep eaðpeapð cýninᵹ
,ᵹepop onmýpicum æt papndune· ᴣælppeapð
·hippunu ppýþe hpaðe þæp ᵹepop ýmbe xvi daᵹaſ
·æt oxan popða. ᴣ þý palic lið æt piittan ceaſpie·
,ᴣ æþelptan pæp ᵹecopen tocýnᵹe op mýpicum· ᴣæt
,cýnᵹep tune ᵹehalᵹoð· ᴣheᵹeaſ hip ppeoſtop
·op ſæ eald peᵹxna cýnᵹep puna·

ꜧ·   dccccxxv· Hep æþelptan cýninᵹ

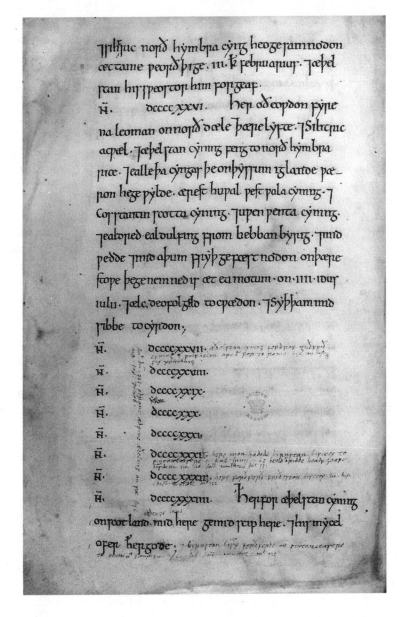

fig. 9. London, British Library, Cotton Tiberius B. iv, fol. 48v

continues in the body of the next intercalated text, the *Battle of Brunanburh*. One must note, of course, that the B scribe is sporadic in his use of annal numbers in the whole.[10] While the text through the end of the entry for 908 seems something of a run-on, the scribe does begin entries with an initial beyond the left margin; thus begin entries for 902, 904, 907, 909–19, and 921 (in C 920 is barren). Though there is no rubrication, the placement of initials beyond the left margin gives some shape to the text and its meaning. The B scribe and the C scribe obviously differ in the execution of details, but they share the same use of the run-on annal enumeration to mark the beginning and end of the *Mercian Register*. The B scribe's inconsistencies may confirm as much about the uniqueness of the *Mercian Register* as the C scribe's relative control.

The most recent editors of Chronicles B and C, Taylor and Rositzke, do not bear witness to this manuscript context in their editions. Taylor notes the string of annal numbers at the beginning and end of the *Mercian Register*, but he sets them out clearly as barren annals, each receiving a line of type for itself and an immediately accompanying blank line. Rositzke simply omits the barren strings at the beginning and end of the *Mercian Register*; even the annal number 920, which is tucked neatly into the right margin at the end of the entry for 919 and before the annal for 921 on the next line, and the annal numbers for 922 and 923, which occupy their own line, receive no notice. One may infer that for Rositzke only entries with text are worthy of notice. Rositzke does bracket notice to the *Mercian Register*, and Taylor makes it even more certain that the dislocation in temporal flow does not go unnoticed by placing 'MR' opposite each reconstructed annal number for B. Even though Taylor implies that the barren dates at the beginning and end of the *Mercian Register* are barren annals as such, he is closer to his B than Rositzke is to his C. These editors, like their predecessor scribes, are seeking to convey meaning by their layout and design, but it is not quite the same meaning that their scribes conveyed. The ongoing tension between the layout and design of the whole *Chronicle* text and the *Mercian Register* intercalation continues more subtly in the editions, but effectively the editors follow twentieth-century notions of layout and design, not to mention their own interpretations of the tactics and strategies of the Old English texts.

If the layout and design of the *Mercian Register* support Plummer's earlier description of the integrity of this text based on temporal dislocation and Mercian focus, then there are internal features of the BC telling that offer slight clues to the text behind BC and further contribute to the integrity-identity of it. It would appear that the *Mercian Register* is a translation from a Latin account, for there are two dative absolutes in the narrative. For 913 the entry begins 'Her Gode forgyfendum' ['Here, God granting'] and for 917 the reading is 'Her Æðelflæd Myrcna hlæfdige Gode fultumigendum' ['Here Æðelflæd, lady of the Mercians, God aiding'].[11] These Old English equivalents for *Deo donante* and *Deo auxiliante* (or similar Latin expressions) exist in the *Mercian Register* alongside the more 'native' prepositional phrase in 918 'mid Godes fultume' ['with God's help']. The mixture of forms is an analogue to the same variations of a Latin original as occur in Vercelli Homily XX and its variants, CCCC 162 art. 36, and CCCC 303 art. 44 where, for *Deo auxiliante*, CCCC 162 gives 'Gode fultumigendum' but with the gloss 'þurh Godes fultume' ['through God's help'] above the line, and CCCC 303 only 'ðurh Godes fultume'.[12] Somewhere in the genesis of the *Mercian Register* is a Latin account or perhaps poem that offers the *gesta Adelfledi*. The *Mercian Register* furthermore carries within it one of the few displays of human emotion in the *Chronicle*. The entry for 917 discusses the campaign at Derby: 'þær wæron eac ofslegene hyre þegna feower ðe hire be sorge wæron binnan þam gatum' ['there four of her thanes who were dear to her were also slain within the gates']. The F version (Cotton Domitian A. viii) of the *Chronicle* refers to 'sorrow' in the continuing comment on Ceolnoth that accompanies the core entry for 870, which relates the martyrdom of Eadmund at the hands of the vikings, and in the entry for 995, which concerns the history of Christ Church and in one passage the days of Ceolnoth when there was 'gewinn ⁊ sorh on þysum lande' ['contention and sorrow in this land'].[13] The Peterborough Chronicle [E] summarizes in part the year 1112 by calling it 'hefig tyme & sorhfull' ['grievous and sorrowful'].[14] These annals in E and F do not refer to personal emotion as indicated in the *Mercian Register*, but give more generalized descriptions of difficult times. The originary account would seem, then, to have left another trace in this comparatively unelaborated mention of Æðelflæd's feelings.

The foregoing discussion of essentially internal evidence argues in favour of Plummer's inference that the Mercian Register existed as a separate document.[15] Plummer adduces external and comparative evidence from the relations of *Chronicle* versions B, C, and D. The external evidence is 'Elfledes Boc', mentioned in a Durham catalog of manuscripts; 'This is not impossibly the *Mercian Register*',[16] says Plummer, while regretting the disappearance of the book. It is noteworthy that the general context of Plummer's discussion is the existence of copies of the *Chronicle* that circulated in the north.

In contrast to BC, the D version of the *Mercian Register* offers a clean, stately hand and a clear layout, wherein one account of Æðelflæd is blended into the *gesta* of the House of Wessex (see figs 7–9). For the period 902–25 there is a clear left margin on each page. The opening of an annal entry is regular: the abbreviation 'Ñ.' begins at the left margin, a blank space of about six letters follows, and the prose text begins. Each text with prose begins with 'her', 'h' written somewhat larger but without rubrication. There is no colour for display, etc. This layout applies for 903–06, 909–15, 919, 921, 923–25. Entries for 902, 907, 908, 916, 920, 922, are barren of prose text. The entries for 917 and 918, which are clearly Æðelflæd entries, begin prose on the next line, but 919, which gives a sketchy account of Ælfwyn, Æðelflæd's daughter successor, is back in the standard layout. There are no run-on annal entries that frame the *Mercian Register*.

In D Æðelflæd receives her first outright mention as the builder of the burh at Beremesbyrig. D makes mention of this activity in 909. There is no BC 912 equivalent. The focus in D returns to Æðelflæd in 913, where she receives an abbreviated line: 'Her æþelflæd getimbrode tameweorðe. ⁊ eac stafforda burh' ['Here Æðelflæd built Tamworth and also Stafford']. This entry is really double-stated since the next sentence begins 'her on þyssum geare ymbe martines mæssan het eadweard cyning' ['Here, in this year, around Martinmass, King Edward commanded'], which is the quivalent of BC 913. BC call her 'myrcna hlæfdige' ['lady of the Mercians'], but D gives her no title. D entries for 914–15 (see figs 7–9, for the end of 915 and ff.) do not concern Æðelflæd, and D 916 is blank, it will be recalled. BC shows signs of the originary document by means of narrative focus, temporal dislocation, and layout and design, whereas D blends these elements trailing 'the annals of Æðelflæd' so that only some narrative focus, as in 917, 918, and perhaps 919 remain. D shows the assertiveness of the House of Wessex in fashioning its political myth, but in that writing of events Æðelflæd moves a quiet step closer towards erasure, a fate already observable for Ealhswið, for example, who, mentioned in BC 902, gets no mention in D 902. Thus, while D 916 is blank, BC tell of Æðelflæd's successful exploits in Wales where she captured the king's wife. When in D Ælfwyn is given the male 'se' in pronominal reference, the blunder-insult, comparatively speaking, at least allows her to stay in the record.

The Peterborough Chronicle [E] virtually eliminates Æðelflæd in its very abbreviated account of the Edwardian years, which apparently owes nothing to the *Mercian Register*. Her death is noted for 918: 'Her Æðelflæd forðferde Myrcena hlæfdige' ['Here Æðelflæd, lady of the Mercians, passed away'].[17]

Though D begins to show the erasure of Æðelflæd and her deeds in the record of the house of Wessex as far as the context of *Chronicle* accounts is concerned, she nevertheless lives on in William of Malmesbury's *De Gestis Regum Anglorum*, II.125, with a brief mention also in II.126.[18] William's inscription of Æðelflæd is within his account of her brother Edward, where she is 'virago potentissima multum fratrem consiliis iuvare' ['a most powerful man-woman who aided her brother much with advice']. William's treatment of Edward contains enough left-handed compliments to create some ambiguity as to his intention. In II.125, while praising Edward somewhat for his royal actions, he consistently compares him unfavourably with his father Alfred. The casual connective phrase 'inter haec' introduces Æðelflæd who, William says, is not to be passed over [either], and now all manner of praise follows for Æðelflæd, presumably at the expense of Edward. In this general encomium William calls Æðelflæd 'favor civium, pavor hostium', two phrases that might very well suggest a rhyming poem behind William's treatment. This dual theme, 'citizens' delight, enemies' fright', appears again somewhat later when William observes that he does not know whether it be 'fortuna an virtute ut mulier viros domesticos protegeret, alienos terreret' ['by fortune or by manliness that a woman would protect her male retainers, terrify her enemies']. The rhythm and the rhyming verbs continue the suggestion of some antecedent text, but they also faintly echo the BC version that relates Æðelflæd's emotion when she lost her men, with whom she clearly had a special bond, at the battle of Derby (918). William offers one theme in the story of Æðelflæd that seems special to him. He says that Æðelflæd had so difficult a time giving birth – presumably to Ælfwyn – that she was always shrinking in horror from her husband's embrace because it was not fitting for a princess ['non convenire regis filiae'] to engage in sexual pleasure that later proved so inconvenient ['incommodum']. The kitchen psychologist may see in this anecdote a form of transference where sexual desire is translated into martial prowess, but William has already given his explanation: it is either *fortuna* or *uirtus*. The latter word, in its primary or root meaning, is 'manliness', of course, and indeed *uirago* carries with it mannish connotations. William is offering sister Æðelflæd along with father Alfred as contrasts to Edward, and the story of Æðelflæd is turned towards a specific rhetorical purpose in *De Gestis Regum Anglorum*. Æðelflæd's ostensible reasons for avoiding her husband's ardor, a blending of physical fear with perceived royal status, may have, for William, a reality, but if one grants his terms there is still a problem of reconciling her fear of childbirth and her fearlessness in battle. Marital chastity is not a theme here, one must note. At the end of his narration William mentions Æðelflæd's death and burial at St Peter's, Gloucester, without reference to where at St Peter's exactly, but in the process William explains why BC 904 occurs in the *Mercian Register*: Æðelflæd lay at St Peter's, which she and her husband had built, and to which she had transferred Oswald's bones.[19] William, thus, does not so much erase Æðelflæd as use her as a rhetorical foil. Of all the sources considered here, he is, most patently, creating and developing gender differences out of a story he has received. His contrast of Æðelflæd with Edward almost requires William to bring out the sister's special strengths and to create, perhaps only by deepest implication, some kind of sibling rivalry.

Henry of Huntingdon, on the other hand, poses a series of interesting problems that lie beyond the scope of this essay.[20] Henry gets some basic facts wrong: he makes Æðelflæd the daughter of Æðered [*sic*], not wife, and the sister of Ælfwyn, not mother. This dislocation of relationships could come from several possible causes: sources defective as texts, inaccurate sources, or Henry's faulty reception of correct information, which could be the result of his own inattention to detail or, more interestingly, a 'mis-reading' of sources coloured by his own contemporary preconceived notions. Henry's account, as Foerster's note observes, 'notices the events of the succeeding years in a tolerably accurate sequence' but 'from subsequent entries . . . [he] himself is generally at fault in his chronology of the period'.[21] These questions of accuracy, relative to the initial dislocation of the *Mercian Register* in the *Chronicle*, need their own study, particularly in 'manuscript context'. Still, Henry gives a straightforward account, noting the death of the four thegns at Derby and Æðelflæd's own burial 'apud Gloucestre in porticu S. Petri'. It is Henry's panegyric, however, that (presumably) points to a pre-existent Latin text. The poem is worth quoting in its entirety:

> O Elfleda potens, O terror virgo virorum,
>   Victrix naturae, nomine digna viri.
> Te, quo splendidior fieres, natura puellam,
>   Te probitas fecit nomen habere viri.
> Te mutare decet, sed solam, nomina sexus,
>   Tu regina potens, rexque trophaea parans.
> Jam nec Caesarei tantum meruere triumphi,
>   Caesare splendidior, virgo virago, vale.[22]

These remarkable eight lines suggest that the erasure of Æðelflæd is not so simple a matter, post–House of Wessex, after all.

A recent, popular work lists Æðelflæd among a book's worth of Amazons and other female prodigies, downplaying her martial exploits and giving prominence to her reaction to the pains of childbirth instead.[23] William is the obvious source of this information. The Terentian option, i.e., decrying the depravity of our audiences, who in this case seek out the lurid in a biography, is less important than recognizing that there is a full record and context for understanding. To describe Æðelflæd as an Amazon is to ignore the evidence of the chronicles and to initiate her erasure through misemphasis. Wainwright gives the best all-around historical treatment of the *gesta*, to be sure, but here my intention has been to create a chain of texts, viz., implied Latin sources, *Chronicle* versions, and William's treatment in an attempt to describe how this figure of history survives in various texts.[24] This small 'text' of great significance makes it possible to show how a methodology, traditionalist in its roots, can assist this major theme of feminist analysis. This emphasis on the 'old-time philology' and its scholarly modes effective for that feminist analysis has an echo in later literary historiography. For the story of Æðelflæd, the analysis begins, as it must, on those first manuscript pages that display an immediate context telling much and celebrating the lady of the Mercians.

NOTES

1 Fred C. Robinson, 'Old English Literature in Its Most Immediate Context', in *Old English Literature in Context*, ed. John D. Niles (Cambridge and Totowa 1980), 11–29 at 11 and notes at pp. 157–61. The article now appears in Robinson's collection of essays, *The Editing of Old English* (Cambridge, Mass., and Oxford 1994), 3–24 at p. 3, as well as in the anthology *Old English Shorter Poems*, ed. Katherine O'Brien O'Keeffe (New York 1994), 3–29 at p. 3.

   Portions of this article, particularly the discussion of the C-Chronicle below, have appeared in 'Æðelflæd in the *Chronicle*', *Old English Newsletter* 29/1 (Fall 1995) 42–44. See also Catherine Karkov's note on 'Æðelflæd's Exceptional Coinage?' in the same issue, p. 41.

2 Robinson, 11; in *The Editing of Old English*, 3; in *Old English Shorter Poems*, 3.

3 John D. Niles, 'Introduction', in *Old English Literature in Context*, 7.

4 It may very well be that the first paper delivered on 'theory' was Colin Chase, 'Source Study as a Trick with Mirrors: Annihilation of Meaning in the Old English "Mary of Egypt"', in *Sources of Anglo-Saxon Culture*, ed. Paul E. Szarmach with the assistance of Virginia Darrow Oggins, Studies in Medieval Culture 20 (Kalamazoo 1986), 23–33, which was delivered at the first Sources of Anglo-Saxon Culture Symposium at the Eighteenth International Congress sponsored by the Medieval Institute at Western Michigan University, 5–8 May, 1983.

5 Roy M. Liuzza, 'The Texts of the Old English *Riddle 30*', *Journal of English and Germanic Philology* 87 (1988) 1–15; 'The Old English *Christ* and *Guthlac*: Texts, Manuscripts, and Critics', *Review of English Studies* n.s. 41 (1990) 1–11 at 10.

6 Sarah Larratt Keefer, 'Respecting the Book: Editing Old English Liturgical Poems in their Manuscripts', *Florilegium* 11 (1992) 32–52.

7 The Ker references are to N.R. Ker, *Catalogue of Manuscripts Containing Anglo-Saxon* (Oxford: Clarendon Press 1957; rev. repr. 1990); the Gneuss references are to Helmut Gneuss, 'A Preliminary List of Manuscripts Written or Owned in England up to 1100', *ASE* 9 (1981) 1–60. At this writing Prof. Gneuss is revising and expanding his list. The status of edited versions is various. The collaborative edition, *The Anglo-Saxon Chronicle*, announced by D.S. Brewer Ltd and produced under the general editorship of David Dumville and

Simon Keynes, has resumed progress. Particulars about this series can be found in David
N. Dumville, 'Edition and Re-edition of the *Anglo-Saxon Chronicle*', *Old English Newslet-
ter* 27/3 (Spring 1994) 21–22 [repr. from *Medieval English Studies Newsletter* 28 (June 1993)
4–6]. The editions are: B: vol. 4: *MS B*, ed. Simon Taylor (Cambridge and Totowa 1983);
C: vol. 5: *MS C*, ed. in progress, ed. Katherine O'Brien O'Keeffe; D: vol. 6 : *MS D*, ed.
G.P. Cubbin (Woodbridge 1996). Cf. the first announcement of the series in *Old English
Newsletter* 15/2 (Spring 1982) 15–17. Harry August Rositzke, ed., *The C-Text of the Old
English Chronicles*, Beiträge zur englischen Philologie 34 (1940) is the only available edi-
tion of the C version at this time. *Two of the Saxon Chronicles Parallel*, ed. Charles Plummer
on the basis of an edition of John Earle, 2 vols (Oxford 1892–99; rev. Dorothy Whitelock,
1952) is the point of departure for modern study of the entire tradition. Translations of the
Chronicle are numerous. G.N. Garmonsway, *The Anglo-Saxon Chronicle* (London and New
York 1965), which follows Plummer–Earle, may be the most readily available. Simon Keynes,
Anglo-Saxon History: A Select Bibliography, Old English Newsletter Subsidia 13, 2nd rev. ed
(1993), items B40–B66 (pp. 4–5), offers an easy entry into the scholarship. The third edi-
tion of this bibliography (through 1995) came online on 15 August 1996, at http://
www.wmich.edu/medieval/rawl/keynes1/index.html. The relationships between the
Chronicle versions are intricate, to say the least. For an overview of the problems see Audrey
L. Meaney, 'St Neot's, Æthelweard, and the *Anglo-Saxon Chronicle*: A Survey', in *Studies in
Earlier Old English Prose*, ed. Paul E. Szarmach (Albany 1986), 193–243. Meaney presents a
distillation of her article in 'The *Anglo-Saxon Chronicle* c. 892: Materials and Transmission', *Old English Newsletter* 18/2 (Spring 1985) 26–35. See also *English Historical Documents, Volume 1: c. 500–1042*, ed. Dorothy Whitelock, 2nd ed. (London 1979), 109–21.
Janet Bately likewise offers an important study: *The Anglo-Saxon Chronicle: Texts and Textual Relationships*, Reading Medieval Studies Monograph 3 (Reading 1991), offering in
conclusion a stemmatic representation of the relationships between Latin and vernacular
texts on p. 62.
8 Ed. Plummer, 1: 92 n. 7. Plummer offers a discussion 'Of the Character and Mutual
Relations of the MSS' in vol. 2:xxxvii–cii, which is remarkable for its detail – and its
intricacy. For a discussion of chronicle narrative in general – the text here at hand is not
treated – see Cecily Clark, 'The Narrative Mode of *The Anglo-Saxon Chronicle* before the
Conquest', in *England before the Conquest: Studies in Primary Sources Presented to Dorothy
Whitelock*, ed. Peter Clemoes and Kathleen Hughes (Cambridge 1971), 215–35, which is
now available in *Words, Names, and History: Selected Writings of Cecily Clark*, ed. Peter
Jackson (Cambridge 1995), 3–19.
9 For the influence of Latin texts on layout and design see Janet Bately, 'Manuscript Layout
and the Anglo-Saxon Chronicle', *Bulletin of the John Rylands University Library of Manchester*
70 (1988) 21–43 [1987 Toller Lecture]. See also M.B. Parkes, 'The Palaeography of the
Parker Manuscripts of the *Chronicle*, Laws, and Sedulius, and Historiography at Winchester in the Late Ninth and Tenth Centuries', *ASE* 5 (1976) 149–71.
10 Ed. Taylor, xxviii and extended discussion, xxviii–xxxiv.
11 The dative absolute is a feature in the development of prose style. See Janet M. Bately,
'Old English Prose before and during the Reign of Alfred', *ASE* 17 (1988) 93–138, and
particularly the discussion of Werferth of Worcester's mimicry of Latin features, pp.
120–21. For the dative absolute generally, see Bruce Mitchell, *Old English Syntax*, vol. 2
(Oxford 1985), §§ 3804–31 (pp. 914–30).
12 Vercelli is defective at this point. All the editors note the variation in their apparatus: Paul
E. Szarmach, ed., *Vercelli Homilies IX–XXIII*, Toronto Old English Series 5 (Toronto 1981),

79 (= line G 6), with brief discussion on p. 82; Joyce Bazire and James E. Cross, eds, *Eleven Old English Rogationtide Homilies*, Toronto Old English Series 7 (Toronto 1982; repr. Kings College London Medieval Studies 4, 1987), 36 (line 133); Donald G. Scragg, ed. *The Vercelli Homilies*, EETS 300 (Oxford 1992), 340 (lines 143–44). See also my 'Vercelli Homily XX', *Medieval Studies* 35 (1973) 1–26, which also offers a discussion of the dative absolute.

13 Ed. Plummer, 1:284 and 130.

14 Cecily Clark, ed., *The Peterborough Chronicle, 1070–1154*, 2nd ed. (Oxford 1970), 36 *s.a.* line 8.

15 Ed. Plummer, 2:lxxii–lxxiii, and esp. n. 1 on lxxii.

16 Ed. Plummer, 2:lxxii n. 1.

17 Ed. Plummer, 1:103.

18 William of Malmesbury, *De Gestis Regum Anglorum*, ed. W. Stubbs, 2 vols, Rolls Series (London 1887–89) 1:136, 145. J.A. Giles provides translations of the relevant passages in *William of Malmesbury's Chronicle of the Kings of England* (London 1854), 123–24, 131. Plummer, 2:lxxxvi–lxxxvii, believes that William had a chronicle of the DE type.

19 When BC report that Æðelflæd was buried 'on þam east portice Sancte Petres ciricean', they may be suggesting royal burial. See Deborah Mauskopf Deliyannis, 'Church Burial in Anglo-Saxon England: The Prerogative of Kings', *Frühmittelalterliche Studien* 29 (1995) 96–119, with special reference to the earlier Anglo-Saxon period. For Bede, a 'porticus' could be a lateral chamber flanking the nave; see Mauskopf Deliyannis, pp. 97–98. My thanks to Prof. Deliyannis for allowing me to see an advance copy of her article. Æðelflæd appears in two charters; see P.H. Sawyer, *Anglo-Saxon Charters: An Annotated List and Bibliography* (London 1968), nos 224 and 225 (p. 127). In the latter, BL Cotton Claudius B.vi fol. 14r2-v2, which is dated XIII and has a difficult pedigree, Æðelflæd is called 'regina'. She sits in royal majesty, as one of several royal portraits on fol. 14. In its photographic files the BL incorrectly identifies the print, no. 74460, as 'seated abbot'.

20 See Thomas Arnold, ed., *Henrici Archidiaconi Huntendunensis Historia Anglorum*, Rolls Series 73 (London 1879), 157–59, for the full account; and also Thomas Forester, trans. and ed., *The Chonicle of Henry of Huntingdon* (London 1853, repr. New York 1968), 167–69. There are other historians to consider: (1) Benjamin Thorpe, ed., *Florentii Wigornensis Monachi Chronicon ex Chronicis* (London 1847), vol. 1, 121–28; translation by Joseph Stevenson, *Florence of Worcester: History of the Kings of England* (1853, repr. Felinfach, Lampeter, Dyfed, [1988]), 74–78; also Thomas Forester, trans., *The Chronicle of Florence of Worcester, with the Two Continuations* (London 1854, repr. New York 1968); and now see R.R. Darlington and P. McGurk, eds, and J. Bray and P. McGurk, trans., *The Chronicle of John of Worcester*, vol. 2, *The Annals from 450 to 1066* (Oxford 1995); (2) Thomas Arnold, ed., *Historia Regum*, in *Symeonis Monachi Opera Omnia* ([Wiesbaden] 1965]), vol. 2, sec. 104–05 (pp. 122–23); translation by J. Stevenson, *Simeon of Durham: A History of the Kings of England* (1858; repr. Felinfach, Lampeter, Dyfed, 1987); (3) *Rogeri de Wendover Chronica sive Flores Historiarum*; J.A. Giles, trans., *Roger of Wendover's Flowers of History* (London 1849, repr. New York 1968), 237–44.

21 Ed. Foerster, 165 n. 5.

22 Ed. Arnold, 158; tr. Foerster, 168, freely:

Heroic Elflede! great in martial fame,
A man in valour, woman though in name;
Thee warlike hosts, thee, nature too obey'd,
Conqu'ror o'er both, though born by sex a maid.

Chang'd be thy name, such honor triumphs bring,
A queen by title, but in deeds a king.
Heroes before the Mercian heroine quail'd:
Caesar himself to win such glory fail'd.

23 Jessica Salmonson, *The Encyclopedia of Amazons* (New York 1991), 3. Anne Nichols and Marty Williams, *An Annotated Index of Medieval Women* (New York and Princeton/Oxford 1992), s.n. (pp. 11–12), establish incorrect information of another kind in saying categorically: 'The Anglo-Saxon poem *Judith* is modeled on her.' Though in the history of the scholarship on this poem many have asserted a connection between Æðelflæd and Judith, that suggestion has never achieved the status of fact; it is a dubious proposition, moreover, that the suggestion is the current reigning opinion. See B.J. Timmer, ed., *Judith* (London 1952), 6–8.

24 F.T. Wainwright, 'Æthelflæd Lady of the Mercians', in *New Readings on Women in Old English Literature*, ed. Helen Damico and Alexandra Hennessey Olsen (Bloomington and Indianapolis 1990), 44–55; this article was originally published in *The Anglo-Saxons: Studies in Some Aspects of Their History and Culture Presented to Bruce Dickins*, ed. Peter Clemoes (London 1959), 53–69. Don Stansbury offers a more popular treatment in his *The Lady Who Fought the Vikings* (South Brent, Devon, 1993); my thanks to Paul Boldrey for this reference. For an overview see Joel T. Rosenthal, 'Anglo-Saxon Attitudes: Men's Sources, Women's History', in *Medieval Women and the Sources of Medieval History*, ed. Joel T. Rosenthal (Athens, Ga., and London 1990), 259–84, with a bibliography of primary and secondary sources, 281–84, and mention of Æðelflæd on 262, 267–68 ('heroic if not quite Churchillian', 267). See also the Keynes bibliography mentioned in n. 7 above.

Old English Texts and Modern Readers: Notes on Editing and Textual Criticism

HELMUT GNEUSS

This modest contribution, and the volume in which it appears, are dedicated to a distinguished scholar and an eminent textual critic.[1] It may not be inappropriate, therefore, to take up a subject that has occupied Anglo-Saxonists for a long time; its recent discussion, lively and sometimes controversial,[2] will no doubt have attracted the special attention of not a few readers and editors of Old English texts.

Before I turn to textual criticism proper, however, it seems advisable to consider the less elevated aspects of editorial work, the practical problems and 'technicalities' that have to be mastered. A history of how this was achieved in the more than four hundred years in which Old English texts were printed needs to be written one day. Here I must restrict my observations to the recent past. The virtues and the shortcomings of such printed editions were brought into focus more clearly than ever before, I think, when work on the new *Dictionary of Old English* began. Here, the question was simply whether the lexicographers would find a suitable and sufficient basis for their work in an edition, or whether they would have to make up for explanations – linguistic or otherwise – that the editor had not provided, and possibly even for emendations.

This was one of the reasons for my attempt to write a 'Guide' to the editing of Old English texts, which, together with a headnote, has now been reprinted;[3] sooner or later, it may have to be completely revised. In this 'Guide', I concentrated on the practical issues that every editor has to face: the presentation of the text or glosses, signs and conventions used, spelling, manuscript abbreviations, word division, punctuation, the arrangement of the critical apparatus, introductory matter, and commentary. To consider all this very carefully remains essential for every editor, though with regard to some details of the advice I have tried to give, one cannot emphasize often enough that each text demands its individual, proper method of editing, for editing, as Eric Stanley has rightly stressed, is a practical art.[4]

If an up-to-date guide to editing Anglo-Saxon texts were now to be written, it would of course have to incorporate the results of recent research, and editors would have to be made aware that all such results need to be taken into consideration in their work, whether in the edited text itself or – where an edition might be in danger of becoming too complex and sophisticated – in the introduction and notes.

To mention a few examples: Fred Robinson and Michael Korhammer have taught us a great deal about syntactical glossing or what was once called, in a special form, 'paving letters', and any editor of interlinear Old English glosses must take such devices into account nowadays, although it seems obvious that extensive syntactical glossing can hardly be reproduced in print.[5] Again, it has become clear that glossators of the Psalms were familiar with pertinent patristic commentaries, and in one case – in London, BL, Royal 2. B. v – such a commentary, in an abbreviated form, has even been added in the manuscript margins by the same scribe who wrote the Latin text and the Old English gloss.[6] Could we still afford to print an edition without this commentary, as Fritz Roeder did ninety years ago?

Continuous interlinear glosses in general used to be edited with little or no editorial commentary at all; why a detailed, thorough annotation of such glosses deserves to be considered, and how much this could serve to support the lexicographer's tasks, has very recently been demonstrated in Lucia Kornexl's edition of the *Regularis Concordia* in BL Cotton Tiberius A. iii.[7] More generally, it may be said that the main weakness of most of our editions of Old English prose texts is the lack of an adequate commentary dealing with matters of language as well as of content.

A debate about whether it is preferable to employ modern or medieval punctuation is now going on; I will return to it later.[8] Glosses added in the Middle English period – especially those by the 'tremulous hand' of Worcester – may not always seem of importance to the Anglo-Saxonist, but to other readers they could offer invaluable evidence for language change; would it be feasible to find an appropriate place for them in our editions?[9] Finally, an old headache: should we try, at last, to devise a uniform system of signs and symbols marking alterations, additions, omissions (editorial or in the manuscripts), and various other peculiarities in Old English prose and verse texts? It seems advisable not to be dogmatic on this point, but it may not be without some interest to note that of four scholarly standard editions of Old English homilies,[10] all published by the Early English Text Society between 1967 and 1993, each has its own system of signs used in text and apparatus, no two agree, and none follows the usage advocated by Martin West for classical texts.[11]

In neither version of my 'Guide' have I gone into the problems and intricacies of textual criticism or the special question of editorial emendation. Although there are a number of reasons for this, the main one is that each text has its individual shape and history of transmission, and it would have seemed arrogant and foolish to pretend to have a recipe with generally applicable rules for textual problems of any kind. But as Anglo-Saxonists now appear to be developing a special interest in points and principles of editorial policy and textual criticism, it may not be out of place to review some of the current arguments.

There is now an almost infinite, if not interminable, literature on editorial method and textual criticism, much of it written by classical philologists and medievalists in various disciplines.[12] It seems clear that the editor of an Old English text (preserved in more than one manuscript) can no longer light-heartedly undertake the quest for the author's original or the construction of a stemma, just like a nineteenth-century classicist. Karl Lachmann's method and its explication by Paul Maas, despite modern (and post-modern) criticism, have deserved our admiration, but nobody dealing with widely transmitted medieval texts could nowadays disregard the lessons we have been taught by Joseph Bédier, Henri Quentin, and George Kane.[13] Nobody who looks at Arnold Schröer's well-intentioned but unrealistic stemma of the manuscripts of Æthelwold's translation of the *Regula S. Benedicti*, and who compares it with the results of Mechthild Gretsch's investigations, can fail to see what I mean.[14] Similar difficulties would be met if one were to construct a stemma for the transmission of Ælfric's *Grammar*, as I have tried to do (but not published),[15] while Malcolm Godden expressly notes that his stemma of the manuscripts of the Second Series of Ælfric's *Catholic Homilies* summarizes their relationship 'as best it can'.[16]

Before I come to the real or presumed controversy concerning the editorial methods and the printing of Old English texts, there is one important point that I wish to make. The dictum of Richard Bentley, the great classical scholar, in his edition of Horace (1711) has been frequently quoted: 'nobis et ratio et res ipsa centum codicibus potiores sunt'.[17] This may seem to be the overoptimistic view of an early-eighteenth-century scholar. But let us consider the difference between what he – and present-day classicists – knew and know of the Latin language (and, of course, of Roman culture and history), and what we know – privileged as we are, as opposed to Bentley's contemporaries, even to great scholars like George Hickes and Humphrey Wanley – about Old English and Anglo-Saxon England.[18] Why is it that classical philologists and some medievalists even now can write the introductions to their editions in perfect Latin, while I have yet to hear of a twentieth-century editor of a medieval English text whose introduction is composed in Old or Middle English? There are perfectly good reasons why this is so; they have to do with the question of standardization, but also, and simply, with our knowledge of the respective languages.

This brings me to the present issue: the assumed fundamental opposition[19] between the 'conservative' and the 'liberal' editor of Old English texts. It is, if I may say so, not at all a new issue; some of the greatest Anglo-Saxonists referred to it, in a way, long ago. Let us look at two quotations from the writings of Henry Sweet and Kenneth Sisam:

The main principle I have adopted in printing is to make the text as far as possible a facsimile of the original MSS., without introducing any theoretical emendations. *All alteration in the text of a MS., however plausible and clever, is nothing else but a sophistication of the evidence at its fountain-head: however imperfect the information conveyed by the old scribe may be, it is still the only information we have, and, as such, ought to be made generally accessible in a reliable form.* In accordance with this principle I have in all cases enclosed contemporary additions above the line in brackets, the two forms, with and without the bracketed letter, being often extremely valuable, as showing fluctuations in the pronunciation.[20]

But when, as is usual for Old English poetry, only one late witness is available, there is no safety in following its testimony. The difference between a better reading and a worse is, after all, a matter of judgement; and however fallible that faculty may be, the judge must not surrender it to the witness. *To support a bad manuscript reading is in no way more meritorious than to support a bad conjecture, and so far from being safer, it is more insidious as a source of error.* For, in good practice, a conjecture is printed with some distinguishing mark which attracts doubt; but a bad manuscript reading, if it is defended, looks like solid ground for the defence of other readings. So intensive study with a strong bias towards the manuscript reading blunts the sense of style, and works in a vicious circle of debasement.[21]

May we then assume that there are two kinds of editors, who – perhaps influenced by their schooling, or following their personal inclinations – tend to treat their texts in a basically different manner? I do not think so and will try to explain why to me it seems more fruitful to concentrate the ongoing debate on individual texts and tasks, and not on theories and presumed principles, with their necessarily limited use and validity. Even the two quotations above should be seen in this light: Henry Sweet actually printed two manuscript texts side by side and supplied them with a translation in Modern English; for an editor with pronounced linguistic interests, this seems a fair procedure. Kenneth Sisam was considering a completely different type of text; moreover, he was well aware of the fact that ever since the days of Grundtvig, Kemble, Thorpe, Ettmüller, and Grein numerous textual problems in Old English poetry had been successfully solved by means of what classicists would call conjectural emendation.[22]

If we believe that the gap between liberal and conservative editing is not really so very wide – if there is a gap at all – this does not mean that there have not been cases in which past editors went far beyond what seems defensible and acceptable today. The daring practices of Moritz Trautmann and Ferdinand Holthausen (both of them serious and respectable scholars) are well-known, and it seems unthinkable that anybody today would want to study *Beowulf* in Hermann Möller's 'restored' version in four-line stanzas.[23] If we disregard such extreme cases, what are our arguments for denying that we have to assume a 'fundamental opposition' between the two attitudes to textual criticism?

First, there are the readers. Editions are not meant to be shelved in libraries, they are meant to be used and read. In an important paper on punctuation in printed Old English texts,[24] Bruce Mitchell distinguishes among the scholar, the ordinary reader, and the beginner. Can we afford to prepare and print different editions of the same text for each type of reader – and what would the publishers say? Providing for the beginner is no real problem; thus there are normalized texts available, like the first three selections in Bruce Mitchell's and Fred Robinson's excellent *Guide to Old English*,[25] and in any case, as Eric Stanley has noted, 'Old English studies are of a kind where the elementary student soon reaches advanced status'.[26] Providing for the scholar and, at the same time, the ordinary reader is a far more difficult task; and who, after all, is 'the ordinary reader' – the 'common' reader with literary interests, a historian, a theologian, an expert in some other field? Again: is 'the scholar' possibly a historical linguist?

If we assume, as I think we have to, that most Old English prose texts, and some verse as well, will be accessible in only one standard edition, then this edition will have to meet the needs of all prospective readers, and this can obviously be achieved most efficiently and economically by providing the scholar with a reliable record of the manuscript evidence (which is not to be understood as a plea for a diplomatic edition!) and of its interpretation by the editor, while the ordinary reader should always have the benefit of an idiomatic and yet exact translation accompanying the original. Such a translation would then serve a double purpose, as it would also show unambiguously how the editor understands and interprets his or her text. It is much to be regretted that the Early English Text Society gave up its earlier practice of supplying translations with Old English texts; I would not be surprised to meet Anglo-Saxonists who admit that they still, occasionally, find Sweet's rendering of Alfred's *Cura pastoralis* or Skeat's version of Ælfric's *Lives of Saints* useful.

Our next concern must be the type of text and its transmission. A readable *Beowulf* cannot now be produced without incorporating a considerable number of generally accepted emendations, yet does not necessarily have to include a full record of other, or all, suggested conjectures. A prose text transmitted in several manuscripts may pose fewer problems in the text, but more in the critical apparatus, where it should be remembered by intending liberal editors that even an 'ordinary' reader may profit from looking at significant variant readings, or may often derive a great deal of help from variant texts printed synoptically, on facing pages. How liberal an editor of interlinear glosses (continuous or not), or of glossaries, should be, is a nice question. The 'ordinary' reader is hardly likely to consult such matter, while the scholar has the Latin lemma and the context to help him.[27] There is no reason, therefore, why in such editions emendations should not be relegated to the critical apparatus or to the notes, although it ought to become common practice always to mark in text and gloss whatever an editor considers as erroneous.[28] Here it may be worth quoting what James Rosier, an experienced editor of psalm glosses, had to say: 'In an edition of this kind of text it is essential that the gloss be reproduced precisely as it stands in the manuscript, since expansions of abbreviations and emendations of supposed errors all too frequently obscure the important evidence of syntax, phonology, the glossator's use of a particular word, and the like.'[29] This, in my view, is not an expression of extreme conservatism, but a circumspect (though perhaps overcautious) and pragmatic approach to a specific task of an editor. We should also realize the limits of our insight into a glossator's mind, his training, and his 'Sprachgefühl'; and this warning applies to *any* author of an Old English text!

Let us look at an example. Section 4 of the tenth-century *Regularis Concordia* begins with an absolute participle, rendered by a temporal clause in Dom Thomas Symons's helpful translation:

Regulari itaque sancti patris Benedicti norma *honestissime* suscepta . . .

When therefore the Rule of the holy Father Benedict had been accepted with the greatest goodwill, . . .[30]

In the Old English interlinear version of the Latin text in BL Cotton Tiberius

A. iii, Latin *honestissime* is glossed by *wyrplice*. As is duly noted in Dr Kornexl's edition, 'Statt des vom lat. Lemma *honestissime* geforderten Superlativs (*wyrplicust*) steht hier der Positiv'. Are we then, whether liberals or conservatives, entitled to introduce an emendation into a gloss that appears perfectly idiomatic and adequate for rendering the sense of the Latin? Are we even justified in doing as little as marking the gloss as 'faulty'? Recent research has convincingly shown that Anglo-Saxon glossators (not, of course, all their copyists) were no hacks or dunces, mechanically turning word for word into the vernacular;[31] does this affect our decision in a case like *wyrplice*?

As was pointed out above, we can hardly hope to have at our disposal different types of editions for all our Old English texts, serving different readers and divergent purposes. This needs to be taken into account when one proposes to adopt liberal principles of editing, principles, incidentally, that might affect the critical apparatus more than the actual text.[32] Here we must ask what an editor should be expected to offer to a group of scholars – and not a very small one – who in the past have themselves greatly contributed to the work of the textual critics, and who will no doubt continue to do so: the historical linguists, or philologists, as some may call them.

For these – to mention just one point that has been extensively discussed – a full record not only of all lexical, morphological, and dialectal variants, but even of all the spelling variants of a text would be an ideal source for their studies; but we have to realize that there is a limit to what can be done in this respect, for instance, in a critical edition of Ælfric's *Catholic Homilies*. Malcolm Godden has convincingly demonstrated the practical problems involved, and he is certainly right in suggesting that 'what is needed for linguistic purposes is not exhaustive lists of variant readings in critical editions but studies, and perhaps editions, of single manuscripts in their entirety'.[33] Instead of such editions, facsimiles would no doubt often be more useful for linguistic investigations of various kinds, but such facsimiles have so far been too expensive for the private scholar. The recently announced series 'Anglo-Saxon Manuscripts in Microfiche Facsimile'[34] may bring a welcome solution, although it is well known that certain details of a manuscript page cannot be reproduced even in excellent photographs.

Nevertheless, it is my belief that no editor can afford to neglect significant linguistic evidence. I do not, therefore, agree with J.R.R. Tolkien's claim that 'It is futile to preserve forms which are supposed to have linguistic (dialect or period) significance', nor do I quite understand why 'most of these forms preserved by editors are palaeographical in origin, or vitiated as linguistic evidence by suspicion of such an origin'.[35] Such views, if applied to edited Old English texts in general, seem as unfortunate as the (apparent?) contempt for manuscripts and palaeography shown by the influential A.E. Housman and others, and rightly deplored by Michael Lapidge.[36] Let us look at a few random examples illustrating what an editor could do for his text, for his reader, and at the same time for the linguist. In the Old English translation of the Rule of St Benedict, Æthelwold renders chapter 2.13 (dealing with the duties of the abbot) somewhat freely:

Omnia vero, quae discipulis docuerit esse contraria, in suis factis indicet non agenda, . . .

Eal þæt he forbeode and his gingrum læþe, he þæt no mid weorce gefremme; . . .[37]

This is the reading in the two oldest manuscripts of the Old English prose version, Oxford, Corpus Christi College, 197 (last quarter s. x) and CCCC 178 (s. xi¹), as well as of the later copy in Durham Cathedral Library B. iv. 24 (s. xi²).[38] But in two other manuscripts, læþe has been altered: in BL Cotton Titus A. iv (s. xi^med) to lærð, with rð on erasure, and in Faustina A. x (s. xii¹) into lærð with r superscript. If the editor had omitted these alterations from his apparatus – possibly considering them as insignificant, or just faulty – valuable lexical evidence would have been lost. The two cases of lærð could perhaps simply be explained as caused by docuerit in the Latin, but a more convincing explanation seems to be that læðan in the sense 'cause to be hateful, cause (a person) to shun' was extremely rare in Old English and perhaps not understood by some of the scribes, apart from the fact that OE læðan 'to hate' was replaced very early, in the period of transition from Old to Middle English, by lāðian (Mod.E. loathe).[39] Here then is a lectio difficilior deserving the attention of the historical lexicographer of English and not, therefore, to be ignored in the projected new critical edition of the Old English Rule of St Benedict.

In a programmatic paper that has already been mentioned, Michael Lapidge has discussed the question whether the critical apparatus of an Old English poem should or could be devoted exclusively to 'significant' variants. In his example, Professor Dobbie's exhaustive apparatus for the 'Metrical Preface to King Alfred's Pastoral Care',[40] he noted that 'there is only one variant which might be thought "significant" for the purposes of classing the manuscripts'. This is the variant eorðbugendum, in line 3, found in Cambridge, Trinity College, R. 5. 22 (s. x/xi) for the original reading iegbuendum in the other manuscripts. However, on going through the apparatus it turns out that there are four more variants in the same manuscript that an editor and textual critic might legitimately consider to be not strictly 'significant', but which a linguist would certainly regard as important. In line 11, the Trinity copy replaces *min* with *me*, which could make sense if a comma were placed after *awende* in line 12, though here an error is more likely; cf. the passage as in Oxford, Bodleian Library, Hatton 20:

Siððan min on englisc Ælfred kyning
awende worda gehwelc,. . .

In line 15, *ðorfton* is replaced by *beporftan*, i.e., a different lexeme, and the Trinity scribe (or the scribe of his exemplar) may have had good reasons for choosing the prefixed verb. Even more interesting is the substitution of *bringan* for the weak and mainly dialectal form *brengan* in line 14, where the Trinity scribe may well have introduced the more common present infinitive because *brengan* seemed old-fashioned to him, or because it had no place in his dialect.[41] That the scribe was, in a sense, a modernizer can be seen in forms like *het* (line 13) for *heht*. Finally, there is the seemingly insignificant reading *adihtnode* (line 4) in the Trinity manuscript, where the other copies have *adihtode*. Anybody with an interest in diachronic word-formation in English, and especially in verbal suffixes, would consider this a piece of valuable evidence.[42] In any case, for the linguist, and particularly the lexicographer, Dobbie's apparatus has more to offer than just a record of scribal practices and preferences; and should we not all be interested to see what became of one of the two English poems 'which can be incontestably assigned to the reign of King Alfred',[43] within a hundred years or so?

Editors of Old English texts will do well to remember that in the past editorial decisions had to be made often enough on the basis of linguistic evidence; even the feasibility of complete editions may depend on such a procedure, as was demonstrated in Angelika Lutz's admirable reconstruction of the text of MS G of the *Anglo-Saxon Chronicle*,[44] which she was able to produce only after a systematic and painstaking analysis of the phonology and morphology in the charred remains of the Cotton manuscript, the manuscript copies made by Laurence Nowell and William Lambarde, and the printed edition of Abraham Wheloc.

I am pleading, then, for a pragmatic approach to the editing of Old English texts, an approach that gives us scholarly and yet readable editions and takes into consideration the prospective readership as well as the nature of the particular text; an approach that does not avoid necessary economies and emends (in a clearly marked form) where this seems appropriate; ideally, it would also be an approach that recognizes the needs and interests of the literary reader as well as those of the historical linguist.[45] Fundamentally opposed positions of conservative and liberal editors have not, in my view, really existed in Anglo-Saxon studies so far, and I do not think that a dichotomy of this kind is to be feared in the future, near or far. One might even wonder whether the notions of 'conservatism' and 'liberalism' in editing could not become reversed, as seems to be the case with the treatment of manuscript punctuation in printed editions.

For a long time editors who may have been regarded by some as conservative took modern punctuation in printed Old English prose and poetry for granted,[46] and I still strongly believe that this practice provides very essential help for readers, even if we suspect that Anglo-Saxon authors, and especially poets, did not always think and write in terms of the categories and structures of our modern 'traditional' grammar.[47] Such an attitude may now have to be reconsidered, not only because our knowledge and understanding of medieval punctuation has greatly advanced in recent years,[48] but also and mainly because scholars who are experts in the field have advocated the development of a new system of punctuation in our editions, and have even demonstrated that it is possible to adopt, without alteration, the punctuation of an Anglo-Saxon manuscript in which the pointing is intelligently and consistently devised and used, as in certain manuscripts of Ælfric's *Catholic Homilies*.[49] Such practice may remain limited to a few particular texts, but it is apt to demonstrate the paradox that what to some may appear novel and progressive (or even liberal?) is in fact an example of well-founded conservatism.

But let us forget about labels and theories: all we need now and in the future is editors whose work is determined by wide competence and common sense, editors who could say like Ludwig Bieler, 'My views are derived primarily from practical work on texts, and not from the study of theories'.[50]

NOTES

1 His important work in this field has now been published or reprinted in *The Tomb of Beowulf and Other Essays on Old English* (Oxford 1993), and *The Editing of Old English* (Oxford 1994).

2 The major contributions to this discussion are: Malcolm Godden, 'Old English', in *Editing Medieval Texts: English, French, and Latin Written in England. Papers Given at the Twelfth Annual Conference on Editorial Problems, University of Toronto, 5–6 November 1976*, ed. A.G. Rigg (New York 1977), 9–33; E.G. Stanley, 'Unideal Principles of Editing Old English Verse', *Proceedings of the British Academy* 70 (1984) 231–73 [Sir Israel Gollancz Memorial Lecture 1984, also published separately]; Michael Lapidge, 'Textual Criticism and the Literature of Anglo-Saxon England', *Bulletin of the John Rylands University Library of Manchester* 73 (1991) 19–45; Michael Lapidge, 'The Edition, Emendation, and Reconstruction of Anglo-Saxon Texts', in *The Politics of Editing Medieval Texts: Papers Given at*

the Twenty-Seventh Annual Conference on Editorial Problems, University of Toronto, 1–2 November 1991, ed. Roberta Frank (New York 1993), 131–57. *The Editing of Old English: Papers from the 1990 Manchester Conference*, ed. D.G. Scragg and Paul E. Szarmach (Cambridge 1994), was not yet available to me at the time of writing this essay.

3 'Guide to the Editing and Preparation of Texts for the Dictionary of Old English', in *A Plan for the Dictionary of Old English*, ed. Roberta Frank and Angus Cameron (Toronto 1973), 11–24; repr. with supplementary material in *The Editing of Old English* (see n. 2 above), 7–26.

4 'Unideal Principles', 269.

5 Fred C. Robinson, 'Syntactical Glosses in Latin Manuscripts of Anglo-Saxon Provenance', *Speculum* 48 (1973) 443–75; Michael Korhammer, 'Mittelalterliche Konstruktionshilfen und altenglische Wortstellung', *Scriptorium* 34 (1980) 18–58.

6 See *Der altenglische Regius-Psalter*, ed. Fritz Roeder, Studien zur Englischen Philologie 18 (Halle 1904), xiv–xv, and esp. W. Davey, 'The Commentary of the Regius Psalter: Its Main Source and Influence on the Old English Gloss', *Mediaeval Studies* 49 (1987) 335–51; see also the facsimile of fol. 8 in George F. Warner and Julius P. Gilson, *Catalogue of Western Manuscripts in the Old Royal and King's Collection* (London 1921), vol. 4, plate 22. William J. Davey, 'An Edition of the Regius Psalter and Its Latin Commentary' (PhD diss., University of Ottawa 1979), remains unpublished.

7 *Die Regularis Concordia und ihre altenglische Interlinearversion*, ed. Lucia Kornexl, Texte und Untersuchungen zur Englischen Philologie 17 (Munich 1993).

8 See below, p. 136.

9 See now Christine Franzen, *The Tremulous Hand of Worcester: A Study of Old English in the Thirteenth Century* (Oxford 1991), and Angus Cameron, 'Middle English in Old English Manuscripts', in *Chaucer and Middle English Studies in Honour of Rossell Hope Robbins*, ed. Beryl Rowland (London 1974), 218–29.

10 *Homilies of Ælfric: A Supplementary Collection*, ed. John C. Pope, 2 vols, EETS 259–60 (London 1967–68), 1:188–89; *Ælfric's Catholic Homilies: The Second Series. Text*, ed. Malcolm Godden, EETS s.s. 5 (London 1979), xcv–xcvi; *The Vercelli Homilies and Related Texts*, ed. D.G. Scragg, EETS 300 (Oxford 1992), lxxxi–lxxxii; *Old English Homilies from MS. Bodley 343*, ed. Susan Irvine, EETS 302 (Oxford 1993), lxxviii.

11 Martin L. West, *Textual Criticism and Editorial Technique Applicable to Greek and Latin Texts* (Stuttgart 1973). Cf. my 'Guide' (above, n. 3, 1994 version), p. 9, and the system devised by the late Julian Brown and M.P. Brown, in Michelle P. Brown, *A Guide to Western Historical Scripts from Antiquity to 1600* (London 1990), 5–7.

12 For the important work in the field, see the comprehensive surveys and annotated bibliographies in Leonard Boyle, *Medieval Latin Palaeography: A Bibliographical Introduction* (Toronto 1984), 287–316; and Horst Fuhrmann, 'Réflexions d'un éditeur', in *Les problèmes posés par l'édition critique des textes anciens et médiévaux*, ed. J. Hamesse (Louvain-la-Neuve 1992), 329–59, a revised version of the German original first published in 1978.

13 For the highly influential work of these scholars, from Lachmann to Kane, see the references in the publications cited above in n. 12; for Lachmann's role in the study of Old English, see the recent comments in Allen J. Frantzen, *Desire for Origins: New Language, Old English, and Teaching the Tradition* (New Brunswick 1990), ch. 3, not quite objective, I think. Sebastiano Timpanaro, *La genesi del metodo del Lachmann*, 2nd ed. (Padua 1985) is important.

14 *Die angelsächsischen Prosabearbeitungen der Benediktinerregel*, ed. Arnold Schröer, 1st ed. 1885–88, 2nd ed. with an appendix by H. Gneuss (Darmstadt 1964), xxxiv; Mechthild

Gretsch, 'Æthelwold's Translation of the *Regula Sancti Benedicti* and its Latin Exemplar', *ASE* 3 (1974) 125–51, esp. 140–43.

15 *Ælfrics Grammatik und Glossar*, ed. Julius Zupitza, 1st ed. 1880, 2nd ed. with introduction by H. Gneuss (Berlin 1966). Unfortunately, Zupitza did not live to write his projected second, introductory volume of the edition, and 115 years after the publication of the first we are still waiting for the gap to be filled. A tentative survey of the MS relationships reveals that there are close links between MSS D and H, C and U; other groups emerge, but the degree of contamination in general makes things appear hopeless for any follower of the stemmatic method. This is one of the indications of how numerous and how widely used copies of the first Anglo-Saxon 'bestseller' must have been. For recent literature on Ælfric's *Grammar* see H. Gneuss, 'The Study of Language in Anglo-Saxon England', *Bulletin of the John Rylands University Library of Manchester* 72 (1990) 3–32, at 13–17.

16 See *Ælfric's Catholic Homilies: The Second Series* (see n. 10 above), lx–lxi.

17 *Q. Horatius Flaccus*, ed. Richard Bentley (Cambridge 1711), 147, note on *Carm.* III.27.15.

18 This is the main reason why I would rather cautiously follow the suggestion by Professor Lapidge 'that the editing of Old English texts could proceed more fruitfully if Old English editors were able to profit from the wider experience of Latin textual criticism' ('The Edition', 139; see n. 2 above), apart from the fact that we have to remember the special problems of Medieval Latin. For these, we can now expect a systematic and comprehensive treatment in *Handbuch zur lateinischen Sprache des Mittelalters*, in 5 vols., by Professor Peter Stotz, of which vol. 3, *Lautlehre*, has appeared (Munich 1996); see also Peter Stotz, 'In Sichtnähe: Ein Handbuch zur lateinischen Sprache des Mittelalters', *Filologia mediolatina* 1 (1994) 183–202. Another reason for caution or scepticism in this matter should not be forgotten: editors of classical or patristic texts are often necessarily selective in their choice of manuscripts and representation of variant readings, when such texts survive in hundreds of medieval and Renaissance manuscripts; for some pertinent figures see *Texts and Transmission: A Survey of the Latin Classics*, ed. L.D. Reynolds (Oxford 1983). No Old English text and hardly any Anglo-Latin text poses similar editorial problems.

19 Lapidge, 'The Edition', 139: 'The two attitudes . . . are fundamentally opposed and apparently irreconcilable.' But a reconciliation does seem possible to me, as I hope to show.

20 Henry Sweet, ed., *King Alfred's West-Saxon Version of Gregory's Pastoral Care*, pt I, EETS 45 (London 1871), viii; my italics.

21 Kenneth Sisam, 'The Authority of Old English Poetical Manuscripts', in *Studies in the History of Old English Literature* (Oxford 1953), 39 [the essay was first published in 1946]; my italics.

22 For an inventory of early emendations in *Beowulf*, see Birte Kelly, 'The Formative Stages of *Beowulf* Textual Scholarship', *ASE* 11 (1983 for 1982) 247–74, and 12 (1983) 239–75. Claus-Dieter Wetzel's critical discussion of Kevin Kiernan's ultraconservative attitude towards the text of *Beowulf* is well worth reading: 'Die Datierung des *Beowulf*: Bemerkungen zur jüngsten Forschungsentwicklung', *Anglia* 103 (1985), 371–400, at 396–7.

23 For Trautmann and Holthausen as well as their opponents, see Lapidge, 'The Edition', 135–37. Some instructive examples of Holthausen's method are included in Fred Robinson's 'Two Aspects of Variation in Old English Poetry', in *The Tomb of Beowulf* (see n. 1, above), 80–81. For Möller, see that author's *Das altenglische Volksepos in der ursprünglichen strophischen Form, I. Teil: Abhandlungen*, and *Das altenglische Volksepos* [text] (both Kiel 1883).

24 Bruce Mitchell, 'The Dangers of Disguise: Old English Texts in Modern Punctuation', *Review of English Studies* n.s. 31 (1980) 385–413.

25 *A Guide to Old English*, 5th ed. (Oxford 1992), 171–89.

26 'Unideal Principles' (see n. 2 above), 248.
27 In the case of scattered and occasional glosses, the provision of the Latin context, not only of the individual lemma, should be recommended. This practice, first introduced by Herbert Meritt (see Gneuss, 'Guide', 1994 version, p. 21, n. 26), has been applied in Martin Richter, *Die altenglischen Glossen zu Aldhelms 'De laudibus virginitatis' in der Handschrift BL, Royal 6 B. VII*, Texte und Untersuchungen zur Englischen Philologie 19 (1996), where the editor also supplies Modern English translations of the respective passages.
28 As has been consistently done in Lucia Kornexl's edition of the *Regularis Concordia* (cf. note 7, above).
29 *The Vitellius Psalter*, ed. James L. Rosier, Cornell Studies in English 42 (Ithaca 1962), vii.
30 *Regularis Concordia Anglicae Nationis Monachorum Sanctimonialiumque: The Monastic Agreement of the Monks and Nuns of the English Nation*, ed. and trans. Dom Thomas Symons (London 1953), 2; *Regularis Concordia*, ed. Kornexl, p. 3, line 35, and note on p. 156.
31 See H. Gneuss, 'Anglicae linguae interpretatio: Language Contact, Lexical Borrowing and Glossing in Anglo-Saxon England', *Proceedings of the British Academy* 82 (1993) 107–48, at 145–47, and the literature cited there.
32 For an example see the 'Metrical Preface to King Alfred's *Pastoral Care*' and its apparatus, discussed below.
33 Godden, 'Old English' (see n. 2 above), 25.
34 *Anglo-Saxon Manuscripts in Microfiche Facsimile*, vol. I– , ed. A.N. Doane and Phillip Pulsiano (Binghamton, N.Y., 1994–).
35 J.R.R. Tolkien, *The Old English Exodus: Text, Translation, and Commentary*, ed. Joan Turville-Petre (Oxford 1981), 36, quoted approvingly by Eric Stanley, 'Unideal Principles', 267. But here one has to admit that a linguist's needs could easily be supplied by other editions of *Exodus*, and even from Tolkien's apparatus.
36 See esp. A.E. Housman, 'The Application of Thought to Textual Criticism', in *The Classical Papers of A.E. Housman*, 3 vols, ed. J. Diggle and F.R.D. Goodyear (Cambridge 1972), 3:1058, and Lapidge, 'Textual Criticism' (see n. 2 above), 21.
37 *Benedicti Regula*, ed. Rudolf Hanslik, 2nd ed., CSEL 75 (Vienna 1977), 23; *Die angelsächsischen Prosabearbeitungen der Benediktinerregel* (see n. 14 above), p. 11, lines 17–18; my italics. Cf. *The Rule of Saint Benedict*, ed. and trans. Justin McCann (London 1952), 19: 'And whatever he has taught his disciples to be contrary to God's law, let him show by his example that it is not to be done . . .'
38 For the MSS see Mechthild Gretsch, *Die Regula Sancti Benedicti in England und ihre altenglische Übersetzung*, Texte und Untersuchungen zur Englischen Philologie 2 (Munich 1973), 17–48. I owe my knowledge of the reading in the Durham MS (not collated by Schröer) to Dr Gretsch.
39 Cf. the historical dictionaries of English and *A Microfiche Concordance to Old English*, compiled by Antonette diPaolo Healey and Richard L. Venezky (Toronto 1980). Of ten recorded occurrences of OE *lǣðan*, only one may represent the same meaning as that in the Benedictine Rule: *The Vercelli Homilies and Related Texts*, ed. D.G. Scragg (see n. 10 above), 369 (XXII.15); but see Dr Scragg's interpretation, 'to revile', p. 443. A homonymic clash with ME *lēthe(n)* 'to free', 'to mitigate', 'to cease' may have played a role in the later development (see *MED* s.v. *lēthen* v.), but the case is rather complex and deserves further investigation.
40 *The Anglo-Saxon Minor Poems*, ed. Elliott van Kirk Dobbie, ASPR 6 (New York 1942), 110 and cxii–cxv; cf. Lapidge, 'Textual Criticism', 39–40. For another MS copy of the 'preface', not noticed by Dobbie, see Katherine O'Brien O'Keeffe, *Visible Song: Transitional Literacy*

in Old English Verse, Cambridge Studies in Anglo-Saxon England, 4 (Cambridge 1990), 77–107, esp. 88–94.

41 See A. Campbell, *Old English Grammar* (Oxford 1959), § 753(5), and Karl Brunner, *Altenglische Grammatik nach der Angelsächsischen Grammatik von Eduard Sievers*, 3rd ed. (Tübingen 1965), § 407, n. 8, where a possibly iterative sense of OE *breng(e)an* is noted.

42 For the origin, formation and semantics of OE *dihtan* and *dihtnian* see now Kornexl, *Regularis Concordia*, 190–91 and esp. 323–24, and for English verbs formed with a nasal suffix, see the *OED* s.v. *-en*, suffix⁵; Josef Raith, *Die englischen Nasalverben* (Leipzig 1931); Herbert Koziol, *Handbuch der englischen Wortbildungslehre*, 2nd ed. (Heidelberg 1972), 265, and Hans Marchand, *The Categories and Types of Present-Day English Word-Formation*, 2nd ed. (Munich 1969), 271–73. In his notes (p. 202), Dobbie points out that Sweet's *foreadihtode* (*King Alfred's . . . Pastoral Care*, p. 9, see n. 20 above), which was received into the dictionaries, should be written as two words, for metrical reasons. This is a reminder of one of the worst problems for editors of Old English texts, the question of word division, particularly with regard to the so-called separable prefixes (where 'prefix' is not used in the strict sense of a 'bound morpheme'). Cf. Gneuss, 'Guide', 1994 version, nn. 19 and 20; Claus-Dieter Wetzel, *Die Worttrennung am Zeilenende in altenglischen Handschriften* (Frankfurt am Main 1981), 7, n. 22; Hans Sauer, 'Die Darstellung von Komposita in altenglischen Wörterbüchern', in *Problems of Old English Lexicography: Studies in Memory of Angus Cameron*, ed. Alfred Bammesberger (Regensburg 1985), 267–315; Bruce Mitchell, *Old English Syntax*, 2 vols (Oxford 1985), §§ 1072–73.

43 Dobbie, cxii–cxiii.

44 Angelika Lutz, *Die Version G der Angelsächsischen Chronik: Rekonstruktion und Edition*, Texte und Untersuchungen zur Englischen Philologie 11 (Munich 1981); see esp. sec. 5 of her introduction.

45 The value of seemingly unimportant variant readings for the work of the lexicographer and the grammarian has been emphasized, and amply demonstrated, by Fred C. Robinson, 'Metathesis in Dictionaries: A Problem for Lexicographers', in *Problems of Old English Lexicography* (see n. 42 above), 245–65. This is not the place for dealing specifically with the causes of mistakes made by scribes in the process of copying. For Latin texts, they have been treated comprehensively by James Willis, *Latin Textual Criticism* (Urbana 1972); see now also Paul Gerhard Schmidt, *Probleme der Schreiber – der Schreiber als Problem*, Sitzungsberichte der wissenschaftlichen Gesellschaft an der Johann Wolfgang Goethe-Universität, Frankfurt am Main, 30, no. 5 (Stuttgart 1994). For the problem of dictation as such a cause see now Peter Bierbaumer, 'Slips of the Ear in Old English Texts', in *Luick Revisited. Papers Read at the Luick-Symposium at Schloss Liechtenstein 15.–18.9.1985*, ed. Dieter Kastovsky and Gero Bauer (Tübingen 1988), 127–37.

46 For exceptions see Mitchell, 'The Dangers of Disguise' (see n. 24 above). Another notable example (for the Latin text underlying an Old English gloss) is *Der Cambridger Psalter*, ed. Karl Wildhagen (Hamburg 1910, repr. Darmstadt 1964).

47 At the risk of falling into disgrace with some modern authorities, I refer the reader to Bruce Mitchell, *Old English Syntax*, 1:lxi–lxii, in order to explain why I consider 'traditional' grammar adequate for the purposes here envisaged.

48 The standard work is now M.B. Parkes, *Pause and Effect: An Introduction to the History of Punctuation in the West* (Aldershot, Hampshire, 1992). See also Fuhrmann, 'Réflexions d'un éditeur' (see n. 12 above), 349–50.

49 See Bruce Mitchell's important paper (n. 24, above), and the same author's *Old English Syntax*, §§ 1879–82; Godden, 'Old English', 19, and esp. his edition of the Second Series of

Ælfric's *Catholic Homilies* (n. 10, above), in which he follows the punctuation of CUL Gg. 3. 38; also C.G. Harlow, 'Punctuation in Some Manuscripts of Ælfric', *Review of English Studies* n.s. 10 (1959) 1–19, and Peter Clemoes in *Ælfric's First Series of Catholic Homilies: British Museum Royal 7.C.xii, Fols 4–218*, ed. Norman Eliason and Peter Clemoes, Early English Manuscripts in Facsimile 13 (Copenhagen 1966), 24–25.

50 Ludwig Bieler, 'The Grammarian's Craft', *Folia* 10/2 (1958) 3–42, at 4. For comments on a draft of this paper, and for putting it into the computer, I wish to thank Mechthild Gretsch, Lucia Kornexl, and Ursula Lenker.

The Dream of the Rood Repunctuated

BRUCE MITCHELL

§ 1.   I have already paid a personal tribute to my friend and collaborator
Fred Robinson in the dedication to *A Critical Bibliography of Old English
Syntax* (Oxford 1990). It is a further pleasure for me to share in this wider
tribute to a man who for thirty years has stimulated my thinking by correspondence ('O those Fred-letter days'), conversation, and publication, and
who, with Helen, has enriched my life by his friendship. It is perhaps not
unfitting that my tribute to the author of *'Beowulf' and the Appositive Style*
(Knoxville 1985) and my collaborator in *'Beowulf': An Edition* (Oxford, forthcoming) should be concerned with Old English poetry, and in particular
with its punctuation. Despite this concentration, however, I believe that
mutatis mutandis what follows is applicable to Old English prose as well as to
the poetry.

§ 2.   *Delenda est Carthago.* It is twenty-five years since I first complained in
print about the use of modern punctuation in editions of Old English poetry.[1] It is fifteen years since I wrote the article entitled 'The Dangers of
Disguise: Old English Texts in Modern Punctuation',[2] in which I pointed
out (*inter alia*) that modern punctuation – familiar but misleading – is not
the proper replacement for the inadequate punctuation found in Old English manuscripts. It is ten years since the appearance of my *Old English Syntax* (Oxford 1985), in which punctuation was much discussed. It is seven
years since I observed that 'to my regret, this paper ['The Dangers of Disguise'] seems to have sunk without a ripple in the ocean – or pond – of OE
literary criticism' and, while conceding that 'I am sure that I have not solved
the problem', regretted that no conference had yet been dedicated to a problem of such 'fundamental significance'.[3] It is four years since I delivered the
Second H.M. Chadwick Memorial Lecture,[4] in which I again argued that,

faced as we are by the inadequacy of the manuscript punctuation and the unsuitability and irrelevance of modern punctuation, we should be able to produce a system of punctuation which would both satisfy the modern reader's desire for clarity and respect the syntax and style of Old English. *Carthago delenda est.*

§ 3.   My failure so far to produce a system which satisfies myself, let alone others, explains why editors have stuck to modern or, more rarely and for prose texts only, manuscript punctuation. But it does not explain why the subject has not been taken more seriously or why, despite my pleas for help, I have received no practical suggestions for improving my system. There has, however, been some recognition of the fact that I might have a point. Robinson (*'Beowulf' and the Appositive Style*, preface) observed that 'often and unconsciously readers have had their interpretations of the poem [*Beowulf*] restricted or even predetermined by glossaries and dictionaries . . . , by modern conventions of punctuation which (as Bruce Mitchell has recently shown) limit the multiple reference of Old English syntactical constructions, and by modern conventions of capitalization . . .' Donoghue, after offering some relevant criticisms which I discuss below, concluded, 'In spite of these reservations, I still find Mitchell's proposal attractive and agree that there is much room for work in this area'.[5] Stanley wrote that 'The Dangers of Disguise' 'advocated a reformed system of punctuation with which I have little sympathy, though I admire the discussion leading up to it'.[6] I am grateful for the concessive clause and, as will become apparent below, now share his lack of sympathy for my 1980 system.

§ 4.   Before I unveil the latest version of my new system of punctuation, I shall attempt a brief explanation of my current thinking. We cannot know exactly how Old English poetry was performed because we do not know its intonation patterns. We cannot always know whether what seems to us a possible reading was in fact acceptable because we have no native informants. How then are we to present Old English poetry? I regard this as one of the most important problems facing Anglo-Saxonists today. I find the apparently general lack of interest in it more than regrettable. I have not yet reached a solution which completely satisfies me and, as will become clear, still hope for help from others.

§ 5.   Manuscript punctuation is clearly not that solution; Stanley (*In the Foreground: 'Beowulf'*, 100, n. 62, penultimate sentence) oversimplifies and so misrepresents what I said in 'The Dangers of Disguise' about its use in modern editions. My belief that modern punctuation is not suitable for Old English poetry hinges on these points: it destroys the ebb and flow of the poetry;[7] it demands decisions from editors when there are no grounds for such decisions ('The Dangers of Disguise', 399–405, and § 10); it does not allow the recognition of the *apo koinou* constructions in which, despite Stanley's arguments,[8] I still believe ('The Dangers of Disguise', 406–08, and § 10); and it is unable to signal that the unit of Old English poetry is the verse paragraph, not the modern sentence (ibid., 399). I agree with Donoghue (*Syntax and Style*, 93) that the problem of distinguishing individual verse paragraphs remains. But, as I see it, we shall at least be working in a unit recognized by poets and hearers.

§ 6.   What are ambiguities for us today would have been resolved for Anglo-Saxon audiences by the scops, sometimes in different ways.[9] This need not surprise us if we think of the different interpretations of drama and poetry created by today's actors and reciters. While, as Donoghue (*Syntax and Style*, 50) acutely observes, some of our uncertainties would have been shared by 'an Anglo-Saxon reader coming upon an unfamiliar poem in manuscript', that reader, being a native informant, would (as Donoghue [ibid., 92] implies), have had more chance of being right than we have; see 'The Dangers of Disguise', 391. But our uncertainties about Old English poetry are in marked contrast to our certainty that Old English poetry was not subject to the conventions of modern punctuation. Hence my enthusiasm for a new system.

§ 7.   In any discussion about the editing of Old English poetry, the phrase 'editorial interference' is soon heard. It is frequently an argument for conservatism, for not doing something which would help readers to a greater understanding or appreciation. Proposals for new methods of punctuation do not go unmolested. I would argue that line divisions, length marks and other diacritics, notes, and glossaries, are all forms of editorial interference and that the use of modern English or modern German punctuation is a gross form of it. I do not deny that the system set out below is also a form of editorial interference but submit that it is less gross. Donoghue (*Syntax and Style*, 93) claims that 'Mitchell's punctuation is as foreign to the texts as the punctuation it would replace'. This is not as true as it seems on first glance because my system, while still needing improvement (§§ 2 and 3), is specifically designed to remove from editors the burden of making decisions when there are no grounds on which to make them (§§ 5 and 10) and to reflect the ebb and flow of Old English poetry, including *apo koinou* constructions (§§

5 and 10) – all in the belief that 'to continue using modern punctuation will only perpetuate the awkward tension between the artificially disjointed parataxis imposed by edited texts and the provocatively allusive poetry that we manage to sense in spite of it all' (Donoghue and Mitchell, 'Parataxis and Hypotaxis', 179).

§ 8.   Donoghue (*Syntax and Style*, 93) also objects that my system of punctuation 'necessarily imposes an interpretation that may not have been that of the Anglo-Saxon author'. I agree; see Mitchell, 'Some Syntactical Problems', 178, and § 4 above. But if this uncertain state of affairs is a reason for maintaining the status quo or for passive inaction, we might as well all give up; in the words of Stanley's epitaph on his own book *In the Foreground: 'Beowulf'*: 'everything dissolved, nothing resolved, nothing solved, no conclusion' (244). Why bother?

§ 9.   While accepting the value of unpunctuated texts for scholarly contemplation or pedagogic persuasion, I assume that the need for some punctuation is generally accepted. What should be its aim? It should be used only when essential and should involve a minimum of interfering whistle blasts from an officious umpire-editor. It should allow the river of poetry to ebb and flow so that the reader can appreciate its variety – now swift-flowing, with swirling currents and rapids, now calm and leisurely, now slow-moving and majestic – but should not be taken as implying an increase in the speed of delivery; see Mitchell, *Old English Syntax*, § 3971. The system I proposed in 'The Dangers of Disguise' did not fulfil these requirements: it was too novel, too cumbersome, too interfering. The modifications to be found in appendix B to Donoghue and Mitchell, 'Parataxis and Hypotaxis' and in *An Invitation to Old English*[10] were stages in the development of the system I now propose. This can be described as involving a minimal use of modern punctuation with one departure from it: the replacement of the semicolon by the more flexible elevated point (·), which I use to indicate a pause which might vary between today's comma and full stop. Not so revolutionary a system now and one more worthy of being taken seriously.

§ 10.   The basic principle of the new system is

NO PUNCTUATION WHERE THE SENSE IS CLEAR WITHOUT ANY.

It involves the use of the following marks of punctuation:

1) the paragraph inset to mark major changes of theme or argument;

2) the point (.) to indicate the end of a paragraph or of a major sense unit;
3) the elevated point (·) to indicate a less definite pause which might vary between today's comma and full stop;
4) the colon to introduce speeches or, in the words of H.W. Fowler, for 'delivering the goods that have been invoiced in the preceding words';
5) the comma;
6) dashes (– –) to mark the parentheses which play an important part in Old English, especially in the poetry;
7) the question mark;
8) the exclamation mark;
9) single inverted commas, with double inverted commas inside when needed.

In general, the elevated point marks off clauses. This frees the comma for use within clauses, e.g., to mark off appositions and vocatives or to clarify the sense. The flexibility of the elevated point (§ 9) means that editors are spared the task of deciding whether *þā* is an adverb or a conjunction and whether *se* is a demonstrative or a relative where ambiguity exists, and perhaps that of adjudicating about *apo koinou* constructions; see §§ 5, 7, and 11.2. And it allows readers to make up their own minds about these difficulties or to pass over them without being aware of their existence.

§ 11.   I now think that the following marks, which I proposed in 'The Dangers of Disguise', 408–10, and Donoghue and Mitchell, 'Parataxis and Hypotaxis', 181–82, should be used only as pedagogic devices. They are no longer features of my system:

1) double commas (,,) to indicate the presence of ambiguous adverb/ conjunctions such as *þǣr* 'there'/'where' or *þā* 'then'/'when' or of the ambiguous demonstrative/relative *se* 'that one'/'who'. I now use the elevated point in these contexts;
2) = = to mark off *apo koinou* elements which 'face both ways'. When elements are words and phrases such as *secga geseldan* in *The Wanderer* 53a ('The Dangers of Disguise', 396), they can be left without punctuation. When they are clauses, the decision is more difficult. As I write, I hesitate between putting an elevated point before and after them or leaving them unpunctuated. In this exercise, I have adopted the latter solution; see § 14.4. I should particularly welcome comment on this point;
3) ‿ to mark what I have called 'enjambment of sense';

4) double hyphens or broken marks of parenthesis.

§ 12.   The text presented here is that printed in *A Guide to Old English*.[11] It is punctuated according to the system set out in § 10 above. The numbers introducing the notes refer to lines. The words 'See § 14' or 'See § 15' could have been added to nearly all the notes, but the resulting repetition would have been extremely tedious.

§ 13.   According to Krapp,[12] there are in the Vercelli book version of this poem no section divisions, no large capitals, and twenty-four small capitals:

11	Ac	24	Hwæðre	47	Inwid-	95	Nu
13	Syllic	28	Ic		Ic	115	Ac
	Ic	30	Genaman	59	Sare	117	Ne
18	Hwæðre	39	Ongyrede	63	Aledon	119	Ac
21	Forht	43	Ac	65	Ongunnon	131	Nah
23	Hwilum	44	Rod	78	Nu	132	Ac

Ten of these are not reproduced in the text which follows: *Ic* (lines 13, 28, 47), *Forht* (line 21), *Hwilum* (line 23; see the note below), *Inwidhlemmas* (line 47), and four of the five occurrences of *Ac* in the manuscript. (There are none of *ac*.) In these, the *ac* clause immediately follows and reinforces by contrast a negated principal clause: lines 10–11 *ne wæs . . . ac*, lines 42–43 *ne dorste . . . ac*, lines 117–19 *Ne þearf . . . ac*, and lines 131–32 *Nāh . . . ac*. In the fifth example (line 115), I retain the manuscript capital because of the abrupt change of subject, with *hīe* referring back to *ǣnig* line 110 and *þǣre mænige* line 112. It is true that the *ac* clause has some connection with the *Ne mæg* clause in line 110 but the contrast between them is less direct and less dramatic. In two of the seven instances of clause-initial *hwæð(e)re* (lines 18 and 24) the manuscript has a capital. I have printed capitals in these and in lines 57, 70, and 75, because in all of them the conjunction is followed by a change of subject. On the two examples which do not involve a change of subject (lines 38 and 101), see the relevant notes below.

§ 14.   As noted in § 10, the elevated point indicates a pause which might vary between today's comma and full stop and in general is used to mark off clauses when this is necessary or desirable. Unless the circumstances are exceptional, I do not use it:

1)   before the coordinating conjunctions *and, ac,* or *oþþe*. The two excep-

tions here are in line 135, where *and* introduces a change of subject and direction, and in line 115, where (as I explain in § 13) I print *Ac*;

2) before initial *ne* when it is unambiguously a conjunction, that is, when it is not used immediately before a verb. There are no examples in this poem;

3) before subordinate clauses which are at the end of their governing clause;

4) before and after *apo koinou* clauses; see § 11.2 and the notes to lines 3 and 36b–37a.

I use the elevated point:

5) before parallel asyndetic clauses, whether the verb is expressed, as in lines 44–47, or unexpressed, as in line 23b;

6) before initial *ne* immediately before a verb, when it can be construed as an adverb or a conjunction, although I think the former more likely. The five examples in this poem are in lines 10, 42, 47, 110, and 117. On *nāh* in line 131, see Mitchell, *Old English Syntax*, § 1847, n. 27;

7) before ambiguous adverb/conjunctions, as in lines 68b–69a;

8) before ambiguous demonstratives/relatives, as in line 107b;

9) before noun clauses in apposition with an anticipatory noun or pronoun, as in lines 1–2 and 18–20a;

10) before and after subordinate clauses which are interpolated within their governing clause. There are no examples in this poem.

There are no ambiguous principal/subordinate clauses with initial verb and the element order Verb Subject ('The Dangers of Disguise', 404) in this poem. Those which do occur require individual treatment.

§ 15.   The thirty-six commas in the text are used within clauses as follows:

1) before and after vocatives: lines 78, 95 (4);

2) after *Hwæt* interjection: line 90 (1);

3) with parallel infinitives dependent on modal verbs: lines 42, 128, 143 (3);

4) with parallel participles dependent on *wæs*: lines 22, 29, 48 (3);

5) with appositional elements as defined in Mitchell, *Old English Syntax*, § 1431:
   nouns: lines 5, 11, 44, 46, 53, 72, 75, 79, 91, 92 (2 commas; see below), 105, 106 (see below), 122, 139, 147, 151, 155 (18);

pronoun and noun: lines 89, 152 (2);
noun and adjective: line 150 (1);
pronoun and adjective: line 64 (1);
adjectives: line 87 (1);
adjective and participle: line 13 (1);
participles: line 15 (1).

There is no need for a comma after the second appositional element unless the sense demands. For the two uses of such a comma in *The Dream of the Rood*, see the notes below on lines 92–93 and 105–06.

(In response to an editorial question by Peter Baker, I now ask for readers' comments on whether or not appositional elements should be marked off by a comma, firstly when they are contiguous and secondly when they are separated by a verb or an adverb. In our forthcoming edition of *Beowulf* (§ 1), Fred C. Robinson and I use modern punctuation as lightly as possible. We have not marked appositional elements off by commas except when the absence of a comma might cause confusion, as in *Beowulf* 250b–51a, where a beginner might be tempted to think that line 251a was the object of *léoge*.)

§ 16.   Before I turn to the text, please allow me to express the hope that comments on my new system will pour into St Edmund Hall, Oxford, and my best wishes to the scholar and man we honour in this book and to his family and friends.[13]

The Dream of the Rood
or
A Vision of the Cross

Hwæt!
Ic swefna cyst   secgan wylle·
hwæt mē gemætte   tō midre nihte
syðþan reordberend   reste wunedon
þūhte mē þæt ic gesāwe   syllicre trēow
5   on lyft lædan   lēohte bewunden,
bēama beorhtost.   Eall þæt bēacen wæs
begoten mid golde·   gimmas stōdon
fægere æt foldan scēatum·   swylce þēr fīfe wæron
uppe on þām eaxlgespanne.   Behēoldon þēr engel Dryhtnes ealle
10   fægere þurh forðgesceaft·   ne wæs ðēr hūru fracodes gealga

ac hine þǣr behēoldon   hālige gāstas,
men ofer moldan   and eall þēos mǣre gesceaft.
   Syllic wæs se sigebēam   and ic synnum fāh,
forwundod mid wommum.   Geseah ic wuldres trēow
15   wǣdum geweorðod   wynnum scīnan,
gegyred mid golde·   gimmas hæfdon
bewrigen weorðlīce   Wealdendes trēow.
   Hwæðre ic þurh þæt gold   ongytan meahte
earmra ǣrgewin·   þæt hit ǣrest ongan
20   swǣtan on þā swīðran healfe.   Eall ic wæs mid sorgum gedrēfed·
forht ic wæs for þǣre fægran gesyhðe·   geseah ic þæt fūse bēacen
wendan wǣdum and blēom: hwīlum hit wæs mid wǣtan bestēmed,
beswyled mid swātes gange·   hwīlum mid since gegyrwed.
   Hwæðre ic þǣr licgende   lange hwīle
25   behēold hrēowcearig   Hǣlendes trēow
oð ðæt ic gehȳrde   þæt hit hlēoðrode·
ongan þā word sprecan   wudu sēlesta:
   'Þæt wæs gēara iū   – ic þæt gȳta geman –
þæt ic wæs āhēawen   holtes on ende,
30   āstyred of stefne mīnum.   Genāman mē ðǣr strange fēondas·
geworhton him þǣr tō wǣfersȳne·   hēton mē heora wergas hebban·
bǣron mē þǣr beornas on eaxlum   oð ðæt hīe mē on beorg āsetton·
gefæstnodon mē þǣr fēondas genōge.   Geseah ic þā Frēan mancynnes
efstan elne micle   þæt hē mē wolde on gestīgan.
35   Þǣr ic þā ne dorste   ofer Dryhtnes word
būgan oððe berstan   þā ic bifian geseah
eorðan scēatas   ealle ic mihte
fēondas gefyllan·   hwæðre ic fæste stōd.
Ongyrede hine þā geong hæleð   – þæt wæs God ælmihtig! –
40   strang and stīðmōd·   gestāh hē on gealgan hēanne
mōdig on manigra gesyhðe   þā hē wolde mancyn lȳsan.
Bifode ic þā mē se beorn ymbclypte·   ne dorste ic hwæðre būgan tō
   eorðan,
feallan tō foldan scēatum   ac ic sceolde fæste standan.
Rōd wæs ic ārǣred·   āhōf ic rīcne Cyning,
45   heofona Hlāford·   hyldan mē ne dorste.
Þurhdrifan hī mē mid deorcan næglum·   on mē syndon þā dolg
   gesīene,
opene inwidhlemmas·   ne dorste ic hira ǣnigum sceððan.
Bysmeredon hīe unc būtū ætgædere·   eall ic wæs mid blōde bestēmed,

begoten of þæs guman sīdan   siððan hē hæfde his gāst onsended.

50   'Feala ic on þām beorge   gebiden hæbbe
wrāðra wyrda: geseah ic weruda God
þearle þenian.   Þȳstro hæfdon
bewrigen mid wolcnum   Wealdendes hrǣw,
scīrne scīman·   sceadu forð ēode

55   wann under wolcnum.   Wēop eal gesceaft·
cwīðdon Cyninges fyll: Crīst wæs on rōde.
Hwæðere þǣr fūse   feorran cwōman
tō þām Æðelinge·   ic þæt eall behēold.
Sāre ic wæs mid sorgum gedrēfed·   hnāg ic hwæðre þām secgum tō
handa

60   ēaðmōd elne mycle.   Genāmon hīe þǣr ælmihtigne God·
āhōfon hine of ðām hefian wīte·   forlēton mē þā hilderincas
standan stēame bedrifenne·   eall ic wæs mid strǣlum forwundod.
Ālēdon hīe ðǣr limwērigne·   gestōdon him æt his līces hēafdum·
behēoldon hīe ðǣr heofenes Dryhten   and hē hine ðǣr hwīle reste,

65   mēðe æfter ðām miclan gewinne.   Ongunnon him þā moldern wyrcan
beornas on banan gesyhðe·   curfon hīe ðæt of beorhtan stāne·
gesetton hīe ðǣron sigora Wealdend·   ongunnon him þā sorhlēoð galan
earme on þā æfentīde·   þā hīe woldon eft sīðian
mēðe fram þām mǣran Þēodne·   reste hē ðǣr mǣte weorode.

70   Hwæðere wē ðǣr grēotende   gōde hwīle
stōdon on staðole·   stefn up gewāt
hilderinca·   hrǣw cōlode,
fæger feorgbold.   Þā ūs man fyllan ongan
ealle tō eorðan   – þæt wæs egeslic wyrd! –

75   bedealf ūs man on dēopan sēaþe.   Hwæðre mē þǣr Dryhtnes þegnas,
frēondas gefrūnon·
gyredon mē   golde and seolfre.
'Nū ðū miht gehȳran,   hæleð mīn se lēofa,
þæt ic bealuwara weorc   gebiden hæbbe,

80   sārra sorga.   Is nū sǣl cumen
þæt mē weorðiað   wīde and sīde
menn ofer moldan   and eall þēos mǣre gesceaft·
gebiddaþ him tō þyssum bēacne.   On mē Bearn Godes
þrōwode hwīle·   for þan ic þrymfæst nū

85   hlīfige under heofenum   and ic hǣlan mæg
æghwylcne ānra   þāra þe him bið egesa tō mē.
Iū ic wæs geworden   wīta heardost,

lēodum lāðost   ǣr þan ic him līfes weg
rihtne gerȳmde,   reordberendum.

90   Hwæt, mē þā geweorþode   wuldres Ealdor
ofer holtwudu,   heofonrīces Weard
swylce swā hē his mōdor ēac,   Marīan sylfe,
ælmihtig God   for ealle menn
geweorðode   ofer eall wīfa cynn.

95   'Nū ic þē hāte,   hæleð mīn se lēofa,
þæt ðū þās gesyhðe   secge mannum·
onwrēoh wordum   þæt hit is wuldres bēam
se ðe ælmihtig God   on þrōwode
for mancynnes   manegum synnum

100   and Adomes   ealdgewyrhtum·
dēað hē þǣr byrigde.   Hwæðere eft Dryhten ārās
mid his miclan mihte   mannum tō helpe·
hē ðā on heofenas āstāg·   hider eft fundaþ
on þysne middangeard   mancynn sēcan

105   on dōmdæge   Dryhten sylfa,
ælmihtig God   and his englas mid,
þæt hē þonne wile dēman·   se āh dōmes geweald·
ānra gehwylcum   swā hē him ǣrur hēr
on þyssum lǣnan   līfe geearnaþ.

110   Ne mæg þǣr ǣnig   unforht wesan
for þām worde   þe se Wealdend cwyð:
frīneð hē for þǣre mænige   hwǣr se man sīe
se ðe for Dryhtnes naman   dēaðes wolde
biteres onbyrigan   swā hē ǣr on ðām bēame dyde.

115   Ac hīe þonne forhtiað   and fēa þencaþ
hwæt hīe tō Crīste   cweðan onginnen.
Ne þearf ðǣr þonne ǣnig   anforht wesan
þe him ǣr in brēostum bereð   bēacna sēlest
ac ðurh ðā rōde sceal   rīce gesēcan

120   of eorðwege   ǣghwylc sāwl
sēo þe mid Wealdende   wunian þenceð.'
        Gebæd ic mē þā tō þām bēame   blīðe mōde,
elne mycle   þǣr ic āna wæs
mǣte werede.   Wæs mōdsefa

125   āfȳsed on forðwege·   feala ealra gebād
langunghwīla.   Is mē nū līfes hyht
þæt ic þone sigebēam   sēcan mōte

āna oftor   þonne ealle men,
well weorþian.   Mē is willa tō ðām
130   mycel on mōde   and mīn mundbyrd is
geriht tō þǣre rōde.   Nāh ic rīcra feala
frēonda on foldan   ac hīe forð heonon
gewiton of worulde drēamum·   sōhton him wuldres Cyning·
lifiaþ nū on heofenum   mid Hēahfædere·
135   wuniaþ on wuldre·   and ic wēne mē
daga gehwylce   hwænne mē Dryhtnes rōd
þe ic hēr on eorðan   ǣr scēawode
on þysson lǣnan   līfe gefetige
and mē þonne gebringe   þǣr is blis mycel,
140   drēam on heofonum·   þǣr is Dryhtnes folc
geseted tō symle·   þǣr is singāl blis
and mē þonne āsette   þǣr ic syþþan mōt
wunian on wuldre,   well mid þām hālgum
drēames brūcan.   Sī mē Dryhten frēond
145   se ðe hēr on eorðan   ǣr þrōwode
on þām gealgtrēowe   for guman synnum·
hē ūs onlȳsde   and ūs līf forgeaf,
heofonlicne hām.   Hiht wæs genīwad
mid blēdum and mid blisse   þām þe þǣr bryne þolodan.
150   Se Sunu wæs sigorfæst   on þām sīðfate,
mihtig and spēdig   þā hē mid manigeo cōm,
gāsta weorode   on Godes rīce,
Anwealda ælmihtig   englum tō blisse
and eallum ðām hālgum   þām þe in heofonum ǣr
155   wunedon on wuldre   þā heora Wealdend cwōm,
ælmihtig God   þǣr his ēðel wæs.

1. As at the beginning of *Beowulf,* the exclamation *Hwæt!* is usually printed as part of the first line. I prefer to treat it as an extra-metrical call for attention: 'The poem is about to begin.'

1–2. *Ic* does not have a capital in the MS or in Mitchell and Robinson, *Guide.*

3. I take line 3 *apo koinou* with the clauses which precede and follow it. I therefore follow the MS, not Mitchell and Robinson, *Guide,* in printing *þūhte* without a capital and leave the clause without punctuation. See § 11.2.

5. Here and in line 11 the comma marks off nouns in apposition.

10. In this line *ne* may be an adverb or a conjunction. But I think it is

more likely to be an adverb. See § 14.

13. The comma separates two appositional adjectival/participial phrases arranged as a chiasmus.

15. Here too the appositional participial phrases (lines 15a and 16a) form a chiasmus.

22. Here the comma separates two parallel participial phrases dependent on *wæs*. They are arranged chiastically.

23b. This half-line is preceded by an elevated point because it is an asyndetic coordinate clause with unexpressed *hit wæs*. It is interesting that the MS has *Hwilum* with a small capital; see § 13.

29. Here we have two parallel participial phrases dependent on *wæs*.

36b–37a. Another *apo koinou* clause. See line 3, note.

37. The word *ealle* has a capital in Mitchell and Robinson, *Guide*, but not in the MS.

38. I have not printed *Hwæðre* because of the sequence *ic . . . ic . . . ic . . . ic*. But see lines 101–03, note.

42. The comma marks off parallel infinitives dependent on *dorste*.

44. Here and in lines 46 and 53 we have nouns in apposition.

48. Another example of parallel participial phrases dependent on *wæs* arranged chiastically. See line 22, note.

64. The comma here marks off an adjective phrase in apposition with a pronoun.

65. The sequence 65 *Ongunnon . . .* 67 *ongunnon* conforms to that in the MS; see § 13.

68. Here *þā* is an ambiguous adverb/conjunction 'then'/'when'; see § 14.

72. Here and in line 75 we have nouns in apposition.

75. There are two changes from Mitchell and Robinson, *Guide*: no capital *B* in *bedealf*, capital *H* in *Hwæðre* (§ 13). The MS has *b* and *h*.

78. The commas separate the vocative expression from the clause in which it appears.

79. Here and in lines 91 and 92 (twice; see note), we have nouns in apposition.

87. Two adjective phrases in apposition.

89. Apposition of pronoun and noun.

90. *Hwæt* here is less emphatic than at the beginning of the poem; hence the comma rather than an exclamation mark.

92–93. Here the appositional pairs are *hē . . . ælmihtig God* and *his mōdor . . . Marīan*, and a comma is needed after *Marīan sylfe*.

95. On the vocative expression see line 78, note.

101–03. I am indebted to Dr Susan Irvine for the punctuation of these lines. There are no capitals in the MS. Mitchell and Robinson, *Guide*, print *Dēað . . . hwæðere . . . Hē . . . Hider*. Although no change of subject occurs after *Hwæðere* – see § 13 and line 38, note – the dramatic change of emphasis demands a capital.

105–06. A comma is needed before and after the second appositional element because it extends the reference of *Dryhten sylfa*.

107b. Here *se* is an ambiguous demonstrative/relative 'he'/'who'; see § 14. I reject the punctuation – *se āh dōmes geweald!* – because in my opinion, that would require *þæt* not *se*; see lines 39b and 74b.

112–13. Despite the placing of the verb *sīe* between antecedent and relative, the sense is clear without punctuation. So also in lines 117–18 and 144–45, where the intervening elements are respectively *anforht wesan* and *frēond*.

115. On *Ac* see § 13.

122. The comma separates two appositional noun phrases used adverbially.

128. Here we have parallel infinitives dependent on *mōte*.

139. Nouns in apposition here and in line 147.

143. Parallel infinitives dependent on *mōt*.

144–45. See lines 112–13, note.

150–53a. The three commas mark off the two appositional sequences *Se sunu . . . , mihtig and spēdig . . . , Anwealda ælmihtig* and *mid manigeo . . . , gāsta weorode*. On the use of only one preposition in the latter sequence, see Mitchell, *Old English Syntax*, § 1173.

155. The last example of nouns in apposition!

NOTES

1 'Five Notes on Old English Syntax', *Neuphilologische Mitteilungen* 70 (1969) 70–84, at 78–81.

2 *Review of English Studies* 31 (1980) 385–413. Repr. in Bruce Mitchell, *On Old English: Selected Papers* (Oxford, 1988), 172–202.

3 'Coda 1987' to 'The Dangers of Disguise', in *On Old English*, 202.

4 *'The Study of Anglo-Saxon': Fifty Years On*, H.M. Chadwick Memorial Lectures 2 (Cambridge 1992).

5 Daniel Donoghue, *Style in Old English Poetry: The Test of the Auxiliary*, Yale Studies in English 196 (New Haven and London 1987), 92–93.

6 Eric Gerald Stanley, *In the Foreground: 'Beowulf'* (Cambridge 1994), 102 n. 69.

7 Daniel Donoghue and Bruce Mitchell, 'Parataxis and Hypotaxis: A Review of Some Terms Used for Old English Syntax', *Neuphilologische Mitteilungen* 93 (1992) 163–83, at 181.

8 Eric Gerald Stanley, ''Aπὸ Κοινοῦ, Chiefly in *Beowulf*'', in *Anglo-Saxonica: Festschrift für*

Hans Schabram zum 65. Geburtstag, ed. Klaus R. Grinda and Claus-Dieter Wetzel (Munich 1993), 181–207.

9 Bruce Mitchell, 'Some Syntactical Problems in *The Wanderer*', *Neuphilologische Mitteilungen* 69 (1968) 172–98, at 178 (repr. in *On Old English*, 99–117); and 'The Dangers of Disguise', 406–08.

10 Bruce Mitchell, *An Invitation to Old English and Anglo-Saxon England* (Oxford 1995).

11 Bruce Mitchell and Fred C. Robinson, *A Guide to Old English*, 5th ed. (Oxford 1992).

12 George Philip Krapp, *The Vercelli Book*, ASPR 2 (New York 1932), xliii–xlviii.

13 This article was submitted on 13 September 1994.

Mapelian in Old English Poetry

MATTI RISSANEN

The verb *mapelian* 'speak publicly', 'harangue', occurs forty-four times in the extant corpus of Old English poetry, always in the form *mapelode* (with the spelling variant *mapelade*) and always introducing direct speech. In prose texts this verb occurs only three times, besides half-a-dozen instances in Latin–Old English glosses. The latest text in which it can be found, with the pejorative meaning 'babble', 'gossip', is the early Middle English *Ancrene Riwle*.[1]

Mapelode is the most important verb introducing direct speech in *Beowulf*: there are more instances of this verb than of all the other verbs used in a similar position (*cwepan, frignan, secgan, sprecan, gyd wrecan*, etc., see table 2, below). In the other Old English poems it is much less frequent (see table 3 below). It is therefore natural that the present discussion should concentrate on the role of *mapelode* in *Beowulf*; its use in the other poems and in prose texts is only briefly dealt with at the end of this essay.[2]

The formulaic structure of the expressions with *mapelode* has been adequately discussed in earlier studies,[3] while the textual/discoursal significance of this verb has attracted less attention.[4] In this essay I hope to show how a contextual analysis of the use of even conventional formulaic expressions can illustrate the special character of the narrative art of *Beowulf* and give more information on the semantics and discourse functions of a verb which was highly restricted in its use as early as the Old English literary period.

As is well known, the events preceding and following the three fights in *Beowulf* contain a number of instances of direct speech: questions and answers, addresses of greeting or farewell, narratives, moralizing monologues, etc. From the point of view of the use of *mapelode*, the events listed in table 1 are of interest.

Mapelode occurs at least once in each of these fourteen passages and introduces the utterances of the characters given in the right-hand column, ex-

Table 1. Events with direct speech in *Beowulf* [5]

Lines	Event	Speaker(s)
229–319	meeting on the Danish coast	coastguard/Beowulf
330–355	meeting at Heorot	Wulfgar/Beowulf
360–389	announcement of Beowulf's arrival	Wulfgar/Hroþgar
389–490	Beowulf enters the hall	Beowulf/Hroþgar
491–661	banquet at Heorot	Unferth/Beowulf/Hroþgar
916–1231	celebration after Grendel's death	Hroþgar/Beowulf/Wealhþeow
1315–1398	meeting after Grendel's mother's attack	Beowulf/Hroþgar
1441–1491	Beowulf prepares for the fight with Grendel's mother	Beowulf
1644–1887	celebration after Grendel's mother's death; Beowulf's departure	Beowulf/Hroþgar
1977–2199	meeting at Hygelac's court	Beowulf/Hygelac
2417–2537	Beowulf prepares for the fight with the dragon	Beowulf
2602–2669	Wiglaf hastens to help Beowulf	Wiglaf
2712–2820	Beowulf's death	Beowulf
2845–3155	Beowulf's death announced; the funeral	Wiglaf, messenger

cept for Hygelac and the messenger announcing Beowulf's death. On most occasions, the verb is used in dialogue-type contexts, although the dialogue often tends to take the form of subsequent speeches rather than real exchanges. A complete list of the instances of direct speech, arranged by the speaker and the introductory verb, is given in table 2. The superiority of *maþelode* over other introductory words is obvious: it introduces twenty-six passages of direct speech while all the other verbs are used only nineteen times in a similar context. It is obvious that *maþelode* marks both the speaker and the discourse situation with importance and emphasis.

The first time this verb occurs in *Beowulf* is in connection with the coastguard's address to the hero at Beowulf's landing on the Danish coast. Typically, *maþelode* is not used when the introductory verb has a clear discourse function, such as question or reply. Thus, the coastguard's opening is preceded by an emphatic and dignified expression which echoes *maþelode* but contains a verb of interrogation:[6]

Þa of wealle geseah   weard Scildinga,
se þe holmclifu   healdan scolde,
beran ofer bolcan   beorhte randas,
fyrdsearu fuslicu;   hine fyrwyt bræc
modgehygdum,   hwæt þa men wæron.

Table 2. Passages of direct speech in *Beowulf* (the numbers refer to the lines in which the introductory verbs occur)

Speaker	Introductory verb
Beowulf	*maþelode*: 405, 529, 631, 957, 1383, 1473, 1651, 1817, 1999, 2425, 2510, 2724
	andswarode . . . wordhord onleac: 258–59
	andswarode . . . word . . . spræc: 340–41
	gegrette: 2516
	gespræc . . . gylpworda sum: 675
	gyd . . . wræc: 2154
	het: 2812
	spræc (emended): 2792
Coastguard	*maþelode*: 286
	meþelwordum frægn: 236
	word . . . cwæþ: 315
Hroþgar	*maþelode*: 371, 456, 925, 1321, 1687, 1840
	gegrette . . . word acwæþ: 652–54
Hygelac	*ongan . . . fricgcean*: 1983–85
Last survivor	*fea worda cwæþ*: 2246
Messenger	*sægde*: 2899
Old spear-warrior	*word acwyð*: 2046
Unferþ	*maþelode*: 499
Wealhþeow	*maþelode*: 1215
	spræc: 1168
Wiglaf	*maþelode*: 2631, 2862, 3076
	fea worda cwæþ: 2662
	het: 3110
Wulfgar	*maþelode*: 348, 360
	frægn: 332
	word . . . abead: 390

Gewat him þa to waroðe   wicge ridan
þegn Hroðgares,   þrymmum cwehte
mægenwudu mundum,   *meþelwordum frægn*:
'Hwæt syndon ge   searohæbbendra,
. . . (229–37)

Beowulf's reply is introduced in the same vein, with an emphatic expression typical of the Old English poetic style, but using *andswarode* instead of *maþelode*:

Him se yldesta   *andswarode*,
werodes wisa,   *wordhord onleac*:

'We synt gumcynnes   Geata leode
. . . (258–60)

After this initial sequence, the coastguard's next utterance is introduced by
mapelode:

Weard *mapelode*,   ðær on wicge sæt,
ombeht unforht: 'Æghwæþres sceal
scearp scyldwiga   gescad witan,
. . . (286–88)

The use of *mapelode* no doubt emphasizes the coastguard's important position, implied in many ways by the phrases describing him and by his manner
of address.[7] Note, however, that his short and more matter-of-fact farewell
address is introduced in a more modest way:

           guðbeorna sum
wicg gewende,   *word æfter cwæð*:
'Mæl is me to feran;   Fæder alwalda
mid arstafum   eowic gehealde
siða gesunde!   Ic to sæ wille,
wið wrað werod   wearde healdan.' (314–19)

The dialogue immediately following between Beowulf and Wulfgar, Hroþgar's
officer, has the same pattern. Wulfgar begins with a question:

           Þa ðær wlonc hæleð
oretmecgas   *æfter æþelum frægn*:
'Hwanon ferigeað ge . . . (331–33)

Beowulf's answer, too, is introduced by a phrase containing the appropriate
verb:[8]

Him þa ellenrof   *andswarode*,
wlanc Wedera leod,   *word æfter spræc*
heard under helme: 'We synt Higelaces
beodgeneatas; . . . (340–43)

Wulfgar's importance and high position is clearly indicated in the context. It
is therefore natural that, like the coastguard's, his second utterance is introduced by *mapelode*:

Wulfgar *maþelode*   – þæt wæs Wendla leod,
wæs his modsefa   manegum gecyðed,
wig ond wisdom – :   'Ic þæs wine Deniga,
frean Scildinga   frinan wille,
... (348–51)

After these two encounters, it is time to see how the use of *maþelode* is related to King Hroþgar and his court at Heorot. It is of interest that no fewer than seventeen of the total number of twenty-six instances of *maþelode* in *Beowulf* introduce speeches uttered either by Hroþgar himself or in his presence. The connection between this verb, the dignity of the Danish king, and the courtly atmosphere is obvious.

When Wulfgar tells Hroþgar about the arrival of Beowulf and his men, his shortish announcement is introduced by *Wulfgar maðelode to his winedrihtne* (360). Hroþgar's response, too, is introduced by *maþelode*:

Hroðgar *maþelode*,   helm Scyldinga:
'Ic hine cuðe   cnihtwesende;
... (371–72)

Of the seven instances of direct speech by Hroþgar, only one has an introductory verb other than *maþelode* (654, below).

When Wulfgar passes Hroþgar's invitation on to Beowulf, his words are not introduced by *maþelode* – he is not speaking to the King:

[Þa to dura eode
widcuð hæleð,] *word inne abead*:
'Eow het secgan   sigedrihten min,
... (389–91)

Beowulf enters; this time there is no discoursal or situational reason to introduce his long address to the king with any other expression than *maþelode*:

Beowulf *maðelode*   – on him byrne scan,
searonet seowed   smiþes orþancum – :
'Wæs þu, Hroðgar, hal! ... (405–07)

The following addresses and speeches at Heorot by Hroþgar (456), Unferþ (499), and Beowulf (529, 630) are all introduced by *maþelode*, until, at the end of the banquet, Hroþgar leaves the hall. The function of his speech – good-night – is marked by the change of introductory verb:

[Ge]grette þa   guma oþerne,
Hroðgar Beowulf,   ond him *hæl abead*,
winærnes geweald,   ond *þæt word acwæð*:
'Næfre ic ænegum men   ær alyfde,
. . . (652–55)

And it is only to be expected that when the king has left and Beowulf addresses his men, the introductory verb changes again:

Gespræc þa se goda   *gylpworda* sum,
Beowulf Geata,   ær he on bed stige:
'No ic me an herewæsmun   hnagran talige
guþgeweorca, . . . (675–78)

At the celebration following Grendel's death, Hroþgar's (925) and Beowulf's
(957) speeches are introduced by *maþelode*. This is also the first occasion
when Queen Wealhþeow speaks. She first addresses Hroþgar, and her words
are introduced by *sprecan*:

Spræc ða ides Scyldinga:
'Onfoh þissum fulle,   freodrihten min,
. . . (1168–69)

In her second speech, Wealhþeow is asking Beowulf to take care of her two
sons. The use of *maþelode* perhaps indicates that Wealhþeow here intends
her speech to be even more publicly observed than her words to Hroþgar.
Her words may contain a political comment the full implications of which
could only be understood by a contemporary audience.

Wealhðeo *maþelode*,   heo fore þæm werede *spræc*:
'Bruc ðisses beages,   Beowulf leofa,
. . .

Beo þu suna minum
dædum gedefe,   dreamhealdende!
Her is æghwylc eorl   oþrum getrywe,
modes milde,   mandrihtne hold,
. . . (1215–29)

When, after the attack of Grendel's mother, Beowulf comes to the Hall with
his men, his 'good morning' to Hroþgar is expressed in the form of a simple
indirect question, *frægn gif him wære / æfter neodlaðum niht getæse* (1319–20).

Hroþgar's dramatic reply is introduced by *mapelode* (1321), as is Beowulf's heroic speech of consolation beginning with *Ne sorga snotor guma!* (1383). The same verb introduces Beowulf's address to Hroþgar when the hero prepares for the fight with Grendel's mother (1473). At the celebration after the fight, both Beowulf's (1651) and Hroþgar's (1687) speeches are once again introduced by *mapelode*.

The formulaic structure of the introductions to speeches has been amply discussed in earlier studies (see note 3 below) and need not be dealt with in the present paper. The very long and weighty introduction (1687–99) to Hroþgar's 'sermon' deserves, however, a comment: its purpose is obviously to draw special attention to what is the most emphatic moralizing statement in the poem. The phrase *Hroþgar maðelode* (1687) is followed by a twelve-line description of the golden hilt which the old king is inspecting, and then another introductory formula is given, strengthened by 'all were silent':

Hroðgar *maðelode* – hylt sceawode,
. . .
        Ða se wisa *spræc*
sunu Healfdenes – swigedon ealle – :
'Þæt, la, mæg secgan se þe soð ond riht
fremeð on folce, . . . (1687–1701)

We have come to the end of Beowulf's visit to Heorot. Our earlier analysis suggests that we might expect a specific verb introducing the farewell speeches of the hero and the king, but it is perhaps the length (over 20 lines) and rhetorical weight of both addresses that elicit the use of *mapelode*:

Beowulf *mapelode*, bearn Ecgþeowes:
'Nu we sæliðend secgan wyllað
feorran cumene, þæt we fundiaþ
Higelac secan. . . . (1817–20)

Hroðgar *mapelode* him on andsware:
'Þe þa wordcwydas wigtig Drihten
on sefan sende; ne hyrde ic snotorlicor
on swa geongum feore guman þingian.
. . . (1840–43)

In comparison to the events at Heorot, Beowulf's homecoming and his meeting with King Hygelac form an anticlimax. This is no doubt intentional, since the poet is hastening towards Beowulf's final fight with the dragon.

This can also be seen in the introductions to speeches. Hygelac does not share Hroþgar's dignity; the introduction to his welcoming words echoes that of the coast-guard (lines 232, 236, quoted above). Note the use of a verb meaning 'ask' and the phrase *hyne fyrwet bræc*:

> Higelac *ongan*
> sinne geseldan   in sele þam hean
> fægre *fricgcean*,   hyne fyrwet bræc,
> hwylce Sæ-Geata   siðas wæron:
> 'Hu lomp eow on lade,   leofa Biowulf,
> . . . (1983–87)

Beowulf's long account of his journey is introduced by *maþelode* (1999).

In comparison to the rich and varying exchanges at Heorot, the pattern of the speeches in the second part of *Beowulf* perhaps offers a less rewarding topic for analysis. A typical feature in this part is the division of speeches into sections by short comments and new introductions. When Beowulf prepares for his fight with the dragon, his speech is introduced by *maþelode* (2425). After a long historical account, another introduction with *maþelode* follows, and after a five-line comment on the oncoming fight, he addresses his warriors; this time the introductory verb is *gegrette*:

> . . . Nu sceall billes ecg,
> hond ond heard sweord   ymb hord wigan.'
> Beowulf *maðelode*,   beotwordum spræc
> niehstan siðe: 'Ic geneðde fela
> guða on geogoðe;   gyt ic wylle,
> frod folces weard   fæhðe secan,
> mærðu fremman,   gif mec se mansceaða
> of eorðsele   ut geseceð.'
> *Gegrette* ða   gumena gehwylcne,
> hwate helmberend   hindeman siðe,
> swæse gesiðas: 'Nolde ic sweord beran,
> wæpen to wyrme, . . . (2508–19)

This is the only sequence in the poem in which what is essentially a single speech is introduced twice by *maþelode* or interrupted twice with a new introduction. The feeling of the last public address is strongly present.

In the final events of the poem, Wiglaf is in focus. He makes three long speeches, all introduced by *maþelode* (2631, 2862, and 3076), while the short and highly emotive cry to Beowulf immediately following his first address to the cowardly retainers is preceded by *fea worda cwæþ*; the contrasting use of verbs sounds highly appropriate:

> Wod þa þurh þone wælrec,   wigheafolan bær
> frean on fultum,   *fea worda cwæð*:
> 'Leofa Biowulf,   læst eall tela,
> swa ðu on geoguðfeore   geara gecwæde,
> þæt ðu ne alæte   be ðe lifigendum
> dom gedreosan; . . . (2661–66)

Beowulf said goodbye to his men in the three-part speech mentioned above, but his last words are addressed to Wiglaf. Mortally wounded, he asks to see the treasure – this is the last time his speech is introduced by *maþelode*. After Wiglaf has returned from the vault, loaded with treasures, the king utters his last words. Unfortunately the manuscript is corrupt at this point; Klaeber emends the introduction as *Biorncyning spræc* (2792).[9] But there is one final interrupting passage, and the very last introductory expression offers a moving contrast to *maþelode* and the other verbs which have introduced Beowulf's speeches earlier in the poem:

> Dyde him of healse   hring gyldenne
> þioden þristhydig,   þegne gesealde,
> geongum garwigan,   goldfahne helm,
> beah ond byrnan,   *het hyne brucan well –*:
> 'Þu eart endelaf   usses cynnes,
> Wægmundinga;   ealle wyrd forsweop
> mine magas   to metodsceafte,
> eorlas on elne;   ic him æfter sceal.' (2809–16)

Intentionally or unintentionally, the *Beowulf* poet has found exactly the right tone. In contrast to all the heroic and courtly speeches made by Beowulf in the course of the poem, it now seems as if the poet were supporting the dying king, explaining what he really intends but has no more strength to say: *het hyne brucan well* – the symbolic significance of the gesture is obvious.

I have made an attempt above to comment on the occurrences of *maþelode* and its connection with characters and situations. It might also be of interest to call attention to some of the contexts in which *maþelode* is not used. As I pointed out above, *maþelode* never introduces indirect speech and it is avoided with utterances which have a clear discourse function, such as question or reply.

Maþelode does not introduce the recitals of unnamed singers or scops

(867–915 and 1063–59): one reason for this is certainly that both begin as indirect speech. Furthermore, the elegy of the last survivor, the speech of the 'old spear-warrior' and the announcement of Beowulf's death by an unnamed messenger do not fulfil the conditions of publicity of occasion or importance of speaker to be introduced by *maþelode*:

þær on innan bær   eorlgestreona
hringa hyrde   hordwyrðne dæl,
fættan goldes,   *fea worda cwæð*:
'Heald þu nu, hruse,   nu hæleð ne mostan,
eorla æhte! . . . (2244–48)

Þonne cwið æt beore   se ðe beah gesyhð,
eald æscwiga,   se ðe ealle geman,
. . .
            ond þæt word *acwyð*:
'Meaht ðu min wine,   mece gecnawan,
. . . (2041–47)

            Lyt swigode
niwra spella   se ðe næs gerad,
ac he soðlice   *sægde* ofer ealle:
'Nu is wilgeofa   Wedra leoda,
. . . (2897–2900)

The survey of the occurrences of *maþelode* in the other Old English poems can be less detailed. Table 3 shows the distribution by poem and the number of occurrences.[10] In all these poems, except *Riddle 38*, *maþelode* retains the basic function it has in *Beowulf*, mostly introducing the speeches of important characters on public occasions. But it is obviously losing its distinctive features in comparison with other verbs of speaking. It is a minority variant even in *Elene* and can be used in contexts that would seem alien to its character in *Beowulf*.

In *Elene* there are some thirty instances of direct speech introduced by verbs other than *maþelode*.[11] This verb is used, appropriately, only with reference to the speeches of the main characters of the poem, Elene and Judas, but there seems to be no systematic reason, besides stylistic variation, for the choice of *maþelode* or some other verb of speaking.

In *Genesis A* and *B*, the subordinate role of *maþelode* is even more obvious. The four instances are in a clear minority in comparison to the approxi-

Table 3. *Maþelode* in Old English poems

Beowulf	26
Elene	9
Genesis	4
Battle of Maldon	2
Widsith	1
Waldere	1
Riddle 38	1
Total	44

mately seventy occurrences of other verbs with a similar function. Even in this poem, however, the association of *maþelode* with an important speaker is obvious: Satan (347), Adam (522), Abraham (1817, 2893). The condition about public occasion or length and weight of utterance is broken only in one instance, in which *maþelode* introduces Abraham's short, almost casual, reply to Isaac:

>   Ða þæs fricgean ongann
> wer wintrum geong   wordum Abraham:
> 'Wit her fyr and sweord,   frea min, habbað;
> hwær is þæt tiber,   þæt þu torht gode
> to þam brynegielde   bringan þencest?'
> *Abraham maðelode*   (hæfde on an gehogod
> þæt he gedæde   swa hine drihten het):
> 'Him þæt soðcyning   sylfa findeð,
> moncynnes weard,   swa him gemet þinceð.' (2888–96)

Maþelode introduces the long speeches by Byrhtnoþ and Byrhtwold in *The Battle of Maldon*, obviously as a late echo of the older heroic style: 'Byrhtnoð/ Byrhtwold maþelode, bord hafenode' (42, 309). The use of this verb also sounds natural at the opening of *Widsiþ* ('Widsið maðolade, wordhord onleac') and in *Waldere* 8 ('Waldere maðelode, wiga ellenrof'). In these two poems, *maþelode* suggests a public setting for the speeches, not otherwise clearly indicated in the poems.

But in *Riddle 38*, *maþelode* seems to have lost its significance and special characteristics:

> Ic þa wiht geseah   wæpnedcynnes,
> geoguðmyrþe grædig;   him on gafol forlet

ferðfriþende   feower wellan
scire sceotan,   on gesceap þeotan.
Mon *maþelade*,   se þe me gesægde:
'Seo wiht, gif hio gedygeð,   duna briceð;
gif he tobirsteð,   bindeð cwice.'

In prose texts apart from the glosses, *maþelode* occurs only three times. There are no traces left of its elevated discourse function:

Þu wendest þet þin ende nefre ne cuman scolde, To longe *maþelede* deaþ þe þet he nolde nimen þe, for efre þu arerdest sake ond unseihte makedest. (*Fragments of Body and Soul*, ed. Buchholz; Toronto OE Corpus, HomU 5.4)

Fela we mihton ymbe þissum þingum *maþelian*, ac we asittað þæt þe boceras ascunian, þæt we ymbe heora digolnyssa þas rumlice sprecað. (*Byrhtferth's Manual* 180.15)

þæt ys eac to gemunanne þam þe þas þing þengð to asmeagenne, þe we ymbe syn *maþeligende*, þæt se bissextus his cynestol gesytt on þam forman vi. kl Martii, & on þam æftran vi kl. man sceal healdan Sanctus Mathias mæssedæges freols. (*Byrhtferth's Manual* 70,12)

In the two passages from *Byrhtferth's Manual*, *maþelian* simply means 'tell', with no reference to speech. In the *Body and Soul* passage, the verb introduces a simple clause of indirect speech.

The Latin–Old English glossaries show, however, that the feeling of the original function of *maþelode* had not been completely lost even in later Old English. There are a few occurrences of *maþelian* in the eighth- or ninth-century Corpus Glossary (CCCC 144), the tenth- or eleventh-century Harley Glosses (London, BL, Harley 3376) and the eleventh-century Aldhelm Glosses (Brussels, Bibliothèque Royale, 1650).[12] *Maþelaþ*, *maþalade* gloss the Latin *contionatur* 'to give a public speech', 'harangue':

[Contionatur] *maðalade* [declamat uel iudicat uel contestatur] (Corp. Gl. 2, [Hessels] 3.854)

[Contionatur i conclamat loquitur contestatur in populo] *maþelaþ* (HlGl [Oliphant] 2326)

But the reference to *sermocinantur* in the Aldhelm Glosses reveals the deterioration in the meaning of *maþelian*:

[contionantur locuntur] rædaþ vel *maþeliað* [sermocinantur] (Ald V 1 [Goossens] 2282)

[contionantur i sermocinantur] rædaþ, *maþeliaþ* (Ald V 13.1 [Nap] 2321)

and this is even more obvious in the glosses with the noun *maþelung*:

[uerbositas] gewyrd, *maþelung* (Ald V 13.1. [Nap] 1419)

[garrulitatis loquacitatis uerbositatis] *maþelunge* (Ald V 1 [Goossens] 2850)

The final degradation of the dignified meaning of *maþelian* is reached in Early Middle English, in *Ancrene Riwle* (OED, s.v. *mathele*):

Hore muð *maðeleð* euer.

Ane maðelild þ *maðeleð* hire all þe talen of þe londe

What, then, causes this deterioration in the meaning of *maþelian* and its loss in early Middle English? Even in Old English, *maþelian* is a verb highly restricted both semantically and (con)textually. It is a word originating from and belonging to the heroic time of oral delivery – meetings, harangues, and recitals. It lives on in Old English poetry, particularly in the genre of heroic epic represented by *Beowulf.* But solemn public speaking easily creates associations with pomposity and empty words; high rhetoric comes to be interpreted as mere verbosity. The days of *maþelian* are numbered when the society characterized by speech and recital gradually changes into one leaning more on writing and literacy.

NOTES

1 The use of the related verb *mæþlan* is also restricted to poetry, and the number of occurrences is low (seven instances in *Genesis, Christ, Guþlac,* and *Andreas*); no instances of the past tense form **mæþlede* occur. The verb *mell,* from *mæþlan,* is attested in late Middle English (see *OED* s.v. *mathele* and *mell* v.).

2 For the occurrence of cognates to *maþelian* and other verbs introducing direct speech in the poetry of the oldest stages of Germanic languages, see A. Heusler, 'Der Dialog in der altgermanischen erzählenden Dichtung', *Zeitschrift für deutsches Altertum und deutsche Literatur* 46 (1902) 189–284.

3 E.g. A.S. Cook, 'The Beowulfian *Maðelode', Journal of English and Germanic Philology* 25 (1926) 1–6; Fr. Klaeber, *Beowulf and the Fight at Finnsburg,* 3rd ed. (Boston 1951), lv; T. Pàroli, *Sull'elemento formulare nella poesia germanica antica,* Biblioteca di ricerche linguistiche e filologiche 4 (Roma 1975), 117–22; P. Mertens-Fonck, 'Structure des passages introduisants

le discours direct dans Beowulf', in *Mélanges de philologie et de littératures romanes offerts à Jeanne Wathelet-Willem* (Liège 1978), 433–45; A.B. Lord, 'Ring Composition in Maldon', in *The Ballad and Oral Literature*, ed. J. Harris (Cambridge, Mass., 1991), 235–36; A.B. Lord, 'The Formulaic Structure of Introductions to Direct Discourse in Beowulf and Elene', in *Epic Singers and Oral Tradition* (Ithaca and London 1991), 147–69.

4 Note, however, Lord's pertinent observations in 'The Formulaic Structure'. Fred C. Robinson briefly discusses the meaning and etymology of *mapelian* in *'Beowulf' and the Appositive Style* (Knoxville, Tenn., 1985), 66–67, and Robert E. Bjork comments on the use of this word in 'Speech as Gift in *Beowulf*', *Speculum* 69 (1994) 993–1022. I had submitted this essay for publication before Bjork's article appeared.

5 In addition to the events listed below, direct speech occurs in the last survivor's lament (2247–65) and in the speech of the 'old spear-warrior' (2047–56).

6 All quotations from *Beowulf* are taken from Klaeber's third edition (macrons omitted). Other Old English poems are quoted from ASPR.

7 Cf. also my suggestion in *'Sum* in Old English Poetry', in *Modes of Interpretation in Old English Literature: Essays in Honour of Stanley B. Greenfield*, ed. P.R. Brown, G.R. Crampton, and F.C. Robinson (Toronto, Buffalo, and London 1986), 219–21, that the coastguard has a group of men under his command.

8 Note the similarity of the formulaic structure between this response and 258–59, above.

9 It is obvious that a half-line is missing. Klaeber's emendation sounds the most likely of all those suggested (see, e.g., the note in Krapp and Dobbie's ASPR edition), in view of the use of the verbs indicating saying in *Beowulf* (cf. table 2 above).

10 In her very thorough survey of speech-introducing formulae in Old Germanic poetry Teresa Pàroli gives only thirty-eight occurrences of *mapelode* (*Sull'elemento formulare*, 118–19). To her list should be added *Beowulf* 1687, *Genesis B* 347, *Genesis A* 1820, *Elene* 685, *Widsith* 1, and Riddle 38.5.

11 In addition to those occurring in *Beowulf* (see table 2 above), the most notable are *wordum (ge)negan*, *wordum mælan*, *reordian*, *hleoprian*, and *clipian*.

12 In addition, there are a few glossarial instances of the nouns *mapelere*, *mapelung(e)* and one with the adjective *mapeli*. The gloss quotations are from *A Microfiche Concordance to Old English*, comp. Richard L. Venezky and Antonette diPaolo Healey (Toronto 1980).

Apposition and the Subjects of Verb-Initial Clauses

MARY E. BLOCKLEY

Is a subject still a subject when it is unexpressed? In his elegant study of apposition in *Beowulf*, Fred Robinson alludes to Jespersen's observation that, 'as in the structure of compounds, so also in the structure of sentences much is left to the sympathetic imagination of the hearer'.[1] But though the modern imagination has its work cut out for it in *Beowulf*, the grammatical context of the compound and the sentence can give direction to its reconstructive efforts. Appositional nouns and pronouns get their salience from their sharing a verb with other nominals at least as much as from their semantic parallelism to the subject or object of the clause in which they appear. Clausal apposition, in contrast, must rely on parallel content alone to indicate its appositive function.

Jespersen enlists the clausal quality of compounds as a useful analogy for sentences where less is said than meets the understanding. In Old English, the incomplete apodosis of Satan's exclamation in *Genesis B* is not a cause for conjectural emendation.[2] Editors see it as an instance of the rhetorical figure of *aposiopesis*:

> Wala, ahte ic minra handa geweald
> and moste an tid   ute weorðan,
> wesan ane winterstunde,   þonne ic mid þys werode –
> – ac licga me ymbe   irenbenda,
> rideð racentan sal. (*Genesis B* 368–72)

[Alas, had I the force of my hands and might be abroad one time, be for one winter's hour, when I with this troop – but iron bonds lie about me, the bond of a fetter chafes.]

There is a break in grammatical continuity at the end of line 370, marked in this edition by the first of two dashes. Assuming that this grammatical break has a rhetorical motivation rather than representing a gap in transmission, what rhetorical figure best describes it? Since the next clause is coordinated with it by means of *ac*, Doane (272), following others, calls the whole construction an example of *anacoluthon*, a sentence that breaks off and is resumed by the speaker with a change of grammar. But as the phrase headed by *ponne* (whether that headword is taken as a temporal adverb or as a conjunction) is incomplete, lacking a verb to agree with the first-person pronoun, it is also *aposiopesis*. Jespersen suggests that we have a complement to the unexpressed conclusion of *aposiopesis* in the type of expression seen in 'Morning', 'Bless you!' ''Fraid not', and others in which 'the beginning of a sentence falls out by what we might learnedly term *prosiopesis*'.[3]

Beowulf has 185 instances of a construction where a finite verb with an unexpressed subject appears at the head of a verse.[4] Examples include *egsode eorlas* (6a), *weox under wolcnum* (8a), *aledon þa* (34a), and 1274a, below:

hwæþre he gemunde   mægenes strenge,
gimfæste gife,   ðe him God sealde,
ond him to Anwaldan   are gelyfde,
frofre ond fultum;   ðy he þone feond ofercwom,
gehnægde helle gast. (*Beowulf* 1270–74a)

[none the less he remembered the power of his strength (his virtue), his liberal gift, which God gave him, and trusted himself to the protection of the Ruler of all, to his grace and aid; by this means he overcame the enemy, [he] humbled the infernal spirit.]

The verb and object in 1274a is certainly appositive in content to some part of the immediately preceding half-line *ðy he þone feond ofercwom*. Robinson cites it, with characteristically specific definition, as an example of 'parallel restatement of the verb and its object'.[5] Does restatement of a verb and its object in Old English inevitably present us with a clause rather than a predicate alone, or is *gehnægde helle gast* something less than a clause? If it is a clause, is such a construction independent, subordinate, or indeterminate?

Bruce Mitchell's views on the status of such predicates as expressed in his authoritative *Old English Syntax* are complex. He allows that some instances of this construction are independent clauses but does not require that all of them be so.[6] S.O. Andrew and A.J. Bliss, whose views on the syntax of *Beowulf* have been influential, argue specifically against interpreting constructions similar to *gehnægde helle gast* as independent, and maintain that they are either coordinate clauses or appositives equivalent to coordinate clauses. They assume that such constructions must take their subject from a preceding clause, and that they must be construed with those clauses. But not all constructions with this form fit the coordinate interpretation. Taking these constructions as wholly independent clauses has difficulties of its own, but these difficulties lead to a new appreciation of the contribution of apposition. Mitchell's examples tend to emphasize the verb-initial constructions that can be translated as clauses with an unexpressed but understood subordinating conjunction, while Andrew lays special stress on the possibility of understood coordination within subordination, and Bliss on apposition with or without this understood coordination.

S.O. Andrew maintained that many seemingly independent clauses, including some finite verbs that are not accompanied by an expressed subject, are in 'asyndetic co-ordination',[7] meaning that they should be punctuated with a comma and translated with a coordinating conjunction. Andrew notes that editors are particularly reluctant to treat verbs as parts of coordinate clauses when they immediately follow a subordinate clause, and concludes that 'it is surely a significant fact that the great majority of them admit of being taken as coordinate clauses, in which . . . the omission of the subject, if the same as in the preceding sentence, is the regular idiom'.[8] Andrew's choice of examples shows that he assumes that the asyndetically coordinate clause typically adds new information about the subject, rather than appositively restating the information in the predicate of the preceding clause. He illustrates his contention with instances like the following, where he sees *nægde* and *frægn* as needing an 'and' to connect them, rather than as one expression varied by another.

> þæt he þone wisan   wordum nægde
> frean Ingwine;   frægn gif him wære
> æfter neodlaðum   niht getæse. (*Beowulf* 1318–20)

[then he approached the wise one with words, the lord of the Ingwine; [he] asked, following the urgent summons, whether the night had been agreeable for him.]

For Andrew, clauses with unexpressed subjects are only one type of asyndetically coordinate clause, nor is the lack of an expressed subject an infallible indicator of the clause. In stating that five out of six of these clauses are asyndetically coordinate he acknowledges that some verb-initial clauses are independent, but he does not indicate how, other than by content, one can separate the minority that he admits as independent from the rest of the clauses that he claims are coordinate.⁹ Andrew's one out of six clauses that is independent is additional to the clauses with demonstrative adverbs. Clauses that begin with the finite verb are always principal in Andrew's system if they are followed by the adverb *þa*, whether or not they have expressed subjects.¹⁰

A.J. Bliss takes a more formal approach. He notes that in *Beowulf* several hundred finite verbs that appear early in their clause participate in the alliterative scheme. While some of these verbs are clause-medial, as in *hi hyne þa ætbæron* (28a), some are in clause-initial position, as happens in *gehnægde helle gast*. Under Bliss's interpretation of Kuhn's Law a clause-initial particle, such as the finite verb, would normally not bear stress and therefore should not alliterate. Bliss observed that thirty-three of these clause-initial alliterating verbs immediately follow other finite verbs, as *gehnægde* follows *ofercwom*. For this subset of apparently clause-initial alliterating verbs he proposed an appositive explanation: 'when two consecutive finite verbs stand in apposition to each other the second does not open a new clause; from the point of view of stress the two verbs are treated as equivalent, so that the stress of the second depends on the stress of the first'.¹¹ Bliss's idea of apposition is based on the formal parallelism in stress of a clause-final verb with an immediately following clause-initial verb. Though he does not comment on the content of these clauses, the majority of them are semantically as well as formally appositive. But not all are. Of the thirty-two verses with finite verbs that Bliss places in this category, several do not seem to be appositional in their content.¹² Moreover, Bliss does not include all appositives here, not even all clause-initial verbs that immediately follow the verb they appose. For example, he puts into another category verse 302a, which has for its context *Flota stille bad, / seomode on sale   sidfæþmed scip, / on ancre fæst* (301b–03a), 'the floater remained still. The broad-bottomed ship hung on its hawser, fast at anchor'). Though he does not state his reason for doing so, he may treat verbs like *seomode* that have an expressed subject differently, even when, as here, that subject has the same referent as the subject of the preceding clause, with which it is in clausal apposition.

Andrew and Bliss take different approaches to the status of clause-initial verbs, but both of them assume that the verbs without subsequent expressed subjects are usually or always different in kind from independent clauses. They both assume that the non-expression of the subject indicates not only that the subject must be understood from a previous clause, but that the clause-initial verb is itself dependent on this previous clause, whether as an apposition within the clause, or as a clause coordinated with it.

The unexpressed subject of a verb-initial construction does indeed frequently take its referent from the subject of the preceding clause. But not always. There is something wrong with approaches that take up the verb-initial constructions without expressed subjects in a syntactic vacuum, without looking at verb-initial clauses with expressed subjects, and at other verbs lacking expressed subjects. The constructions that begin with a finite verb may look like predicate-only constructions, especially when they are appositive, but they have much in common with undoubted clauses that begin the same way but eventually get an expressed subject.

A specific example may help indicate the similarity between verb-initial clauses with the unexpressed subject and verb-initial clauses with delayed subjects. When *bugon þa to bence* first occurs, in line 327a, its subject is unexpressed. This unexpressed subject continues the reference of *sæmeþe*, the subject of the immediately preceding clause in line 325. But when the verse reappears in line 1013 as *Bugon þa to bence   blædagende*, the delayed subject differs from the expressed subject of the immediately preceding main clause in line 1011, the first-person singular pronoun *ic*.[13]

Each of these two forms has a complement. With clauses like *Beowulf* 327 can be compared those like *seomode on sale   sidfæþmed scip* (302), quoted above in its context. Verb-initial clauses may have an expressed subject even when that subject has the same referent as the subject of the preceding main clause. When, as in *Beowulf* 302, the predicate also refers to the same action as does the predicate of the preceding clause, the clause is in apposition to its predecessor. Other verb-initial clauses with expressed subjects continue the referent of the preceding subject, but the predicate is different and so the clause is independent, as in *Beowulf* 307a. The complement of the changed and expressed subject in *Beowulf* 1013 is the changed but unexpressed subject in 446b, discussed below. The verb-initial constructions in the poem divide nearly evenly between those with unexpressed subjects and those with delayed subjects. There are roughly forty per cent unexpressed subjects to sixty per cent delayed subjects.

The great majority of both kinds of verb-initial clauses in *Beowulf* are declaratives. In Modern English and Old English the interrogatives that can be answered with a 'yes' or 'no', which Jespersen calls 'nexus-questions', must be verb-initial, as commands must be, yet these interrogatives and commands are not frequent in the poem, and frequently are not confusible with the declaratives. *Beowulf* contains at most two questions that begin with the finite verb.[14] Other questions in this poem are like 1986a in having an interrogative pronoun or adverb in clause-initial position. Commands are easier than questions to distinguish from declaratives, as the imperative mood often has a distinctive grammatical form. Like Modern English, Old English can have subordinate and principal clauses such as 'were this to happen' as verb-initial, but these are infrequent. Mitchell gives no certain examples from *Beowulf* of the conditional subjunctive type, and only two of concessions.[15] Since there are few verb-initial clauses in Old English poetry that do what verb-initial clauses must do in Modern English, the clauses that begin with a finite verb in Old English are less syntactically determined, and less ambiguous than they could be. Separating out the possible non-declaratives from the declaratives reduces the counts below by fewer than one in fifty instances.

The clauses like 327a, with an unexpressed subject that continues, only slightly outnumber clauses like 448a, in which the unexpressed subject breaks with *deað*, the subject of the clause immediately before it, and with *þu*, the subject of the main clause before it as well. This particular unexpressed subject has the same referent as the *he* of the intervening subordinate clause in 446; others have as their referent the object of a preceding clause, or no referent anywhere in the nearby preceding clauses. For example, Grendel is the referent of the unexpressed yet understood subject of *Gewat ða neosian* (115a), yet this referent last appears as the subject nine clauses away, in line 105, and as an object in line 106. Clause-initial verbs with unexpressed subjects like 115a and 448a accordingly get editorial punctuation that indicates they are independent clauses. Since some instances must be independent, maintaining that others with the same grammatical form must be considered subordinate becomes difficult, even in contexts where subordination would accord with modern assumptions about the sentence structure.

>   Na þu minne þearft
> hafalan hydan,   ac he me habban wile
> dreore fahne,   gif mec deað nimeð;
> *byreð blodig wæl* (*Beowulf* 445b–8a)

[Not at all need you cover my head, for he will have me stained with gore, if death takes me; [he] carries the bloody slaughter]

These verb-initial constructions can best be read as independent clauses, whether their subjects are expressed subsequently or only understood, and whether those subjects continue the referent of the subject of the preceding main clause, or introduce a new subject. Here in summary are the four possible outcomes for verb-initial clauses and their distribution in *Beowulf*:

1.   Delayed expressed subject, continuing the reference of the subject of the preceding main clause:

[flota stille bad,]/ seomode on sale   sidfæpmed scip, / on ancre fæst (301b–03a, '[The floater remained still.] The broad-bottomed ship hung on its hawser, fast at anchor')

II. Delayed expressed subject, changing from the reference of the subject of the preceding main clause:

[hæl sceawedon.] Hæfde se goda   Geata leoda / cempan gecorone   þara þe he cenoste / findan mihte; (204b–06a, '[They examined the auguries.] The good one chose warriors from among the Geatish people, those whom he might find to be keenest')

III. Unexpressed subject, continuing the reference of the subject of the preceding main clause:

[ðy he þone feond ofercwom,] / gehnægde helle gast. (1273b–74a, '[by this means he overcame the enemy], [he] humbled the infernal spirit')

IV. Unexpressed subject, changing from the reference of the subject of the preceding main clause:

[Na þu minne þearft / hafalan hydan,   ac he me habban wile / dreore fahne,   gif mec dead nimeð;] / byreð blodig wæl (445b–48a, 'Not at all need you cover my head, for he will have me stained with gore, if death takes me; [he] carries the bloody slaughter')

Verb-initial constructions in *Beowulf* (total = 446)

Delayed expressed subject		Unexpressed subject	
Continues subject of main clause	Changes from subject of main clause	Continues subject of main clause	Changes from subject of main clause
57	204	115	70
Per cent of total			
13	46	26	15

The strongest argument for taking these verb-initial constructions as independent clauses is that the majority of them subsequently have an expressed subject. Moreover, an expressed subject can appear even when it continues, somewhat redundantly, the referent of the subject of the preceding clause. Of the clauses without an expressed subject, the majority have as their referent the subject of the preceding main clause. But the non-expression of the subject is not reason enough to claim that these constructions are less than clauses, or are formally subordinate. However one calculates the antecedent to the unexpressed subject – whether it is stated anywhere in the immediately preceding clause or not – there remain a good number of clauses like 448a that cannot easily be taken as part of the clause immediately before them. Andrew's idea of an understood coordinate conjunction will almost always produce an acceptable reading, but that is only because a coordinating conjunction can plausibly join almost any two clauses.

Nor are the verb-initial clauses the only group of clauses with this pattern of subject reference. Another clause type has an even more pronounced tendency for the unexpressed subject to continue the referent of the subject of the preceding main clause. There are 410 clauses beginning with some word other than a conjunction or a finite verb in which the subject, if expressed, follows the finite verb. The 178 that have only the unexpressed subject include [*þone God sende / folce to frofre;*] *fyrenðearfe ongeat* (13b–15b), where the subject of *ongeat* continues the subject of *sende*, and [*Fand þa ðær inne æþelinga gedriht / swefan æfter symble;*] *sorge ne cuðon / wonsceaft wera* (118a–20a), where the subject of *cuðon* does not continue the subject of *fand*. These clauses tend to have the referent of the unexpressed subject continue the subject of the preceding main clause more strongly than do verb-initial subjectless clauses, by a more than three-to-one ratio,[16] and Andrew takes as asyndetically coordinate some of these clauses that do not begin with the finite verb. But again, the larger context suggests that the clause type is essentially independent. As with the verb-initial clauses, the majority of these clauses gets a subsequent subject, and this subsequent expressed subject tends overwhelmingly to differ from the subject of the preceding main clause. Whenever the verb appears in a clause before the subject, there is the possibility that the subject of that clause will have an antecedent in a preceding clause, but it is more usual for the verb not preceded by a subject to have a new subject.[17]

The strongest argument for taking some of the verb-initial clauses as dependent is based on apposition. When the verb-initial clause follows a principal clause to which it is related by apposition, Andrew or Bliss might seek to take it as subordinate or coordinate, but for other scholars nothing requires the second clause to be grammatically dependent. Indeed, under most definitions of variation a dependent clause cannot appose a principal clause. It might seem, therefore, that the verb-initial construction must come in under the conjunction of the preceding clause when it immediately follows a subordinate clause and varies its subject and verb, as in Klaeber's punctuation seen in the following examples from Robinson's study of apposition:[18]

ðonne forstes bend   Fæder onlæteð,
onwindeð wælrapas (*Beowulf* 1609–10a)

þæt se byrnwiga   bugan sceolde,
feoll on feðan (*Beowulf* 2918–19a)

þæt he blode fah   bugan sceolde,
feoll on foldan. (*Beowulf* 2974–75a)

Andrew pointed out that editors were reluctant to treat a verb-initial construction as asyndetically coordinate when it immediately follows a subordinate clause, disliking coordination within subordination. Yet editors place commas and not semicolons between these three sets of verbs, and take the second verb as an appositive within the subordinate clause. In each of the three examples the subject of the subordinate clause differs from that of the main clause before it. The subject of the subordinate clause has the same referent as the unexpressed subject of the verb-initial construction. The subordinate clause is therefore not only the nearest but the only source for the unexpressed subject of the verb-initial construction. Under such circumstances, it might seem that the verb-initial construction must be taken as an appositive.

A complete survey of the contexts for these verb-headed clauses reveals that these examples are not exceptional in the continuing subject reference of the verb-headed clause and are exceptional in the kind of clause they follow. The verb-headed clause with an unexpressed subject is most frequently immediately preceded by a main clause, as happens in 99 of the 174 instances in *Beowulf*. In 69 of those 99 examples the subject of the verb-headed construction continues the subject of that preceding independent clause, a majority of instances. Some of these continuing subjects are part of clausal appositions; others are not. The frequency of the continuing subject reference drops when the preceding clause is subordinate, even when the subject of the subordinate clause continues the referent of its preceding main clause. Specifically, in 42 of the 75 instances of a subordinate clause intervening between the main clause and the verb-initial clause, the subject of the subordinate clause has the same referent as the subjects of both the main clause and the verb-initial clause, and yet only 26 of the unexpressed subjects of the 42 verb-initial constructions also continue this subject. Another 32 of the 75 subordinate clauses have a subject different from those of their preceding main clauses. Of the 32 verb-initial constructions that follow these subordinate clauses, 17 have an unexpressed subject that has as its referent the subject of the subordinate clause, 9 continue the referent of the distant main clause instead, and in the remaining 6 instances the subject of the verb-headed clause continues neither of the two preceding subjects.

If any expectation comes with the verb-headed clause following a subordinate clause, it is that the second clause may have any of a variety of relationships to its predecessor. For example, consider the 42 clauses headed by what Klaeber punctuates as the subordinating *þær*. Of these, 3 are immediately followed by a verb-initial construction with an unexpressed subject that can be taken as appositional to the subordinate clause (420, 513, and 2050), but another 2 also have subjects that are unexpressed but that differ from the subject of the *þær*-clause (2276 and 2851), while 1378 has an imperative verb-initial construction following the clause headed by the subordinating conjunction.

It happens frequently that a verb-initial construction with an unexpressed subject will continue the reference of the subject of the preceding clause, but most frequently when the preceding clause is independent, as happens in the majority of the examples of the construction. When following independent clauses, verb-initial clauses with unexpressed subjects continue the referent of the preceding subject 70 per cent of the time, but when following a subordinate clause, the unexpressed subject of a subsequent verb-initial clause will continue the referent of the subject of the subordinate clause only 57 per cent of the time, even though that subject is also often the subject of the main clause preceding the subordinate clause. In 47 per cent of the instances with intervening subordinate clauses the verb-initial construction will continue the reference of the subject of the main clause. Moreover, types of clause other than those that begin with the finite verb are even more inclined to continue in their unexpressed subject the reference of the subject of the preceding clause. This general predisposition indicates that the verb-headed clause is not especially prone to be dependent on a predecessor for its subject reference. In other words, rather than the verb-headed construction arising in response to some need to have a subordinate or appositive, or coordinate clause, it is the other way round – a verb-headed clause appears most where it can be most free.

If not a variation of the predicate of a preceding main or subordinate clause, what is the origin of the verb-initial clause in verse? It seems possible that the presence of so many verb-initial clauses may compensate for the absence of clauses in which the finite verb immediately follows a clause-initial personal pronoun. *Beowulf* contains a very few examples of a personal pronoun in clause-initial position immediately followed by a finite verb, as in *he ah ealra geweald* (1727b) and eight others. In four, such as *he onfeng hrape* (748b), removing the pronoun would leave a verbal prefix in clause-initial position in violation of Kuhn's First Law. This does not establish that the clauses are defective, since many other verbal prefixes appear in just this position.[19] More revealing is what does not happen in the way these subjects pattern with the subjects of surrounding clauses and in the possibility that these clause-initial pronouns could be appositionally varied by a susequent noun within the clause.

A prose text like the Alfredian translation of Boethius's *De Consolatione Philosophiae* offers evidence that the scarcity of these pronoun-headed independent clauses is no accidental gap in the language. Virtually any hundred clauses of Alfredian prose (about five pages of Sedgefield's edition of the translation of Boethius) offer as many examples of clause-initial personal pronouns immediately followed by the finite verb as can be found in the whole of *Beowulf*, which has over 2,600 clauses. Examples from the prose include:

hi spanað þe to þinne unðearfe ('they allure you to your detriment')
Ic wolde nu giet ðæt wit ma sprecen ('I wish that we should speak more')
Þu meaht þæs habban þanc ('You might be thanked for this')
þu settest us on þæt setl ('you set us on that seat')
þu cwist ðæt we hæbban þe beswicene ('you say that we have deceived you')
wit geanbidiað þinne ondsware[20] ('we await your answer')

The usualness of pronoun subjects together with verb-final word order in subordinate clauses in verse and prose suggests that in these independent clauses it is the verb that comes to the head of a clause and brings the pronoun with it, rather than that a pronoun attracts the finite verb. The impulse towards variation may be at the heart of the answer to the question why we have so many of these verb-before-subject clauses in poetry. In *Beowulf*, none of the nine clause-initial subject pronouns is subsequently varied in the clause. At least five of the nine have the referent of the subject as different from the referent of the subject of the preceding clause; for various reasons the referent of the subject of half of them is hard to pin down.[21] It seems possible that these are instances of poetic clauses that were to have been augmented, because they usually are augmented, by a subsequent pair of half-lines that include an expressed subject in apposition to the clause-initial pronoun. The poet might then remove the pronoun from the clause-initial verse and allow the subsequent subject to stand alone, both when it continues the referent of the subject of a preceding clause and when, as is more usual, that clause-early verb introduces a new subject. Verb-initial constructions with understood subjects may require fewer assumptions about the interpretation of the subordinate clauses that they sometimes follow. Clausal apposition, more subtle and difficult than that managed with non-finite elements, necessarily crosses clause boundaries, and may cross even those clause boundaries between a subordinate clause and a subsequent main clause.

None of the scholars who have concerned themselves with the syntactic status of clause-initial verbs has been able to state a separate condition that attends all and only non-independent clauses. Using apposition for such purposes in the punctuation of clauses like *Beowulf* 1610a assumes what it sets out to prove, that parallel content in subject referent and in the verb's meaning requires parallel clause types. Nouns can be appositive, and whole independent clauses can be, too. There may even be room for appositively parallel dependent clauses, such as the two *þær*-headed clauses with different subjects but the same adverbial antecedent in *Beowulf* 1188–90.

Must we then either stretch the definition of apposition to cover a subordinate clause varied by an independent in passages like *Beowulf* 1608–10a and 514b–15a or regard the apposition as proof that the verb-initial construction is subordinate? Perhaps the mismatch between the form and the content is not a Procrustean bed. Perhaps the contrast is just the point. The *Beowulf* poet might be playing the expectation of full independence generated by the verb-initial construction following a subordinate clause against the surprising parallelism of content between it and the subordinate clause that precedes it. The result is a resumptive statement that uses both the rhetoric of apposition and the grammar of an independent clause. This variation in the use of variation emphasizes, with the structure of the independent clause, a 'faintly disquieting apposition'.[22]

NOTES

1 *Philosophy of Grammar* (London 1924), 310, cited in Fred C. Robinson, '*Beowulf*' and the Appositive Style (Knoxville 1985), 19.
2 *Genesis B*, cited from *The Saxon Genesis: An Edition of the West Saxon 'Genesis B' and the Old Saxon Vatican 'Genesis'*, ed. A.N. Doane (Madison, Wis., 1991), 213. The translation is mine.
3 Jespersen, *Philosophy of Grammar*, 310.
4 *Beowulf*, cited from *Beowulf and the Fight at Finnsburg*, ed. Frederick Klaeber, 3rd ed. (Boston 1950). I have provided literal translations of some examples with some reluctance,

after Robinson's convincing demonstration of the difficulty of rendering words like *mægen* and *gife* (*'Beowulf' and the Appositive Style*, 54–55).

5 Robinson, *'Beowulf' and the Appositive Style*, 19.

6 *Old English Syntax*, 2 vols. (Oxford 1985), §§ 1503–14; while in §§ 1690–98 he develops Andrew's idea of asyndetic parataxis as serving, through semisubordination, various functions like concession and condition that are elsewhere served by unambiguously subordinate adverbial clauses. The only place I have found where Mitchell might possibly be seen as supporting a non-clausal reading of verb-initial constructions is in his discussion of verbs in apposition in § 1529. In *Style in Old English Poetry: The Test of the Auxiliary*, Yale Studies in English 196 (New Haven 1987), 41, Daniel Donoghue indicates in his discussion of *Beowulf* 1807–09a that the auxiliary-headed clause taken as principal has a subsequently expressed subject, while the clause following it, which lacks an expressed subject, can be taken as dependent or asyndetically coordinated or principal. Donoghue and Mitchell, 'Parataxis and Hypotaxis: A Review of Some Terms Used for Old English Syntax', *Neuphilologische Mitteilungen* 93 (1992) 162–83 at 172 and appendix A, note that most, if not all stylistic parataxis is consistent with the grammar of a principal clause. They cite a *nære* clause discussed in *OES* § 3682, *Eaðe mihte þes cwyde beon læwedum mannum bediglod, nære se gastlice getacning* (Ælfric, *Catholic Homilies* i. 94.33), as one that is difficult for a modern informant to construe as principal; the presence of the negative adverb makes this verb non-clause-initial for me.

7 *Syntax and Style in Old English* (Cambridge 1940), § 85; restated without substantial alteration in *Postscript on Beowulf* (Cambridge 1948), §§ 60–63; see *OES* § 1698 for Mitchell's reservations.

8 *Syntax and Style*, § 90.

9 *Syntax and Style*, § 91.

10 *Syntax and Style*, § 15. Andrew's *Postscript on Beowulf* does not present a significantly different interpretation of this data.

11 *The Metre of Beowulf*, rev. ed. (Oxford 1967), § 14.

12 *Beowulf* 307a, 423a, 926a, 1604a, 208a, and 3096a. Bliss lists thirty-three examples, but verse 2476a does not contain a finite verb.

13 The subject of the verb-initial clause often continues the referent of a preceding clause. In a paper presented at the 1994 Berkeley–Michigan Germanic Linguistics Roundtable, Robert P. Stockwell suggested that the subject of the clause immediately preceding a verb-initial clause with an unexpressed subject determines the referent of the subject of the verb-initial clause. The numbers in my table, however, indicate whether the subject of a verb-initial clause continues or changes the reference of the subject of the preceding main clause. The difference is little. Most clauses immediately preceding a verb-initial clause are independent, and when a subordinate clause does intervene, it often has the same subject as the main. See below, p. 178.

14 One is the inversion with the copula in *Eart þu se Beowulf* (506a) that all modern editors punctuate as interrogative, though seven of the eight other instances of this collocation, including *Andreas* 1188b, have always been taken as declaratives. The other, *Meaht ðu, mine wine* (2047a), has contextually better claims to being a question. Even in Modern English, an imperative need not have a subsequent expressed subject. Though imperatives without the negative usually do in Old English, neither they nor questions need have expressed subjects. Among commands, there are examples without expressed subjects like *Gewitaþ forð beran* (291b) as well as those like *Beo ðu on ofeste* (386a).

15 *OES* §§ 3451–55, 3678–83. In § 3451, Mitchell identifies *Beowulf* 2766b and 1394b, both of

which Klaeber punctuates with a comma, as subordinate. In § 3681, Mitchell cites *Beowulf* 1735 as one of 'the few possible examples in OE poetry [that] can be taken as either non-dependent questions or principal clauses making a statement'.

16 Of the 410 clauses in which something other than a conjunction , a subject, or the finite verb head the clause, only 11 have subsequent expressed subjects that continue the referent of the subject of the preceding main clause. There are 222 with an expressed subject that breaks with the referent of the subject of the preceding main clause. The division between those with subsequent expressed subjects and those with only an understood subject is the same 60/40 split seen with the verb-initial clauses. Of the clauses with unexpressed subjects, 137 continue the referent of the subject of the preceding main clause, and 41 break with that referent.

17 Compare *OES* § 3933, on the functions of VS order.

18 Robinson, *'Beowulf' and the Appositive Style*, 20 and 61, where 2918–19a and 2974–75a are cited as minor instances of 'specifying apposition', though, as he points out, the appositive function is typically filled by nouns.

19 The role of Kuhn's Laws has been explored in a number of articles by Peter J. Lucas, such as 'Some Aspects of the Interaction between Verse Grammar and Metre in Old English Poetry', *Studia Neophilologica* 59 (1987) 145–75, and in two books: Donoghue, *Style in Old English Poetry*, and Calvin B. Kendall, *The Metrical Grammar of Beowulf*, Cambridge Studies in Anglo-Saxon England 5 (Cambridge 1991). Rand Hutcheson has given new substance to Mitchell's reservations, expressed in *OES* § 3947, in 'Kuhn's Law, Finite Verb Stress, and the Critics', *Studia Neophilologica* 64 (1992) 129–39.

20 Walter J. Sedgefield, *King Alfred's Old English Version of Boethius, De Consolatione Philosophiae* (1899, repr. Darmstadt 1968), cited by page and line number: 16/6, 17/3, 17/14, 19/14, 19/16, and 19/24.

21 In the two examples cited, the pronoun in *Beowulf* 1727b continues the referent of the subject of the preceding subordinate clause, while in 748b the antecedent is unclear because of the unexpressed subject in the clause before it, which is also a notorious metrical crux. The referent of the subject of the preceding main clause is continued in 811b, 2395b, and 3056a. The referent of the subject of the preceding subordinate clause is continued in 1837b as well as in 1727b, and the referent of the object of the preceding subordinate clause is continued in 2208b. In 1563a the preceding main clause has an unexpressed subject. In 3029b the *swa* heading the preceding clause could be a conjunction for a subordinate clause that precedes its main clause, though Klaeber takes it as an adverb heading an independent clause.

22 *'Beowulf' and the Appositive Style*, 82.

The Inflection of Latin Nouns in Old English Texts

PETER S. BAKER

Early each fall, one of the first Old English passages my students encounter is from Ælfric's translation of Genesis as edited in that best of textbooks, *A Guide to Old English*: 'and sēo nædre cwæð tō þam wīfe: "Hwȳ forbēad God ēow þæt gē ne æten of ælcum trēowe binnan Paradīsum?" Þæt wīf andwyrde: "Of þāra trēowa wæstme þe sind on Paradīsum wē etað."'[1] I count myself as fortunate that my students have never yet asked a very difficult question that this passage raises: how do we explain the ending *-um* in the two occurrences of the noun *paradisus*? We can be sure that the ending is not an Old English one (it would have to be dat. pl., and there is only one Paradise); it is Latin acc. sg. Normally, however, *binnan* 'within' and *on* 'in' take dat. objects when, as here, they express location.[2]

Paradisus is, of course, a loan-word from Latin (which borrowed it from Greek παράδεισος), and like a number of learned Latin loans, it occurs sometimes with a Latin ending, sometimes with an Old English one.[3] Wulfstan uses it with Latin endings, and the endings he chooses correspond closely in case to the expected Old English ones, e.g., acc. sg. 'Ðurh gifernesse Adam forlet ærest *paradisum*' (WHom 10c, 78–79); dat./abl. sg. 'God hine gelogode on fruman in *paradyso*' (WHom 15, 14–15).[4] The translator of the West-Saxon Gospels also matches Latin dat./abl. to Old English dat.: 'Ða cwæþ se hælend to him, "todæg þu bist mid me on *paradiso*"' (Lk [WSCp] 23.43).[5] Ælfric once uses the word with an Old English ending: dat. sg. 'ðæt we inn moton gaan to ðam upplican *paradise*' (ÆHex 512).[6] So do various other writers, e.g., acc. sg. 'gegadered togædere ofer eall *paradis*' (HomU 17.2, 67–68); gen. sg. 'hine gewræc drihten of *paradises* myrhþe' (LS 14, 259–60); dat. sg. 'he heom geofð in *paradise* eardingstowe' (ibid., 139–40).[7] Two late writers or scribes appear to have resolved the problem of choosing between Latin and Old English endings by choosing none at all: 'Þas hundseofentig gearen betacnigeð þa seofon elden þysses lifes fram þan time þe Adam of *paradis* ascofen wæs oðð þa geendunge þysses middeneardes' (HomU 57, 15); 'þurh deofles swicdom and Adames gemeleaste we wæren æt frumþe ut of *paradis* ascofene' (HomM 9, 18).[8]

More often than not *paradisus* retains its Latin form; however, as in the passage from Ælfric's Genesis quoted above, it often appears with a case-ending different from the one the Old English context leads us to expect. It takes acc. sg. endings in the following sentences, though one requires the nom. sg. while the other two require the dat. sg.:

nom. sg. *Paradisum* nis naðor ne on heofonum ne on eorþan (HomU 17.1, 3; but cf. '*Paradisus* hangað betwynon heofonan and eorðan wundorlice', ibid., 6).[9]

dat. sg. Ðas synd þa feower ean of anum wyllspringe þe gað of *paradisum* ofer Godes folc wide (ÆLet 4, 881–82);[10] and þonn fleogeð se fugel and asett hine on þæt heagoste treow þe is on *paradisum* ongean þa hatan sunnan (HomU 17.1, 24).

Most scholars consider 'foreign words' to be those that retain the inflections of the source language, and 'loan-words' those that appear with Old English inflections.[11] Because we must somehow delimit the vocabulary of Old English, the distinction is useful, even indispensable. But as the scholar whom this essay celebrates has often demonstrated, many wonderful hybrid creatures inhabit the marches that lie between Medieval Latin and the vernaculars;[12] it should come as no surprise that in practice it can be difficult to distinguish 'foreign words' and 'loan-words'. Consider the following short computistical text:

Git hit is god þæt þu wite hrædlice hwilc *concurrentes* yrne on geare. Loca hwilce dæg cuma nona kalendas Aprilis, gif he cymð on Sunnandæg, þonne yrnð se *concurrent* unum. Gif he cymð on Monandæg, þonne yrnð se *concurrent* duo. Cume swilce dæg swilce he cume, swa þu miht witan hwilc *concurrent* yrnð on geare. (Comp 2.1.2)[13]

Here *concurrent(es)* occurs four times, once with a Latin nom. pl. ending (though it is understood as nom. sg.) and three times without an ending; to this stem one other writer added Old English inflections: nom. pl. *concurrentas* and gen. pl. *concurrenta* (Comp 3.2).[14] *Concurrent* is unambiguously a 'loan-word' as traditionally defined, but the status of *concurrentes* is unclear. It might be considered a 'foreign word' in that it retains a Latin ending; but a Latin nom. ending could be borrowed as part of the stem, as frequently happens with proper names in the Old English Orosius, e.g., 'On þæm twelftan geare *Tiberiuses* rices' (Or 6, 29).[15] That the Latin pl. *concurrentes* is used as a sg. may point in this direction. On the other hand, that the writer omitted *-es* after he had used it once shows that he understood it was not part of the stem; it is as if he were deliberately reshaping the word to conform to Old English usage. We may be unable to decide on a category for *concurrentes* in this passage, but it is easy to see that the writer of Comp 2.1.2 was not interested in consistency or in rigid distinctions. Neither, it appears, was Ælfric, who used *paradisus* with both Latin and Old English inflections. For the purposes of this study I also avoid making a distinction between 'foreign words' and 'loan-words'. I consider any Latin word used in an Old English passage to be a loan-word, but I distinguish unassimilated loans (those with Latin inflections) from assimilated ones (those with Old English inflections).[16] The word 'unassimilated' should not be understood to mean 'unchanged', for as we shall see, a loan-word may undergo significant adaptations well before it is assimilated to the Old English inflectional system.

It appears from the examples of *paradisus* quoted above that unassimilated and partly assimilated loan-words posed great difficulties for writers of Old English. But before we conclude that the situation was simply chaotic, let us take a leisurely look at a text that uses such words in large numbers.

Byrhtferth's *Enchiridion* (or *Manual,* as it has sometimes been called) is a Latin and Old English work in four parts, of which the first three constitute a guide to the use of the ecclesiastical calendar, with ample digressions on such subjects as metrics, rhetoric, and weights and measures; the fourth book is a Latin treatise on the significance of numbers.[17] As Byrhtferth himself complains, 'Þas þing synt earfoðe on Englisc to secganne' (ii. 1. 190–91, 'these things are difficult to say in English'), and so he uses a number of Latin and Greek words for technical concepts. In addition, such words as the Latin names of the months and the planets, while apparently in common use, retain their Latin inflections,[18] as do Latinate proper names. In part I of the *Enchiridion,* Byrhtferth's method is to discuss a matter in Latin and then supply an Old English translation. For example, he explains the zodiac twice:

Est unus circulus qui zodiacus uel horoscopus siue mazaroth appellatur necnon sideralis, per quem sol et luna et stella *Saturni, Iouis* et *Martis, Veneris* et *Mercurii* decurrunt (i. 1. 24–26, 'There is a certain circle called the "zodiac" or "horoscope" or "mazaroth" or the "sidereal circle" through which pass the sun and moon and the stars of Saturn, Jupiter, Mars, Venus and Mercury').

An circul ys þe uðwitan hatað zodiacus oððe horoscopus oððe mazaroth oððe sideralis, þurh þæne yrnð seo sunne and se mona and þas steorran *Saturnus* and *Iouis*, *Martis* and *Veneris* and *Mercurius* (i. 1. 41–43).

Notice that in the Latin passage the names of the planets (or of the gods they are named for) are in the gen.: 'the stars of Saturn, Jupiter, Mars, Venus, and Mercury'. But in the Old English passage, two of the names appear to be nom. (*Saturnus*, *Mercurius*) and the other three gen. (*Iouis*, *Martis*, *Veneris*). Byrhtferth was a modestly competent writer of Latin and an able translator; we can rule out the possibility that he did not know the proper gen. forms of these names. Rather, he is deliberately using either the Latin nom. forms as genitives ('the stars of Saturn and Jupiter . . .') or the gen. forms as nominatives ('the stars Saturn and Jupiter . . .').

The following sections set out a sampling of evidence from the *Enchiridion* showing the use of Latin nouns of various declensions in Old English passages. The examples are grouped by Latin declension and Old English case and number – that is, the case and number called for by the context. Word-counts are usually approximate, for delimiting the body of evidence is complicated by the frequent difficulty of determining whether a word is used as part of an Old English, a Latin, or indeed any syntactical structure;[19] in lieu of word-counts, I have sometimes marked forms and endings attested more than twenty times as 'frequent'. Where no indication of frequency is given, it is to be understood that I have quoted all the examples I have found.

Feminine nouns of the first declension

nom. sg. *Vncia*, þæt byð an dæl, byð þus gemearcod (iii. 3. 272–73).
    [The nom. sg. is frequent and always ends in -*a*.]
acc. sg. nu cyðe we her þæt .xxiiii. scripuli wyrcað ane *uncia* (iii. 3. 298–99);
    hu þa getyddusta boceras gewyrceað *sinelimpha* on heora uersum (ii. 1.
    432–33); Doð þæt Martius monð hæbbe *lunam* tricessimam, swa hys
    gewuna ys (iii. 2. 229–30).
    [The acc. sg. of *luna* always ends in -*am* (ca 9×), the acc. sg. of other
    nouns in -*a* (ca 4×).]
gen. sg. and Wodnesdæges [nama wæs] of Mercurio *Maia* sunu (ii. 3. 227).
dat. sg. swa Genesis geseð (þæt ys seo forme boc on *biblitheca*) (i. 1. 91–92);
    Healfe þa uers gebyriað to þam termene, þæt ys to þam *lunam* quartam
    decimam (iii. 2. 53–54); Theophilus hæfð gesett þæt on .xiiii. *lunam* wæs
    se hælend belæwed and on .xv. *luna* ahangen (iii. 1. 134–35).
nom. pl. swa fela *epacte* beoð þy forman geare on þam circule (i. 2. 343–44);
    Þy geare beoð fif and twenti *epacte* (ii. 2. 27); Swa fela *semiuncias* beoð on

þam punde (ii. 1. 495–96); Nu togeare, þa Brihtferð writere þis awrat, synd feowertyne *epactas* (iii. 2. 111–12); and twa *semiuncia* wyrcað ane uncia (iii. 3. 309–10).

[Nom. pl. *epacte* occurs ca 10×; this noun occurs occasionally with Old English endings (cf. gen. pl. *epactana* i. 2. 325; dat. pl. *epactum* i. 2. 332, 343). Latin acc. pl. *-as* (used as nom. pl. 4×) is the same as the most common Old English masc. nom./acc. pl. ending. The ending *-a*, which is the same as the Old English fem. nom. pl., occurs only once.]

acc. pl. Ða wynsume boceras fægere hig todælað þa scansiones uel *cesuras* (ii. 1. 470–71); Wel geradlic hyt eac þingð us þæt we herto gecnytton þa *epactas* (i. 2. 291–92).

[The ending *-as* occurs ca 10×, and it is the same as the Old English masc. nom./acc. pl. ending; see note on nom. pl. forms above.]

gen. pl. Nu hyt gerist þæt we þas þing mid rihtlicre race areccun and þisra *epacta* gerynu apinsiun (i. 2. 317–18).

[The *-a* of *epacta* is the same as the Old English strong gen. pl. ending.]

Masculine nouns of the second declension

nom. sg. Of þissum syx tidum aspringð up *bissextus* (ii. 1. 32).

[The nom. sg. is very frequent and always ends in *-us*.]

acc. sg. uton nu ymbe þone seofoðan *embolismum* wurdlian (ii. 2. 112–13); Ac ærest ys to witanne þæt se mona sceal habban his *bissextum* (ii. 1. 21–22); Seo oðer ræding sprycð ymbe þone oðerne *embolismus* (ii. 2. 24–25).

[The ending *-um* occurs ca 14×; *-us* occurs ca 2×.]

gen. sg. Ymbe þises *bissextus* upasprungnysse oððe gefyllednysse we wyllað rumlicor iungum cnihtum geopenian (ii. 1. 46–47); We witon geare þæt þær næs æt ne gediht ne *Virgilius* gesetnyss (iii. 2. 31–32); he byð *Iunius* mona (ii. 2. 54–55); and he [sc. the moon] geendað .xxix. on .iii. nonas Februarii, and he byð *Februarii* (iii. 2. 156–57).

[The ending *-us* occurs ca 21×; *-i* occurs ca 4×.]

dat. sg. þæt ys on þam ytemestan *embolismo* on þam eahtoðan geare (iii. 2. 117–18); Soðlice ealle þa monðas habbað .iiii. nonas butan *Martio* and *Maio* and *Iulio* and Octobre (i. 3. 40–41); þa þe beoð on þam oðrum geare æfter þam *bissextum* (i. 2. 103–04); we habbað trume gewitnysse on *Hieronimum* þam soðfæstan trahtnere (ii. 1. 87–88); Ðæne þriddan Marte hig getealdon . . . and þone seofeðan *Saturnus* (ii. 3. 218–20).

[The ending *-o* occurs ca 32×, *-um* ca 12×, *-us* only once.]

nom. pl. Ðas þry *embolismi* beoð on þam eahta gearum (ii. 2. 64); Feower *puncti* (þæt synt prican) wyrcað ane tid on þære sunnan ryne (ii. 3. 19–20);

and syððan synt þa *terminos* awritene þe belimpað to þære Easterlican tide
(iii. 2. 206–07); On þære þriddan stowe synt þa *termina* (þæt synt þa
gemæro) þe gebyriað to Gangdagum (iii. 2. 207–09).

[The ending -*i* occurs ca 15×; -*os* occurs only once. *Termina* may be a form
of the assimilated loan-word *termen*, which is usually masc. but once (iii.
2. 246) fem.; the expected Old English fem. nom. pl. would be **termena*.]

acc. pl. he hæfð syx and hundnigontig *punctos* (ii. 3. 18); gif þu wylle witan þa
terminos þe we ymbe spræcon (iii. 1. 183–84); Nu we habbað ymbe þas
embolismus gesprecen, uton nu ymbe þone seofoðan embolismum wurdlian
(ii. 2. 112–13); Scripulus hæfð syx *cilicus* (iii. 3. 304).

[The ending -*os* occurs ca 5×; -*us* occurs 2×.]

dat. pl. Þæt we be þissum cweðað undergytað be eallum þam oðrum *terminum*
(iii. 1. 188–89).

[Once only; Latin acc. sg. -*um* is the same as the universal Old English
dat. pl. ending. For the assimilated loan-word *termen*, see note on the
nom. pl. above.]

Neuter nouns of the second declension

nom./acc. sg. *Minutum* ys se teoðan dæl þære tide (ii. 3. 30); Fif hund and
feower and syxtig atomi gewyrcað an *momentum* (ii. 3. 101–02); On þam
oðrum dæge he geworhte *firmamentum* (ii. 2. 249–50).

[The nom./acc. sg. is frequent and always ends in -*um*.]

nom./acc. pl. Se dæg hæfð *ostenta* an þusend and feower hundred and feowertig
(ii. 3. 61–62); Heræfter we wyllað todælan þa *abecedaria* on twa todæled-
nyssa (iii. 3. 140).

[*Momenta* (7×), *minuta* (5×), and *ostenta* (4×) always occur with numbers,
where Old English might have the gen. pl., which also ends in -*a. Abecedaria*
is the only other second-declension neut. nom./acc. pl. I have located.]

Third-declension nouns

nom. sg. *September* hæfð .xxx. daga and fif regulares (i. 2. 284–85); And se
oðer ys geciged Foeton oððe *Iouis* (ii. 3. 205).

[The nom. sg. is frequent and generally ends as expected, but for names of
planets/gods the forms appear to be *Iouis, Martis, Veneris* (ii. 3. 206, 211).]

acc. sg. Aprilis hæfð þrittig daga and anne *regularem* (i. 2. 187).

gen. sg. We witon geare þæt þær næs æt ne gediht ne Virgilius gesetnyss, ne
þæs wurðfullan *Platonis* fandung oððe *Socratis* his lareowes smeagung (iii.
2. 31–33).

[The gen. sg. occurs ca 17× and always ends in *-is*.]

dat. sg. Ðæne þriddan *Marte* hig getealdon and þone feorðan Mercurio and þone fiftan *Ioue* and þone syxtan *Venere* (ii. 3. 218–20); Nu þær ys an to lafe; gif þæne *Aprili* (i. 2. 185–86).

[The ending *-e* occurs at least 15× and *-i* ca 11×; *-e* is the same as the most common Old English strong dat. sg. ending.]

nom./acc. pl. Æfter þisre gewritenan forespræce on endebyrdnysse þæs gerimes synt gemearcode þa *concurrentes* (i. 2. 83–84); Ða wynsume boceras fægere hig todælað þa *scansiones* uel cesuras (ii. 1. 470–71).

[The forms *concurrentes* (15×) and *regulares* (14×) are the most frequent nom./acc. plurals. I have found no examples of neut. pl. nouns of the third declension.]

gen. pl. Vs gelustfullað þissera rynela (*concurrentium*) angin preostum ætywan (i. 2. 111–12).

dat. pl. Nim þæt an and sete on foreweardum þam *concurrentium* (i. 2. 133–34); Nu we wyllað gecyðan hu man sceal mid þam *concurrentium* and þæra monða rihtingum findan hwylce dæge þa monðas gan on tun (i. 2. 200–02); Of þissum fif *uocales* wyrcað preostas heom anne circul (ii. 1. 436).

Fourth-declension nouns

nom. sg. Ðes *saltus* (þæt ys þes monan oferhlyp), he wyxst wundorlice æfter boccræfte (ii. 1. 163–64).

[The nom. sg. ends in *-us* 5×.]

acc. sg. hu boceras awringað up þæne *saltus* on heora cræfte (ii. 1. 496–97); þonne gewyrcst ðu *saltum* (ii. 1. 213).

[The acc. sg. ends in *-us* 5×, in *-um* once.]

gen. sg. Nu hæfð se eadiga wer us geopenod ymbe þæs *saltus* weaxunge (ii. 1. 189); and þæræfter we geswutelodon ymbe þæs *saltus* hlyp (ii. 1. 426–27, where the MS reading *þæs saltus hlyp* 'the leap of the *saltus*', though redundant, is to be preferred to Crawford's emendation *þæs saltus lune, þæt ys þæs monan hlyp*).

dat. sg. Nu we habbað be þam bissextum and þam *saltum* gemotud and be Ianuarium and Februarium manega þing gehrepode (ii. 1. 223–24); Æfter þissum *uersum* byð þes (iii. 2. 63, where context shows that *uersum* is sg.).

nom. pl. Silempsis ys an hiw, þonne þa *casus* on anre gesetnysse hig totwæmað (iii. 3. 42–43).

Fifth-declension dies

dat. sg. gif he byð beforan þam intercalatum uel interpolatum *diem*, þæt ys gif he byð beforan þam gesettan dæge (ii. 1. 123–25).

The endings for each noun are chosen from among the ones proper to the declension to which it belongs: in general forms such as **lunum*, **embolisme*, and **concurrentos* do not occur.[20] This circumstance argues that there is method here, even if that method appears not so much to have prescribed an ending to use in each environment as to have permitted an array of choices. The following notes go through the Old English paradigm by case and number, in each instance offering a tentative interpretation of the evidence laid out above; my working hypothesis is that the choice of Latin endings is influenced by the Old English inflectional system. Some examples are cited from other Old English texts by way of assuring that the situation in the *Enchiridion* is not idiosyncratic.

nom. sg. The forms in all declensions are quite regular, perhaps suggesting that the Latin nom. sg. was regarded as the 'unmarked' form; the occasional use of nom. sg. forms for other cases and numbers (e.g., acc. sg. *saltus*, dat. sg. *Saturnus*, acc. pl. *embolismus*) may point in the same direction. In other Old English texts acc. sg. forms are occasionally used for nom. sg.: '*Paradisum* nis naðor ne on heofonum ne on eorþan' (HomU 17.1, 3, quoted above, p. 188) and, perhaps, 'Þa locode Sanctus *Mamilium* on þæt cild' (Mart 5, 15 Sept.).[21] These may reflect a tendency to equate nom. and acc. (cf. notes on acc. sg., nom. pl., and acc. pl. below). The apparent use of gen. sg. forms for names of planets/gods in the *Enchiridion* may be explained in two ways: (1) The names may retain the gen. sg. from such phrases as *stella Iouis*; thus 'And se oðer ys geciged Foeton oððe *Iouis*' (ii. 3. 205, quoted above, p. 192) could be translated 'and the other is called Foeton or [the star] of Jupiter'; cf. 'Þas endlufon we settað on foreweardum þam circule þe man hæt *epactarum*' (i. 4. 58–59, 'We set those eleven [days] at the beginning of the cycle called "[the cycle] of the epacts"'). (2) In Old English generally, *Iouis*, not *Iup(p)iter*, is the nom. sg. form of the god's name, e.g., 'Eft his sunu *Iouis*, þe ge wurðiað for God, se wolde acwellan his unclænan fæder . . . Se *Iouis* wæs afylled mid fulre galnysse' (ÆLS [Sebastian] 172–76);[22] however, the usual nom. sg. forms of the names of Venus and Mars are *Uenus* and *Mars* (e.g., ÆLS [Agatha] 66, ÆHom 22, 126).[23] An occasional tendency in the Old English *Martyrology* to use Latin gen. sg. for nom. sg. may support the first of these two interpretations: 'On ðone þriddan dæg ðæs monðes bið þæs halgan papan tid þe is nemned Sancte *Antheri*' (Mart 5, 3 Jan.); 'On ðone eahtateogðan dæg ðæs monðes bið þæs halgan biscopes tid Sancte Eleutheri, ond his modor ðære nama wæs Sancte *Anthie̜*' (Mart 5, 18 Apr.; Mart 2 reads *Anthie* and Mart 3 *Anthiæ*).[24] This apparently idiosyncratic usage is very likely influenced by formulas with gen. sg. in martyrologies and calendars, e.g., 'Natale Eleutherii episcopi et martyris et Anciae matris eius' in Hrabanus Maurus's *Martyrology*,[25] and similar formulas with *natale*, *passio*, etc. unexpressed, e.g., 'Sancti Eleutherii episcopi' in the calendar in Salisbury Cathedral 150.[26] To a writer accustomed to working with such texts, the gen. sg. of a saint's name might well come to seem an 'unmarked' form. In any case it is difficult to explain the use of Latin gen. sg. forms for nom. sg. with reference to the Old English inflectional system.

acc. sg. Beside the expected Latin acc. sg. endings we find a number of Latin nom. sg. forms, especially in the first and fourth declensions. Cf. 'On þæm dagum gecuron Brettanie *Maximianus* him to casere ofer his willan' (Or 6, 35).[27] Two factors might have influenced the choice of endings: (1) In the Old English strong paradigms, all masc. and neut. nouns, and some fem. nouns, are the same in the nom. and acc. sg. Perhaps this lack of distinction produced a tendency to use the same Latin form for the nom. and acc. sg. The choice for both cases would normally be the 'unmarked' Latin nom. sg., but the acc. sg. form would be expected to occur occasionally for the nom. sg., as in the passages quoted in the preceding paragraph. (2) The Latin fem. nom. sg. ending *-a* sounds more like the Old English fem. acc. sg. *-e* of the *ō*-stems than does the Latin fem. acc. sg. *-am*.

gen. sg. Third- and fourth-declension nouns behave exactly as expected, presumably because the Latin endings *-is* and *-us* resemble gen. sg. *-es* of the Old English masc. and neut. strong nouns. For masc. second-declension nouns, the expected *-i* is rare, and instead we find Latin nom. sg. *-us*, presumably also because of its resemblance to Old English *-es*. This ending is frequent in Old English texts, e.g.,

Swylce emb feower wucan
þætte Solmonað sigeð to tune
butan twam nihtum, swa hit getealdon geo,
Februarius fær, frode gesiþas,
ealde ægleawe (Men 15–19)[28]

and 'and swa wearð gefyld *Augustinus* witegunge þe he cwæð: "Gif Wealas nellað sibbe wið us, hi sculan æt Seaxana handa farwurþan"' (ChronA 606 [MS 607], a late addition).[29] Here also belong 'On *Dioclitianus* dagum þæs hæþenan caseres' (Mart 5, 19 Jan.)[30] and 'Raþe æfter þæm on þara twegea consula dæge, *Claudius*, þe oðre noman hatte Marcellus, ond *Ualerius*, þe oðre noman hatte Flaccus . . .' (Or 3, 6), though the latter text more commonly adds Old English *-es* to the Latin nom. sg. form.[31] There is little evidence in the *Enchiridion* for the fem. first-declension gen. sg., but here belong 'ond þære *Affrica* norþwestgemære is æt þæm ilcan Wendelsæ þe of ðæm garsecge scyt' (Or 1, 1) and 'On þære tide Antiochuse, *Asia* cyninge, geþuhte ðæt he rice genoh næfde' (Or 5, 4);[32] also 'On þone .xx. dæg þæs monþes bið þære fæmnan gemynd *Sancta Fausta*' (Mart 5, 20 Sept.).[33] At first glance, the Latin gen. sg. *-e* (< *-ae*) would seem to be more like Old English fem. $\bar{o}$-stem *-e* than is the *-a* used in these examples. But Latin gen. sg. *-e* was pronounced long and open, while in late Old English gen. sg. *-e* was approaching the quality of a schwa, presumably more like Latin nom. sg. $\bar{a}$.[34] Even the early West-Saxon translator of Orosius may have found Latin nom. sg. *-a* more like Old English gen. sg. *-e* than Latin gen. sg. *-e*.

dat. sg. For the dat. sg. of first-declension nouns Byrhtferth uses Latin nom. sg. *-a* (or, less likely, abl. sg. *-ā*); the preference for this ending over Latin dat. sg. *-e* may be explained in the same way as the use of *-a* for the gen. sg. For the dat. sg. of second-declension nouns he uses dat./abl. sg. *-o*, and for third-declension nouns he uses dat. sg. *-i* or abl. sg. *-e/-i*. He appears to make no attempt to distinguish contexts that in Latin would require a dat. from those that would require an abl. In the third declension he uses only *-i/-e*, but in other declensions he frequently uses Latin acc. sg. forms, e.g., *lunam*, *Hieronimum*, *saltum*, *diem*. Use of Latin acc. sg. endings for dat. sg. is also well attested in Ælfric; in addition to the examples of *paradisum* cited at the beginning of this article, cf. 'Middangeard is gehaten eal þæt binnon þam *firmamentum* is' (ÆTemp 5.1); 'Ealle mæst hi sind fæste on ðam *firmamentum*' (ibid., 9.3); 'Þone þriddan þe benoþan *Iouem* gæð hi heton Mars' (ÆIntSig 21.125–26).[35] In another writer's work: 'On þam selfan dæge to ðam *passionem*, þæt is ures drihtnes þrowung, sy gecweden Dominus uobiscum fram þam diacone' (RegC 1, 30–32).[36] This usage is presumably the result of analogy with Old English *-(u)m*, strongly associated with the dat.: though Old English *-(u)m* is not a dat. sg. nominal ending, it is universal for the dat. pl. and in strong adjectives marks the masc. and neut. dat. sg. The Latin second-declension masc. nom. sg. form can be used for the dat. sg. Cf. 'On *Ianuarius*, þonne se mona bið iii nihta eald and iiii' (Days 3.1, 4) and other examples in the same text;[37] 'hio

The Inflection of Latin Nouns in Old English Texts 197

ða eft . . . fulwihte onfeng þurh ða wundor ðe ðe heo geseah æt þam bisceope *Sanctus Narcisus*' (Mart 5, 8 Aug.).

nom. pl. Though Latin nom. pl. endings are well attested, there is some tendency in the first and (masc.) second declensions to use Latin acc. pl. -*as* and -*os* for the nom. pl., presumably by analogy with the Old English noun system, in which nom. and acc. pl. are never distinguished (and in which the most common masc. nom./acc. pl. ending is -*as*). Cf. 'Þa toferdon þa *apostolos* to fyrlynum landum' (ÆLet 2, 43); 'and his *discipulos* þær slæpende wæron mid him' (LS 1.1, 103).[38] The single instance of -*a* in first-declension *semiuncia* may be the result of analogy with nom. pl. -*a* of the Old English ō-stems or, less likely, an 'unmarked' nom. sg.

acc. pl. The forms are generally as expected; the resemblance of Latin -*as*, -*os*, -*es* to Old English nom./acc. pl. -*as* of the masc. *a*-stems may explain their stability. Acc. pl. *embolismus* and *cilicus* may be explained either by the resemblance of -*us* to Old English nom./acc. pl. -*as* or as the spread of the 'unmarked' nom. sg. form through the paradigm. At least one writer used the Latin nom. pl. form for acc. pl.: 'Genimað Andreas and his *discipuli* and asettað hie beforan Marmadonia ceastre' (LS 1.1, 98);[39] cf. the frequent use of Latin nom. sg. forms for acc. sg. Byrhtferth always uses Latin neut. nom./ acc. pl. *momenta*, *minuta*, and *ostenta* in contexts where Old English could use a partitive gen., and it is impossible to say whether these words might have been perceived as gen. pl. Such ambiguity is common with Old English strong feminines, where the nom./acc. pl. matches gen. pl. -*a*, e.g., 'þonne beoð þær an hund *tida* and twentig *tida*' (i .1. 52). In addition, in the *Enchiridion* and some other late Old English texts, the neut. nom./acc. pl. often ends in -*a*, e.g., 'Þisra stafa *tacna* we wyllað on rumran fæce geswutelian' (iii. 2. 167).[40]

gen. pl. Unambiguous forms are rare; in view of the occasional occurrence of *epacte* with Old English endings, it is possible that the ending of gen. pl. *epacta* has nothing to do with the Latin endings it resembles. Third-declension *concurrentium* retains the Latin ending. Cf. 'Þis sind eac þa reliquias þæra haligra *confessorum*, þæt is Cristes andettera' (Rec 10.8, 74).[41]

dat. pl. The evidence is scarce but suggestive. In the second declension Byrhtferth once uses *terminum* with Latin acc. sg. -*um*: an ambiguous form, since he uses the assimilated loan-word *termen* beside unassimilated *terminus*. He twice uses *concurrentium* with Latin gen. pl. -*ium*; the explanation of this form can only be that it resembles Old English dat. pl. -*um*. In Ælfric, cf. 'He halgode hlaf ær his ðrowunge and todælde his *discipulum*' (ÆCHom II, 15, 76–77); the form is given interest by the invariability with which Ælfric otherwise uses *discipulus* with Latin endings, e.g., 'Æfter þæs hælendes æriste wæron his *discipuli* belocene on anum huse' (ÆCHom I, 16, 230.3); 'and cwæð þæt he wære soðlice Cristes *discipulus* him to hæle asend' (ÆLS [Abdon & Sennes] 139).[42] Byrhtferth's use of nom./acc. pl. *uocales* in a context that demands the dat. pl. suggests that a nom. pl. ending might be used for any case.

The rules governing the choice of endings for Latin words in Old English texts now seem reasonably clear: (1) Writers may attempt to match a Latin case to the equivalent Old English one, nom. to nom., acc. to acc., gen. to gen., dat./abl. to dat.; but there is a tendency to equate Latin nom. and acc. forms. (2) Where an ending in the Latin paradigm is spelled like (and presumably homophonous with) the appropriate Old English one, writers may use that Latin ending even though it does not match the Old English one in case or number – e.g., second-declension acc. sg. *-um* for dat. pl. Such endings are for practical purposes Old English, even when the word shows no other sign of being assimilated to the Old English inflectional system. (3) Writers may choose a Latin ending that sounds similar to, but not the same as, the appropriate Old English one, e.g., a Latin ending in *-s* resembling Old English masc./neut. gen. sg. *-es*. (4) They may choose an ending that, while not sounding like the appropriate Old English one, is suggestive of the appropriate Old English case – here, particularly, endings in *-m* (suggestive of the dat.) for the dat. sg. (5) They may use a Latin nom. form for any case. These rules are not mutually exclusive; rather, a single Old English writer may apply sometimes one, sometimes another. The rules can also interact: for example, in the first declension rule (1) applies, nom. and acc. sometimes being equated; but nom. sg. *-a* is used for acc. sg. after rule (3), while acc. pl. *-as* is used for nom. pl. after rule (2).

Our modern perspective leads us to think of the matching of case and number as the only appropriate rule to apply when choosing Latin endings to use in Old English contexts; we are tempted to dismiss variations from this expected norm as the result of error or ignorance. I would suggest, however, that the evidence presented here shows clearly that many Old English writers whose Latin literacy is not open to challenge thought other criteria to be equally appropriate. Chief among these was the matching of sound-patterns, but looser sorts of pattern-matching were acceptable as well, and it was possible to ignore the problem entirely by using 'unmarked' nom. forms for all cases.

It remains to say a few words about the gender of Latin words in Old English texts. Consider this passage:

Middangeard is gehaten eal þæt binnon þam *firmamentum* is. *Firmamentum* is ðeos roderlice heofen mid manegum steorrum amet. Seo heofen and sæ and eorðe sind gehatene middangeard. Seo *firmamentum* tyrnð symle onbutan us under ðyssere eorðan and bufon, ac þær is ungerim fæc betwux hire and ðære eorðan. (ÆTemp, 5.1–4)

Firmamentum is a Latin neut., and one would expect it to be used as a neut. in Old English; the dat. form *þam firmamentum* in the first sentence must be either masc. or neut. Thus *Seo firmamentum* in the fourth sentence is something of a surprise; one is tempted to dismiss it as scribal error, but five manuscripts agree in the reading, and a sixth has *Se*. All manuscripts, then, agree that *firmamentum* is not neut.; from the context one can speculate that Ælfric has given it the gender of Old English *heofon*. This passage tells a somewhat different story:

On ðam oðrum dæge ure Drihten geworhte ðone *firmamentum* ðe men hatað rodor, se belycð on his bosme ealle eorðan bradnysse, and binnan him is gelogod eal ðes middaneard, and he æfre gæð abutan swa swa yrnende hweowol, and he næfre ne stent stille on anum, and on anre wendinge, ða hwile he æne betyrnð, gað witodlice forð feower and twentig tida, ðæt is ðonne ealles an dæg and an niht. (ÆHex 139)

Here Ælfric treats *firmamentum* as masc. acc. sg., perhaps agreeing with masc. *rodor*; it is uncertain whether the masc. pronouns that follow agree with *firmamentum* or *rodor*. Ælfric's *Grammar* shows that he was well aware of the correspondences between Latin and Old English genders:

Ys eac to witenne þæt hi [sc. nouns] beoð oft oðres cynnes on Leden and oðres cynnes on Englisc. We cweðað on Ledyn *hic liber* and on Englisc þeos boc; eft on Leden *haec mulier* and on Englisc ðis wif, na ðeos; eft on Leden *hoc iudicium* and on Englisc ðes dom, na ðis. (ÆGram 18.19–19.3)

Ælfric's statement that words for the same concept often have different genders in Latin and Old English would make no sense to readers who did not equate masc., fem. and neut. in the two languages. However, it does not follow from his having made this equation that he must assign Latin gender to the unassimilated loan-words in his prose. Indeed, research on borrowing in modern languages suggests that speakers normally assign gender to loan-words according to the synchronic rules by which they assign gender to native words, whether those rules are predominantly semantic (as in Modern

English), morphological (as in Russian), or phonological (as in French); the gender of the word in the source language is rarely a factor.[43] It has been proposed that Latin gender was sometimes a factor in assigning gender to loan-words in Old English, particularly when the borrowers were well educated.[44] Ælfric was as learned as anyone in late Anglo-Saxon England, and yet he seems to have been quite uninfluenced by the Latin gender of *firmamentum*, an unassimilated loan-word that we should expect to have been especially subject to the influence of the source language.

In Byrhtferth's *Enchiridion*, Latin masculines tend to retain their gender: in Old English passages, *embolismus*, *bissextus*, *punctus*, and *saltus* are consistently treated as masculines. Latin feminines and neuters are treated less consistently. They can retain their gender, as in acc. sg. *ane uncia* and *an momentum* (iii. 3. 298–99, ii. 3. 101–02, quoted above, pp. 190, 192). However, it is uncertain whether we are to understand the endings of nom. pl. *epactas* and *semiuncias* as Latin fem. or Old English masc.; a passage from a short computus text, possibly by Byrhtferth, is less ambiguous, if somewhat confused: 'and þæs geares þu hæfst anne *epactum*' (Comp 2.3).[45] Here *anne epactum* is treated as masc. acc. sg., as shown by the ending of *anne*. The Latin masc./neut. acc. sg. ending of *epactum* violates the rule that Latin words may have only those endings proper to their declensions; presumably *-um* is a bit of pedantry, influenced by the masc. gender that has been assigned to the generally pl. *epacte*. Consider further these passages from the *Enchiridion*:

Healfe þa uers gebyriað to þam termene, þæt ys to þam *lunam* quartam decimam (iii. 2. 53–54).

and underfoð Aprilis *lunam*, se sceal geendian .xxix. (iii. 2. 230).

Momentum ys gewyss stow þære sunnan on heofenum; þonne he byð feowertig siðon gegaderod, þonne gefylleð he ane tid, and he ys gecweden for þæra tungla hwætnysse momentum (þæt ys styrung) and on Lyden a motu siderum (ii. 3. 58–61).

In the first, *þam lunam quartam decimam* treats the fem. *luna* as if masc. or neut.; in the second, the adjective clause modifying *lunam* begins with a masc. pronoun; in the third, Latin neut. *momentum* is three times referred to with masc. pronouns. If Ælfric's treatment of *firmamentum* suggests that a Latin noun might be assigned the gender of an Old English synonym, Byrhtferth's treatment of *luna* and *momentum* suggests a general preference for the masc. – a preference that reflects the tendency of words borrowed by late Old English to show up as masculines.[46]

The evidence presented here is too slight to permit us to reach conclusions concerning the rules by which gender was assigned to unassimilated loan-words. It does, however, point towards the likelihood that these rules were the same as for assimilated loan-words. It may also warn us against the easy assumption that the assignment of gender to loan-words was influenced to any significant degree by the source language, for even unassimilated loan-words that still carried unmistakable signs of their Latin gender might be assigned new genders in the work of such learned writers as Ælfric and Byrhtferth.

If the subject broached in this essay should be thought worth pursuing, further research might include a more thorough examination of the works of Ælfric, of proper names in such works as the Old English Orosius and Bede, of plant names in medical texts, and of adjectives, which, to judge from the attestations in the *Enchiridion*, were treated in ways no less interesting than nouns.[47] The gathering of information will become easier as work progresses on the *Dictionary of Old English*, which often supplies information concerning the Latin inflections of loan-words.[48] Here I have attempted no more than a preliminary survey, just enough to suggest that Old English writers inflected the Latin words in their texts according to a system that we can describe, and that the study of assimilated loan-words may usefully be complemented by the study of unassimilated ones.[49]

NOTES

1 B. Mitchell and F.C. Robinson, *A Guide to Old English,* 5th ed. (Oxford 1992), 174. The passage is of course normalized; in the standard edition, S.J. Crawford, *The Old English Version of the Heptateuch,* EETS 160 (London 1922), 88, the text reads: 'and seo næddre cwæð to ðam wife: "Hwi forbead God eow ðæt ge ne æton of ælcon treowe binnan paradisum?" Þæt wif andwyrde: "Of ðæra treowa wæstme ðe synd on paradisum we etað"' (Gen 3.1–2). Here and elsewhere in this essay, I cite texts by the abbreviations used by the *Dictionary of Old English* (hereinafter cited as *DOE*) project in its various publications; see *Dictionary of Old English: Preface & List of Texts and Index of Editions* (Toronto 1986) and, for a convenient printed list, *A Microfiche Concordance to Old English: The List of Texts and Index of Editions,* comp. Antonette diPaolo Healey and Richard L. Venezky (Toronto 1980). Both the *DOE* and the *Microfiche Concordance* have been indispensable in the preparation of this article; it is also a pleasure to acknowledge my extensive use of the electronic corpus of Old English texts prepared by the *DOE* project and accessible via search software at the University of Virginia Library. I have occasionally made slight alterations in the punctuation, capitalization, and word division of Old English quotations; words being illustrated are italicized.
2 The rule is not universally observed: see B. Mitchell, *Old English Syntax* (Oxford 1985), § 1117 (4). However, it appears to be strictly observed in Ælfric; see J.C. Pope, ed., *Homilies of Ælfric: A Supplementary Collection,* EETS 259–60 (London 1967–68), glossary, s.v.

binnan, on. It is worth mentioning that Ælfric does not reproduce the case-forms of the Vulgate text, which reads, 'qui dixit ad mulierem, "cur praecepit vobis Deus ut non comederetis de omni ligno paradisi?" Cui respondit mulier, "de fructu lignorum quae sunt in paradiso vescemur"' (R. Weber, ed., *Biblia sacra iuxta vulgatam versionem*, 4th ed. rev. R. Gryson et al. [Stuttgart 1994], 7). It is also worth pointing out that Ælfric was well aware of the correspondences between Old English and Latin cases, as is shown by the many translations of Latin case-forms in his *Grammar*, e.g.: 'NOMINATIVO *hic faber* ðes smið, GENITIVO *huius fabri* þises smiþes, DATIVO *huic fabro* þisum smiðe, ACCUSSATIVO *hunc fabrum* þysne smið, VOCATIVO *o faber* eala ðu smiþ, ABLATIVO *ab hoc fabro* fram ðisum smiðe' (ÆGram 26.16–27.1, ed. J. Zupitza, *Ælfrics Grammatik und Glossar*, Sammlung englischer Denkmäler in kritischen Ausgaben 1 [Berlin 1880]). Notice that Ælfric translates the nom., gen., dat., and acc. with case-forms only and uses periphrasis to express the sense of the voc. and abl., implying that the first four have Old English equivalents while the last two do not.

3 Such words are treated by O. Funke, *Die gelehrten lateinischen Lehn- und Fremdwörter in der altenglischen Literatur* (Halle 1914). Funke discusses a number of the words treated in this article; for references see his index. For a convenient survey of scholarship on loan-words, see H. Gneuss, '*Anglicae linguae interpretatio*: Language Contact, Lexical Borrowing, and Glossing in Anglo-Saxon England', *Proceedings of the British Academy* 82 (1993) 107–48; see also his 'Linguistic Borrowing and Old English Lexicography: Old English Terms for the Books of the Liturgy', in *Problems of Old English Lexicography: Studies in Memory of Angus Cameron*, ed. A. Bammesberger, Eichstätter Beiträge 15 (Regensburg 1985), 107–29, and especially the remarks on p. 118. The study by M.S. Serjeantson, *A History of Foreign Words in English* (New York 1936), is still indispensable; see esp. pp. 11–50, 271–92.

4 WHom 10c (*Be Cristendome*), WHom 15 (*Sermo de cena Domini*): ed. D. Bethurum, *The Homilies of Wulfstan* (1957, corrected repr. Oxford 1971), 203–04, 236.

5 R.M. Liuzza, ed., *The Old English Version of the Gospels*, vol. 1, EETS 304 (Oxford 1994), 153. The variant version in Oxford, Bodleian Library, Hatton 38 has *paradise*, with an Old English ending (W.W. Skeat, ed., *The Gospel According to Saint Luke in Anglo-Saxon and Northumbrian Versions, Synoptically Arranged* [Cambridge 1874], 226).

6 S.J. Crawford, ed., *Exameron Anglice; or, The Old English Hexameron*, BaP 10 (Hamburg 1921), 71.

7 HomU 17.2 (on the phoenix): ed. F. Kluge, 'Zu altenglischen Dichtungen', *Englische Studien* 8 (1885) 472–79 at 475–76; the quotation here is from the *DOE* text, which incorporates corrections from R.D.-N. Warner, ed., *Early English Homilies from the Twelfth Century MS. Vesp. D. XIV*, EETS 152 (London 1917), 146–48. LS 14 (*Passio Beatae Margaretae Virginis et Martyris*): ed. B. Assmann, *Angelsächsische Homilien und Heiligenleben*, BaP 3 (1889; repr. with supplementary introduction by P. Clemoes, Darmstadt 1964); now re-edited by M. Clayton and H. Magennis, *The Old English Lives of St Margaret*, Cambridge Studies in Anglo-Saxon England 9 (Cambridge 1994), 152–71 at 158 and 166.

8 HomU 57 (homiletic fragment): ed. Warner, *Early English Homilies*, 139–40. HomM 9 (*De inclusis*): *DOE* text, ed. from CCCC 303.

9 *De Sancto Johanne*: ed. Kluge, 'Zu altenglischen Dichtungen', 477–79.

10 Ælfric's letter to Sigeweard on the Old and New Testaments: ed. Crawford, *The Old English Version of the Heptateuch*, 53–54.

11 For a clear statement of this position, see Funke, *Die gelehrten lateinischen Lehn- und Fremdwörter*, 44: 'Lehnwörter' are those that always occur with Old English inflections;

'Fremdwörter' retain Latin inflections; and a third category of words occurs sometimes with Old English, sometimes with Latin endings. *DOE* makes a similar distinction, including only those words that occur with Old English inflections but frequently reporting Latin-inflected examples of words that belong to Funke's third category. For doubts about the validity of the distinction for Old English, see H. Gneuss, *Lehnbildungen und Lehnbedeutungen im Altenglischen* (Berlin 1955), 16–19. On the theoretical difficulty of distinguishing borrowing from 'code mixing' (i.e., the use of foreign elements in native speech), see R. Appel and P. Muysken, *Language Contact and Bilingualism* (London 1987), 172: 'The classical view is that code mixing and borrowing can easily be kept apart: with code mixing the non-native items are not adapted morphologically and phonologically, with borrowing they are. This view is problematic for at least two reasons: first, there may be different degrees of phonological adaptation for borrowed items, second it is not evident that all non-adapted items are clearly cases of code mixing.'

12 On macaronic poetry, see F.C. Robinson, 'Consider the Source: Medieval Texts and Medieval Manuscripts', in his *The Editing of Old English* (Oxford 1994), 25–35, at 29–32 (originally publ. in *Medieval Perspectives: Papers from the Twelfth Annual Conference of the Southeastern Medieval Association*, vol. 2, ed. M. Blakeslee et al. [1987], 7–16), and '"The Rewards of Piety": "Two" Old English Poems in Their Manuscript Context', *The Editing of Old English*, 180–95 (originally publ. in *Hermeneutics and Medieval Culture*, ed. P.J. Gallacher and H. Damico [Albany, N.Y. 1989], 193–200; the reprint adds a text and translation). On the likelihood that Old English syntax was the basis for the syntactical glossing of Latin texts, see his 'Syntactical Glosses in Latin Manuscripts of Anglo-Saxon Provenance', *Speculum* 48 (1973) 443–75. On the tendency of some scribes to substitute Latin abbreviations and words for Old English, see his 'Latin for Old English in Anglo-Saxon Manuscripts', in *The Editing of Old English*, 160–63 (originally publ. in *Language Form and Linguistic Variation: Papers Dedicated to Angus McIntosh*, ed. J. Anderson [Amsterdam 1982], 395–400).

13 On the concurrents, from CCCC 422: ed. H. Henel, *Studien zum altenglischen Computus*, Beiträge zur englischen Philologie 26 (Leipzig 1934), 49. Cf. Comp 2.4 (on concurrents and epacts): 'Gif þu nyte hwylc *concurrentes* beo on geare. . . . þonne bið *concurrentes* .i. . . . þonne bið *concurrentes* .ii. . . . swa fela *concurrentes* þu scealt habban þy geare' (ibid., 51; now re-ed. by B. Günzel, *Ælfwine's Prayerbook (London, British Library, Cotton Titus D. xxvi + xxvii)*, Henry Bradshaw Society 108 [London 1993], 121). See also *DOE*, s.v. *concurrent, concurrentes*.

14 *De concurrentibus*, from London, BL, Harley 3271: ed. Henel, *Studien*, 49.

15 J.M. Bately, ed., *The Old English Orosius*, EETS s.s. 6 (London 1980), 134.29. For the inflection of Latin names in Orosius, see pp. cvi–cix.

16 Cf. Gneuss, *Lehnbildungen*, 19: 'Aus diesem Grunde erscheint es angebracht, die Unterscheidung zwischen Lehnwort und Fremdwort fallen zu lassen. Wir können mit dem einen Begriff "Lehnwort" auskommen: das Fremdwort ist nur genau so eine Vorstufe wie die, von der Funke spricht; eine Vorstufe vor der endgültigen Aufnahme in die empfangende Sprache. Der Begriff Lehnwort umfaßt dann jedes Wort, das von einer Sprache direkt in eine andere übernommen wird, gleich in welcher Form und in welchem Stadium der Übernahme.'

17 P.S. Baker and M. Lapidge, eds, *Byrhtferth's Enchiridion*, EETS s.s. 15 (Oxford 1995). The *Enchiridion* was earlier edited by S.J. Crawford, *Byrhtferth's Manual*, EETS 177 (1929; repr. with table of errata by N.R. Ker, London 1966). Here the text is cited from the new edition by part, chapter, and line number.

18 A month's name occurs only once with an unambiguously Old English ending: 'Of

Septembres dagum and his mona ylde þu scealt findan þæs æftran monðes rihtinga' (i. 4. 41–42). Such forms occur occasionally in late Old English texts.

19 See, e.g., 'Þæt an þe þær ys to lafe sete on foreweardum þam circule þe man nemð *concurrentium*' (i. 4. 23–24), where *concurrentium* may implicitly be part of a Latin phrase *cyclus concurrentium* 'cycle of concurrents'. The *Enchiridion* contains a large number of relative clauses and parenthetical statements supplying the Latin names of things, e.g., 'Þa steorran þe man hæt *planete* on Lyden' (ii. 3. 198) and 'and on .xii. kalendas Iulius byð sunstede, þæt ys on Lyden *solstitium* and on Englisc midsumor' (ii. 1. 320–21); the Latin words in such constructions are not well-enough integrated into the syntax of the Old English sentence to yield evidence useful for this study. Normally dates in Old English passages consist of a number (either Roman or written out in Latin) followed by apparently indeclinable *kalendas, nonas,* or *idus* and a gen. sg. month's name (treated as noun), e.g., '.xii. kalendas Iulii' (i. 1. 94). However, the month's name is sometimes nom. sg. in form, e.g., '.ix. kalendas *Martius*' (iii. 1. 156), '.xv. kalendas *December*' (ii. 1. 355). I have avoided citing such phrases as evidence.

20 A possible exception in the *Enchiridion* is neut., pl. *termina*, which may, however, have an Old English fem. nom. pl. ending (see note on second-declension nom. pl. above, p. 192). For a more certain exception from a text possibly by Byrhtferth, see p. 200.

21 G. Kotzor, ed., *Das altenglische Martyrologium*, 2 vols., Bayerische Akademie der Wissenschaften, phil.-hist. Klasse 88 (Munich 1981), 2:209.9. The correct nom. sg. is *Mamilianus*; the variant version in Mart 2 reads *Mamilius*, and the gen. sg. of the name in the same text is *Mamiliani*. Kotzor's edition, 1: 426–34, contains a table usefully summarizing the inflection of abbreviations for *sanctus* etc. and saints' names in the *Martyrology*.

22 W.W. Skeat, ed., *Ælfric's Lives of Saints*, EETS 76, 82, 94, 114 (1881–1900, repr. London 1966), 1: 126.

23 Ibid., 1:198; *De Falsis Diis*, ed. Pope, *Homilies of Ælfric*, 2:683. See also WHom 12 (*De Falsis Deis*), 47, 50, 58 (ed. Bethurum, *Homilies of Wulfstan*, 222–23).

24 Kotzor, *Das altenglische Martyrologium*, 2: 10.19–20, 54.10–12. Cf. Mart 5, 17 July, masc. *Sperati* (2: 151.10 – Mart 2 has *Speratis*, perhaps a corruption of nom. sg. *Speratus*); Mart 2, 2 Aug., fem. *Theotote* (apparatus to 2: 168.11 – Mart 5 has *Theodota*); Mart 5, 23 Sept., masc. *Sossy* (2: 215.8 – Mart 2 has *Sossi*; both versions may simply have dropped the ending *-us* of *Sosius*).

25 In J. McCulloh and W.M. Stevens, eds, *Rabani Mauri martyrologium, De computo*, CCCM 44 (Turnhout 1979), 37.

26 F. Wormald, ed., *English Kalendars Before A.D. 1100*, Henry Bradshaw Society 72 (1934; repr. Woodbridge, Suffolk 1988), 19. The usage is exceedingly common in every calendar.

27 Bately, *Old English Orosius*, 153.28–29.

28 *The Menologium*, ed. E.V.K. Dobbie, *The Anglo-Saxon Minor Poems*, ASPR 6 (New York 1942), 49. See Dobbie's note to line 18, p. 171. The months' names in Men always alliterate on the first syllable; for a discussion of their accentuation see Funke, *Die gelehrten lateinischen Lehn- und Fremdwörter*, 69–70.

29 J.M. Bately, ed., *The Anglo-Saxon Chronicle: A Collaborative Edition*, vol. 3, *MS A* (Cambridge 1986), 26.

30 Kotzor, *Das altenglische Martyrologium*, 2: 10.9–10. The *Martyrology* contains numerous examples of nom. sg. *-us* for gen. sg. (ibid., 1: 427–28).

31 Bately, *Old English Orosius*, 60.14–15. In her introduction (cviii), Bately attributes gen. sg. *Claudius* to 'adoption of the Latin nominative as an "indeclinable" form'.

32 Ibid., 9.13–15; 118.17–18. According to Bately, some such apparently gen. sg. forms may be

explained rather as gen. pl.: 'Certainly whatever the translator intended, his audience would probably have interpreted constructions such as *-a cyning* and *-a lond* as plurals of the type *Norðanhymbra cyning* and *Englalond*' (cviii, n. 4). The second of the two examples given here could be understood so (though it is unlikely that the translator intended it), but the first clearly cannot.

33 Kotzor, *Das altenglische Martyrologium*, 2: 212.3–4. There are numerous examples of *-a* for gen. sg. in Mart 2 and Mart 5 (ibid., 1: 431–32).

34 See A. Campbell, *Old English Grammar* (Oxford 1959), § 379. For the evolution of Latin *ae*, see V. Väänänen, *Introduction au Latin vulgaire*, new ed. (Paris 1967), § 59.

35 ÆTemp: ed. H. Henel, *Aelfric's De Temporibus Anni*, EETS 213 (London 1942); ÆIntSig: ed. G.E. MacLean, 'Ælfric's Version of *Alcuini interrogationes Sigeuulfi in Genesin*', *Anglia* 7 (1884) 1–59.

36 Fragment of a translation of *Regularis Concordia*: ed. J. Zupitza, 'Ein weiteres Bruchstück der *Regularis Concordia* in altenglischer Sprache', *Archiv* 84 (1890) 1–24 at 5. The apparatus in Kotzor, *Das altenglische Martyrologium*, 2: 237.4–5, records a dat. sg. *Hilarionem* in Mart 2 where Mart 5 reads *Hilarione*.

37 Lucky and unlucky days: ed. M. Förster, 'Die altenglischen Verzeichnisse von Glücks- und Unglückstagen', *Studies in English Philology: A Miscellany in Honor of Frederick Klaeber*, ed. K. Malone and M.B. Ruud (Minneapolis 1929), 258–77 at 262–64.

38 ÆLet 2 (Ælfric's first letter to Wulfstan): ed. B. Fehr, *Die Hirtenbriefe Ælfrics in altenglischer und lateinischer Fassung*, BaP 9 (1914; repr. with supplementary material by P. Clemoes, Darmstadt 1966), 88. Variant readings are *apostolas* and *apostoli*. LS 1.1 (St Andrew): ed. F.G. Cassidy and R.N. Ringler, *Bright's Old English Grammar and Reader*, 3rd ed. (New York 1971), 210. A note to this passage says, 'The OE translator has carried over the Lat. acc. pl. ending from his original, though it is no longer syntactically appropriate'; the source printed by Cassidy and Ringler reads 'et respexit ad discipulos suos et uidit eos dormientes'. This explanation of *discipulos* seems likely to be correct; however, the difficulty with such explanations of individual passages and forms (cf. n. 32 above) is that they take no account of the system from which apparent anomalies arise. If the argument in this essay is correct, we can predict that it will be permissible for authors to 'carry over' acc. forms from their sources as nom., but not to 'carry over', say, dat. or abl. forms as nom. We can also recognize the use of *discipuli* as acc. pl. in the same homily as consistent with the system, even though the source is defective at this point (the passage is quoted in the next paragraph).

39 Ibid. The editors do not comment on this passage.

40 For an argument that neut. pl. *-a* is not simply the result of the late Old English confusion of vowels in unstressed syllables, see Baker and Lapidge, *Byrhtferth's Enchiridion*, xcviii.

41 List of Exeter relics: ed. P.W. Conner, *Anglo-Saxon Exeter: A Tenth-Century Cultural History*, Studies in Anglo-Saxon History 4 (Woodbridge 1993), 182. The reference in the text follows Conner's numeration of the paragraphs.

42 ÆCHom II, 15 (*Sermo de sacrificio in die Pascae*): ed. M. Godden, *Ælfric's Catholic Homilies: The Second Series*, EETS s.s. 5 (London 1979), 152. ÆCHom I, 16 (*Dominica prima post Pasca*): DOE text, from unpublished edition by P. Clemoes; cf. B. Thorpe, ed., *The Homilies of the Anglo-Saxon Church: The First Part, Containing the Sermones Catholici, or Homilies of Ælfric* (London 1844–46), 1: 230. ÆLS (Abdon & Sennes): ed. Skeat, *Ælfric's Lives of Saints*, 2: 62. Dat. pl. *discipulum* is frequent in Ælfric; dat. pl. *discipulis* occurs once in a twelfth-century copy of one of his homilies: 'Cristes iwunæ wæs ðæt he wolde oft spæcæn on deopum biȝspellum to his *discipulis*' (ÆHomM 7, 2–3, ed. S. Irvine, *Old English Homilies from MS Bodley 343*, EETS 302 [Oxford 1993], 37). See further Pope, *Homilies of Ælfric*,

glossary, s.v. *discipul(us)*.

43 See G.G. Corbett, *Gender*, Cambridge Textbooks in Linguistics (Cambridge 1991), 70–82. In ch. 2 and 3 (pp. 7–69) Corbett discusses the rules by which languages assign gender to native words.

44 See J. Welna, 'On Gender Change in Linguistic Borrowing (Old English)', in *Historical Morphology*, ed. J. Fisiak, Trends in Linguistics, Studies and Monographs 17 (The Hague 1980), 399–420 at 402. On loan-words that appear with more than one gender, see Welna, 'Complex Gender in Old English Loanwords', *Acta Philologica* 7 (Warsaw) (1978) 143–64.

45 Fragment of a computus text, from BL Cotton Caligula A. xv (Part B): ed. Baker and Lapidge, *Byrhtferth's Enchiridion*, appendix B.

46 See Campbell, *Old English Grammar*, §§ 559–62. Welna, 'On Gender Change', 400, states that of the loan-words he has studied (most from Latin), 93% of masculines, 67% of feminines, and 34% of neuters retained their gender. The most common kind of gender-change in loan-words is from fem. or neut. to masc.; fem. nouns become neut. with some frequency, but other kinds of change are rare (403–09). For a summary of more recent work, see Gneuss, '*Anglicae linguae interpretatio*', 141; figures he cites from unpublished dissertations confirm a preference for the masc. in loan-words; further, 'the percentage of words taken over into the $\bar{o}$-declension is markedly lower towards the end of the Old English period'.

47 See the brief remarks in Baker and Lapidge, *Byrhtferth's Enchiridion*, civ.

48 See the entries for *abecedarium, apostol, aprelis, bibliopece, bissextus, calend, casus, concurrent, confessor, discipul*.

49 Drafts of this essay were read by Monique Willemien Dull, Helmut Gneuss, and Nicholas Howe; I am grateful to them for their comments.

When Lexicography Met the Exeter Book

ROBERTA FRANK

It is an old story, long familiar to the imagination: an enchanted beauty sleeping through the ages, waiting impatiently for a prince to come. True, one or two tentative suitors got their hands on the Exeter Book in the sixteenth century;[1] and there was that brief encounter with George Hickes at the end of the seventeenth (it left permanent marks), and a hurried rendezvous with Humfrey Wanley in 1701.[2] But then, nothing at all, just a boring, uninterrupted nap through the Lisbon earthquake, Jacobite riots, Seven Years War, and American and French revolutions. When, after mid-century, writers all over Europe began to seek native bards here, there, and everywhere, they did not, apparently, look in the Exeter Book: 'Indeed, it was not until the following century that this great manuscript began to receive the attention for which it had been waiting since the close of the eleventh century.'[3] The Dean of Exeter Cathedral, the antiquary Charles Lyttelton (1714–68), writing to a friend in 1761 about 'some good MSS in the library', seems not to have regarded the Exeter Book as anything special.[4] Certainly Sharon Turner (1768–1847) was not aware of its existence when he wrote his *History of the Anglo-Saxons* (1799–1805). In 1812 the Grimms published a tale about a lovely princess shelved for a hundred years in a palace surrounded by thorns.[5] That very year, just as brutal cold enveloped Napoleon's troops in Russia, a titled gentleman, the third Rawlinson Professor of Anglo-Saxon at Oxford, uncovered and then warmly embraced the Exeter Book, which, as every Anglo-Saxonist knows, lived happily ever after.[6]

There is another version of the story, rarely told, in which the Exeter Book does not gather dust throughout the eighteenth century but runs off and has a long-term relationship with two men. In 1759 the manuscript travelled to Northamptonshire, where it stayed for almost three years with Edward Lye (1694–1767), who was compiling an Old English dictionary.[7] The borrowers' book of Exeter Cathedral Library records the loan: 'June 30 1759. The Saxon MS. No I was lent to Dr Lye for a twelvemonth, the editor of Junius.'[8] Lye was not eager to discard his new companion.

On 10 July 1760 Dean Lyttelton reminded him that the book was now overdue: 'As the Term is now expired which the Chapter of Exeter granted you in the use of the Saxon MS, you will allow me to trouble you with a few Lines just to say, that if you have occasion for a longer use of the MS. you should write to Dr. Milles Præcentor of the Cathedral who is now resident there & President of the Chapter in my absence, to request of him & his Brethren, Leave to keep it another Year or such time, be it more or less, that you have occasion for it.'

On 22 July 1760 Lyttelton observes that returning the manuscript would not be logistically difficult for Lye: 'I wrote on Thursday to the President of our Chapter signifying your request for three months longer use of the MS, which, there is no doubt, but will be readily complied with. In case you go into the west this Autumn, you can easily convey the Book yourself, otherwise I know no other method than sending it by a Friend to London & from thence by the Exeter Waggon thither.'

A year later (1 June 1761) Lyttelton's reminder is still polite: 'You will excuse my reminding you, that the Term is nearly expired which the Chapter granted you the use of their Manuscript. If you have occasion to keep it another Year, please to make a fresh Request before this Month expires, in a few Lines directed to me & enclosed to the *Bishop here*. and I have no doubt but it will be readily complied with.'

Eight months later (23 January 1762) the Dean's impatience begins to show: 'You inform'd me last Summer that you had finished your Extracts from the Saxon MS belonging to the Ch. of Exeter, and was ready to return it the first convenient opportunity. as is probable I shall soon go thither for a short time, if you will send it by some Friend that is coming to Town, directed to be left at my House in Old Burlington Street, I will carry it down with me & return you your Receipt.'

Ten weeks later Lye sent the manuscript to London. The new Dean of Exeter acknowledged receipt, expressing his hope that the lexicographer had 'found some curious matter in it, & that the publick will one time or another be the better for it'.[9]

On Lye's death, the Exeter Book was borrowed again by Owen Manning (1721–1801), who used it to correct and augment his friend's unfinished work.[10] The completed *Dictionary* includes some sixty-two words peculiar to the Exeter Book, at least eighty-eight new headwords or lemmas derived from the same manuscript, and several hundred additional entries taken from all sections of the codex, beginning with the first folio (8a) and ending with the last (130a).[11] Such devoted combing suggests something more serious than a fun flirtation with the new kid in town.

Still, contemporary reviewers of the *Dictionary* managed to look the other way, discreetly ignoring the influence of a strange vellum.[12] (Twentieth-century notices have followed suit, referring slightingly to 'Lye's "own" dictionary, . . . largely based upon Junius' work'.[13]) The 'Big Sleep' leitmotif is heard again and again. In his initial report of 1812, John Conybeare maintained that the Exeter Book had 'hitherto been known only by the scanty and somewhat inaccurate synopsis of its contents given by Wanley'.[14] In later editions of his *History*, Sharon Turner credits Conybeare with the find and affirms, like everyone else, that 'the MS. had lain unnoticed since the time of Wanley until he inspected it'.[15] After Wanley and Hickes, 'for more than a century, nothing further was done'.[16] The latest scholarship is only slightly more cautious: 'If Wanley's *Catalogue* registered the existence of the "Exeter Book", it does not seem to have stirred much excitement for it. It was not until 1814 that the manuscript began to be made generally known to scholars.'[17] Before 'the anthology first attracted the attention of critics at the beginning of the nineteenth century', life for the Exeter Book was a prolonged yawn.[18]

Scholars can be ungrateful beasts. Conybeare, who used the Lye/Manning *Dictionary* to translate extracts from the Exeter Book, mentions his lexicographical helpmate only when departing from it.[19] In 1834 John Mitchell Kemble, who had in the previous year announced plans to publish his own 'Lexicon Poeticum' of Old English, attacked the *Dictionary*, according to his biographer, 'for heaping together words from every dialect and period but having none from *Beowulf* and the *Codex Exoniensis*'.[20] (Kemble's actual words were: '. . . and to crown this, *not one word* from Beowulf, and not a tithe of the words from the Codex Exoniensis . . .'[21]) Two years earlier, at age twenty-five, he had complained to Jacob Grimm: 'Is it not too bad that Lye, who appears to have read the Cod. Ex., says nothing of wicg, heafela, umbor, etc.?'[22] By January 1842, after some two-hundred pages of the Exeter Book had been printed by the Saxon Committee of the Society of Antiquaries of London, Kemble's tone is more subdued: 'The number of new words in the Codex Exoniensis is very great, and they come in excellent time for my dictionary which goes on slowly but steadily: yet my mind really sinks within me when I consider the labor that lies before me and the little value any one here will set upon it, when all is accomplished.'[23] Kemble, by not finishing, was spared such indifference. As Samuel Johnson, who knew Lye and subscribed to his *Dictionary*, observed in the preface to his own: 'Every other authour may aspire to praise; the lexicographer can only hope to escape reproach, and even this negative recompence has been yet granted to very few.'[24]

Not even the greatest philologist of the first half of the nineteenth century found the language of the Exeter Book easy. Almost a century after Lye borrowed the manuscript, Jacob Grimm confided to Kemble: 'I have read with curiosity through the Exeter poems . . . One must take them up and read them through for a long time before drawing profit from the richness of forms and words. With regard to the riddles I likewise don't understand much.'[25] Nor, apparently, did the Exeter Book scribe always fully comprehend the language he was copying, which seems to have early fallen into disuse.[26] Henry of Huntingdon, born barely fifty years after Bishop Leofric, is thought to have donated the Exeter Book to that cathedral, was startled by the diction of *The Battle of Brunanburh* – understandably, since he took *hæleða* 'of men' (the most frequent genitive plural poetic noun in Old English) to mean *sanitas* 'health', and *blondenfeax* 'greyhaired' to mean *verbis blandus* 'easy with words'; English writers, he asserted, 'used as strange words as figures'.[27]

Lexicographers initially avoided the special language of Old English poetry. Workers in the vineyard of prose had a better chance of getting it right, propped up as they were by Anglo-Saxon glosses and glossaries that gave Latin equivalents for Old English words (and vice versa) and by Old English prose texts that closely followed their Latin originals. 'The earliest known lexicographer of the English language', the thirteenth-century Worcester scribe who set his tremulous hand to preparing an alphabetical Old English–Latin glossary, worked with prose translations, not verse.[28] The only part of Cambridge, Corpus Christi College, 12 (the Old English version of Gregory's *Pastoral Care*) not heavily glossed and annotated by him is the verse epilogue, while his glosses to the metrical prologue indicate that he 'made little sense of that text'.[29] Laurence Nowell, despite his known interest in Old English poetry, kept his manuscript dictionary, compiled in the reign of Queen Elizabeth, almost completely verse-free: only one word, *dogor* 'day', is marked 'poetice'; no poetic words from *Beowulf, Judith*, or the Exeter Book are included, not even those glossed by him on the opening folios.[30]

Poetic words form part of the first published Old English dictionary, compiled by William Somner in 1659. He extracted from his own transcript of the Cædmon Manuscript some 256 vocabulary items; yet almost half of the definitions provided for these words contain an expression of doubt such as *fortasse* or *forte*.[31] No industry, patience, or skill could bring about clarity, Somner explained, for the book 'was written chiefly in a style so old, obsolete, poetic, overcharged, unnatural, hidden, and riddling, and [it] abounded in a profusion of unusual and excessive transpositions of words . . .'[32] Forty years later George Hickes also declared Old English verse *spinosa* 'thorny'.[33] But he glossed, with the help of a thirteenth-century Icelandic treatise, more than a hundred simplices found only or chiefly in Old English verse.[34] His illustrations are taken mainly from Junius's edition of the Cædmon poetry and from the unpublished *Judith*, *Menologium*, and *Maxims II*. There are no citations from the Exeter Book, whose turn to be courted by a dictionary came in another seventy years.

The many translation errors made by Lye and Manning show just how puzzling they found the Exeter Book. The *hapax legomena* of the manuscript inspire a small pride of blunders: *geþryðed* 'mighty' (Phoen 486) is glossed 'compelled'; *hreðleas* 'inglorious' (Guth 906), 'gentle'; *hopgehnast* 'dashing of waves' (Rid 3.27), 'hope of victory'. Poetic *reotan* 'to weep, mourn' (Christ 835, 1229; Fort 46), a new word, is translated 'rattle, creak, clatter', while *leolc*, the pret. 3 sg. of *lacan* 'to sport' (Jul 674, Rid 56.8), remains, as in Somner's *Dictionarium*, 'lion-like'.[35] Errors sometimes cripple more than the sense. By glossing *deall* in *feðrum deall* 'proud of its wings' as 'deprived', Lye and Manning permanently ground both phoenix (Phoen 266) and hawk (Fort 88). Their guess that poetic *hroðor* 'joy, benefit' is related to prose *hryðer* 'cattle, ox, bull, cow' means that Christ comes to men 'as a protection and beast of burden' (Christ 1196) and that the punishment of punishments for anyone heading to hell is to be *hroðra bedæled* 'deprived of cattle' (Jul 390, 681). Other errors may have been inspired by depression and overwork. When murderous death assails a victim *on þa sliðnan tid* 'in that cruel time' (Guth 992), Lye and Manning translate *sliðen* 'hard, evil' as 'easy, fortunate'. The life of a lexicographer probably made oblivion look good.

Some of their erroneous definitions are worth a second look. Manning took the unique compound *brægdboga* (Christ 765), denoting the devil's weapon, to mean 'bent bow' (from *bregdan* 'draw, bend, move'); he was followed by Thorpe and Gollancz.[36] Grein seems to have been the first to interpret *brægdboga* as 'deceitful bow' (*bræd* 'trick, fraud' = *brægden* 'deceitful' from *bregdan*);[37] subsequent dictionaries, editions, and translations have given full authority to this interpretation. But the Lye/Manning reading serves as a reminder that there is an etymological link, visibly embodied in the devil's bow and audibly in Cynewulf's compound, between 'bending, twisting' and 'deceiving', the moral sense darkening the physical. An Old English poet, learned in the conventions, could, as Fred Robinson has many times demonstrated, 'shade and knit anew the patch of words'.[38]

A Cynewulfian spelling seems to be responsible for another 'blunder' in the 1772 *Dictionary*. The adjective *eormen* 'wide, great, powerful' in *ofer/geond ealne yrmenne grund* (Jul 10, Christ 481) is confused by Lye and Manning with the etymologically distinct verb *yrman* 'to make desolate, trouble, afflict': 'over/through all the forsaken world'. Wrong, of course. Yet each time the spelling *yrman* is used in the Exeter Book, the two meanings, 'wide' and 'wretched', seem to converge.[39] The question for the lexicographer is whether semantic infection or blending is at work in Cynewulf's verse as it is in the *Dictionary*.

Other entries reveal how slowly old errors fade away, how fallible the consensus of scholars brought up in the same lexicographical tradition can be. Faulty manuscript readings linger longer than they should. On fol. 13b, line 18, Lye and Manning take the fourth letter in *wræclic wrixl* 'wondrous exchange' (Christ 416) to be a 'c'; all subsequent dictionaries, concordances, and editions have concurred – wrongly, it turns out, if Muir (1994) is right that 'the MS clearly has *wrætlic*'.[40]

Like a bad guest, once a definition is admitted, it is hard to get it to leave. Somner's *Dictionarium* (1659) says that *gamol* means 'a camel' and *gamolfeax*, 'camelhaired, bushy- or longhaired'. Fred Robinson has recently drawn attention to the Old English ode published by Humfrey Wanley in 1700 in commemoration of the death (at the age of eleven) of William, duke of Gloucester, a poem in which Wanley (who had earlier transcribed Somner's *Dictionarium* in order to have a copy for himself) calls the child *gamolfeax hæleð* 'a flowing-haired man'.[41] Hickes, in his chapter on Old English poetic language, published in 1703, reported, correctly, that Old English *gamol* (= Old Norse *gamall*) meant 'old'.[42] But 'camel' stubbornly persisted. Lye's first meaning for *gamol* is 'old', but he still accepts 'camel' as an alternative, and defines *gamolfeax* as 'longhaired'. It was left to Manning in his supplement to rid the Exeter Book of its residual hippies; for him, as for Pound, the *gamolfeax* seafarer, 'grey-haired he groaneth'.[43]

Sometimes, loosening the tight grip of tradition, the Exeter Book nudged Manning in the right direction. *Hwær cwom mearg?* 'Where has the horse gone?' laments a voice in *The Wanderer*. Readers of early Old English dictionaries might well ask the same question. Poetic *mearh* 'horse' occurs only once in the Cædmon Manuscript: *mæton milpaðas meara bogum* 'they measured the miles on horseback' (lit. 'mile-paths on shoulders of horses', Ex 171). Hickes mistranslated four of the five words ('in confinium angulis inter semitas eum inveniunt'), giving *mearh* the meaning *confinium* 'limit, border', as if it were *mære* 'boundary'.[44] Lye and Manning initially follow him, mistranslating not only the *Exodus* verse ('invenerunt inter semitas finium angulis'), but also the Exeter Book's *meares gleaw* 'skillful with a horse' (Gifts 69) as 'boundary-wise'. But *mearh* occurs another nine times in the manuscript. And as he was finishing the last letter of the *Dictionary*, Manning noticed a pattern: *yðmearh* 'wave-horse, ship' (Christ 863) looked and acted a lot like nearby *sundhengest* 'sea-horse' (Christ 852, 862) and *wæghengest* 'wave-horse' (Guth 1329). Since he had glossed the last two compounds 'marinus caballus, marinus equus, vector. Navis', he now glossed the first, 'marina equa, vectrix, Navis', as if *mearh* 'steed' were 'mare'. The definition is not yet perfect, but it is improved, and the Exeter Book has shown the way.

Lye and Manning make genuine advances. They identify many new poetic headwords in the Exeter Book (e.g., *breotan, deall, eaden, gefælsian, firgenstreamas, frige, garfaru, geocend, geoc, giefl, hoðma, hremig, hreðer, hroðer, gelac, neotan, geniðla, reotan, sælan, seomian, sneome, swylt, peccan, preanied, pryð, waðum, wræclast, wræcmæcgas, wrætlic/e,* and *wrætt*). Fuller and more correct meanings are given to words such as *blæst, blæd, bebugan, behealdan, freoðan, gedriht, gehnæst, gleam, gyld, spelboda, stiellan, sinniht, swat, þing, þrymm, weardian, wineleas, wlitan, wordcwide,* and *woð.* And their shotgun approach to definition, their glossing of *þrymm,* for example, by eleven words (*multitudo, turba, turma, cohors, caterva, chorus, coetus, immensitas, magnitudo, crassitudo,* and *densitas*) may have been trend-setting, for it is exactly matched by the eleven of Clark Hall and Meritt: multitude, host, troop, torrent, force, power, might, ability, glory, majesty, splendour.[45]

The Lye/Manning *Dictionary* is one of those rare reference books that seems to get better as its final letters are reached. Except for the first thirty sheets, which were published before Lye's death, and the supplement, which is Manning's independent work, exactly how much and what each editor contributed to any one entry is unclear. From *st-* on, when the reference system changes to include line as well as folio numbers, entries tend to be fuller, with more and longer citations from the Exeter Book: the letter 'w', for example, draws 172 quotations from that manuscript; 'n' and 'r', three each, and 'i', only one. Multiple citations become common. Ten references to the Exeter Book citations are found, for example, s.v. *þrymm,* fourteen, s.v. *wuldor.* More than ninety headwords in the supplement, from *abreman* and *anhaga* to *weoh* and *wolcengehnast,* contain material from the Exeter Book. Manning clearly looked afresh at the early entries in the *Dictionary* (especially 'a' to 'h'), sometimes expressing polite doubt about the definitions provided. The sense 'God, lord' given by both Somner and Lye for *gedriht* 'troop, band' worries him, for he can find the former meaning nowhere ('nescio tamen an unquam occurit in hoc sensu: raro certe'), while the latter is richly illustrated in the poetry. And he gets *wolcengehnast* 'nubium conflictus' (Rid 3.60), the final entry from the Exeter Book, right at last. The first reviewers of the *Dictionary* gave Manning the lion's share of credit for the work;[46] he probably deserved it as far as the Exeter Book is concerned.

The unusual amount of attention paid to verse by the two *Dictionary* editors may or may not have something to do with current literary taste, the post-1750s fascination with early vernacular poetry. In the 1760s, when the *Dictionary* was being compiled, native bards and their compositions were all the rage. James Macpherson's Ossian corpus was published in 1760, 1762, and 1763; Evan Evans's volume on the ancient Welsh bards in 1764, and Thomas Percy's *Reliques of Ancient English Poetry* in 1765. In 1759, the year in which Lye borrowed the Exeter Book, Samuel Johnson has the sage Imlac observe: '. . . in almost all countries, the most ancient poets are considered the best'.[47] In 1767, the year of Lye's death, the concluding chapter of William Duff's *Essay of Original Genius* bore the long title (here abbreviated) 'That Original Poetic Genius Will in General Be Displayed in its Ultimate Vigour in the Early . . . Periods of Society . . .'[48] Yet somehow Anglo-Saxon poets did not make the grade: 'Our Saxon poems are for the most part little more than religious rhapsodies', explained Thomas Warton, who said that was one reason why he was not including them in his *History of English Poetry* (1774).[49]

The 'scop' poems of the Exeter Book were unknown in eighteenth-century literary circles. Lye and Manning, in their romp through the manuscript, show no particular interest in either *Widsith* or *Deor*, even though Wanley had noted that the former recorded many Old Saxon names, and the latter, information on the origins of the ancient Saxons.[50] They cite two words from *Widsith* (*weold Ytum*) and two from *Deor* (*Mæringa burg*), and seem unimpressed that each poem depicts a northern *scop* or *gleomann* in action. The two editors are equally lukewarm towards the 'elegies': *The Wanderer* and *The Seafarer* each contribute five words to the *Dictionary*; *The Wife's Lament*, like *The Ruin*, one phrase; *The Husband's Message*, like *Wulf and Eadwacer*, one word. Nor do Lye and Manning seem overly fond of stories about saints: only twelve of the twenty-five pages of *Guthlac A*, nine of the seventeen of *Guthlac B*, and fourteen of the twenty-two of *Juliana* supply material for the *Dictionary*, and then (with the exception of the opening five pages of *Guthlac A* and the last of *Guthlac B*) sparingly. What did excite them was biblical and patristic verse and Christological allegory: all but three of the forty-nine pages of the *Christ* poems, all pages of the *Panther, Whale*, and *Storm Riddles*, and all but one of the nineteen pages of *The Phoenix*, are rich sources of citations. In *Christ I*, the Marian antiphon (lines 71–103) supplies sixteen words; the dialogue between Mary and Joseph (lines 164–213), fifty-six words. The *Dictionary* derives most of its Exeter Book material from poems in the first half of the manuscript, the 'religious rhapsodies'.[51] Conybeare's *Illustrations* (1826), an anthology that features a number of secular, romantic, and personal-seeming pieces from the Exeter Book (e.g., *Widsith, Deor, The Ruin, The Wife's Lament, The Maxims*, and *The Riming Poem*) heralds a change in taste: the Christian verities preferred by Lye and Manning have fifty years later given way to Teutonic glory.[52]

The working methods of the two editors remain opaque. Perhaps it was only chance or quirkiness that led them to gloss one word in a line and not another. Why *renig* 'rainy' and not its more interesting twin *reotig* 'mournful' in *Wulf and Eadwacer*? Why *cyrred* 'turned' and not *pyrred* 'dried' in *Riddle 28*? And why, of the 535 lexical items in *The Battle of Maldon*, did Lye and Manning single out only *dreng* 'warrior' and *darod* 'spear' (149) for inclusion in their *Dictionary*?[53] Certain principles are clear. Pronominals and prepositions are not plucked from the Exeter Book, but hard words (*edergong*, *bleat*) and characteristic spellings (*bi-* for *be-*; *o*, not *a*, before nasal consonants) are. Manning has an eye for formulas (*bi sæm tweonum*), kennings (s.v. *hengest*), synecdoche (*hama*), metonymy (*lind*), and pleonasm (*wundrum wrætlice*). Certain folios of the manuscript seem to have been searched with particular letters of the alphabet in mind: *The Phoenix* supplies all four verbs beginning with *on-*; all seven words cited on fol. 91b and all nine on fol. 58a begin with a 'w'. In fact, 'w'-entries make up about one-third of the Exeter Book citations in the *Dictionary* (excluding the supplement). 'W' is a big letter in Old English poetry, but not so big as all that. For some reason, perhaps having to do with availability, when compiling the penultimate letter of the *Dictionary*, Manning became deeply, obsessively, intimately involved with the manuscript.[54]

In general, the 'w'-words in the Exeter Book inspiring the most extensive entries are those that are rare or non-existent in the Old English verse published before 1772.[55] The simplex *wong* 'plain', for example, occurs thirty-seven times in the Exeter Book and only seven times in the pre-1772 corpus.[56] Poetic *weardian* 'to dwell', for which one page alone of *The Phoenix* provides three citations, occurs nineteen times in the Exeter Book and only three times in the pre-1772 corpus. Most strikingly, poetic *wod* 'sound, poetry, eloquence' is found, along with four of its compounds, some fifteen times in the Exeter Book and only once in the verse known before 1772 (*wodbora*, DEdg 33). The *Dictionary* includes two Exeter Book citations s.v. *wod*, two s.v. *wodbora* 'bearer of eloquence', and one each s.v. *wodcræft* 'poetic skill, eloquence', *wodgiefu* 'eloquence-gift', and *wodsong* 'inspired song (of prophet)'. Vernacular poetics was clearly of some interest to Manning, and he made the Exeter Book reveal new and precious information about its own traditional verbal art.

A major theme in the Exeter Book from the opening Advent antiphons to the final riddles is the importance of wonder and the wondrous in accessing the divine. The poetic adverb *wundrum* 'wondrously' occurs twenty-five times in the manuscript and only six times in the pre-1772 corpus; the poetic adjective *wrætlic* 'wondrous, rare' (along with *wrætt* 'work of art, ornament' and *wrætlice* 'wondrously', all cognate with *writan* 'to incise, write'), appears some thirty-six times in the manuscript and only twice in all the verse known before 1772. The *Dictionary* cites from the Exeter Book no fewer than fourteen examples of *wundrum* and seventeen of *wrætlic* and its companions. The two words occur together seven times, either in the same half-line or alliterating across the caesura; and both signal the presence of the marvellous, of elegant, subtle artistry, of magisterial skill. The mysterious multicoloured phoenix and panther as well as the intricately constructed objects in the riddles are *wrætlic*; so are jewelled angelic words, paradoxical truths, and majestic city walls, all things that can inspire in 'readers' a sense of wonder, an intimation that the hand of a master craftsman has been at work. An Anglo-Saxon poet might well have used the same two words to praise the art and soaring excellence of the scholar to whom this piece is dedicated.

By all accounts, nothing happened when lexicography met the Exeter Book. No social transformations were effected, no public oppressors reined in, no boundaries redrawn. England had her weather and navy still. Encounters between the principals took place far from the universities, far from forests of spires, far from fashionable watering places. To Thomas Warton and his literary set, the *Dictionary* might as well not have been.

But it was; its makers gambled on immortality and won. For Lye at home in Yardley Hastings, as later for Manning, reading the Exeter Book, slowly and searchingly, was like receiving a guest from a distant land. Comprehension required alertness, tact, discretion, and an initial trust that communication, however approximate, was going to be possible. The two scholars did their best to make sense of the stranger's words, peculiar syntax, and startling imagery; like perfect hosts, they showed tender solicitude in extracting, cataloguing, restoring, and conserving the remnants of a vanished past. Many late hours and pots of tea, much lonely toil and physical suffering undoubtedly went into the making of the *Dictionary*. Those who love words can still glimpse in the strivings of eighteenth-century lexicography something of their own hopeless passion, of a windswept *gamolfeax* embarked with his craft on a quest that will not end until solid ground is sighted, and that therefore never ends.

NOTES

1 Laurence Nowell, Dean of Lichfield 1560–76, wrote glosses on fols 9r (6 lines) and 10r (4 lines) of the manuscript and further Latin and Old English titles on fols 20v, 32v, and 44v;

John Joscelyn probably saw the copy of Leofric's donation list bound with it ca 1566. See Max Förster in *The Exeter Book of Old English Poetry*, with introductory chapters by R.W. Chambers, Max Förster, and Robin Flower (Bradford 1933), 91. The Exeter Book may have come to London at this time, into the possession of either Sir William Cecil or Matthew Parker. See Timothy Graham, 'A Parkerian Transcript of the List of Bishop Leofric's Procurements for Exeter Cathedral: Matthew Parker, the Exeter Book, and Cambridge University Library MS. Ii.2.11', *Transactions of the Cambridge Bibliographical Society* 10/4 (1994) 421–55, at 450–51.

2 Hickes (1642–1715) outlined in pencil runic passages that were to be reproduced in *Grammaticae Icelandicae Rudimenta*, vol. I, pt iii, p. 4, of his *Thesaurus linguarum septentrionalium* (Oxford 1703–05); p. 5 of the same *Grammar* presents brief descriptions of these passages as well as extracts (with translations) from the Exeter Book riddles. Wanley (1672–1726) described the manuscript in his catalogue, vol. III of Hickes's *Thesaurus*, pp. 279–81. A letter sent by Hickes to Wanley in London on 21 June 1701 pressures him to finish and return the Exeter Book: 'I am punctually engaged to restore it on Thursday next in the evening, and I will break my word no more.' See *A Chorus of Grammars: The Correspondence of George Hickes and his Collaborators on the Thesaurus linguarum septentrionalium*, ed. Richard L. Harris, Publications of the Dictionary of Old English 4 (Toronto 1992), 350–51.

3 L.J. Lloyd, *The Library of Exeter Cathedral* (Exeter 1967), 16.

4 Lloyd, *The Library of Exeter Cathedral*, 16. Lyttelton mentions the Exeter Book in his short catalogue of 1751 as item 26: 'Miscellanea Leofrici etc. charactero Saxonico.' See Bernard Muir, *The Exeter Anthology of Old English Poetry* (Exeter 1994), I: 2, n. 5.

5 'Dornröschen' in Jacob and Wilhelm Grimm, *Kinder- und Hausmärchen* (Berlin 1812), no. 50.

6 John J. Conybeare announced his discovery in a letter sent 2 November 1812 and read 5 November 1812 to the Society of Antiquaries; the notice was published two years later, along with two other communications relating to the manuscript, in *Archaeologia* 17 (1814) 180–88, 189–92, and 193–97. The years 1830 to 1832 were particularly busy ones for the Exeter Book: Nikolai F.S. Grundtvig claimed to have made the first full transcript (no longer extant) of the manuscript in 1830; Robert Chambers transcribed it in 1831–32; Benjamin Thorpe, in 1832.

7 See T.A. Birrell, 'De Studie van het Oud-Engels, 1705–1840', *Handelingen van het Achtentwintigste Nederlands Filologencongres* (1964) 30–40; Eng. trans. as 'The Society of Antiquaries and the Taste for Old English, 1705–1840', *Neophilologus* 50 (1966) 107–17, at 117, n. 23. Northamptonshire patriotism may be behind Lye's etymology for Lancashire: see s.v. *hland* 'urine'.

8 Dean and Chapter 7134/1. Noted by N.R. Ker, *Medieval Manuscripts in British Libraries* (Oxford 1977), 2: 808; also Ker, 'Cathedral Libraries', *Library History* 1 (1967) 38–45; repr. in Ker, *Books, Collectors, and Libraries: Studies in the Medieval Heritage*, ed. Andrew G. Watson (London 1983), 293–300, at 297. The Dean and Chapter demanded a receipt for the Exeter Book before allowing Lye to go off with it; no date is given in the borrowers' book for the return of the manuscript.

9 I owe these excerpts from London, BL, Add. 32325 to the kindness of Professor Margaret Clunies Ross, University of Sydney, who is editing letters to and from Lye in this unpublished manuscript. The first four extracts cited here are found on pp. 159–60, 161, 174–75, and 180–81, respectively. For the journey home of the Exeter Book, see letters of 8 April 1762 (pp. 186–87) and 19 May 1762 (pp. 190–91).

218   Roberta Frank

10 Mrs Angela Doughty, Cathedral Archivist, reports that the volume of the borrowers' book
covering the period 1764–1800 (Dean and Chapter 7134/2) mentions neither the Exeter
Book nor Owen Manning. Evidence for the manuscript having been in Manning's possession for an extended period is provided by *Dictionary* entries and by Society of Antiquaries, London, MS. 447 (1), fols 19r–21v. The *Dictionary* was published in 1772 under the
title: Edward Lye, *Dictionarium Saxonico- et Gothico-Latinum ... Accedunt Fragmenta
Versionis Ulphilanae, necnon Opuscula quaedam Anglo-Saxonica Edidit, Nonnullis Vocabulis
auxit, plurimis Exemplis illustravit, et Grammaticam utriusque Linguae praemisit Owen
Manning, S.T.B.*, 2 vols (London).
11 Of the 246 pages of poetry in the manuscript, 162 provide entries for the *Dictionary*. At
least 512 headwords contain one or more illustrations from the Exeter Book, for a total of
681 citations.
12 *Monthly Review* 47 (1772) 374–75; *The Critical Review, or, Annals of Literature* 36 (1773)
417–20; *Göttingische gelehrte Anzeigen* (1774) 25–30.
13 M. Sue Hetherington, *The Beginnings of Old English Lexicography* (Austin 1980), 283. Her
cited source is J.A.W. Bennett, 'The History of Old English and Old Norse Studies in
England from the Time of Francis Junius till the End of the Eighteenth Century', Oxford
University D.Phil. thesis (Bodl. MS. D. Phil. d. 287), 374: '[Lye's work] is based, though
without acknowledgement, on Junius' "Dictionarium" of Anglo-Saxon, or rather on the
Harleian transcript of it (B.L. MS. Add. 4720–22)'. Bennett still praises the 1772 *Dictionary*
as 'the most considerable achievement of Anglo-Saxon studies in the early Georgian era'
(376). The copy of Junius's 1655 edition of the Cædmon poetry, into which Lye and Manning inserted an (original) interlinear gloss, is now part of MS. 823 of the Society of Antiquaries. See Eric Stanley, 'Translation from Old English: "The Garbaging War-Hawk", or,
The Literal Materials from Which the Reader Can Re-create the Poem', in *Acts of Interpretation: The Text in its Contexts, 700–1600. Essays on Medieval and Renaissance Literature in
Honor of E. Talbot Donaldson*, ed. Mary J. Carruthers and Elizabeth D. Kirk (Norman,
Okla., 1982), 67–101, at 83, n. 40; repr. in Stanley, *A Collection of Papers with Emphasis on
Old English Literature*, Publications of the Dictionary of Old English 3 (Toronto 1987),
83–114, at 97, n. 40.
14 *Archaeologia* 17 (1814) 180.
15 *The History of England: From the Earliest Period to the Norman Conquest* (London 1839), 3:
332.
16 R.W. Chambers in *The Exeter Book of Old English Poetry* (London 1933), 34.
17 Patrick W. Conner, *Anglo-Saxon Exeter: A Tenth-Century Cultural History* (Woodbridge,
Suffolk, 1993), 252.
18 Muir, *The Exeter Anthology*, ix.
19 When Conybeare names Lye in *Archaeologia* 17 (1814) 190, it is only to reject his reading of
poetic *hremig* 'compos' in *Soul II*, line 9.
20 Raymond A. Wiley, 'Anglo-Saxon Kemble: The Life and Works of John Mitchell Kemble
1807–1857, Philologist, Historian, Archaeologist', in *Anglo-Saxon Studies in Archaeology
and History*, 1, ed. S.C. Hawkes, D. Brown, and J. Campbell, BAR British Series 72 (Oxford
1979) 165–273, at 198.
21 'Review of Benjamin Thorpe's *Analecta Anglo-Saxonica*', *Gentleman's Magazine* n.s. 1 (1834)
391–93, at 392. Kemble's 'Lexicon Poeticum', announced to Jacob Grimm, was never completed. See *John Mitchell Kemble and Jakob Grimm: A Correspondence, 1832–1852*, ed.
Raymond A. Wiley (Leiden 1971), 34.
22 *A Correspondence*, ed. Wiley, 26.
23 *A Correspondence*, ed. Wiley, 223. The first edition of the Exeter Book appeared in 1842:

Benjamin Thorpe, ed., *Codex Exoniensis: A Collection of Anglo-Saxon Poetry from a Manu-script in the Library of the Dean and Chapter of Exeter, with an English Translation, Notes, and Indexes* (London).

24 *Dictionary of the English Language* (London 1755), preface, par. 2. When Johnson stayed with Thomas Percy in Northamptonshire from 25 June to 18 August 1764, Lye, Percy's near-neighbour, called several times. See M. Clunies Ross, 'Percy and Mallet: The Genesis of *Northern Antiquities*', in *Sagnaþing helgað Jónasi Kristjánssyni* (Reykjavík 1994), 1: 107–17, at 115.

25 *A Correspondence*, ed. Wiley, 238.

26 A number of manuscript forms appear to make no contextual sense: e.g., *brondas þencan* 'to think of flames' (Fort 43) has been variously emended to *brondas þeccan, brond aþeccan, brond aþecgan, brond aþengan*, and *brond aswencan*. Abbreviations for individual OE po-ems are those in *A Microfiche Concordance to Old English: The List of Texts and Index of Editions*, comp. Antonette diPaolo Healey and Richard L. Venezky, Publications of the Dictionary of Old English 1 (Toronto 1980).

27 *Hæleða* occurs IIIx in OE verse, Ix in OE prose. The next most frequent gen. pl. poetic noun is *fira*, which occurs 50x in OE verse, and never in prose. On Henry's artful rendition of *The Battle of Brunanburh*, s.a. 937 in his *Historia Anglorum* (ca 1125–40), see A.G. Rigg, 'Henry of Huntingdon's Metrical Experiments', *Journal of Medieval Latin* 1 (1991) 60–72. On Henry's errors of translation, see Edith Rickert, 'The Old English Offa saga, I', *Mod-ern Philology* 2 (1904) 29–76, at 65–66.

28 Christine Franzen, *The Tremulous Hand of Worcester: A Study of Old English in the Thir-teenth Century* (Oxford 1991), 119. For tremulous-hand glosses to the *Metrical Preface* and *Epilogue* to the *Pastoral Care* in CCCC 12, fols 3v–4r and 224v–225r, see *Old English Verse Texts from Many Sources: A Comprehensive Collection*, ed. Fred C. Robinson and E.G. Stanley, Early English Manuscripts in Facsimile 23 (Copenhagen 1991), items 6.1.2.1–2 and 6.2.1.1–2.

29 R.I. Page, 'Yet Another Note on Alfred's Aestel', *Leeds Studies in English* n.s. 18 (1987) 9–18, at 15.

30 E.g. *sundbuende, gebedscipe*, and *manwise*. See Albert H. Marckwardt, 'The Sources of Laurence Nowell's *Vocabularium Saxonicum*', *Studies in Philology* 45 (1948) 21–36.

31 See Mary Joan Cook, 'Developing Techniques in Anglo-Saxon Scholarship in the Seven-teenth Century: As They Appear in the *Dictionarium Saxonico-Latino-Anglicum* of Will-iam Somner' (Ph.D. diss., University of Toronto 1962), esp. 45–46 and 123–27. On Somner's use of underlinings in his copy text of the Junius II poems, see Angelika Lutz, 'Zur Entstehungsgeschichte von William Somners *Dictionarium Saxonico-Latino-Anglicum*', *Anglia* 106 (1988) 1–25, esp. 17–20.

32 Preface 'To the Reader', par. 7, in William Somner, ed., *Dictionarium Saxonico-Latino-Anglicum* (Oxford 1659). Lye also confessed his dismay at the language of Bodleian Junius II. In a letter to Lyttelton dated 9 May 1758 (BL Stowe 754, fols 16r–16v), he wrote: 'Cædmon gives me not a little trouble. There are several words to be met with in him, the precise meaning of which will be very difficult, if not impossible, to trace out.' The same letter reveals that it was Wanley's note (*Catalogue*, p. 279) pointing to an overlap between the Exeter Book *Azarias* and the Cædmon *Daniel* that first prompted Lye to locate, look at, and then borrow the former manuscript. I am again deeply grateful to Professor Clunies Ross for this reference.

33 Ch. 23 ('De poetica Anglo-Saxonica') in the *Thesaurus* (*Anglo-Saxon Grammar*), 177, 198–203.

34 Ibid., ch. 21 ('De dialecto poetica'). Hickes's study, completed ca 1697, is modelled on the

ars poetica of Snorri Sturluson, published by Peder Resen in 1665.

35 Benjamin Thorpe translated *leolc* as 'lion-like' in 1832: *Cædmon's Metrical Paraphrase of Parts of the Holy Scriptures* (London), 29. But by 1839 both Kemble and Grimm had identified the form as the reduplicative preterite of *lacan*: see *A Correspondence*, ed. Wiley, 178, 180–81.

36 Thorpe, ed., *Codex Exoniensis* (1842); Israel Gollancz, ed., *Cynewulf's 'Christ': An Eighth-Century English Epic* (London 1892); Gollancz, ed., *The Exeter Book: An Anthology of Anglo-Saxon Poetry, Part I, Poems I–VIII*, EETS 104 (London 1893).

37 Christian W.M. Grein, *Sprachschatz der angelsächsischen Dichter* (Cassel 1861–64).

38 See esp. Robinson, 'Artful Ambiguities in the Old English "Book-Moth" Riddle', in *Anglo-Saxon Poetry: Essays in Appreciation for John C. McGalliard*, ed. Lewis E. Nicholson and Dolores Warwick Frese (Notre Dame 1975), 355–62; repr. in Robinson, *The Tomb of Beowulf and Other Essays on Old English* (Oxford 1993), 98–104. The 'B' fascicle of the Toronto *Dictionary of Old English*, ed. A.C. Amos, A. diP. Healey, et al. (Toronto 1991) gives both meanings for *braegd-*, 'deceitful' and, with wordplay, 'bent'.

39 Kemble, who had an interest in paganism, took the adjective to mean 'heathen': *A Correspondence*, ed. Wiley, 34. When *eormen* is used compounded in the Exeter Book, it has a different spelling and a positive sense: *eormencynn* 'mighty race' (Fort 96). Cf. *eormengrund* 'wide world' (Beo 859).

40 2: 395.

41 'The Afterlife of Old English: A Brief History of Composition in Old English after the Close of the Anglo-Saxon Period', in Robinson, *The Tomb of Beowulf*, 274–303, at 283–85. On Wanley's handcopying of Somner, see Hetherington, *The Beginnings of Old English Lexicography*, 177.

42 Ch. 21 in the *Thesaurus* (*Anglo-Saxon Grammar*), 122, 128. In ch. 23, p. 199, Hickes translates *gamolfeax* (DEdg 26) as *canus senex* 'greyhaired oldster'. But like Somner and Wanley, he reads *deormod* 'brave' (DEdg 24) as *charissimus* 'dearest'.

43 Sfr 92. On Pound's poem, see Fred C. Robinson, '"The Might of the North": Pound's Anglo-Saxon Studies and *The Seafarer*', *The Yale Review* 71 (1982) 199–224; repr. in *The Tomb of Beowulf*, 239–58.

44 Ch. 21, p. 122.

45 John R. Clark Hall, *A Concise Anglo-Saxon Dictionary for the Use of Students* (London 1894), 4th ed. with a supplement by Herbert D. Meritt (Cambridge 1960).

46 See n. 12.

47 *The History of Rasselas, Prince of Abyssinia* (London 1759), ch. 10.

48 *An Essay of Original Genius and its Various Modes of Exertion in Philosophy and the Fine Arts, Particularly in Poetry* (London 1767), 274.

49 *The History of English Poetry from the Close of the Eleventh to the Commencement of the Eighteenth Century, to which are prefixed two dissertations* (London 1774), Diss. I, e3.

50 *Catalogus*, 281.

51 In the first half of the Exeter Book (fols 8a–65a) about twice as many pages are cited as in the second (fols 65b–130b).

52 John J. Conybeare, *Illustrations of Anglo-Saxon Poetry*, with additional notes, introductory notices, etc., by his brother William D. Conybeare (London 1826).

53 Their entry s.v. *dreng* and *daroð* is the sole indication that Hearne's edition of *Maldon* was ever consulted in the eighteenth century: Thomas Hearne, *Johannis confratris et monachi Glastoniensis chronica sive historia de rebus Glastoniensibus* (Oxford 1726), 1: xlviii–li; 2: 570–77.

54 In a letter dated 21 February 1771 to Richard Gough (Oxford, Bodleian Library, MS. Gough

gen. top. 43, fol. 21v), Manning writes: 'We are now got into Letter W of the Dictionary, and I hope shall be able to get thro' it by Midsummer at farthest'. (I am indebted once again to Professor Clunies Ross for this reference.)

55 These are: *A Proverb from Winfrid's Time* (1605), *Thureth* (1639), *Cædmon's Hymn* and four *Chronicle* poems (1643), *Durham* (1652), the scriptural poetry of Bodleian Junius 11 (1655), Boethian *Metres* (1698), *Judith* (1698), *Maxims II, Menologium, Lord's Prayer* 3, *Creed, Fragments of Psalms, Rune Poem, Finnsburh* (1703), and *Maldon* (1726). The untranslated *Finnsburh* and *Maldon* were as good as unknown. For full references, see Stanley B. Greenfield and Fred C. Robinson, *A Bibliography of Publications on Old English Literature to the End of 1972* (Toronto 1980).

56 By mistaking *seo deorce niht/won gewited* 'the dark, dusky night departs' (Phoen 98–99) as *seo deorce niht/wonge wited* 'tenebrosa nox planitie discedit', the *Dictionary* creates an additional (ghost) *wong*.

Chaucer's English Rhymes: The *Roman*, the *Romaunt*, and *The Book of the Duchess*

MARIE BORROFF

Rhyme – the repetition of the sounds of words at regular intervals – has been a distinctive feature of verse in English from the earliest times to the present. The displacement of alliteration, or initial rhyme, by rhyme in the more familiar sense, or end-rhyme, was part of the process whereby French literary culture came to dominate English culture after the Norman Conquest. But the total vocabulary of rhymes, and the range from the most obvious to the most ingenious combinations offered by the shapes and meanings of particular words, are unique to each language, and poetry in English naturally developed a tradition of its own. Chaucer, the first major English poet to use end-rhyme, was thoroughly conversant with French poetry, and, in his early writings especially, we can see the French influence interacting with the native inheritance. In this essay, I shall explore this interaction in two of Chaucer's earliest poems: his translation of *Le roman de la rose*, known as the *Romaunt*, and his first important narrative poem, *The Book of the Duchess*.

End-rhyme was evidently invented more than once.[1] It appears infrequently in classical Greek and Latin poetry but becomes common in Medieval Latin, whence it makes its way into French. We find it also as a constituent feature of poetry in two unrelated non-European languages, namely, Arabic and Chinese. In Modern English, rhyme appears everywhere and at all cultural levels: in the poems of the classical canon, in light verse, in the early babblings and traditional games of children, in proverbs, in nursery rhymes, in Cockney slang, in the nicknames of popular celebrities, on greeting cards, in the fugitive verses written for informal occasions. As one branch of what I call 'systematic sound symbolism',[2] rhyme derives its power from our counter-rational, deeply rooted sense that identities of sound imply connections among meanings and even among things. Such connections are implicit in the traditional rhymes familiar to English speakers in literary and popular poetry alike: 'kiss' and 'bliss', 'spring' and 'sing', 'moon' and 'June'. The reinforcing implications of identities of sound can also work ironically to underline oppositions or discrepancies between meanings, as in 'death' and 'breath' or 'night' and 'bright'.

The responses of individual readers to rhyme in literature will vary in depth and breadth. There is a primary pleasure associated with the 'incantatory' repetitions of the rhyming sounds themselves. We are also affected, consciously or unconsciously, by the symbolic power of rhyme in the realm of meaning. And we may find pleasures of a more sophisticated kind in the transcendence of technical difficulties, or the creative handling of a tradition.

In an important article entitled 'One Relation of Rhyme to Reason',[3] W.K. Wimsatt compared Chaucer's rhymes with those of 'the English poet whose rhyming shows perhaps the clearest contrast to [his]', namely, Alexander Pope (p. 157). Wimsatt began with some general observations about rhyme such as I have made above, noting that the repetitions of rhyme 'impose upon the logical pattern of expressed argument a kind of fixative counterpattern of alogical implication' (p. 153). It was his view that rhyming words that also exhibit 'parallels of meaning' are characteristic primarily of 'balladry and other primitive types of poetry', though he conceded that 'even in sophisticated poetry such as Tennyson's *In Memoriam* one may find some stanzas where a high degree of parallel is successful' (p. 154). Once he embarked on a detailed comparison between Chaucer's rhymes and Pope's, he clearly showed his preference for combinations in which identities of sound in pairs of rhyming words are played off against various kinds of differences between them. A rhyme like Chaucer's *resoun/condicioun*, for example, is 'dullish', in comparison with the 'quaint minor contrast in length and quality of words' in Pope's *maids/masquerades* (p. 158). Syntactic differences, such as those among the parts of speech, can also add piquancy to rhymes. Pairings like *thriftily/yemanly*, *bracer/bokeler*, and *sheene/grene* in Chaucer's portrait of the Yeoman are 'tame' because the rhyming words belong to the same part of speech; furthermore, the words linked in the first two are formed with the same suffixes (p. 160). Rhymes between nouns and verbs in Pope, such as *eyes/rise* and (*with civil*) *leer/(to) sneer*, have more 'piquancy'. When Pope does rhyme words that are grammatically alike, the pairs not infrequently present interesting formal differences, for example, that between singular and plural in the nouns *laws* and *applause* (p. 161).

Though, so far as I am aware, Wimsatt never included *Le roman de la rose* in his purview, he would surely have taken the same sort of pleasure in the rhymes of the *Roman* that he took in the rhymes of Pope. I have in mind, in particular, the rich rhymes which appear in the verse with such frequency as to constitute a conspicuous feature of its style. Before I go on to discuss some of these within the framework of Wimsatt's comparative analysis of Pope and Chaucer, I need to present and define my terms. Rhymes in French verse have been classified according to many schemes, some involving distinctions of word origin and meaning as well as of sound.[4] Mine is based entirely on degrees of phonic identity. I distinguish the following categories, in order of increasing degrees of 'richness', and decreasing frequency of occurrence, in the octosyllabic couplets of the *Roman*. I add the terms applied to them in French prosody.[5]

1. 'Simple rhymes' (*rime suffisante*) between the eighth syllables of successive lines, in which phonic identity is restricted, as is usual in English rhyming, to the vowels and the consonants that follow them. Examples: *plot* 'pleased'/*n'ot* '(there) was not' (27–28), *feirë* 'to make'/*peirë* 'pairs, sets' (61–62)[6]
2. 'Rich rhymes' (*rime riche*) between the eighth syllables of successive lines, in which phonic identity includes the consonants immediately preceding the rhyming vowels. Example: *argent* 'silver'/*gent* 'pretty' (91–92)
3. 'Double rhymes' (*rime léonine*)[7] in which a simple rhyme between the seventh syllables of successive lines is followed by a rich rhyme between the eighth syllables. Example: *romanz* 'romance'/*comanz* '(I) commence' (35–36)
4. 'Double rich rhymes' in which both the seventh and eighth syllables of successive lines rhyme richly. Example: *songier* 'dream [infin.]'/*mençongier* 'false' (3–4)
5. 'Triple rhymes', in which a simple rhyme between the sixth syllables of successive lines is followed by rich rhymes between the seventh and eighth syllables. Example: *couertëment* 'secretly'/*apertëment* 'openly' (19–20)[8]

In the two passages of the *Roman* I have tabulated, 40 out of 64 rhymes, or 63 per cent, and 20 out of 25, or 80 per cent, respectively, are rich, belonging to the second, third, fourth, and fifth of the above categories. 13 out of 64, or 20 per cent, and 6 out of 25, or 24 per cent, belong to the last three. (I have rounded off some of these percentages to two figures.) The ear of the reader familiar with the conventions of the verse is thus constantly made aware of variations among lesser and greater degrees of phonic identity in rhyming pairs. As regards meaning, form, and grammatical function, these same pairs exhibit a range between similarities of the sort Wimsatt found 'dullish' in Chaucer and differences of the sort he found 'interesting' or 'piquant' in Pope. My concern for the moment is with the differences.[9]

Linkages between words of different parts of speech are found in monosyllabic rich rhymes (category 2, above) such as *mais* 'May'/*mais* 'more' (45–46), *chantant* 'singing'/*tant* 'so much' (71–72), *atempree* 'mild'/*pree* 'meadow' (125–26), *portast* 'carried, possessed'/*tast* 'touch' (543–44), and *mignot* 'pretty'/*n'ot* 'did not have' (551–52), as well as in double rhymes (category 3), such as *aparant* 'apparent'/*garant* 'guarantee' (5–6), *forment* 'strongly, deeply'/*dormant* 'sleeping [ger.]' (25–26) and *atornee* adorned'/*iornee* 'day, day's work' (569–70). A notably ingenious double rich rhyme, involving a lexical contradiction, links *uerdure* 'greenery' with *yuer dure* 'winter lasts' (53–54). In the rhyme *die* 'should say'/*musardie* 'foolishness' (11–12), the basic grammatical disparity between verb and noun is doubly enhanced: the two words differ in length and as diction, the former being a more ordinary word, the latter more unusual and colourful. The effect is rather like that of the *maids/masquerades* rhyme cited from Pope by Wimsatt. Grammatical similarities between pairs of richly rhyming words belonging to the same part of speech are sometimes qualified, as in Pope, by minor contrasts in form or length. Thus *ganz* 'gloves' and *Ganz* 'Ghent' (563–64) differ in that the first is a common noun, the second a proper noun, while the first is plural, the second singular. The triple rhyme *ai ge fiance* 'have I trust'/*senefiance* 'significance' (15–16) links the three-syllable noun *fiance* (counting the final *e*) with a noun of five syllables.

As I have indicated above, the passages I have examined in detail also contain numerous rhymes of the sort viewed by Wimsatt as 'tame'. A large proportion of these involve simple homeoteleuton, that is, the repetition of an inflectional ending or suffix: *aloie* '(I) went'/*souloie* '(I) was accustomed' (23–24), *amee* '(to be) loved'/*clamee* '(to be) called' (43–44), *leué* '(I) rose'/*laué* '(I) washed' (89–90), *esbanoiant* 'taking my pleasure'/*costoiant* 'passing alongside' (127–28), *sauoree* 'made savoury'/*coloree* 'coloured' (535–36), *enbesoignie* '(was) busied'/*pignie* '(was) painted' (567–68). Given the technical virtuosity of the poet, and thus his presumable ability to have avoided these simplest forms of rhyme had he so wished, it seems wrongheaded to compare them invidiously with rhymes of greater elaboration, viewing them as occasional dull patches in an otherwise brilliant fabric. They ought rather to be seen as part of an array in which each element throws into relief the qualities of the others. In the art of rhyme as practised in the *Roman*, variety is of the essence in more ways than one, as we shall see. And in fact, simple linkages of form as well as sound may, when the meanings of the rhyming words are akin or antithetical, felicitously emphasize either of these relationships, as happens with *amoreus* 'amorous'/*savoureus* 'pleasing' (79–80), *frarin* 'miserable'/*serin* 'serene, enjoyable' (69–70), and the triple rhyme *couertement* 'covertly'/*apertement* 'openly' (19–20).

I cannot conclude this discussion of the *Roman* without singling out, as of particular interest, the two rhymes that occur in the first four lines of the poem. The first is a double rhyme, the second, double rich.

> Maintes genz dient que en songes
> N'a se fables non et mençonges;
> Mès l'en puet tex songes songier
> Qui ne sont mie mençongier . . . .

Many men say that there is nothing in dreams but fables and lies, but one may have dreams which are not deceitful.[10]

The phonic identity of *songes* 'dreams' with the second syllable of *mençonges* 'lies' in the first couplet 'confirms', on the level of sound, the opinion the poet is referring to: that 'dreams are lies', just as virtual phonetic identity in the Italian proverb 'Traduttore, traditore' 'confirms' the idea that translators are traitors to their texts. In the second couplet, the identity of *songier* '(to) dream' with the last two syllables of *mençongier* 'telling lies' 'contradicts' the poet's affirmation that 'one may have dreams which are not deceitful'. But these phonic identities in Old French have resulted from the fortuitous convergence of pairs of words that were once entirely distinct in sound as well as in meaning. Old French *songe* is derived from Latin *somnium* 'dream', which in turn is based on *somnus* 'sleep', whereas *mençonge* is thought to derive from an unattested popular Latin word **mentionica*, based on *mentio* 'a lie'. The rhymes thus symbolize a disparity between outward appearance (the shapes of words) and truth (the origins of words), just as a dream may seem when one experiences it to be a deceptive illusion, yet signify a truth that will emerge later: 'Qui li plusor songent de nuiz / Maintes choses couertement / Que l'en uoit puis apertement' (18–20) ('for most men at night dream many things in a hidden way which may afterward be seen openly'). In that this same distinction between surface appearance and latent meaning is basic to allegorical narrative generally, the difference between the seeming and actual relationships between the words of the two opening rhyme-pairs is profoundly relevant to the poem as a whole.

I turn now to Chaucer's use of French-style rhymes in the *Romaunt* and in his first major independent poem, *The Book of the Duchess*.[11] Anyone familiar with Chaucer's verse will know that to examine it in search of witty and ingenious linkages of meaning and form, such as enhance the verses of the *Roman*, is to place him at a disadvantage. Especially is this true for the *Romaunt*, since Chaucer's choices among words here are constrained by his line-for-line adherence to the meaning of the French original.[12] I shall make this more invidious part of my discussion as brief as possible.

Whereas rich rhymes of various kinds occur 63 per cent and 80 per cent of the time, respectively, in the two passages of the *Roman* I tabulated, the proportions of such rhymes in the corresponding passages of the *Romaunt* are a comparatively low 15 per cent and 17 per cent.[13] A number of the rich rhymes that do occur involve linkages, based directly on the French original, of words of French derivation by homeoteleuton; thus *apparaunt/warraunt* (5–6) corresponds to *aparant/garant, amorous/saverous* (83–84), to *amoreus/savoureus, pitous/delytous* (89–90), to *piteus/deliteus*, and *fasoun* 'fashion'/*resoun* (551–52), in part to *moison* 'dimension'/*reison*. Of the remaining rich rhymes, a large proportion are formed by repetition of native suffixes – most frequently of *-ly*, which sometimes, but not invariably, echoes the corresponding suffix *-ment* in the French: *covertly/openly* (19–20), *redily/erly* (93–94), *queyntely/fetisly* (569–70), *fetisly/richely* (577–78), *oonly/uncouthly* (583–84). The rich rhyme *here/here* (37–38) is a simple reiteration of word and meaning; the rhyme *also/so* (33–34) is likewise reiterative in slightly disguised form, since *also* was originally a phrase with *so* as its second element. The second syllable of the double rhyme *pleiyng/costeiyng* (133–34), corresponding to *esbanoiant/costoiant*, is a homeoteleuton in which the native ending of the participle is substituted for the French ending. Only in *seyne* 'say'/*Seyne* 'Seine' (117–18) has the translator contrived an original linkage in which phonic identity is set off by a grammatical difference (the corresponding rhyme in the *Roman* is not a rich rhyme but a simple one: *fontaine/Saine* [111–12]).

In *The Book of the Duchess* (*BD*), Chaucer is adapting materials from French poetry rather than translating line by line, and is thus presumably freer to rhyme according to his own bent. But this freedom does not result in an increase in the number of rich rhymes. The percentage for the poem as a whole is slightly over 7 per cent, about half as great as the percentages cited above from my two sample passages of the *Romaunt*. A number of the rich rhymes that appear in *BD*, like those taken directly from the original in the *Romaunt*, involve homeoteleuton, linking words of French derivation having the same suffixes, for example, *creature/portrayture* (625–26) and *suffisance/plesance* (703–04). As in the *Romaunt*, native suffixes also appear in such linkages. There are four rhymes on *-ly*, including a notable five-line sequence in which *why/comlily* (847–48) is immediately followed by *swetely, womanly, debonairly*, and *frendly* (849–52). Although I did not find it in the rhymes of my sample passages of the *Romaunt*, *-nesse* appears in four rhymes in *BD* (601–02, 607–08, 827–28, and 1155–56). Grammatical differences or differences in meaning sometimes add interest to rhymes between words of identical shape, for example, in *here* 'here'/*here* 'hear' (93–94), *countour* 'mathematician'/*countour* 'counting-house'(435–36) and *noumbre* 'to enumerate'/*noumbre* 'number' (sb.) (439–40).

To sum up what I have said so far: in the *Roman*, we find a heavy proportion of rich rhymes of various degrees of intricacy and ingenuity to simple rhymes. Though such rhymes are by no means absent from Chaucer's early verse, it does not exhibit what might be called the systematic formal variation with respect to rhyme that we find in the French poem. This comparative lack of variety manifests itself in two additional ways: there is more repetition of rhyming syllables, that is, of rhyming sounds, in Chaucer's verse than in the verse of the *Roman*, and there is more repetition of rhyming words and of particular rhyming pairs. Repetition of rhyming syllables results in part from linkages between pairs of words ending in native suffixes of frequent occurrence such as *-ly* and *-nesse*; a number of these were cited above from the *Romaunt* and *BD* as examples of Chaucerian rich rhyme. To these should be added simple rhymes in *BD*, such as *trewely/why* (33–34) and *gesse/sicknesse* (35–36), in which only one rhyming word contains the suffix in question (for additional examples with *-ly*, see lines 669–70, 721–22, 745–46, 777–78, 1047–48, 1111–12, 1151–52, 1197–98, and 1269–70; for *-nesse*, see lines 797–98 and 1059–60). The native suffix *-ing(e)* is likewise conspicuous in its frequency; it appears in the *Romaunt* in simple rhymes in lines 25–26, 75–76, 91–92, 105–06, and 133–34, as well as in the rich rhyme *pleiyng/costeiying* which was cited earlier, and in *BD*, mostly in simple rhymes, in lines 229–30, 349–50, 599–600, 605–06, 611–12, 633–34, 639–40, 761–62, 795–96, 801–02, 869–70, 959–60, 995–96, 1313–14, and 1327–28 – fifteen times in all. But repetition of rhyming syllables in English is also a function of something we do not find in French: the repeated use of sets of rhymes made up entirely or chiefly of lexical words. One such set rhymes on the *e* of *be*; its members rhyme among themselves and with a variety of words ending in a stressed *e* (spelled *-y* in modern English) corresponding to the *e* in certain French suffixes. Thus *be* rhymes with *nycete* in *Romaunt* 11–12, with *me* in 15–16, and with *she* in 45–46; *me* rhymes with *she* in 35–36, with *jolite* in 51–52, and with *se* in 121–22; *me* rhymes with *entre* 'entry' in 537–38, *see* with *she* in 549–50, and *she* with *cuntre* and *journe* in 559–60 and 579–80, respectively. The second rhyme of the *Romaunt* links *sen* and *ben*, alternative fuller forms of the infinitives of *see* and *be*; *ben* rhymes with *wren* 'cover (v.)' in 55–56, and *grenë* rhymes with the inflected infinitive *senë* in 57–58. Words rhyming in *-ight* make up another such group: *aright* rhymes with *lyght* in *Romaunt* 31–32, *ryght* with *wight* in 47–48, and *light* with *myght* in 77–78; *sightë* rhymes with *brightë* in 73–74, and *wightës* with *nyghtës* in 17–18. Among repeated pairs of words, *wel* rhymes with *del* in *Romaunt* 27–28 and with *everydell* in 125–26; *is* rhymes with *ywis* in 43–44 , 69–70, and 555–56, *faire* rhymes with *payre* in 65–66 and 107–08, and *here* rhymes with *clere* in 87–88 and 101–02. Sets of words rhyming with *se* and *bright* are similarly conspicuous in *The Book of the Duchess*, leading off with *lyght/nyght* in 1–2 and *me/be* in 9–10. Of the three rhyming pairs that repeat in the passages of the *Romaunt*, *fair/pair* and *here/ clere* do not occur in *BD*, but *wel* rhymes with (*every*)*del* a total of eleven times (221–22, 231–32, 543–44, 697–98, 845–46, 863–64, 1001–02, 1013–14, 1041–42, 1147–48, 1159–60), and *ys* rhymes with *ywys* in 657–68. Two other groups of rhyming words, ending with -*oon* (as in *oon* 'one') and with -*ought*, should also be mentioned as especially conspicuous,[14] and four pairs of rhyming words, in addition to *well* (*every*)*del*, occur with notable frequency: *slep/kep* in 5–6, 127–28, 137–38, and 223–24, along with *slepë/kepë* in 43–44; *wif/lif* in 63–64, 75–76, 85–86, 201–02, and 1037–38; *sorwe/morwe* in 99–100, 213–14, 595–96, and 1255–56, along with *a-morwe/sorwe* in 1103–04 and *morwes/sorwes* in 411–12; and, last but not least, *rowthe/trowthe* in 97–98, 465–66, 591–92, 999–1000, and 1309–10.[15]

The patterns presented by the *Roman* are quite different. The rhyming syllables that recur are almost invariably suffixes linked in both rich and simple rhymes by homeoteleuton (a group that appears in two adjacent rhymes, consisting of the words *ueille* 'wishes', *fuelle* 'foliage' [51–52], *s'orgueille* 'prides itself', and *mueille* 'moistens' [55–56] is a notable exception). Among rhyming suffixes, -*ment* appears in *couertement/apertement* (19–20), *cointement/ apertement* (559–60), and *seulement/noblement* (573–74); -*er*, the ending of the infinitive, appears in *rimeer/agaeer* (31–32), *enfiler/aler* (93–94), and *miroer/ treçoer* (557–58); the variant infinitive ending -*ier* appears in *songier*, rhyming with *mençongier* 'false' (3–4). The rhyming syllable of most frequent occurrence in the passages I examined was the suffix -*ant*, found in the present participle, the gerund, and adjectives of participial origin. It appears in *esbatant/escoutant* (99–100), *pleisant/reluisant* (117–18), and *esbanoiant/costoiant* (127–28), and is linked with words of other parts of speech in *aparant/a garant* (5–6) and *chantant/tant* (71–72). It also rhymes with -*ment* in *forment/dor- mant* (ger.) (25–26) and *dormant* (pple)/*durement* (87–88) The proportion of repeated rhyming syllables to the total number of rhyming syllables in lines 1–128 and 524–74 of the *Roman*, however, falls short of the proportion in the *Romaunt*: about 35 per cent of the couplets I tabulated in the former are repetitive in sound, versus about 62 per cent of those in the latter. More significantly, the verse of the *Roman*, in the passages I tabulated, exhibits almost no repetition among rhyme-words themselves, and no repetition at all of rhyming pairs. The sole exception I found was *apertement*, which ap- pears twice, rhyming with *couertement* in lines 19–20, and with *cointement* in 559–60 (but see n. 16, below).

The above data suggest some across-the-board generalizations concerning English and French rhyming practices. First, though rhymes on suffixes are found in English, the proportion of these to rhymes between the stems of independent words is considerably smaller in English than it is in French.[16] Second, rhyme in English is much more repetitive than it is in French with respect both to rhyming syllables and to rhyming words. Furthermore, the groups of words that rhyme repeatedly among themselves in English are linked by similarities other than sound. They are in general 'common' as diction, in that they are neither colloquial nor literary, and 'common' in their familiarity, in that they occur frequently in the language at large. With a few exceptions, such as the interjection *ywis*, they are lexical words, having referential meanings. And they are of native, rather than of French, origin. In French verse, we do not find groups of repeated rhyming words such as are ubiquitous in English.[17] We do find repeated rhyming syllables, but these are almost all suffixes attached to a variety of bases.

Thus far, I have described Chaucer's rhymes in disparaging language, speaking of their lack of variety in form, and of their repetitiousness in syllables and wording as compared with the rhymes of the *Roman*. A positive description will prove equally valid, and more illuminating. Considered in their own right, the repeated words in Chaucer's rhymes can be thought of as 'systems', formulaic in nature and, like all sets of formulas, serving the poet as a technical resource. Readers familiar with rhymed verse in Middle English will be aware that the systems to which combinations like *be* and *me* or *sight* and *bright* belong are part of an inherited tradition. The groups of common words that rhyme with each other in the *Romaunt* and *The Book of the Duchess* appear also, along with other such groups, in the poems of Chaucer's predecessors and contemporaries, not least the metrical romances whose 'rime doggerel' he deliciously satirized in *Sir Thopas*.

The rhymes of *Le roman de la rose* are equally traditional and, paradoxically, equally repetitive in their very variety of form and wording. The high proportions of rhymes of various degrees of richness, the heavy reliance on rhyming suffixes, and the ingenious ways of devising syllabic sequences of identical shape which are characteristic of the verse of Guillaume de Lorris appear also in the verse of Chrétien de Troyes, who wrote a century earlier than Guillaume, and in the verse of Machaut and Froissart, who wrote a century later.[18]

The two ways of rhyming represented by the English and French traditions might be called 'simple' and 'elaborate', respectively – or, to use more qualitative language, 'naive' and 'sophisticated'. They require different skills of the poets who practise them, and they produce different effects. In the French tradition, rhyme is literally recherché. The lack of readily available sets of simple rhyming words, the comparative intolerance of repetition,[19] the necessity of adorning passage after passage with rhymes of various degrees of richness: these aspects of the French tradition continually challenge the resourcefulness of the poet and press him towards linguistic diversity. Rhyme itself, and the techniques of rhyme, are highlighted; as a result, the reader's attention is divided, as also in the verse of Pope and his contemporaries, between the content and the surface of language. Robert Frost's observation, in 'In a Poem', that 'The sentencing goes blithely on its way, / And takes the playfully objected rhyme' seems designed to fit this kind of verse. The Middle English poet, for his part, may avail himself of the established groups of rhyming words, and, if he wishes, supplement them with similar groups of his own devising. Within the groups, he is free to repeat pairs of rhyming words that are particularly relevant to his subject-matter. The skilful poet is able to do this unobtrusively, in part by working the repeated words and rhymes into the stream of narrative or descriptive detail in such a way that their presence at each point seems natural, in part by using them for a variety of purposes and in a variety of ways: in different meanings, or collocations, or in different idioms or grammatical constructions. Effectively used, they become 'transparent'; the reader sees through the verbal surface to the meanings that help the narrative or descriptive content unfold.[20]

Each of these traditional styles has its characteristic vices. Elaborate formal linkages of the sort that enhance the elegance and wit of the verse of a Guillaume de Lorris may, when contrived by a lesser poet, seem artificial and pretentious, and the hindrances to direct statement presented by the constant need for a variety of form and wording in rhyme may retard the pace of exposition, description, or narration to the point of prolixity. In Middle English verse, the traditional words, when used again and again in the same way and for the same purpose, seem dragged in 'for the sake of the rhyme'; repetition becomes tiresome, and simplicity seems merely flatfooted. There is an additional danger for the Middle English poet in the form of an inherited body of expressions, suitable for use in rhyme, which are general and adaptable in meaning and thus can suggest themselves all too readily for use in filling out the line when inspiration flags. In the metrical romance *Sir Degravant*, for example, the expressions 'both hardy and wight', 'both squire and knight', 'to see with sight', and 'By day or/and/ne by night' recur, with a frequency that soon becomes noticeable, among an unconscionably large number of rhymes on *-ight*.[21] The more accomplished poet may draw on such phrases but, if he does so, will succeed in incorporating them inconspicuously, along with the traditional rhyming words, into the flow of language.

Although the rhymes of *The Book of the Duchess* for the most part represent the native tradition, an admixture of French-style rhymes enhances at various points the dramatic expressiveness of the poem's language. A natural starting-place for discussion is the opening passage, in which Chaucer imitates the opening of Froissart's *Le paradis d'amour*. I quote the French and English passages, with a modern translation of the French.

1   Je sui de moi en grant mervelle
        Coument tant vifs, car moult je velle,
        Et on ne poroit en vellant
        Trouver de moi plus travellant,
5   Car bien sachiés que par vellier
        Me viennent souvent travellier
        Pensees et merancolies
        Qui me sont ens ou coer liies.
        Et pas ne les puis desliier,
10   Car ne voel la belle oubliier
        Pour quelle amour en ce travel
        Je sui entrés et tant je vel.

I wonder greatly about myself, how I live so long, for I stay awake a great deal, and no one would be able to find anyone who suffers more than I do in staying awake. For know well that as a result of staying awake, thoughts and fits of melancholy often come to torment me, which are attached within me to my heart. Nor can I detach them, for I do not wish to forget the beauteous one for whose love I have entered into this torment and stay awake so much.[22]

1   I have gret wonder, be this lyght,
        How that I lyve, for day ne nyght
        I may nat slepe wel nygh noght;
        I have so many an ydel thoght
5   Purely for defaute of slep
        That, by my trouthe, I take no kep
        Of nothing, how hyt cometh or gooth,
        Ne me nys nothyng leef nor looth.
        Al is ylyche good to me –
10   Joye or sorowe, wherso hyt be –
        For I have felynge in nothyng,
        But as yt were a mased thyng,
        Alway in poynt to falle a-doun;

For sorwful ymagynacioun
15   Ys alway hooly in my mynde.

The passages well exemplify their respective traditions as regards patterns and techniques of rhyme.[23] All the rhymes in the French passage are rich; three (*vellant/travellant, vellier/travellier* and *desliier/oubliier*) are double rich. Three couplets out of the six rhyme on suffixes, and three couplets exploit identities of sound between pairs of words related to the verbs *travellier* 'suffer' and *vellier* 'stay awake'. The English passage contains one rich rhyme: *nothyng/ thyng*. All the rhyming syllables are lexical words, and the words themselves (except for *ymagynacioun*) are simple and familiar. Three out of the seven pairs of rhyming words (*lyght/nyght, noght/thoght*, and *me/be*) belong to groups that were cited earlier as frequently represented in the *Romaunt* and *BD*, while *slep/kep* was cited from *BD* as a repeatedly-used rhyming pair. The word *thing* reappears as a rhyme-word in *BD* 62, paired with *king*; this pair appears also in 83–84, 141–42, 219–20, and, in the plural, in 57–58. The words *adoun* and *doun* appear in rhyme five more times in the course of the poem (161, 348, 635, 749, and 1165), and *loothe*, in its plural inflected form, reappears as a rhyme word in line 581. *Day ne night* is a traditional phrase which lends itself to use as a 'filler' (cf. the earlier reference to *Sir Degrevant*), but here the complementary of day and night is in point.

The passage in Froissart is grave in tone, formal in style, and dignified in manner. Admittedly, it suffers in translation into English prose, but one might venture the judgment that even in the original it is a little prolix, ringing the changes on elected identities of sound to if not beyond the point of diminishing returns. The English passage, by contrast, sounds informal and unpremeditated, and the manner of speaking adopted by the Chaucerian persona is characteristically vehement and hyperbolic. (It is hard to imagine Froissart's speaker describing himself as 'a confused creature . . . always on the verge of falling down'.) The mild oath that provides Chaucer's first line with its rhyme-word is apparently drawn from the colloquial idiom.[24] Overall, the passage has in full measure the 'naive intensity' described by J.A. Burrow as characteristic of the style taken over by Chaucer from earlier English poetry, and of the style of Ricardian poetry generally.[25] The ingenuousness, spontaneity, and strong feelings of the narrator of *The Book of the Duchess*, of course, are appropriate for one destined to respond sympathetically to, and receive instruction from, a member of the nobility in the person of the Black Knight. It is interesting to note that though the speakers of both the French and the English poems have been cured of their sleeplessness, and their resultant states of disorientation and distress, by the time they begin to tell their retrospective tales, each describes his malady in the present tense, as if he were experiencing it 'now'. This being the case, Chaucer's language must be judged the more dramatically appropriate of the two.

I said earlier that the proportion of rich rhymes to the total number of rhymes in *BD* is a little over 7 per cent, considerably lower than that in my sample passages of the *Romaunt*. But this is only an average; the proportions vary significantly from part to part. In the language of the narrator, from the opening of the poem until he hears the complaint of the Black Knight (lines 1–474), 15 out of 237 couplets (not counting the anomalous though conspicuous linkage of *Morpheus* with *moo fees thus* in 265–66) rhyme richly, or about 6.7 per cent. (I omit *Riverside*'s umlaut in *feës*, since I scan the word as a monosyllable.) Shortly afterward, in the Knight's first long speech, the distribution of rich rhymes varies in an interesting way. The speech divides naturally into several sections. A description of the intensity and all-pervasiveness of his sorrow taking up almost forty lines (560–97) concludes with a promise to explain what has caused it ('Allas! and I wol tel the why' [598]). The passage that immediately follows consists of a series of variations, couched in language marked by conspicuous repetitive schemes, on the antithesis between former joy and present grief first expressed as 'My song ys turned to pleynynge' (599–619). Then comes a lengthy portrayal of the allegorical figure of 'fals Fortune' (620–51), which leads to a narrative couched in metaphorical terms drawn from the game of chess (652–86). The speech ends, as it began, with a generalized lament (687–709). Lines 560–97 contain no rich rhymes at all, but in the remainder of the speech (lines 598–709), 12 couplets out of 55 rhyme richly, or a proportion of almost 22 per cent. Within this passage, lines 615–30, which contain five rich rhymes, form an especially conspicuous sequence. Literal truth is veiled, in the language of this same passage, by a maximum of rhetorical elaboration, and it seems fitting that the rhymes too should be unusually elaborate. The proportions of rich rhymes in the Knight's three remaining long speeches are lower: about 3 per cent in lines 759–1041 (but 5 out of 13 couplets in lines 827–52), 2 per cent in 1052–1111, and 3 per cent in 1144–1297. The rhymes of the Black Knight's two 'songs', on the other hand, exemplify the native tradition at its simplest; plain rhyme-words and familiar rhyme-combinations seem designed to enhance their artful 'sincerity' of language.

Tracking the pairs of rhyming words that occur most frequently in *The Book of the Duchess*, we see that, even at this early stage of his career, Chaucer has mastered the art of repeating without repetitiousness. One and the same word is made to serve a variety of purposes, and is incorporated in a variety of constructions and phrasal combinations. *Del*, which rhymes only with *wel*, appears in the phrases 'never a del' (543, 937)' and 'a gret del' (1159), as well as in the compound formation 'everydel', which sometimes means 'entirely', as in 'I had be dolven everydel' (222), and sometimes, more literally, 'every part', as in 'Whan I had . . . overloked [the story] everydel' (231–32). In '[of trouthe] she had so moche hyr del' (1001), *del* has its full independent meaning 'share'. *Morwe*, which rhymes only with *sorwe*, means 'morning' in 'I fond hyt redy every morwe' (1256), as does *a-morwe* in 'That whan I saugh hir first a-morwe' (1103), whereas in 'And deyede within the thridde morwe' (214), it means 'day'. *Morwe* also appears in the expression 'ne nyght ne morwe' (22), which harks back to the earlier phrase 'day ne nyght' (2) and is similarly meaningful in the context of the narrative. The expression 'to meet with [i.e., to experience] sorrow' (see *meten* v. [4], sense l[b] in *MED*) is wittily invoked in a rhyme between *morwe* and *sorwe* in lines 595–97, when the Black Knight says of himself that

> whoso seeth me first on morwe
> May seyn that he hath met with sorwe,
> For y am sorwe, and sorwe ys y.

Kep, which rhymes only with *slep*, appears several times, with a variety of meanings, in the expression 'take kep'. In 'I take no kep Of nothyng' (6–7), it means 'I have no interest in anything;' in 'or she tooke kep' (128), it means 'Before she became aware [that she was falling asleep]; in 'Yif I ne had . . . take kep Of this tale' (224–25) it means 'If I had not remembered this story'. The verb *kepë*, in 'Our first mater is good to kepe' (43) means 'continue with, stick to'. The lexical and idiomatic potentialities of other repeated rhyme-words are exploited with similar resourcefulness.

Equally important for the avoidance of repetitious or monotonous effects is Chaucer's ability to incorporate frequently occurring rhyming words in passages of natural-sounding dialogue, as when Juno gives her 'messager' his instructions:

> 'Go bet', quod Juno, 'to Morpheus –
> Thou knowest hym wel, the god of slep.
> Now understond wel and tak kep!' (136–38),

or when the dreamer informs the Black Knight that the hunt for the hart has been unsuccessful:

> 'Sir', quod I, 'this game is doon.
> I holde that this hert be goon;

These huntes konne hym nowher see.'
   'Y do no fors therof', quod he;
'My thought ys theron never a del.'
   'By oure Lord', quod I, 'y trow yow wel;
Ryght so me thinketh by youre chere.' (539–45)

This last passage exemplifies, in the rhyme *del/wel*, another way of creating variety in the repetition of rhyming pairs: by separating the two members syntactically, here with a shift between speakers.

When the meanings signified by two rhyming words are of importance in the narrative, repetition may serve to bring them into prominence and, through the suggestive power of sound-symbolism, to reinforce the connections between them. The rhyme thus acquires thematic significance. This happens, in the first part of the poem, with *slep* and *kep*. The activity of sleeping signified by the former and the faculty of attention, or memory, signified by the latter, are related in several ways that bear on the action: lack of sleep results in an indifference on the part of the narrator which the stories of Ceyx and Alcyone, and of the Black Knight, effectively dispel; sleeplessness leads to reading a book; recollection of the book results in the restoration of sleep; out of sleep comes a dream worthy of being remembered. So, too, the ideas signified in the first part of the poem by the repeated rhymewords *wif* and *lif* have connections with each other and with the story; these relationships remain relevant, though the rhyming pair itself disappears, in the part of the poem concerned with the successive self-revelations of the Black Knight.[26]

The repeated rhyme-words of most profound thematic import in *The Book of the Duchess* are surely *rowthe* and *trowthe*. The compassion signified by *rowthe* is felt by the narrator in the first part of the poem for Queen Alcyone: her sorrow causes him to experience 'such pitee and such rowthe' that he continues to be afflicted by it all the following day (95–100). In the second part of the poem, the Black Knight's complaint strikes the dreamer as 'the moste pitee, the moste rowthe' that he ever heard (465–66). *Rowthe* thus means both the feeling of compassion itself and that which elicits it. In these passages, *trowthe* rhymes with *rowthe* in the colloquial expression 'by my trowthe', which adds emphasis rather than meaning to the statement in which it appears. The word's potential as a designator of the important concept of fidelity remains latent, here and in two additional occurrences of the expression (552, 591). When, however, the Black Knight, exhorting the dreamer to attend fully to the account he is about to give, says, 'Swere thy trouthe therto' (752), the meaning of *trouthe* comes to the fore. The oath is proposed in all seriousness, and the dreamer's assent to it allows him to show his own 'fidelity' as a sympathetic auditor prepared to hear the story out. Fidelity is of course pre-eminent among the virtues attributed to 'Lady White' in the story itself:

> And trewly for to speke of trouthe,
> But she had had, hyt hadde be routhe.
> Thereof she had so moche hyr del –
> And I dar seyn and swere hyt wel –
> That trouthe hymself over al and al
> Had chose hys maner principal
> In hir that was his restyng place. (999–1005)[27]

When the Black Knight completes the final phase of his account, telling of the years of happiness that he and his lady enjoyed together, the poem moves to its conclusion in several different ways. The question 'Where is she now', asked immediately by the dreamer, brings on the literal revelation that he is at last prepared to understand; the hunting of the h(e)art comes to an end as the hunter-king rides home to his 'long castle'; the surrounding dream dissolves as the clock in the castle strikes twelve; and once the narrator has told of his determination, on awakening, to 'put this sweven in ryme', the 'ryme' itself comes to its self-proclaimed conclusion: 'This was my sweven; now hit ys doon.' A single couplet, extraordinary in its rhetorical and metrical emphasis, its concentration of meaning, and its emotional charge, is pivotal:

> 'She ys ded!' 'Nay!' 'Yis, be my trouthe!'
> 'Is that youre los? Be God, hyt ys routhe!' (1309–10)

Needless to say, the familiarity of the rhyme does nothing to detract from these lines. On the contrary, this final linking of the words *trouthe* and *routhe* underscores yet again the relationship between faithfulness and compassion that is essential to the meaning of the poem. It is also a sign of something new: the simplest of English rhymes playing their part in a complex drama resonant with human reality.[28]

NOTES

1 A comprehensive essay, 'Rhyme', written mainly by T.V.F. Brogan, and including sections on definition, taxonomy, terminology, analogues, functions, language and art, data, and origin and history, as well as numerous cross-references and a large bibliography, may be found in *The New Princeton Encyclopedia of Poetry and Poetics*, ed. Alex Preminger, T.V.F.

Brogan, et al. (Princeton 1993), 1052–64. Brogan endorses the view that 'rhyme . . . is a natural linguistic structure which can arise in any language having the right set of features', and goes on to point out that 'there is considerable evidence that children manufacture rhymes spontaneously as one basic form of sound permutation; conspicuous too is rhyme in the chants and charms of many primitive cultures' (1061). However, 'it is a thundering fact that most of the world's 4000 languages lack rhyme in their poetries altogether' (ibid.).

2 See the preliminary discussion of the varieties of sound symbolism in my essay 'Sound Symbolism as Drama in the Poetry of Robert Frost', *PMLA* 107 (1992) 131–44.

3 In *The Verbal Icon: Studies in the Meaning of Poetry* (Lexington, Ky., 1954), 153–66.

4 See, e.g., the categories discussed in the opening pages of P. Rickard's 'Semantic Implications of Old French Identical Rhyme', *Neuphilologische Mitteilungen*, 66–67 (1965–66) 355–401.

5 My examples and statistics derive from a detailed study of two passages of the part written by Guillaume de Lorris: lines 1–128 and lines 524–74 (the description of Oiseuse). Citations and line numbers refer to *'The Romaunt of the Rose' and 'Le Roman de la Rose': A Parallel-Text Edition*, ed. Ronald Sutherland (Oxford 1968). I have silently deleted the parentheses and italics whereby Sutherland indicates departures from his base manuscript and expansions of scribal abbreviations. I have also consulted the text of the *Roman* as edited by Félix Lecoy, *Guillaume de Lorris et Jean de Meun, 'Le Roman de la rose'* (Paris 1965–70). For the French terminology, see Brogan, 'Rhyme', pt III, p. 1059.

6 The eighth syllable of the line may or may not be followed by a syllable containing the weakly stressed vowel which is spelled *e* and pronounced like the *a* in *tuba*, as in *peirël feirë*, above, *songësl mensongës* (1–2), and *kalandrël entendrë* (77–78).

7 The term *rime léonine* is also used in French of rhymes of types (4) and (5) in my classification.

8 The double and triple rhymes of Old French poetry differ from rhymes in English verse like *afterl laughter* and *tenderlyl slenderly*, in that such rhymes in English are almost always extrametrical, appended to the line after the final foot. Rhymes in English in which such pairs as *event* and *prevent*, or *dare to die* and *ne'er to die* are contained within the line would be close analogues, but I can think of none. If others know of them, I would be happy to have them drawn to my attention.

9 Many of the simple rhymes of the *Roman* are also 'interesting' in Wimsatt's sense. However, I shall limit my examples to the categories of more or less elaborate rich rhymes that I have identified above. I do this partly for reasons of space, partly also because the kinds of tension between phonic identity and disparities of other sorts that interested Wimsatt are obviously enhanced when phonic identity, as in rich rhyme, is more than usually conspicuous.

10 Modern translations of the *Roman* are taken from *'The Romance of the Rose' by Guillaume de Lorris and Jean de Meun*, trans. Charles Dahlberg (Hanover and London 1983).

11 There is a brief discussion of rich rhyme, called 'echo rime', in Paull F. Baum, *Chaucer's Verse* (Durham 1961), 37–38. Baum finds such rhyming 'fairly common' in Chaucer; he cites *heere* 'here'/ *heere* 'hear', from 'An ABC' 26 and 31, and *herte* 'hurt'/ *herte* 'heart' from *BD* 883–84, as chronologically early examples, and *seke* 'seek'/ *seke* 'sick' in lines 17–18 of the *General Prologue* as an especially familiar one.

12 Caroline D. Eckhardt, in 'The Art of Translation in *The Romaunt of the Rose*', *Studies in the Age of Chaucer* 6 (1984) 41–63, states that 'the most obvious quality of the *Romaunt* as a translation is certainly its very high degree of literal reproduction of its source' (46);

'overall, the primary principle of translation is that of near-minimal change' (48).

13 The lines in the *Romaunt* corresponding to those I tabulated in the *Roman* are 1–134 and 537–84. All citations from Chaucer are from *The Riverside Chaucer*, 3rd ed., ed. Larry D. Benson et al. (Boston 1987).

14 *Oon* 'one' rhymes, irregularly for Chaucer, with *doon* in 39–40, with *anoon* in 105–06 and 237–38, and with *noon* 'none' in 983–84; *goon* rhymes, again irregularly, with *doon* in 187–88 and 193–94, and with *anoon* in 355–56 and 395–96. *Ought* rhymes with *nought* in 459–60, and with *thought* in 523–24 and 537–38; *nought* rhymes with *thought* in 3–4, 503–04, 509–10, 691–92, 705–06, 789–90, 843–44, 885–86, 1109–10, 1133–34, 1149–50, and 1185–86; *thought* rhymes with *ykaught* in 837–38, and *nought* rhymes with *wrought* in 89–90, for a total of 17 occurrences.

15 Baum discusses repetitive rhyming in Chaucer on pp. 43–47. After expressing some scepticism as to the artistic merits of a series of more or less adjacent echoes in the *General Prologue*, including 'the cheap rimes in *-ly* 105–06 and 123–24', and the sequence *-lyl-lyl -yel-ye* in 761–64, he goes on to defend such repeated linkages in *The Knight's Tale* as *brother/oother, cold/old*, and *lyf/wyf* on the ground that 'that is a long poem with recurrent motifs and something now and then that savors of epic repetition' (42).

16 A spot check will serve to bear this out. Of the first 100 rhyming words in the *Roman*, 46 contain suffixes; of the first 100 in the *Romaunt*, 21; of the first 100 in *BD*, 10, including the proper name *Alcyone* (65). One reason for the difference is obvious. Although there were more suffixes in Middle English that could be stressed, and therefore could rhyme, than there are in Modern English, both native (*-ly, -ing, -ness*) and Romance (*-aunt, -oun, -ure*), there were fewer such suffixes in Middle English than in Old French. An important case in point is the ending of the infinitive, which in Middle English was an unstressed - *e(n)*. In Old French, the corresponding ending *-(i)er* of most verbs could appear in rhyming position as the eighth syllable of the line; virtually any infinitive could thus rhyme with any other. Chaucer's notorious reference, at the end of 'The Complaint of Venus', to the 'skarsete' of rhyme in English, and his difficulty in following the 'curiosite' of the French poet Oton de Grandson, whose poems he is translating, may, as the notes in *Riverside* suggest (1081), be disingenuous. But it may also refer to the lack in English of some of the suffixes found useful for rhyming purposes by the French poets. It is interesting to note, in this connection, that the original versions of two of the three 24-line ballades making up the group contain ten rhyming infinitives apiece.

17 Among the words that occur with greatest frequency in the approximately 4000 lines of de Lorris's part of the *Roman*, some do appear in rhyming position a number of times, and more than once in combination with one and the same rhyme-word, but these repetitions are distributed over a far wider compass than those I have observed in the *Romaunt* and *BD*, and are comparatively few. To refine my generalization about the comparative dearth of repetition in French, I checked twenty-five of the lexical words that appear twenty times or more in *Roman* 1–4028, as cited in appendix II, 'A Word-Frequency List, Arranged in Descending Order of Frequency', in *A Concordance to the 'Roman de la rose' of Guillaume de Lorris*, by Joseph R. Danos (Chapel Hill, N.C., 1975), 273 ff. The patterns I found most reminiscent of the English tradition were those presented by the words *faire* and *bele*. *Faire*, which occurs 75× in all, rhymes 22×, 4× with *treire*, 3× with *plere* and *contreire*, 2× with *portraire*, and *peire*, and once with eight other words. *Bele* occurs 23× in all, and rhymes 8×: 4× with *nouele* and once with four other words. More typical are the words *ioie* and *chose*: each occurs 7× out of 35 in rhyming position; *ioie* rhymes with six different words, and *chose* with five.

18 Of the first 100 couplets of Chrétien's *Yvain* and Machaut's *Le Dit dou lyon*, 42 and 58, respectively, are linked by rich rhymes (*Yvain: Le chevalier au lion*, ed. T.B.W. Reid [Manchester 1942]; *Oeuvres de Guillaume de Machaut*, ed. Ernest Hoepffner [Paris 1911], 2:159–237). For an analysis of a specimen passage of Froissart, see below. In view of these practices, Brogan's statement, in the article entitled 'Rich Rhyme' in *The New Princeton Encyclopedia of Poetry and Poetics*, that 'rich rhyme first appears in French poetry in quantity in the 15th century' (1070) stands in need of revision.

19 There is naturally a considerable amount of repetition of common suffixes, and even a certain amount of repetition of rhyming words and rhyming pairs, from poem to poem, and from poet to poet, in the body of Old French poetry as a whole, though this network of relationships lies beyond the scope of my expertise. The link between the words *songe* and *mençonge* in the *Roman's* opening rhyme, for example, occurs also in *Yvain* 171–72, and for all I know de Lorris may have taken it, consciously or unconsciously, from Chrétien. Here, as also with regard to repeated rhyme-words and rhyming pairs, my judgment is comparative, my point being that repetition is a feature – one might say an accepted convenience – of the English rhyming tradition as it is not in the French.

20 I can do no more than mention two additional aspects of Middle English rhymed verse that differentiate it from Old French verse. The first of these is the regular alternation between heavier and lighter stress in what I call 'chief' and 'intermediate' syllables, meaning by the former the even-numbered, and by the latter the odd-numbered syllables of the eight-syllable line. The second is the linking of stressed chief syllables by alliteration. Lines in *BD* like 'My wyndowes werë shette echon, / And throgh the glas the sonnë shon / Upon my bed with bryghtë bemës, / With many gladë gildë stremës' (336–38) and 'My lyf, my lustës, be me loothë / For al welfare and I be wroothë' (581–82) display Chaucer's command of a repertoire not only of rhymes, but of cadences of rhythm and sound, that are quintessentially English.

21 Twenty-three words rhyme on *-ight* in the first 100 lines of *Degravant*, and the disproportion continues throughout. For the expressions cited, see lines 11, 24, 28, 102, 198, 235, etc. (*The Romance of Sir Degrevant: A Parallel-Text Edition from MSS. Lincoln Cathedral A.5.2 and Cambridge University Ff. I.6*, ed. L.F. Casson, EETS 221 [London 1949]).

22 I am indebted to Professor Daniel Poirion for help in this part of my essay.

23 See the comparative observations on the two passages in Derek Brewer's essay, 'The Relationship of Chaucer to the English and European Traditions', in *Chaucer and Chaucerians: Critical Studies in Middle English Literature*, ed. Brewer (University, Ala., 1966), 1–38, at 2–3. Brewer's account of the blending of native and continental sources in the formation of the style of Chaucer's verse applies, on a smaller scale, to my account of his rhyming in the *Romaunt* and *BD*: 'In respect of language, therefore, Chaucer grafts on to his basic English style, found in the romances, a new diction, more elaborate, learned and formal, though also colloquial. This new diction signalises Chaucer's progressive immersion in European literary culture, first in the poetry of the leading poet of his day, Machaut, and in the dominant poetic influence of his day, *Le Roman de la Rose*' (27).

24 Brewer analyses 'be this lyght' as a cross between 'by my truth' and 'on a day', and goes on to make the following interesting observations: 'It looks commonplace enough, but the earliest quotation in the *NED* is from an interlude of 1510 . . . The later quotations of *by this light* are from colloquial contexts, and this example . . . suggests that Chaucer was more colloquial on occasion than even his earliest masters, the romance-writers' (6). A citation from *Firumbras* which perhaps antedates Chaucer's use of the expression was published after the appearance of Brewer's essay, in *MED*; significantly, it occurs in dialogue

(s.v. *light* n. sense 1b[c]). The wording of the oath may in fact have some relevance to the poem and its bookish narrator, since light in Chaucer is associated with the activity of reading (cf. *The Parliament of Fowls* 85–87: 'The day gan faylen, and the derke nyght, / That reveth bestes from here besynesse, / Berafte me my bok for lak of lyght').

25 See ch. 1, 'Ricardian Style', of *Ricardian Poetry: Chaucer, Gower, Langland, and the Gawain Poet* (New Haven 1971), esp. 16–18. Burrow observes that Chaucer accommodated 'a rather limited and fundamentally simple inherited idiom to more complex and sophisticated purposes' (18). Cf. Eckhardt's description of 'patterns of departure from the original *Roman* [in the *Romaunt*]', including 'the expansion that leads to an informality of tone' and 'the deviations from *courtoisie* toward colloquialism', that 'tend to impart to the *Romaunt* a fresh new narrative voice'. Eckhardt cautions, however, against 'overestimat[ing] the extent to which the mature Chaucerian voice is present in . . . a rather early literary effort' (60–61).

26 Baum's discussion of 'recurrent motifs' expressed by rhymes such as *brother/oother* in *The Knight's Tale* is referred to in n. 11, above. Baum remarks on 'the continual repetition of *Troye/joie* [in *Troilus and Criseyde*] – thirty times, beginning in the very first stanza and running like a pedal point throughout the poem', and notes that the same rhyme also appears three times in *BD*, and elsewhere in Chaucer (46–47 and n. 4).

27 *Trouthe/routhe* is also a thematic rhyme in *Troilus and Criseide*, where it occurs 17x (not counting one instance of *untrowthe/rowthe*). There, its meaning is somewhat different, since *rowthe* comes to signify 'compassion' in the specific, indeed almost technical sense of Criseide's willingness to accept Troilus as her lover. This latter idea is expressed in *BD* by the word *merci* ('My lady yaf me al hooly / The noble yifte of hir mercy' [1269–70]). The relationship between 'fidelity' and 'mercy' in *Troilus* is definitively expressed by Criseide in bk 4, when she tells Troilus that 'moral vertu, grounded upon trouthe – That was the cause I first hadde on yow routhe!' (1672–73).

28 I have arrived, by a different route, at an account of Chaucer's rhymes having many affinities with that presented by Charles A. Owen, Jr, in his comprehensive and insightful essay, 'Thy Drasty Rymyng . . .', *Studies in Philology* 63 (1966) 533–64. Owen says of rhyme in *Troilus and Criseide* that 'it both surprises and delights us to find seemingly natural speech falling into measures of rhythm and rhyme' (545). Rhyme 'has been given a structural as well as a decorative role [in *Troilus*] . . . It reinforces the meaning. It remains for the most part unobtrusive' (554). In general, Chaucer 'subordinated rhyme, . . . eschewing the more difficult and self-conscious exercises so dear to his French contemporaries. The result was a freeing of the sound pattern to . . . support . . . the interest in human personality as it revealed itself in speech, characteristic of his poetry' (563–64). For Owen's observations on repetitiveness in Chaucer's rhymes, see pp. 538 (*Anelida and Arcite*, 'The Complaint unto Pity', and 'The Complaint of Mars') and 542 (Sir Topas). 'Thematic emphasis' in the repeated rhyme *freres/preyeres* in *The Summoner's Tale* is discussed on pp. 561–62.

Seeking 'Goddes Pryvetee': Sodomy, Quitting, and Desire in *The Miller's Tale*

DAVID LORENZO BOYD

In the Middle Ages, as Eugene Vance has elegantly stated, 'thinkers were agile in their applications of sodomy as a metaphor.'[1] For example, simony, writing in a foreign language, and misusing money were all figuratively described as sodomy. Obversely, sodomy was metaphorized by Alan of Lille into the misuse of grammar – a solecism – or the misreading/misinterpreting of what was a proper 'anvil' for one's 'hammer'.[2] The key here, of course, is that sodomy represents misuse, misappropriation (generally for selfish ends), or even misinterpretation itself, and Alan of Lille effectively attempts to control certain inappropriate behaviours by marginalizing them through sodomitical discourse.

Written sometime in the late 1380s or early 1390s as part of the *Canterbury Tales* compilation, Chaucer's *Miller's Tale* is a case in point. In this bawdy fabliau – concerning the adventures of a student (Nicholas) and a parish clerk (Absolon) who both attempt to win the sexual favours of a young wife (Alisoun) married to an old churlish carpenter (John) – sodomy as both figure and fact travels through the normative discourses of the body, social class, and religious authority while it produces, challenges, (mis)reads, and even perverts the hegemonic junction(s) through which these discourses are sustained. This might come as a surprise to many readers. Though some scholars have gingerly prodded various aspects of the issue (and certainly not in any depth), the fact that much of the *Miller's Tale* concerns sodomy remains practically unprobed.[3] But not only were two of the major motifs constituting the fabliau – the misdirected kiss and the flood – associated with sodomy: the story's climax, Absolon's movement to shove a hot coulter [ploughshare blade] up Nicholas's ass, which he has mistaken for Alisoun's 'hole', also has an unmistakably homoerotic and sodomitical ring – much as it does in other fabliaux employing the same motif.

As I hope to demonstrate below, this literal employment of sodomy somatically figures larger social, religious, and *interpretive* issues that the Miller also addresses. The *Miller's Tale* ultimately employs sodomy as a complex discursive strategy – a double move reinforcing, on one hand, the traditional heteronormative positioning of the male body as impenetrable while, on the other, decrying the traditional system of class and religious dominance, oppression, and control that marked the Middle Ages – and through which the male body's terrain was ideologically marked.[4] In order for this double move to succeed, the Miller skilfully associates, both in prologue and tale, this use of sodomy with ideas of misinterpretation, (mis)taking, or (mis)reading.[5] Hence, the idea that improper social, somatic, and spiritual interpretive practices can lead to sodomitical behaviour becomes a powerful and satirical trope for social control.

SODOMIZING GOD, QUITTING, AND SOCIAL CONTROL

Robyn the Miller sets the stage for his complex use of sodomy in his prologue. After the Knight finishes telling a philosophical romance whose sociopolitical function is to preserve unquestioningly the traditional status quo of aristocratic rule,[6] the Miller insists upon delivering a different kind of noble story. The ostensible purpose of this religiously allusioned fabliau, a 'legende and a lyf / Bothe of a carpenter and of his wyf' – and of a student, a clerk, who adulterously 'hath set the wrightes cappe' – is, in accord with the agreement set upon at the Tabard Inn, to requite the nobleman's tale and to win a free supper upon returning from Canterbury.[7] But the tale's actual purpose goes beyond such a limited goal. Not only a discursive challenge to the Knight, who represents the ruling class, but also a professional and possibly personal affront to Oswald the Reeve, a carpenter by profession who objects strenuously to such an adulterous ditty, the tale also exploits the fine tension between medieval sexual and religious representations

This exploitation occurs not just in the adulterous sexualization of the allusions to the Holy Family, but in the Miller's ability to control both objections to, and interpretations of, his story's larger significance. To answer the Reeve's objection that the *fabula* will unnecessarily defame husbands and wives, Robyn employs a sexual/religious strategy whose implications use sodomy to silence effectively the Reeve and to control the latter's objections. Defending his stand on adulterous women, Robyn proclaims to Oswald (and, we may assume, to all those around):

Why artow angry with my tale now?
I have a wyf, pardee, as wel as thow;

Yet nolde I, for the oxen in my plogh,
Take upon me moore than ynough,
As demen of myself that I were oon;
I wol bileve wel that I am noon.
An housbande shal nat been inquisitif
Of Goddes pryvetee, nor of his wyf.
So he may fynde Goddes foyson there,
Of the remenant nedeth nat enquere. (I. 3157–66)

The Miller's defence argues that a husband, as long as he receives his 'due', should not ask for trouble by inquiring too deeply into his wife's private (sexual) affairs: in other words, he should assume her innocence for fear of discovering her guilt. But 'pryvetee' is an enticing double entendre, meaning both 'private affairs' and 'private parts', and, as such, suggests a powerful relationship between sexuality and the probing attempts to penetrate another's secret (p)arts.[9]

Most remarkable about this analogy, however, is its founding on notions of God's 'pryvetee' (in both senses). In constructing the juxtaposition of the secular/sexual to the spiritual, Robyn's extension in effect also advises that one not meddle into God's private affairs/private parts – to let the Mysteries, and the 'mystery' of God's organs and orifices, remain mysterious – lest one discovers what one should not (and cannot) know. This point, as Laura Kendrick has noted, undoubtedly perplexes many teachers of Chaucer, who would like to (or do) gloss over it.[10] Though Kendrick, as did I even before reading her stimulating *Chaucerian Play*, ultimately realizes the importance of focusing on this issue, she reads the passage as part of a central notion of subversion and social control of meaning in the *Canterbury Tales*: reading from 'obscene signs' to higher meanings versus, in her words, 'a materialistic parody or burlesque misappropriation of sacred signs aimed at rerooting them in the body, in the flesh.'[11]

I agree with Kendrick that the comedy of this analogy ultimately stems from issues of control and licence (and interpretive ones at that), but more than a joke about God's genitals underwrites this passage. Since sodomy in the Middle Ages concerns the improper sexual use or manipulation (probing or prying, if you will) of genitalia or orifices of one person by another (particularly persons of the same sex), the Miller's proposition compares meddling husbands to men attempting sodomy with none other than God! This strategy marks a clever move by the Miller, for it allows him to enlist sodomy to control the responses of those around him and to interpret their actions (though, as Kendrick has correctly pointed out, he carnivalesquely challenges in the process transcendent reading practices). Hence sodomy becomes not simply a subversive challenge to interpretive practice but a trope through which other discourses – including that of professional rivalry – can be easily manipulated or silenced. How could the Reeve possibly object further after the Miller has located his protestations within such a risky sodomitical context?

Since sodomy served in such a flexible capacity, it could easily have served the Miller's purpose in controlling the Reeve's objections. That the object of sodomy in the allusion was none other than God himself could only have heightened the effect. Other medieval examples of this move exist and provide an interesting context for Robyn's tactic. In the *Liber Gomorrhianus*, for example, we find that Peter Damian also employs the idea of sodomizing God not only to represent the men of Sodom and Gomorrah's attempt to 'know' the two angels visiting Lot as even more reprehensible than typically interpreted – 'Constat autem, quia per illos duos angelos, qui ad B. Loth venisse leguntur, persona Patris, et filii non incongrue designatur' (165.B.) – but also to describe sodomites who attain holy office or holy orders and thus attempt to enter wrongly into mysteries of God. Damian, however, by referring to Paul's discussion of homosexual activity in the context of the Sodom and Gomorrah story, expands the metaphor to include other unworthies who attempt to gain 'access' to God as well – unworthies who pry into God's 'pryvetee':

Sodomitae ergo ad angelos conantur violenter irrumpere, cum immundi homines ad Deum tentant per sacri ordinis officia propinquare. Sed hi profecto caecitate percutiuntur, quia justo Dei judicio in tenebras interiores cadunt; ita ut nec ostium invenire praevaleant, quia a Deo peccando divisi, unde ad eum revertuntur ignorant. Qui enim non per humilitatis, sed per arrogantiae, et tumoris anfractus ad Deum accedere gestiunt, patet profecto, quia unde ingressionis aditus pateat non agnoscunt; vel etiam quia ostium Christus est, sicut ipse dicit: ⟨Ego sum ostium⟩. . . . Quod ergo illic dicitur: ⟨Percusserunt eos qui foris erant caecitate;⟩ hoc Apostolus manifeste declarat, cum dicit: ⟨Tradidit eos Deus in reprobum sensum;⟩ et quod illic subjungitur: ⟨Ut ostium invenire non possent;⟩ hoc etiam patenter exponit, cum ait; ⟨Ut faciant quae non conveniunt.⟩ *Ac si diceret: ut intrare tentent, unde non debent.*

[So Sodomites try to break in violently on the angels when unclean men attempt to approach God through the offices of sacred orders. But these latter are surely struck with blindness because they fall into such interior darkness through a just judgment of God that they are powerless to find the door. Divided from God by sin, they do not know how to return to home from that condition. For it is obvious that those who desire to approach God by the routes of arrogance and pride and not by the route of humility do not recognize where the entrance is, or that the door is Christ, as he himself says, 'I am the door' . . . So what is said there, 'They struck the man at the entrance with blindness', the Apostle clearly declares when he says, 'God delivered them up to their own depraved sense'. And what is added there, 'That they were unable to find the doorway', he also clearly expresses when he says, 'to do what is unseemly'. *This is as if he were to have said that they try to enter where they ought not.*][12]

Along with its provocative effectiveness in using the 'horror' of sodomizing God as a means to prevent sodomites from entering into holy office, the phrase 'to enter where they ought not' emphasizes a figurative turn whose imperative shares much with that of the Miller. Certainly Robyn in his tale does not attempt such a grand exegetical statement with his own notion of prying simply to imply that the Reeve is a sinner. Rather, much as he takes the rather serious religious figures, allusion, and exegetical techniques of official Church culture and puts them to carnivalesque, secular use, so too does the Miller use the troping of sodomy as a reductive enterprise – to dominate a personal rival. For both Damian and Robyn, sodomy becomes a powerfully disempowering trope.

But it is also likely that secularizing this perverse religious trope masks a larger motive of domination, or at least rebellious protest, as well. If we recall the sequencing of the *Miller's Tale* as following that of the Knight, the warning against prying into God's 'pryvetee' suggests a much broader sociopolitical context, one that accords well with the Miller's plan to 'quite' the tale of this nobleman. Though set in the pre-Christian, classical past (even if concerned with late medieval internecine warfare, chivalric conquests, and courtly love), the *Knight's Tale* concerns the rivalry of two Theban cousins, Palamon and Arcite, for the love of Emily, sister-in-law of their enemy Theseus, ruler of Athens. In keeping with the poem's thinly veiled political subtext clearly supporting aristocratic ideology, Theseus as ruler is represented as 'knowing best' exactly how the social order should be structured and ruled. Therefore he enlists to his advantage the knowledge he claims to have (and, judging from the information given to the reader about the celestial realm, has correctly) about another kind of heavenly 'pryvetee': the workings of the 'Firste Moevere' [First Mover] (I. 2986). In fact, throughout the story the Knight himself takes great pains to describe and explain the workings of the gods, details that were for the most part *inaccessible* to sublunary beings (as well as to most characters in the tale). These inaccessible workings, however, are ultimately employed by Theseus as he seeks to justify his attempts to forge a political alliance between Thebes and Athens. And his celestial explanation for this alliance, interestingly enough, specifies that each person accept his or her fate.

> Thanne is it wysdom, as it thynketh me,
> To maken vertu of necessitee,
> And take it weel that we may nat eschue,
> And namely that to us alle is due.
> And whoso gruccheth ought, he dooth folye,
> And rebel is to hym that al may gye. (I. 3041–46)

In that the intention is to squash rebellion and maintain the status quo, sentiments such as these effectively participate in a dynamic network of social control.

By recasting such knowledge of the supernatural realm's workings in sodomitical terms, however, the Miller subtly shifts the significance of this passage from a description of an oppressive, hegemonic social control to a satirical critique of that control itself (a critique which none the less functions as social control as well). For through the insistent juxtaposition of his tale to the Knight's – a juxtaposition that forces a retrospective rereading of the noble's ideological project – Robyn slyly hints that the Knight, by representing and divulging through Theseus the private workings of the Prime Mover and the gods for his own present-day (class) interests, commits what is, through analogy at least, an act tantamount to figurative sodomy. The Miller's subtle suggestion is even more poignant when we recall that sodomy is frequently a metaphor for misuse: here, both Theseus within the story and the Knight without, for each 'misuses' as he represents 'inaccessible' information. If it is indeed the Miller's intention to 'quite' the Knight, to subvert his tale and social vision with another one, Robyn, by implying that the Knight's discourse and privileged position is posited on God's (or the gods') 'pryvetee', is well on his way. Further, by illustrating the way that sodomy – or, more specifically, constructing an action as sodomitical – can function as a derisive tool for social control in varying discursive schemes, he sets the stage for other sodomitical readings his story will propose as it attempts to protest the penetrating control not only of the aristocracy, but also of the Church over the social body.

SODOMY, MISINTERPRETATION, AND PUNISHMENT

The relationships among interpretation, sodomy, and social control the Miller so cleverly sets up in the prologue initiates the defining principle through which the events of the tale proper occur. In fact, sodomy characterizes not only the punishment for misreading or misinterpreting bodies, but also the queering 'rewards' of those who would misuse their position or interpretive abilities for their private gain: specifically, the clerks Absolon and Nicholas. I want to examine the text's two explicitly sodomitical scenes (and the corresponding wealth of negative associations) connected to these young men as a means to understand the regulatory function that such connections might perform. For Absolon, as Kara Donaldson has pointed out, Alisoun's body is a text that he can interpret and gloss.[13] But his interpretation is a gross misreading which leads to a queer, though unintentional, misuse of orifices, for the duped Absolon mistakes Alisoun's nether region for her mouth, substituting an improper orifice for a proper one. This scene, played out to full comic effect, highlights the young parish clerk's transition from an ignorant participant in a perverse act to a man for whom sodomy functions to inhibit his future adulterous behaviour. His mistake, in fact, becomes a punishment for his transgressive desires as he experiences the anxiety of encountering a 'beard'.

In order to have sex with Alisoun, Nicholas, by telling John that the Flood will reoccur, has duped the 'gnof' (I. 3188) into hanging three tubs from the ceiling so that each of them will survive. Once in the tubs, however, Alisoun and Nicholas climb down while John sleeps and 'Withouten wordes mo they goon to bedde' (I. 3650). But as they engage in sex, Absolon comes to the bedroom window and, attempting to woo the young girl into adultery as well, finally wins the favour of kissing her through the bedroom window. But, as he kneels in front of this window and eagerly anticipates his reward, Absolon's desires are met with an unexpected surprise from Alisoun:

> Derk was the nyght as pich, or as the cole,
> And at the wyndow out she putte hir hole,
> And Absolon, hym fil no bet ne wers,
> But with his mouth he kiste hir naked ers
> Ful savourly, er he were war of this.
> Abak he stirte, and thoughte it was amys,
> For wel he wiste a woman hath no berd.
> He felte a thyng al rough and long yherd,
> And seyde, 'Fy! allas! what have I do?
> 'Tehee!' quod she, and clapte the wyndow to
> And Absolon gooth forth a sory pas. (I. 3731–41)

For the medieval reader, at least, the answer to Absolon's question is an obvious one. Having kissed Alisoun's ass, and possibly vagina as well,[14] he has, however unintentionally, misread her body and committed sodomy, for both anal/oral and anal/vaginal contact fall into the medieval sodomitical sphere. His adulterous behaviour, and his desire to sin even further, do not yield physical gratification but lead to a greater sin through which his anticipated pleasure has been all but destroyed.[15] In other words, Absolon's punishment for his misreading has been the act of misreading itself. While this mistaken substitution of the anal and/or vaginal orifice for an oral one is meant as a punishment, though a humorous one, both the humor and the punishment once again depend on an understanding of sodomy as a perversion of normative sexual activity – particularly of the anus as a site of disgust and filth. That such transgressive humour depends on this tacit cultural understanding receives added emphasis through the subsequent narrative, when Absolon, after kissing the transgressive hole(s), attempts to erase the evidence of his mistake, to clean his mouth with every substance available to him: 'With dust, with sond, with straw, with clooth, with chippes' (I. 3748).

Two other bits of transgressive *energia* inherent in Alisoun's joke resonate within the passage's sodomitical register as well. The first, a continuation of the religious subtext infusing the tale, draws on the connection between Absolon's kiss and his subsequent threat to bequeath his soul unto Satan if he 'were levere than al this toun . . . / Of this despite awroken for to be' (I. 3751–52). The kiss itself, a thinly veiled parody of the Visitation of the Holy Spirit or of Christ and his Bride (*sponsus* to the *sponsa*), supplies the satanic reference with an added bite: anilingual activity, sometimes followed by same-sex anal or oral intercourse, was frequently thought to precede one's admission either to a satanic order or to a pact with the devil.[16] The second, as Elaine Hansen has pointed out, concerns Absolon's emphasis on a woman's beardlessness, indicating that his first fear is that he has kissed 'ful savourly' someone who can indeed have a beard – a man.[17] Such fear of homoeroticism – perhaps today we call it medieval homosexual panic – does not appear in any of the tale's analogues, where the active kisser typically assumes that the ass kissed is that of the wife.[18] Here, however, the clever and rich use of the 'beard' ('male beard' or 'joke') gains added significance, especially since Absolon is represented as effeminate and squeamish about things anal.[19]

In fact, both Alisoun's potentially masculinizing, gender/orifice-confusing beard and Absolon's need to punish her for the transgressive kiss precipitates his making, however unwittingly, a homoerotic object-choice through a *heterosexual* one.[20] While Absolon's first misinterpretation leads to heterosexual sodomy, his second one leads to a symbolic homosexual union. The passive recipient is not Alisoun, however, but her lover Nicholas, who, through symbolically being penetrated anally, is also punished for his adultery, overweening pride, and wilful misinterpretation of signs to John – i.e., that another Flood is coming.[21] After his misdirected kiss, Absolon leaves the carpenter's house, and later, having plotted a scalding revenge, returns to the bedroom window with the hot 'kultour'. Standing underneath the window, he asks for yet another kiss. This time, however, his need to vindicate his misreading of Alisoun's orifices results in another misreading, when Nicholas attempts to repeat Alisoun's joke:

> This Nicholas was risen for to pisse,
> And thoughte he wolde amenden al the jape
> He sholde kisse his ers er that he scape.
> And up the wyndowe dide he hastily,
> And out his ers he putteth pryvely
> Over the buttok, to the haunche-bon;
> And therwith spak this clerk, this Absolon,
> 'Spek, sweete bryd, I noot nat where thou art.'
> This Nicholas anon let fle a fart
> As greet as it had been a thonder-dent,
> That with the strook he was almost yblent;
> And he was redy with his iren hoot,
> And Nicholas amydde the ers he smoot. (I. 3798–3810)

Nicholas's joke should be on Absolon, who instead of confusing a woman's mouth with her 'privy' parts confuses male and female orifices. But this act, a typical fabliauesque technique of disempowerment and submission, reaches in both directions when the hot blade makes contact with Nicholas's ass. Nicholas has been overly proud of his ability to dupe others, to gain control over their activities. Now he passively 'suffers' being duped himself.

While, unlike many of the analogues where the blade (sometimes a hot poker as well, but always phallic) actually seems to pierce the male's exposed ass, here only scalding occurs, but the action is none the less symbolically that of sodomy, especially in light of the widespread rumours of Edward II's death through anal penetration with a hot poker.[22] The use of the ploughshare heightens this queer valence. Ploughing infertile fields is, for example, the *Roman de la Rose*'s trope for homosexual sodomy:

> Cil que si leur pechiez enfume,
> Par leur orgueill qui les desroi,
> Qu'il despisent la droite roie
> Dou champ bel et plenteüreus,

Et vont comme maleüreus
Arer en la terre deserte
Ou leur semence vait a perte,
Ne ja n'i tendront droite rue,
Ainz vont bestorant la charue
Et confirment leur regles males
Par excepcions anormales,
Quand orpheüs veulent ensivre
Qui ne set arer ne escrivre
Ne forgier en la droite forge
 – Penduz soit il parmi la gorge!

[But those who with their stylets scorn to write
Upon the precious tablets delicate
By means of which all mortals come to life,
Which Nature never lent us for disuse
But rather that we all should scriveners
Become, since each of us his livelihood
Gains in this way – yes, every he and she –
And those who two strong hammers have been lent
But will not as they should use them to forge
Upon the proper anvil properly –
And those who are so blinded by their sins
Or by the pride by which they are deranged
That they despise the furrow, fair and straight
Amidst the blooming and luxuriant field,
And to the proper roadway never keep
But go like wretches to the desert wastes
Where they misuse their plows and lose their seed
And prove their evil rules no other way
Than by exceptions most anomalous
When they desire to follow and observe
The example set by Orpheus, who scorned
To write on tablets, plow a furrow, forge –
May all such men be hanged up by the neck!][23]

While the *Roman*'s ploughing denigrates the active partner (he who ploughs), the passive participant is even more reviled in medieval culture, for he is made effeminate – acts *ut muliere*. Nicholas, to put it literally, gets ploughed. Since being penetrated by another man constituted the ultimate act of male degradation, resulting in the loss of masculinity (which Nicholas, of course, attempts to affirm through his encounter with Alisoun), Nicholas therefore becomes feminized by the already effeminate Absolon! He has misread the situation with his clerkly rival, also a misreader, and, because of this misreading, he is now 'scalded in the towte'.

But another aspect of Nicholas's punishment for misinterpretation deserves mention as well: his prediction of a second Great Deluge. Since Nicholas duped John by claiming that another Flood was planned for the earth and he subsequently profited sexually from the effects of this announcement, the text also reenacts on him the Flood's cause. When Nicholas, at the moment of his anal surprise, cries out for water and thus brings the two seemingly different motifs of the Flood and the scalding together, the text invokes through this convergence the medieval belief that the cause of the Great Deluge was sodomy.[24] In the poem *Cleanness*, written by the Gawain-poet at the end of the fourteenth century, human sodomy, both heterosexual and homosexual, encourages devils to mate with the daughters of the earth:

> Þer watz no law to hem lay hot loke to kynde,
> And kepe to hit, and alle hit cors clanly fulfylle.
> And þenne founden þay fylþe in fleschlych dedeȝ,
> And controeued agayn kynde contraré werkes,
> And vsed hem vnþhryftyly vchon on oþer,
> And als with oþer, wylsfully, upon a wrange wyse:
> So ferl fowled her flesch þat þe fende loked
> flow þe deȝter of þe douþe wern derelych fayre,
> And fallen in felaȝschyp with hem on folken wyse,
> And engendered on hem jeauntez with her japen ille.[25]

In a similar manner, Nicholas has misused his wisdom and pays the price for his perverse use of learning and interpretive skills. Absolon's clever retribution not only punishes Nicholas but further casts the parish clerk negatively. Subtly collocated with the parody of the Bride's visit to the Bridegroom in the bedroom window scenes, the suggestion of sodomy in the context of the Flood deftly queers metaphysical/physical union: the conversion conflates the image of Bridegroom with that of a fiend (recall Absolon's oath) 'mating' with a feminized, disempowered man. God's 'pryvetee' is strikingly invoked as sodomy becomes a punishment for inappropriate activity – just as it is a punishable activity in itself.

These scenes reflect a close connection among sodomy, misinterpretation, and disempowerment; in terms of this connection, they use sodomy to

254 David Lorenzo Boyd

produce a heteronormative subject – but a subject whose heteronormatively constructed behaviour does not disobey specific patriarchal rules such as the inaccessibility of another man's wife. Hence, inherent in these comic transgressions is another threat as well: that he who tries to disrupt the proper trafficking in women – and ignore the fact that a wife is to be the sole sexual property of the husband – will be punished and risks sins that far outweigh those of simple adultery.[26] The satanic and homosexual allusions, along with the punishment and pain of male penetration, further serve to highlight this implicit message, and the humour of the transgression itself further enforces the regulation of the proper heteronormative accessibility of married women. Likewise, the relationship between literal sodomy and sodomy as trope gains emphasis, for each controls, through warning and threat, activities that in some way endanger the entitlement of social or patriarchal benefits and gain. Sodomy in the tale supplies energy to the trope's power (and vice versa): each plays into the fear that the male body (including God's) might unwittingly be misread, that one's 'pryvetee' might be misused for non-normative gain, or that, as punishment for transgression, one might participate – as active or passive partner – in a perverse 'ploughing'.

SODOMITICAL TROPE AS SOCIAL CRITIQUE

Why would the Miller choose to connect sodomy and (mis)interpretation to clerks when his naughty tale is a political re-butt-al to the Knight's aristocratic ideology? After all, fabliaux such as 'Berenger au Long Cull' and 'Du Sot Chevalier' employ this connection in regard to knights and aristocracy, and greater use of such a context would, with some modification, have served him well. The answer apparently lies in Robyn's more generalized desire to quite not just the Knight, but all the social forces affecting his class. As Lee Patterson has pointed out in a powerful and influential reading of the tale, both the Church and the ruling classes succeeded in keeping the lower classes in their place through social, ideological, and exegetical control.[27] That the Miller would include representatives of the Church in his scalding critique of the *Knight's Tale* allows him to satirize and disempower further the hegemonic forces of peasant oppression.

To sustain such a critique, the relationship between sodomy and (mis)interpretation serves the Miller well. After John's fall from the tub, it is the clerkly class that supports Nicholas's and Alisoun's explanation of prior events and that thus succeeds in assuring that John will be read as an ignorant, mad fool:[28]

The folk gan laughen at his fantasye;
And turned al his harm into a jape.
For what so that this carpenter answerde,
It was for noght; no man his reson herde.
With othes grete he was so sworn adoun
That he was holde wood in al the toun;
For every clerk anonright heeld with oother.
They sayde, 'The man is wood, my leeve brother' (I. 3840–48)

John suffers – and his punishment is not just physical, but social and emotional as well. He is the *senex amans*, and, as such, is typically cuckolded and duped, but here his misery is not justly deserved, but rather is brought about through the misinterpretation of clerks – first Nicholas, and then the clerkly caste as a whole.[29] It is this oppressive clerkly power and pronouncement that the Miller ultimately critiques. Since clerkly interpretation has already proved to be inaccurate, stemming from sexual need, power politics, and misuse of God's pryvetee, then the pronouncements of this brotherhood illustrate further how wrongheaded and destructive such 'authority' can be. By casting the activities and misinterpretive foibles of Absolon and Nicholas as sodomitical, the Miller queers the pillars of class oppression in his rebellion, using against clerks a powerful trope for social control while turning their interpretive control of events against them.

But the Miller goes even further and turns the very ecclesiastical basis of peasant oppression against the Church. He does so by rewriting the materials on which such oppression was justified: Ham's sin. According to tradition, after the Flood, Noah's son Ham looked upon his father's nakedness and laughed. He was subsequently cursed and was considered by ecclesiastical authority to be the father of peasants – and the justification for their subjugation. In the *Miller's Tale*, which also involves the Flood, it is the clerk Nicholas who 'discovers' pryvetee, and the justification for oppression is reversed. As Patterson points out: 'What the Miller's Tale does, then, is to turn the myth of Ham against the clerical culture from which it originally arose. For here the searcher into hidden 'pryvetee', far from being a peasant, is instead the astrologer-cleric Nicholas, who uses illicit knowledge to mock and scorn John the Carpenter, the father Noah of the play he is staging. Moreover the characteristics that are ascribed to the biblical Ham by medieval clerical culture are here applied, with striking aptness, to Nicholas.'[30] As he examines further implications of this application, Patterson notes that 'the Miller offers a biting exercise in cultural criticism, turning the materials of clerical discourse against its proprietor and revealing by his very act of criticism how defamatory – and self-protective – are its misrepresentations.'[31]

Patterson's analysis makes sense. However, besides being constructed as the fountain of all perversions, Ham's inquiry into his father's 'pryvetee' was also interpreted, through the disseminated influence of the Jewish exegetical tradition, as signifying homosexual sodomy.[32] Since medieval clerks were frequently rumoured to practise sodomy – recall that supplying evidence for this belief probably underwrote John Rykener's implication of so many priests – the connections here between clerks and the sin of Ham forges once again the relationship between physical and figurative sodomy – a relationship already treated in detail by the Miller. Furthermore, by connecting Nicholas's misuse of 'pryvetee', first to sodomy and then to the exegetical oppression of the peasant class, back to misinterpretation of a sodomitical clergy, the Miller succeeds in constructing those very ecclesiastical forces that oppose his own caste as perverse within themselves. Both figuratively and physically, the clergy falls under suspicion as the Miller employs powerful associations to rethink both the 'superiority' of his superiors and the interpretive means through which that superiority is established.

Let us return then to the clerk's final pronouncement. By first associating clerkly misinterpretation with the sodomitical and then illustrating how the brotherhood of clerks misinterprets John's predicament – saving one of its own while reinforcing the dominant social understanding of the peasants as stupid – does not the Miller imply with this clever juxtaposition that, in a metaphorical sense at least, the Church 'sodomizes' through (mis)interpretation the lowly third estate? After all, sodomy has been employed to figure clerical abuse before: both William Peraldus and John Wyclif, for example, read simony as sodomitical. In Wyclif's *De simonia*, he states:

Sicut enim in corporali sodomia contra naturam semen perditur, ex quo individuum humani generis formaretur, sic in illa sodomia semen verbi dei deicitur, per quod in Christo Jesu spiritualis generacio crearetur. Et sicut sodomia fuit tempore legis natura contra ipsam naturam unum de peccatis gravissimis, sic symonia est tempore legis gracie contra ipsam graciam gravissimum peccatorum.

[But just as in carnal sodomy contrary to nature the seed is lost by which an individual human being would be formed, so in this sodomy the seed of God's word is cast aside with which a spiritual generation in Christ Jesus would be created. And just as sodomy in the time of the law of nature was one of the most serious sins against nature, so simony in the time of the law of grace is one of the most serious sins against grace.][33]

I am not arguing, of course, that the Miller would have been aware of a tract such as Wyclif's (though the sodomitical metaphors are not dissimilar), but rather that the clever use of sodomy within this text illustrates the way that such a figure functions within the medieval cultural register. Such a flexible trope for ecclesiastical abuse could easily be adapted to other situations like those in the *Miller's Tale* which involve the clergy as well – particularly situations when 'the seed of God's word' and clerkly pronouncement are misappropriated to anti-spiritual ends.

Furthermore, since sodomy in late medieval thought is inextricably bound up with issues of power and position – who is actively on top – the Miller's implication would deftly intertwine the somatic and figurative relationship between sodomy and social control. If the clerks' activities are sodomitical both figuratively and exegetically – we must not forget the wide use of exegetical allusions and the parodic (mis)use of the biblical and religious imagery manipulated throughout the tale – does not the text imply that their entire participation in the social scheme of things is perverse? Instead of accepting the representation of the peasants as social inferiors, the Miller attempts to reverse this hierarchization by substituting a different type of categorization – one based upon the Same/Other, Normative/Perverse binarism we have seen at work in other texts. The peasant might be an inferior, but he lives within the heteronormative sphere; members of the religious caste might be social superiors, but their physical and figurative activities relegate them at the same time to the realm of the perverse other. By equating ecclesiastical oppression with sodomy, the Miller succeeds in vindicating his own class, a class that, while it might not be perfect (witness John), does not on its own misuse and delve into God's 'pryvetee' as a perverse means of oppressing others (though, as the Miller illustrates, it can certainly turn such misuse against its oppressors).

Despite the playfulness of his tale, then, Robyn successfully addresses class injustice by associating peasant mistreatment with the queering of the dominant norm. That common people at the end of the Miller's story believe the clerks (and the story of Nicholas and Alisoun) and laugh contributes to the poem's sociopolitical imperative: by falling prey to clerkly (mis)interpretation, the people, such like John, are being duped as well.[34] From this perspective, Robyn's tale, with the abuses it illustrates, corroborates other evidence that the imperative underwriting the 1381 Peasants' Revolt, fuelled in part by a trickle-down of ideas from Wycliffite thought, was not just political, but gained some of its impetus from the desire to eliminate the abuse the Church heaped upon the peasants.[35] This gain acquires particular poignancy in the light of the clerkly misinterpretation and appropriation of 'authority' for

selfish ends throughout the tale.[36] I am therefore intrigued by the possibility
that the same cultural associations allowing Wyclif to appropriate sodomy as
a metaphor for one aspect of clerical abuse – simony – might also supply a
figurative imperative to Robyn the Miller's trope.

NOTES

1 Eugene Vance, *Mervelous Signals* (Lincoln, Nebr., 1989), 240.
2 For a general discussion, see Vance, *Mervelous Signals*, 240–42. For Alan of Lille, see *De
planctu*, met. 1. Interestingly here, Alan himself, in his grammatology of sex, describes
sodomy as a trope.
3 See, e.g., Roy Peter Clark, 'Squeamishness and Exorcism in Chaucer's *Miller's Tale*', *Thoth*
14.1 (1974) 37–43; Dolores Warwick Frese, 'The Homoerotic Underside in Chaucer's *Miller's
Tale*', *The Michigan Academician* 10 (1977) 143–50; Britton J. Harwood, 'The "Nether Ye"
and Its Antitheses: A Structuralist Reading of "The Miller's Tale"', *Annuale Mediaevale* 21
(1981) 5–30; and Elaine Tuttle Hansen, *Chaucer and the Fictions of Gender* (Berkeley 1992),
223–36. The first three studies point out some of the local significance of sodomy in the
tale. Hansen's comments on sodomy and gender instability illustrate the tale's method of
mystifying the 'feminizing' threat of the female body to men. Hence she focuses primarily
not on sodomy, but on women and misogyny. I shall draw on this criticism periodically to
develop my own, differently nuanced, reading of the *Miller's Tale*: sodomy's wider-ranging
implications for the text's sociosexual politics – especially in its relationship between the
male body and social oppression.
4 Surprisingly, even the best criticism on the *Miller's Tale* as sociopolitical critique has not
made this larger connection among sodomy, political rebellion, and the male body. See,
for example, Lee Patterson, *Chaucer and the Subject of History* (Madison, Wisc., 1991),
244–79; Peggy Knapp, *Chaucer and the Social Contest* (London 1990), 32–44; and Jon
Cook, 'Carnival and *The Canterbury Tales*: "Only equals may laugh" (Herzen)', in *Medieval Literature: Criticism, Ideology, and History*, ed. David Aers (New York 1986), 181–83.
Frese, 'Homoerotic Underside', 146, points out the connection between sodomy and clerks,
a point to which I shall return, but fails to mention the connection's political valence in
the Miller's rebellious plan.
5 On the pervasiveness of (mis)perception and (mis)interpretation in the tale, see Patrick J.
Gallacher, 'Perception and Reality in the *Miller's Tale*', *Chaucer Review* 18 (1983) 38–48;
and Laura Kendrick, *Chaucerian Play: Comedy and Control in the 'Canterbury Tales'* (Berkeley 1988), 70–73.
6 Several excellent studies have dealt with various aspects of the conservative sociopolitical
underpinnings of the *Knight's Tale* – while pointing out that the text does not present its
noble vision unproblematically. See Patterson, *Chaucer and the Subject of History*, 165–230;
Knapp, *Chaucer and the Social Contest*, 15–31; Stephen Knight, 'The Social Function of the
Middle English Romances', in *Medieval Literature*, ed. Aers, 102–10. I should point out,
however, that Knapp, 31, argues against reading the tale as a 'discourse of power'.
7 'Prologue', lines I. 3141–43. All quotations are from *The Riverside Chaucer*, ed. Larry Benson
(Boston 1987). Subsequent references are cited parenthetically in the text by fragment and
line numbers.
8 On the widely held view of the Miller's story as discursive challenge, see, for example,

Martin B. Schichtman, 'Medieval Literature and Contemporary Critical Theory: Intro-duction', *Philological Quarterly* 67 (1988) 403–07. Critical explorations of this parodic tension between sexual and sacred/typological representation in the *Miller's Tale* are far too numerous (and well known) to require a complete bibliographical citation here. For a selection of some of the more interesting (if less well known) studies, however, see Diane Whaley, 'Nowelis Flood and Other Nowels', in *Language Usage and Description: Studies Presented to N.E. Osselton on the Occasion of his Retirement* (Amsterdam 1991), 5–16; Katharina Wilson, 'Hagiographic (Dis)play: Chaucer's "The Miller's Tale"', *Auctor Ludens: Essays on Play in Literature*, ed. Gerald Guinness and Andrew Hurley (Philadelphia 1986), 37–45; Sandra Pierson Prior, 'Parodying Typology and the Mystery Plays in the Miller's Tale', *Journal of Medieval and Renaissance Studies* 16 (1986) 57–73; Thomas J. Hatton, 'Absolon, Taste, and Odor in *The Miller's Tale*', *Papers on Language and Literature* 7 (1971) 72–75; and Susanna Greer Fein, 'Why Did Absolon Put a "Trewelove" under his Tongue? Herb Paris as a Healing "Grace" in Middle English Literature', *Chaucer Review* 25 (1991) 302–17. On the possible function of religious allusions within vulgar, sexual discourse, however, see Kendrick, *Chaucerian Play*, 1–19.

9 The pun on 'pryvetee' has been treated best in Paula Neuss, 'Double Meaning: *Double entendre* in *The Miller's Tale*', *Essays in Criticism* 24 (1974) 325–40, though her readings ultimately recuperate the tale within dominant ideology.

10 Kendrick, *Chaucerian Play*, 5. On p. 6 she also summarizes the views of other critics who have mentioned this joke in their writings: Neuss, 'Double Meaning', 331; Roy Peter Clark, 'Christmas Games in Chaucer's *The Miller's Tale*', *Studies in Short Fiction* 13 (1976) 285; and Joseph Baird, 'The Devil's Privetee', *Neuphilologische Mitteilungen* 70 (1969) 104. Sur-prisingly, none of these critics, including Kendrick, fully explores the implied sodomitical allusion in this double entendre.

11 Kendrick, *Chaucerian Play*, 16.

12 See Damian's *Liber Gomorrhianus*, in *Patrologia Latina*, ed. J.-P. Migne (Paris 1844–64), 145: 153C–D. For the translation, see Peter Damian, *Book of Gomorrah: An Eleventh-Cen-tury Treatise Against Clerical Homosexual Practices*, trans. Pierre J. Payer (Waterloo, Ont., 1982); here it is quoted from an on-line copy.

13 Kara Virginia Donaldson, 'Alisoun's Language: Body, Text and Glossing in Chaucer's "The Miller's Tale"', *Philological Quarterly* 71 (1992) 139–153.

14 Hansen, *Chaucer and the Fictions of Gender*, 226–27, n. 29.

15 For the way that the kiss 'cures' Absolon, see David Williams, 'Radical Therapy in *The Miller's Tale*', *Chaucer Review* 15 (1981) 227–35; and Edward C. Schweitzer, 'The Misdi-rected Kiss and the Lover's Malady in Chaucer's *Miller's Tale*', in *Chaucer in the Eighties*, ed. Julian N. Wasserman and Robert J. Blanch (Syracuse 1986), 223–33.

16 Clark, 'Squeamishness', 41–43.

17 Hansen, *Chaucer and the Fictions of Gender*, 230.

18 For the analogues, see W.F. Bryan and Germaine Dempster, *Sources and Analogues of Chaucer's 'Canterbury Tales'* (Atlantic Highlands, N.J., 1941), 106–23.

19 On Absolon's effeminacy, see, e.g., Paul E. Beichner., 'Absolon's Hair', *Mediaeval Studies* 12 (1950) 222–33.

20 Despite readings of critics such as Hansen who attempt to emphasize Alisoun's agency in the tale as a whole – she sticks her ass out the window; Nicholas simply imitates, and attempts to better, her primary move – I do not understand either Alisoun or her hole per se as the text's primary emphasis here, but rather as a means through which a homophobically based critique – and the move from heterosexual to homosexual sodomy – can eventuate.

It is for this reason, I think, that her agency is precisely limited in the tale to exposing her own tail to Absolon. In keeping with the text's emphasis I have therefore spent little time discussing her.

21 I use the term 'symbolic penetration' here, for while the movement is that of thrust (and we can assume with a desire to castrate/penetrate), what actually occurs is a scalding of Nicholas's ass.

22 Cf. Frese, 'Homoerotic Underside', 147.

23 Guillaume de Lorris and Jean de Meun, *Le Roman de la Rose*, ed. Armand Strubel (Paris 1992), lines 19644–58. The translation is that of Harry W. Robbins in *The Romance of the Rose*, ed. Charles W. Dunn (New York 1962), ch. 91, lines 101–23.

24 See Michael W. Twomey, 'Cleanness, Peter Comestor, and the *Revelationes Sancti Methodi*', *Mediaevalia* 11 (1985) 205–17. On pp. 205–06, Twomey discusses the passage from *Cleanness* that I cite below.

25 *Cleanness*, ll. 263–72 in *The Poems of the Pearl Manuscript*, ed. Malcolm Andrew and Ronald Waldron, York Medieval Texts 2nd ser. (Berkeley 1978).

26 In fact, this is the point of many fabliaux, especially those involving priests. To put my statement in a theoretical and anthropological context, see Gayle Rubin, 'The Traffic in Women: Notes on the "Political Economy" of Sex', in *Toward an Anthropology of Women*, ed. Rayna R. Reiter (New York 1975), 157–210.

27 Patterson, *Chaucer and the Subject of History*, 244–73.

28 Cf. ibid., 270–73.

29 The critique here is geared much more towards the clerks and less towards John than Patterson suggests. M.F. Vaughn, 'Chaucer's Imaginative One-Day Flood', *Philological Quarterly* 60 (1981) 117–23, points out that John, like Nicholas, is punished because he believes himself capable of taking on biblical roles. While John is a *senex amans*, and is certainly guilty of – if nothing else – stupidity, he is none the less a product of a clerkly culture that teaches ignorant men to accept what their 'betters' tell them in this regard. See Alan J. Fletcher, 'The Faith of a Simple Man: Carpenter John's Creed in *The Miller's Tale*', *Medium Ævum* 61 (1992) 96–103.

30 Patterson, *Chaucer and the Subject of History*, 269.

31 Ibid., 270.

32 In the Jewish exegetical tradition, both the Midrashim and commentators such as Rashi interpreted Ham in these terms, as did some early Christians. Rashi circulated in Latin translations in the West after about 1250, so it is probable that the idea was well enough 'in the air' for it to serve as a subtext to the *Miller's Tale*. I would like to thank Willis Johnson (Clare College, Cambridge), Robert Rachlin (Downs, Rachlin, and Martin), and Tom Hill (Cornell) for supplying me, via the marvels of e-mail, with this information.

33 Iohannis Wyclif, *Tractatus de Simonia*, ed. Dr Herzberg-Fränkel and Michael Henry Dziewicki (London 1989), 8–9. The translation is from *On Simony*, trans. Terrence A. McVeigh (New York 1992), 36–37.

34 Patterson's argument in *Chaucer and the Subject of History*, 271–72, that the tale's ending critiques the modes through which peasant suppression was enacted, strengthens this interpretation.

35 See e.g., Rodney Hilton, *Bond Men Made Free: Medieval Peasant Movements and the English Rising of 1381* (London 1973), 50–208, passim.

36 Patterson, *Chaucer and the Subject of History*, 260–62.

Why the Monk?

SIEGFRIED WENZEL

In his portrait of the Monk (*Canterbury Tales*, I. 165–207),[1] Chaucer presents a religious who not only fails to live up to basic aspects of the monastic life as specified by the Rule, such as staying in the monastery and devoting himself to prayer and meditation ('studie . . . upon a book in cloystre alwey to poure', lines 184–85) and engaging in manual labour ('swynken with his handes, and laboure', 186), but does so consciously and with rationalization ('What should he . . . ?', 184; also 173–77, 182). He is, in other words, deliberately worldly and directs his efforts away from prayer and the liturgy to hunting and other carnal pleasures, including, if we accept the possible pun on *venerie* (166), lechery. This worldliness is further depicted in a number of images that refer to his attire, his favourite dish, his physical appearance, and the high-quality horse and greyhounds that he keeps.[2]

Yet when he is asked to give his tale, this seemingly cheerful and uninhibited hunting monk offers a rather learned definition of 'tragedy' and then launches into a series of short accounts of legendary or historical figures ranging from Lucifer and Adam to nearly contemporary fourteenth-century noblemen, all of whom fell from high estate into utter misery. This series shows no sign of ending any time soon; in fact, in introducing it the monk tells his audience he has a hundred of such tragedies in his cell and might even continue with the life of Saint Edward. This prospect surely is absolutely dreary, as is, at least for most modern readers, the style and lamentable tone of the individual pieces.[3] Why, then, does Chaucer give such a sorry and sorrowful performance to a man who is willing to abandon the ideals of his professed lifestyle and join the world in jolliness?

In attempting to resolve this seeming inconsistency between portrait and performance, critics have offered a variety of explanations. Most of these attempts rely on the view, first proposed by Kittredge, that in the *Canterbury*

Tales Chaucer assigned tales to the pilgrims in such a way that a tale would further develop or reveal its teller's character beyond the description already given in the *General Prologue*, and that the resulting storytelling creates and develops a drama along the highway to Canterbury in which his fictional pilgrims are the *dramatis personae*.[4] Assuming, then, that the character portrayed in the *General Prologue* and later speaking his *Tale* is psychologically consistent and developed dramatically, a typical reading of this kind[5] would point out that this worldly hunting Monk, before he begins his tale, is taunted by the Host for his physical en-bon-point and his apparent sexual potential as a 'tredefowl', a potential which, alas, he cannot fully exercise 'in religioun' (*Canterbury Tales*, VII. 1941–62). The Monk is supposedly taken aback by this taunt, but instead of joining the Host's bantering, he withdraws into a topic that is, somehow, in line with his monastic calling. Thus, according to Donald Howard, 'his choice [of telling tragedies] is prompted by the Host's taunting and hostile speech to him . . .' The earlier *Shipman's Tale*, which had dealt with a philandering monk, and now the Host's sarcasm, 'hit the Monk in a sensitive spot; what we learn from the General Prologue suggests he has good reasons to be embarrassed and feel guilty. Some people would defend themselves in such a situation by giving tit for tat, or by getting angry, or by lapsing into silence, but the Monk's aristocratic demeanor leads him to stand on his dignity. He plays the detached scholar . . . The area in which he can claim a scholar's expertise is *de casibus* tragedy.'[6] Howard's expansion on what are at best vague hints at psychological complexity and drama had been carried even further by Bertrand Bronson, and led to the following sketch of the Monk's personal history and psychological disposition: 'The self-control which he evinces at this crisis goes far to justify his obvious professional success. Such good judgment and self-mastery demonstrate genuine character. He has formerly served his novitiate (however distasteful) in study, and now reaches back for such evidences of learning as he can lay hands on in face of this sudden challenge. His memory is something of a lumber-room, and things are not in such good order nor as accessible as he could wish. At first, he gropes a little uncertainly . . . His knowledge is dusty, but it covers a surprising range.'[7]

Having thus explained the apparent inconsistency between the Monk's description and his choice of a tale by the psycho-drama developing between himself and the Host (and perhaps other pilgrims), it is no wonder that other critics might go even further and analyze the Monk in terms and at a profundity that are usually reserved for King Lear or Hamlet. Howard himself went on to muse that the Monk's tales are 'about powerful men, about kings and potentates, and for this reason they must appeal to the Monk's obsession with power and dignity . . . His tales are a sop to his yearnings: if Fortune casts down the powerful, that is a reason to be satisfied with one's lack of power . . . It is a hapless universe that the Monk reveals, and his obsession with it suggests that Chaucer has given us a study in the psychology of powerlessness.'[8] Other readers have explored other avenues. Kurt Olsson, for example, declares: 'In his reliance on memory, in his aimless compiling, and in his self-assured posing as a "maister", [the Monk] reveals a psychological condition which suits him in all his roles – as a grammarian, tragedian, errant monk, "outridere", and hunter. That condition is idle curiosity, a "lust" that is exacerbated by the sloth which keeps him from "labour" and spiritual "studie". . . . In the Monk's Tale, Chaucer explores the teller's love of "science" as a counterpart to the hunter's love of the trappings of a lordly existence.'[9] And Berndt has similarly argued that our pilgrim suffers from monastic *acedia*.[10] Other critics have, more positively, found in him the new secular view of renaissance man, though here this new image had not yet acquired solid philosophical underpinnings; hence the Monk finds himself in a position 'that would cut a man off from the roots of his true identity and set him adrift in a universe suddenly rendered meaningless. By making the character who epitomizes this situation a monk, Chaucer contrasts in the strongest possible terms the fragmentation and insecurity of the "new" man with the wholeness and self-assurance of a traditional world view, even one so much dishonored in practice as the monastic ideal.'[11]

Having rejected the '"olde thynges" of true asceticism, the Monk ends up embracing a perverted form of it in worldly pessimism'.[12] Thus, whether he is seen as a man frustrated by his own political powerlessness or as one adrift in a new world from which the traditional props have gone, in all of these readings Chaucer's Monk becomes the subject of a fascinating character study; and the poet's choice to give our worldly, hunting monk that dull series of tragic tales ends up being called 'spendidly barbed'[13] and a 'stroke of comic genius'.[14]

Such readings, to which several more in a similar vein could be added, assume that Chaucer chose to use a series of tragedies as a fictional device to further develop the character he had created or portrayed in the *General Prologue*. Of course we do not know much about the order of composition here, and in fact some critics have been convinced that the series of tragic falls was composed long before Chaucer worked on the *Canterbury Tales* and was eventually assigned to the Monk, for whatever reasons.[15] But whether Chaucer created the Monk as the teller of these 'tragedies' or, conversely, wrote the tales to fit the character he had created in the *General Prologue*, his connecting these tales with a monk reflects historical reality: late-medieval monks had a great and demonstrable interest in old tragedies. As Derek Pearsall says: 'The attribution of a catalogue of falls of princes to the Monk is perfectly appropriate: his monastic library would have been full of the patchwork encyclopedias and collections of exempla from which such catalogues were compiled, and his more cloistered colleagues would have been engaged in just such historical joinery-work. It is a remarkable premonition of the monk Lydgate.'[16] In medieval England, monks were great and important chroniclers and historians: Matthew Paris and, nearer to Chaucer's time, Thomas Walsingham come to mind.[17] In addition, they had the best book collections, from which they could extract series of miracle stories, saints' legends, and also tragedies; a fine example of such work is the literary activity of John Whethamstede, the indefatigable compiler of encyclopedias at Saint Albans a generation after Chaucer's death.[18]

This view of a clear historical and sociological fit between the monastic profession and an interest in historical examples of misfortune can be strengthened and sharpened by showing that monastic authors not only gathered stories of the fall of the great at the hand of Fortune, including contemporary ones, in encyclopedias and exempla collections, but utilized them explicitly in their preaching. Like the *Monk's Tale*, a number of sermons preserved in monastic collections speak of and warn against the rule of Fortune, and cite not only ancient history but contemporary cases.

Before giving several examples, I should stress that warnings against Fortune and the folly to trust her wheel are of course ubiquitous in late-medieval preaching and appear in sermons that can be affiliated with all sorts of milieux, not merely the cloister. Thus, the Franciscan preacher's handbook *Fasciculus morum*, in discussing the vice of avarice, dwells at some length on the folly of serving the world and on the fickle nature of Fortune, telling a relatively long and curious tale and quoting Latin and English verses about her wheel and the four kings seated on it.[19] Such conventional material can be found in sermons preached by monks as well as by friars and seculars. What seems to set monastic sermons apart in this respect is their citation of contemporary cases. Three examples will illustrate this particular quality. The first two come from Oxford, Bodleian Library, MS. Bodley 649, which contains a large number of macaronic sermons made between 1415 and 1421 and is strongly associated with Benedictine preaching.[20] In sermon O-11 the preacher exclaims:

The crafty clerk Boethius, in book 2 of the *Consolation*, prose 1 and 2, describes Fortune, the prosperity of this world, in the likeness of a blind woman turning a wheel. And in this figure she is commonly depicted, since Fortune is a great lady, the lady over all earthly goods. In her disposition are all realms, dukedoms and counties,

bishoprics, abbacies and priories, all benefices and high offices on earth. She is a
great lady, but she is blind, for she confers her gifts blindly and without reason; thus,
she promotes the ignorant as well as the learned, the unworthy as well as the worthy,
the vicious as well as the virtuous; hence she is blind. And what is that wheel she
turns? Surely, the wealth and honour of this world. This wheel she turns constantly:
she rolls it up and down at her will. Some people she whirls up on this wheel and
changes them from beggars and knaves to knights and great lords; some she hurls
down from high honours and rule into care and woeful misery. Such is the glory of
this world. This is Fortune's game, as Boethius testifies in the quoted passage. If you
wish to see an example of this, you need not look into Sallust or Eutropius or Orosius
or Valerius; you need not go any further than the woeful misfortunes, the mishaps of
our kingdom which you have seen with your bodily eye. Where was any kingdom
whirled so high on this wheel of honour than ours, I ask?[21]

In another sermon, O-25, the same preacher uses this passage a second
time, but here he replaces the unspecified 'mishaps of our kingdom' with a
definite historical person:

We need no foreign histories to prove this. Do not look into Sallust or Eutropius,
Orosius or Valerius Magnus, go no further than to the lamentable history of the
noble prince Clarence, may God have mercy on his soul! He was wheeled high on
the wheel of honour, he received much honor and was respected for his humanity.
Except for our most worthy prince the king, he was considered the doughtiest warrior and the worthiest Christian prince. No Christian king, as they say, had a better
knight. But saving God's will, the wheel all too soon turned in the wind of wilful-
ness, he was driven from well-being to woe, he perished and went from this world.
Let no one then trust in the honor of this world.[22]

Duke Clarence was the brother of King Henry V and died in France in 1421.
    The third relevant passage comes from a different monastic sermon col-
lection and contains a reference to events that occurred much closer to the
time when Chaucer composed the *Canterbury Tales*. This manuscript, roughly
mid-fifteenth century but containing a reference to 'our king Richard, recently crowned' (i.e., 1377), is a wide-ranging collection of sermons that were
probably copied at the Benedictine priory of Worcester and certainly have a
strong monastic affiliation.[23] Sermon W-107 declares:

That there is no rest in the prosperity of this world is shown by the great clerk
Alanus in his *Anticlaudianus*, where he describes its instability under the form of a
lady who is in constant motion, whom he calls Lady Fortune. Among other features
that belong to her, he says that two rivers flow beneath her dwelling, one sweet, the

other bitter. Many people wish to drink from the sweet, and the more they drink, the more they thirst, just like people suffering from dropsy. The sweetness of this water breaks down their reason and maddens them to the point that they want not just to get drunk on this water but ultimately drown in it. Everybody flocks to this water to sail on it if he can. But some barely touch the banks of this river, others enter just one foot and no further, and still others submerge in it totally. But when they reach the height of their joy, the water throws them out and returns them to the land. The other river, as Alanus says, is bitter like gall and stinks like sulphur. In it are great storms, its waves swell like high mountains, the northwind blows there and raises great tumult in the sea (?), each wave tries to overwhelm the other. Everybody tries to avoid this raging water, and yet both great and small fall into it, just as that unruly lady decides. And this river, according to Alanus, 'with various breaches' invades the other one of the sweet water and makes all its sweetness and savour unsavoury and bitter. Behold, in this passage this clerk learnedly describes the instability of worldly happiness, which always changes and turns with Lady Fortune and never has any rest. The two rivers at her dwelling signify two different ways of life in this world, wealth and woe, prosperity and adversity. Both are rivers and are in continuous motion like a current and never remain the same. But one is sweet, the other bitter; wealth has sweetness, woe bitterness. Prosperity is sweet. All wish to drink from it, all yearn to sail in it. Some take to the royal court, enter the service and become familiars of high lords, they walk lowly to fetch a lamp. Why? To serve someone (?). They backbite and speak fair words, they see how they may please and climb higher. Why all this? Because they want to sail on the water of prosperity. And yet some of them never even get to that water. Others enter only a little and no further. Perhaps one among many will get what he desires; he becomes a bishop, a count, or a duke. What then? He sails along joyfully, he is well off as he thinks; but he is not assured of his safety. The flood often turns and throws him back to the land, it teaches him to play now up now down, now a lord now a beggar; for many such people, when they think they are at the peak of glory, are thrown out of court and either hanged on high gallows or condemned to eternal prison or banished from their country. It is not necessary to bring proof of these things from Rome or Jerusalem. Lately in England the Duke of Dublin, the archbishop of York, the count of Suffolk, and many other magnates fared just so. When they thought they were at the height of happiness, the wind turned and involved them in such tempests that they could not escape. Lo, how the raging flood of suffering entered their prosperity and not only made it bitter but in the end destroyed all its sweetness. Ah Jesus, have mercy![24]

The three individuals mentioned here are Robert De Vere, created duke of Dublin in 1385; Alexander Neville, archbishop of York; and Michael de la

Pole, count of Suffolk from 1385 on. All three were accused of high treason in 1387 and fled the country. Several other magnates were condemned with them, including Tresilian and the former mayor of London, Nicholas Brembre.

My argument, then, is that Chaucer assigned the series of *de casibus* tragedies to a monk because laments against Fortune, with specific examples taken from ancient as well as contemporary history, were currently used in monastic preaching. Whether in the poet's hands the fictional Monk of the *General Prologue* developed into a man frustrated by his own powerlessness, or a sufferer from monastic *acedia*, or a soul fragmented and insecure in the new world of the Renaissance, remains debatable; but certainly, his *Tale* sounds an authentically monastic voice and reflects concerns that are not merely antiquarian or scholarly but spiritual and professionally exhortative.[25]

NOTES

1 Geoffrey Chaucer, *The Canterbury Tales*, as edited in *The Riverside Chaucer*, gen. ed. Larry D. Benson (Boston 1987). All subsequent quotations are taken from this edition.

2 This characterization emerges even without the allegorical reading of detailed images that Edmund Reiss proposed in 'The Symbolic Surface of the *Canterbury Tales*: The Monk's Portrait', *Chaucer Review* 2 (1968) 254–72, and 3 (1969) 12–28.

3 One should remember that medieval *tragedia* often meant no more than 'lamentable song' or 'wailing song'; sermon O-20, e.g., says: 'Qui ergo habet aures audiendi, audiat Lincolniensem *Dicto* 89 quorundam curatorum mores tragedia flebili sic salutantem: "Ve", inquit, "malis pastoribus"' ('Anyone who has ears to hear, listen to Grosseteste who, in his *Dictum* 89 addresses the habits of certain curates in a weeping tragic voice as follows: "Woe", he says, "to evil shepherds"', Oxford, Bodleian Library, MS. Bodley 649, fol. 109). O-42 speaks of the 'planctus tragicus' of the souls in purgatory (fol. 210). Compare with this emphasis the Monk's own words: 'I wol biwaille in manere of tragedie . . .' (*Canterbury Tales*, VII. 1991). The sigla used here and in the following refer to the sermons inventoried in Siegfried Wenzel, *Macaronic Sermons: Bilingualism and Preaching in Late-Medieval England* (Ann Arbor, MI, 1994), appendix A.

4 George Lyman Kittredge, *Chaucer and His Poetry* (Cambridge, MA, 1915), chs 5–6, expanding views presented earlier in 'Chaucer's Discussion of Marriage', *Modern Philology* 9 (1912) 435–67. Though many critics since Kittredge have argued against reading the *Canterbury Tales* as roadside drama, his suggestions continue to have a strong hold on Chaucer criticism.

5 The following remarks are merely illustrative of this critical endeavour and do not intend to give a complete account of it.

6 Donald R. Howard, *The Idea of the Canterbury Tales* (Berkeley 1976), 280.

7 Bertrand Bronson, *In Search of Chaucer* (Toronto 1959), 74.

8 Howard, *Idea*, 280–81.

9 Kurt Olsson, 'Grammar, Manhood, and Tears: The Curiosity of Chaucer's Monk', *Modern Philology* 76 (1978) 1–11, at 3 and 7.

10 David E. Berndt, 'Monastic Acedia and Chaucer's Characterization of Daun Piers', *Studies in Philology* 68 (1971) 435–50.

11 Monica E. McAlpine, *The Genre of 'Troilus and Criseyde'* (Ithaca, N.Y., 1978), 102–03.

12 Ibid., 110.

13 Peter Godman, 'Chaucer and Boccaccio's Latin Works', in *Chaucer and the Italian Trecento*, ed. Piero Boitani (Cambridge 1983), 280.

14 Rodney K. Delasanta, '"Namoore of this": Chaucer's Priest and Monk', *Tennessee Studies in Literature* 13 (1968) 117–32, at 123.

15 As Robert K. Root said, with inimitable fervour and scorn: Chaucer 'foisted the whole off upon the substantial shoulders of the defenseless Monk. Here is a thrifty way of disposing of one's literary bastards!' *The Poetry of Chaucer* (Boston 1906), 206–07. A brief review of discussions of the date of the *Monk's Tale* can be found in *Riverside Chaucer*, 929.

16 Derek Pearsall, *The 'Canterbury Tales'* (London 1985), 284.

17 See Antonia Gransden, *Historical Writing in England*. Vol. 2: *C. 1370 to the Early Sixteenth Century* (Ithaca, N.Y., 1982), ch. 5.

18 For Whethamstede's career and literary compilations, see David Knowles, *The Religious Orders in England*, 2 vols (Cambridge 1948–55), 2:193–97, 267 ff.; Walter F. Schirmer, *Der englische Frühhumanismus*, 2nd ed. (Tübingen 1963), 73–90; Roberto Weiss, *Humanism in England during the Fifteenth Century*, 2nd ed. (Oxford 1957), 30–38; E.F. Jacob, '*Florida verborum venustas*: Some Early Examples of Euphuism in England', *BJRL* 17 (1933) 264–90; and Gransden, *Historical Writing*, 371–86.

19 Siegfried Wenzel, ed. and trans., *Fasciculus morum: A Fourteenth-Century Preacher's Handbook* (University Park, Pa., 1989), 328–36.

20 The MS has drawn the attention of several historians and literary scholars; see the discussion in Wenzel, *Macaronic Sermons*, ch. 3 and appendix A.

21 'þe crafti clerk Boycius, 2° *De consolacione* prosis [?] 1 et 2ª, describit Fortunam, prosperitatem istius mundi, in similitudine cece domine girantis rotam, et in ista figura comuniter depingitur dum ista domina fortuna est magna domina, domina omnium rerum terrestrium. In sua disposicione sunt omnia regna, ducatus et comitatus, episcopatus, abbathie et prioratus, omnia beneficia et dignitates super terram. Ista est magna domina, sed est ceca, quia cece et indiscrete confert sua dona; adeo bene promouet laicum sicut doctum, indignum sicut dignum, viciosum sicut virtuosum, ideo est ceca. Quid est illa rota quam rotat? Certe, þe wele and honor istius seculi. Istam rotam semper vertit; istam rotat versa vice ad libitum. Quosdam illa [MS illam] qwirlid vp super istam rotam et facit ex mendicis et knauis milites and gret dominos; quosdam illa hurlid doune de altis dignitatibus et dominio to care and woful mischef. Talis est gloria mundi. Iste est ludus Fortune, teste Boicio in eodem processu. Si velis videre exemplum huius, nec respiceas Salustie nec Eutropium, Orosium, nec Valerium; go no forthir quam to þe woful infortunys, þe mishappis istius regni que vidisti oculo corporali. Vbi, queso, fuit aliquod regnum qwirlid alcius super istam rotam honoris quam istud fuit?' Bodley 649, fol. 69v. The texts reproduced here are silently expanded and preserve the medieval spelling but have been punctuated according to their sense. Where I have emended the text, the MS reading is given in square brackets.

22 'Non indigemus extraneis historiis ad probandum hoc, ne respicias Salustium nec Eutropium, Orosium, nec magnum Valerium, go no ferþer quam ad lamentabilem historiam insignis principis ducis Clarenc', cuius anime propicietur Deus. Sublimiter rotabatur ipse super rotam honoris, multum honorabatur et timebatur pro sua humanitate. Saluo dumtaxat nostro principe dignissimo / rege, reputabatur þo dowtist werriour and þo worþiest prince Cristyn. Omnes Christiani reges, ut dicitur, non habuerunt meliorem militem, sed salva Dei voluntate, si rota nimis cito vertebatur [MS vertebat] per ventum of

wilfulnes, he ware dreue fro wele into woo, perich [space] hostium periit et transiuit e mundo. Nemo ergo confidat in mundi honore.' Bodley 649, fol. 131r–v. Previously edited by Roy M. Haines, '"Our Master Mariner, Our Sovereign Lord": A Contemporary Preacher's View of King Henry V', *Mediaeval Studies* 38 (1976) 85-96, at 92–93.

23 See Wenzel, *Macaronic Sermons*, 84–89 and 182–200.

24 'Quod non sit requies in huius mundi prosperitatibus ostendit magnus clericus Alanus in *Anteclaudiano*, vbi describit instabilitatem istius in specie domine semper discurrentis, quam vocat dominam Fortune. Ac inter alias proprietates pertinentes sibi dicit quod duo fluuii currunt sub manso, dulcis et amarus. De dulci fluuio multi appetunt bibere, et quanto plus potant more ydropicarum, tanto plus siciunt. Dulcedo aque sic prerumpit racionem suam et dementat eos vt vellent non solum inebriari cum ista sed [MS *om*] vltimate inmergi cum illa. Quilibet currit ad istam aquam ad nauigandum in ea si posset. Set aliqui vix tangunt ripam fluminis, aliqui intrant vno pede et non vltra, aliqui inuoluuntur totaliter in illa, sed cum fuerint maxime iocundi, aqua eicit eos, ad terram remittit. Alius fluuis, inquid, est amarus vt fel et fetidus vt sulphur. In illo sunt grandes tempestates, fluctus intumescunt vt magni montes, borialis ventus est ibi, mare excites plures discor'es, quodlibet wawe temptat transcurrere [MS transcurre] alium. Istam furentem aquam quilibet vitat, et tamen incidunt in eam magis vel minus, prout hec laweles lady dignatur. Et fluuius ille, inquid, "variis anfractibus [MS anfructibus]", idest brokyngapp, incurrit fluuium [MS *om*] predulcis aque et efficit insipidum et amarum totam istius dulcedinem et saporem. Attendite. In isto [MS primo] processu iste clericus clericaliter describit instabilitatem mundane felicitatis, que semper mouetur et circumuoluitur cum domina Fortuna et nunquam habet requiem. Duo fluuii circa mansum suum signant duos [MS tres] diuersos modos viuendi in hoc mundo, welte and woo, prosperitatem aduersitatem. Fluuii sunt et semper fluunt, sunt in continuo motu vt currens et nunquam in eodem statu permanent. Sed vnus dulcis, alius amarus [MS amara]: welth habet dulcedinem, woo amaritudinem. Prosperitas est dulcis. De illa omnes vellent potare, in illa omnes cupiunt nauigare. Aliqui conferunt se curie regali, adquirunt seruicia et familiaritatem dominorum, ambulant base pro lampade. Quare? vt reparant alicuius, adulantur false et loquntur pulcre, temptant qualiter placeant vel ascendant. Quare totum hoc? Quia nauigare in aqua prosperitatis. Et tamen aliqui istorum nunquam peruenient ad illam. Aliqui ingredientur modicum et non vltra. Vnus forsitan inter plures habebit quod cupit, fiet episcopus, comes, vel dux. Quid tunc? Nauigat iocunde, bene est sibi estimat; sed adhuc non est securus de requie. Sepe aqua euoluitur et reicit eum ad terram, docet eum ludere sy haut sy bas, now a lord, now a lurdeyn, quia plures talium quando putant esse in maxima gloria, eiciuntur a curia, et sic vel sunt suspensi in altis patibilis vel dampnati perpetuo carceri vel exulati a terra. Non oportet adducere probaciones illorum a Roma vel Ierusolimis. Sic nauigauit tarde in Anglia dux Dunliuie, archiepiscopus Eboraci, comes Sowthefold, et plures alii magnates. Quando [MS quam] putarent in maxima felicitate, ventus [MS vincus] conuertebatur et inuoluit eos talibus tempestatibus quod non poterunt euadere. Ecce qualiter torrens fluuius angustie subintrauit eorum prosperitatem et non solum amarificauit sed vltimate destruxit totam suauitatem illius. A, Iesu, miserere.' Worcester, Cathedral Library, MS. F.10, f. 203x. Though clearly written, this unique copy is highly corrupt, and its Latin syntax is evidently influenced by English speech patterns. The cited text is Alan of Lille, *Anticlaudianus*, end of bk 7. The two rivers occur at 7.439–80, and the quotation of 'variis anfractibus' is from line 7.476; ed. R. Bossuat (Paris 1955), 170–71.

25 A different version of this essay was presented before medieval seminars at Harvard University (19 November 1992) and the University of Pennsylvania (8 April 1993).

The Real Fulk Fitzwarine's
Mythical Monster Fights

MARIJANE OSBORN

'To modern readers *Beowulf* often seems at once profoundly native and profoundly strange', says Fred C. Robinson in an evocative introductory essay
on the poem.[1] One element of that strangeness lies in the way the poet mingles
archaic story with native history in an elegant, sophisticated presentation
not to be found in the analogous but incidental monster-fighting of such
heroes as Grettir and Fulk Fitzwarine. *Beowulf* scholars have long been familiar with the Icelandic strong-man outlaw Grettir, but the English outlaw
Fulk Fitzwarine, though 'a popular romantic figure' within decades of his
death,[2] is today known to almost nobody.[3] Without attempting to overem-
phasize the analogy between Fulk and Beowulf, this essay aims to make Fulk's
story better known and to introduce him into the company of other more
famous monster-slaying heroes within the same tradition.

Neglect of Fulk may be attributed in part to the history of transmission of
his story. With the loss of two versions in verse, one in Anglo-Norman and
the other, probably derived from it, in Middle English, all we have is the
prose romance of this English hero related in a French dialect now dead.[4] In
this form it is not very attractive either to English readers, who prefer Middle
English verse romances, or to French readers, who prefer French or Arthurian
heroes.[5] But modern neglect of Fulk is also partly attributable to the fact that
his is not a uniformly good or elevating story as we measure such things
today; while Fulk's protest is indeed 'just', as Crane observes,[6] nevertheless as
he seeks retribution in kind he commits atrocities that Beowulf would not
dream of (nor shall I relate them), and that might give pause even to Grettir.[7]
What Fulk's story does have, however, is numerous excellent passages of
narrative and a section containing a surprisingly complete and hitherto
unrecognized English analogue of the three-monster plot of *Beowulf*. The
storyteller incorporates into the Fulk material other legends and traditions

'current in his native district, Shropshire',[8] so perhaps something like the Beowulfian monster sequence was also available. If so, it seems to have been in a later Scandinavianized form that might better be associated with the Danelaw or the Danish rulership of England than with the Anglo-Saxons – except for Fulk's dragon-fight. This last monster-fight finds more echoes in other Anglo-Norman romances of English heroes such as Bevis of Hampton (ca 1154–76) and Guy of Warwick (ca 1232–42)[9] than in the Scandinavian stories, though the dragons of Bevis and Guy suggest correspondence with that of St George (whose feast-day was first celebrated in England in 1222), whereas Fulk's dragon has certain characteristics of a troll.

The essay that follows will proceed in two parts. The first part retrieves the historical Fulk from near-total obscurity and offers a summary of the romance about him, giving in fuller detail than the rest his three 'monster' fights which occur as a digression in the romance. The second part sets these fights beside those of Beowulf, Grettir, and Thorvald of *Fljótsdæla Saga*, all three discussed by J. Michael Stitt in the context of the ancient Indo-European model that he describes in *Beowulf and the Bear's Son: Epic, Saga, and Fairytale in Northern Germanic Tradition*.[10] Thorvald is included in this essay because of the very close correspondence of part of his monster-encounter with Fulk's. Though the relation of each hero to the history of his time is very different, Beowulf, Grettir, Fulk, and the less significant Thorvald could all be said to take time out from the real or mytho-historical events in which they are involved to engage in their mythic fights.[11] Stitt's model associates these heroes' monster fights with a single narrative sequence established long before their time.

FULK FITZWARINE AND HIS ROMANCE RETOLD

Fulk Fitzwarine was a real person, not an invented hero. In this respect he is like Grettir but different from both Beowulf and Robin Hood, the latter a 'good' outlaw who derives elements of his later story of dispossession and political resistance, in a peculiarly circuitous way, from Fulk's. An English nobleman whose historical outlawry is recorded from May 1201 until November 1203,[12] Fulk roamed the forests with his band, preying chiefly upon those who served King John. According to Maurice Keen, 'Shropshire was his usual haunt as a brigand; in 1201 one Simon de Lenz was being paid by the King to hunt down the outlaws there. But he ranged far and wide'.[13] As the result of political manoeuvrings by his friends, Fulk, along with thirty-eight companions, was pardoned in 1203.[14] But the troubles in England of which Fulk's outlawry was but a symptom continued until in 1215 the barons gathered, Fulk among them, to force King John to seal the Magna Carta. This much is history. Not long after his death (ca 1260), Fulk became the swashbuckling hero of an Anglo-Norman romance, *Fouke le Fitz Waryn*.

Reflecting the royal abuse of royal law which finally aroused the barons to take action against the king, Fulk's outlawry may first have been fictionalized around that difficult time. His story shares with the five other Anglo-Norman romances of English heroes (Boeve, Gui, Waldof, Horn, and Havelec) a thematic interest in legal tenure of inherited lands: 'The hero, through his courage and his legal knowledge, regains a rightful inheritance wrongfully seized from him. A concern for law and landed stability transforms crises which could be pure tests of valor into lessons in legality.'[15] The editors of the Anglo-Norman *Fouke le Fitz Waryn* propose that the basic form of this romance about Fulk must have been fixed in oral narrative 'probably during the minority of Henry III, between 1215 and 1227', incorporating facts provided perhaps by Fulk's mother Hawyse, last heard of in 1226,[16] together with some 'very precise topographical allusions'.[17] This oral narrative, they believe, was transformed into an Anglo-Norman verse romance half a century or more later, during the reign of Edward I (1272–1307). The Yorkshire verse-chronicler Peter Langtoft (d. ca 1307) mentions Fulk's outlawry in passing:

Du boyvere dan Waryn luy rey Robyn ad bu,
Ke citez et viles perdist par l'escru,
Apres en la forest, forsenez et nu,
Se pesceit ove la beste de cel herbe cru.
Son livre le temoyne luyquels de luy est lu.

[King Robin has drunk of the drink of dan Warin,
Who lost cities and towns by the shield;
Afterwards in the forest, mad and naked,
He fed with the cattle on the raw grass.
The book which is read about him bears witness of it.][18]

Whether the last three lines refer to Fulk or, as is more likely, Robert the Bruce, the casual comparison suggests that Fulk's factual history had acquired a certain popular currency around the turn of the thirteenth century. Yet his name does not appear in the sample medieval lists of romance heroes offered by Bryan and Dempster.[19]

Ample traces of the rhymed couplets of the verse romance, including passages from Fulk's monster-fight sequence, remain embedded in the Anglo-Norman prose romance composed, the editors estimate, at some time in the

1320s and 1330s.[20] In this version, the only one extant, we see the historical dispossession of Fulk and his ensuing outlawry developed into a full if episodic chivalric romance, complete with jousts, a dragon, and damsels in distress. The editors suggest that the author of the lost verse romance was 'a professional romance writer in a baronial milieu',[21] and that the author of the later prose romance was also its manuscript compiler. They then go on to imagine this later romance writer, revealed by the contents of that manuscript (London, BL, Royal 12 C. xii) and another in which he had a hand (the famous BL Harley 2253 containing the 'Harley Lyrics'), as 'an idealistic young man, a medieval "high churchman"', whom we may think of 'as born and bred in Ludlow, where his father or some older relative might have been in the service of Geoffrey de Geneville or his successors'.[22] The version in English verse mentioned above was of unknown date and provenance, and its author is now beyond the reach even of an active scholarly imagination. Only its trace remains. As Maurice Keen tells us: 'Leland, the great Tudor antiquary, knew the story from a poem in English alliterative verse . . . but this poem has, alas, disappeared.'[23] Availability of the Middle English version, however, would probably not help us to determine the provenance of Fulk's monster-slaying adventures, so abruptly introduced into disparate material, since suggestions of rhyme indicate that they were there already in the earlier Anglo-Norman verse-romance.[24]

John Leland (1506?–52) displayed the first modern interest in Fulk's romance. Ever since his summary of the story was published in the second edition of Hearne's *De Rebus Britannia Collectanea* in 1770, making the romance minimally available, commentators have been disturbed by, as the editors say, 'the crude mixture in its pages of mainly accurate local history, much of it unrecorded elsewhere, and traditional folklore'[25] – criticism more apt in this case than the remarkably similar early complaints about *Beowulf* recorded by Andreas Haarder.[26] Scholars interested in *Fulk Fitzwarine* are pleased, however, at the history it records or that the folklore, as in the following incident, preserves and attempts to explain. The story tells us that Fulk and his brothers were brought up at court with the sons of Henry II. One day, in anger over a chess game, the boy Fulk hit young Prince John on the head with a chessboard. The English plot retrievable from Leland has this the other way around, John first hitting Fulk, but in both versions John lost the fight. Years later in 1200, John, now king, exacted his revenge; he gave Whittington Castle, Fulk's ancestral home on the Welsh borders, to Fulk's rival Maurice of Powis. This transfer of property and Fulk's subsequent protest and outlawry are attested by documents of the period, but the fight over a chess game is a folk-tale element probably borrowed from an-

Whittington Castle Gate

other romance, *Les Quatre Fils Aymon*;[27] on both occasions when chess games appear in the romance of *Fouke le Fitz Waryn* they instigate violent folkloristic episodes.

The romance, which will now be summarized in some detail, begins with the background to Fulk's ownership of that disputed castle at Whittington, the ruin of which may still be visited, as the photograph demonstrates.[28] The castle, we are told, first belonged to the giant Geomagog, or rather to an evil spirit inhabiting that dead giant's body, much as a demonic being reanimates the dead body of Glám in *Grettir's Saga*. The Anglo-Norman knight Payn Peverel, who came to England with William the Conqueror, drove this evil spirit from the land, but, before leaving, the creature chanted a prophecy which among other things granted Payn the castle.[29] Payn's granddaughter was Mellette of the Blaunche Tour, i.e., Whittington Castle, whose hand with the castle and all its lands Fulk's grandfather Guarin (Warine) won in a joust before the king. Guarin and Mellette had a son named Fulk le Brun. He courted and married Hawyse, daughter of Sir Joyce de Dinan, and they had in turn five sons, Fulk (our hero), William, Philip the Red, John and Alan, all of whom grew up at the court of King Henry along with the king's eldest sons, Richard (later 'the Lion-Heart') and John. When Richard died and John came to the throne, Fulk, having fought with and bested John when they were boys, was in trouble. After being bereft of his inherited castle and renouncing his homage to the king in protest, he fled with his brothers, first to Brittany, and then, returning to England, into the forest.

Living in the forest with his companions (at one point joined by his wife, Matilda)[30] and preying upon the minions of the king, Fulk had many adventures of the Robin Hood sort, some of which may well have occurred, but others deriving from folklore. Straight out of Walt Disney is the time when Fulk's friend John de Rampaigne disguises himself as an Ethiopian minstrel to rescue an imprisoned companion, Audulf de Bracy, from Shrewsbury Castle. Going with harp and blackened face alone into the castle, he sings before King John, assuring that monarch that his great deeds are known even in distant Abyssinia (though he whispers something quite different under his breath). Then he manages to drug the court as they drink, and he and Sir Audulf escape from a high window on a rope of sheets. Similar tales of a disguised harper-spy are told of other heroes, including King Alfred (by William of Malmsbury, II: 4).[31] The main difference in the fuller story here is John's disguise as a specifically black musician, perhaps the first time in the literature of England that that particular disguise was assumed.

Shortly after his friend John's minstrel feat, Fulk finds it expedient to leave England for a time, and under an assumed name he becomes a tournament champion at the French court. When Fulk's identity is eventually revealed, the king, wishing to keep him, offers him more land than he ever possessed in England. Fulk replies that he must return to his outlaw quest, because 'he is not worthy to receive lands as the gift of another, who cannot hold those which are his by right of inheritance';[32] this heroic sentiment may be the chief message of the romance. Hiring a mariner named Mador to build a ship to his specifications, Fulk and his brothers now take up pirating upon King John's vessels. That worthy enterprise is interrupted by a 'Favonian' (west) wind that drives them for three days north beyond Scotland and into a series of adventures quite alien to the rest of the story in location as well as tone – off the map of the quasi-historical fiction and into the wilderness of myth. Keen describes the events that occur next as 'no more, really, than colorful interludes in the tale of Fulk's long battle with the tyrant who was reigning in his native land';[33] but these 'colorful interludes' are precisely what connect Fulk's story with *Beowulf*. In the following account from *Fulk Fitzwarine*, partly summary and partly translation,[34] one must understand the cave-dwelling 'viláynz' (churls) or shepherds of the first two fights to be analogous to the trolls in similar Scandinavian stories. The close relationship of this part of Fulk's romance to tales of Scandinavian trolls will be explored later.

again across the sea, and this time, after converting to Christianity all the heathens they encounter, Fulk manages to bring together two warring kingdoms by marrying his brother Alan, who has become champion of one kingdom, to the duke's daughter in the other kingdom – which happens to be Carthage, and she the rescued dragon princess. Thereby he neatly wraps up the loose ends of the monster-killing fantasy before returning to England to wrap up his outlawry. Interestingly, Sidney Painter finds documentary evidence of the real Fulk actually having been at sea during the years 1202–03. 'Hence', he says, amusing himself with metaphor, 'the romance may well be on sound ground when it puts him afloat – improbable as the adventures described may be'.[35] The historicity, in any case, pertains only to Fulk's presence at sea; his landfalls during this period are on the shores of fantasy.[36]

Soon after entering the historical world again and returning to his political purpose, Fulk disguises himself as a charcoal burner and lures King John into ambush. Kidnapping him, the outlaws force the king to promise a pardon to them all, a promise that he afterwards disregards, having made it under duress. But in due course Fulk's friends in court persuade King John that a pardon is best, and in 1203 life returns to normal, the exile over. Receiving his castle back in 1204 as 'his right and inheritance',[37] Fulk lives to a ripe old age. In the conclusion of the romance he is blinded by God for his sins, dies sometime around 1260,[38] and is buried beside his saintly second wife in nearby New Abbey.

ICELANDIC ANALOGUES AND STITT'S GENERIC MONSTER FIGHTS

The similiarity of Fulk's monster fights to those in *Beowulf* will seem remote at best to those familiar with the earlier, more carefully constructed poem. Beowulf fights first the manlike creature Grendel, who comes to raid the Danish hall Heorot, and inflicts a mortal wound upon the monster by tearing off his arm. That night, when the Danes think all is well and are peacefully asleep after the victory banquet, Grendel's mother arrives unanticipated to avenge her son, killing a Danish warrior and retrieving the arm. The next morning Beowulf dives down to her underwater lair and, after his borrowed *hæftmece* (sword) fails and she nearly kills him with her sax (a short sword), he slays her with a giant sword that he finds on the wall; before leaving the cave he also cuts off dead Grendel's head, which he takes back to Heorot. Those are the two 'troll fights'. Fifty years later, having become king in his own country, Beowulf must become the monster-slayer again when a fire-dragon attacks. With the help of his young kinsman Wiglaf he succeeds in killing the dragon, but its poisonous venom also kills him. His people, now unprotected and in fear of vengeful neighbours, mourn the death of their beloved king. In this story there are no abducted damsels, nor can one imagine Grendel donning princely attire and playing chess like the 'vilaynz' in the romance. The dark and serious tone of *Beowulf*, especially as it moves towards its climax in the hero's death, allows for no such exuberant fairy-tale trimmings.

The Icelandic *Grettir's Saga* has obvious affinities with *Beowulf* but also provides links to the plot of *Fulk Fitzwarine*. Before being outlawed, Grettir fights the Grendel-like revenant Glám, who curses Grettir as he lies dying. Some years later and now an outlaw, Grettir takes on two waterfall-trolls in a neighbouring dale. First he wrestles with a female troll who, like Glám, is haunting a farmstead around Yuletide. The fight indoors is reminiscent of that with Glám, but the troll-wife manages to get Grettir outside and wrestle him to the edge of the falls. Finally reaching his sword, he cuts her arm off as she dives in. The next day he descends under the waterfall, finding there a cavern in which a male troll attacks him with a *hepti-sax*.[39] Grettir succeeds in slaying this second waterfall-troll also. He encounters neither dragon nor damsel, but his is a family saga in which such foreign fairy-tale events are unlikely to appear. Revenants and trolls are part of the Icelandic landscape; princesses and dragons normally are not. (Among the few examples are the spirit in dragon form that protects the eastern quarter of Iceland according to Snorri Sturluson, and the Irish slave Melkorka discovered to be a princess in *Laxdaela Saga*.) The first two fights in *Beowulf* and these troll fights in *Grettir's Saga* belong, as T.M. Andersson explains, to a popular Scandinavian '"ecotype" in which a hero enters a cave and kills two giants, usually of different sexes'.[40]

The stories of Grettir and Beowulf seem quite different in kind from that of Fulk. But J. Michael Stitt recounts as a variant of the Beowulfian tale-type a digressive monster-slaying story in the late (fifteenth or sixteenth century) *Fljótsdæla Saga* that has elements so reminiscent of the story of Fulk's rescue of the dragon-princess as to suggest direct influence, though it is more likely that both stories represent similar romance variants of the 'ecotype', as Andersson calls it. *Fljótsdæla Saga*, like the Fulk story, is new to the discussion of the monster-slaying plot, perhaps because no English translation has been available until recently; like the romance of Fulk it contains elements of interest to readers of both *Beowulf* and *Grettir's Saga*. Here is the relevant part of the story. In chapter 5 of the saga an Icelander named Thorvald is shipwrecked on Shetland and takes shelter with a jarl Bjögolf. As Yule approaches he has a dream of entering a troll's cave and finding a woman there. Because Bjögolf's daughter has indeed been kidnapped by a troll, the jarl becomes incensed when Thorvald recounts his dream, thinking that his guest is mocking him. Upon being assured that the dream was real, the jarl decrees that breaking the silence about the outrage obliges Thorvald to rescue his daughter. Reluctantly Thorvald sets out on the quest. He goes that evening along the shore until he comes to a cave; inside he finds a huge bed with a giant sword hanging on the wall above it, which he takes down. At the centre of the cave he sees a woman in a red dress bound to a pillar of iron. She identifies herself as Droplaug, the jarl's abducted daughter, and urges him not to waste words: 'You are in worse danger than you know. A troll has power here, and he is so huge that there is no other like him; also I am bound so fast that you will never get me free.'[41] Despite her eloquent speech, which then details at length the troll's treatment of her as a plaything, contradicting her own advice to be terse, Thorwald hacks her loose and gets her outside, where he hides her. Then he turns with the sword from the cave to confront the troll, who has returned home to find his cave abandoned and now comes storming out. They fight and Thorvald cuts off both the troll's legs, one after the other. The troll falls, saying, 'You have deceived me utterly, by taking the one weapon that could give me a wound. I came after you fearlessly, never thinking that a little man could bring about my death . . .'[42] As he begins to lay a curse upon Thorvald's future family, the young man, more alert than Grettir was in a similar situation, hacks off his head so that he 'should not speak any [more] harmful words'.[43] The hero's prizes are Droplaug, who will produce the almost-cursed family, and the troll's treasure.

After summarizing this story much as above, Stitt lists several 'parallels to certain versions of the Two-Troll tradition';[44] he does not appear to know of Fulk's adventures. One of the major features that he points out as marking a distinction between the earlier medieval tradition and the later fairy-tale is the rescue of the princess; rescue of a damsel in the medieval versions is incidental, whereas in the later tale this is the hero's specific quest. Thorvald purposely sets out to rescue the jarl's daughter, making this saga episode closer to the modern fairy-tale; Fulk's rescue of the damsels is incidental to his fights with the shepherd-gang, and even in the dragon episode the challenge of the fight seems more significant to him than the rescue of the lady, nor does he accept her as his reward. Particularly similar in the stories of both Fulk and Thorvald is the way an abducted woman describes her situation and urges her would-be rescuer to flee before the monster comes who will surely kill him, in a speech too verbose for the situation.

Analysis discovers the parallels among all these stories to be closer than they at first appear. The tradition that Stitt examines presents the monster-slaying story in either three or four major episodes which he lists as Villainy,

First Fight, Second Fight (these three comprising what he, following Jorgensen, calls the 'Two-Troll tradition'), and possibly a third echoic fight. The four major episodes that he finds typical of the Two-Troll tradition in Scandinavia will be compared now with Fulk's story, using Stitt's italicized labels and borrowing from his commentary. In what follows Stitt speaks of two branches of the Two-Troll tradition, the earlier epic branch, which may be associated with Beowulf, and a later Märchen branch, associated in the present discussion with Fulk.

'The initial episode is *Villainy* . . . The standard Villainy in the Two-Troll tradition is a raid for food, either the human beings themselves or their provisions.'[45] Although the churls' raid upon the ships appears to be prompted by sexual appetite rather than food-hunger, it bears a close relation to other instigating raids in the Two-Troll tradition, and in the Märchen AT301 as well. But this episode in Fulk's romance is clearly influenced by what Stitt describes in another context as 'a different Scandinavian, and especially Danish, Märchen tradition' in which 'the female may be the mother of a band of robbers . . . In both these Märchen traditions the hag remains a mother-figure and is associated with a House-in-the-Woods episode';[46] the 'House-in-the Woods' is a wilderness dwelling come upon by accident, as in Fulk's adventure. 'The abduction of a woman . . . occurs in several Two-Troll texts, but the abduction is not functional in the Proppian sense; it does not motivate plot development because the hero does not seek the woman.'[47] Fulk finds the abducted damsels by chance when he explores the inner chambers of the cave after the fight instigated by the chess game. This free-for-all with the seven churls is the traditional *First Fight* marking the second episode of the story and typically occurring 'at or near the place the humans have chosen for shelter . . . This first fight ends inconclusively, but with the hero holding the upper hand'.[48]

The first fight is inconclusive in *Beowulf* because Grendel's mother survives her son to avenge him; it is inconclusive in Fulk's romance because of the churls' mother's horn. A female troll, whom the folklorist Edvard Lehmann has named 'the Devil's Grandmother' and Stitt calls a 'formidable female', is integral to the *Second Fight*. Following upon and as a result of the first fight, this marks the third episode of the Two-Troll tradition, in which the hero encounters a couple or a family in their cave. In this second fight, the more variable of the two sequential fights in the tradition, 'a troll's hand or arm may be cut off, the hero may spare the female, or he may discover and rescue a human woman being held captive'.[49] Whereas in his second fight Beowulf encounters a truly formidable female in Grendel's mother, the old woman whom Fulk meets is too ineffectual even to blow her horn to summon help.

Fulk has to blow it himself to instigate the fight. Then the 'family' of churls that appears is two hundred strong. After suitably dispatching them with some help from his friends, Fulk discovers and rescues the princess and her maidens.

'There is a tendency to follow here', says Stitt, 'with an episode that in some way echoes the dragonslayer [i.e., monster- or troll-slayer] adventure of the first three episodes.'[50] It may be useful to name this final episode the *Echoic Fight*, akin but not identical to the chthonic monster-fight that Stitt describes in chapter 5 as 'the Gravemound Battle'. This final battle of the tradition is missing in most Scandinavian analogues including *Grettir's Saga* – unless one cares to identify its appearance in the saga as Grettir's earlier descent by a rope into the treasure-mound of Karr the Old, with whom he must wrestle (chapter 18); his exploit here includes the Two-Troll motif of the watcher deserting the rope. But the final fight is clearly present in both *Beowulf* and *Fulk Fitzwarine* as each hero confronts a flying, cave-dwelling dragon who possesses a hoard of gold. The difference between these fights is marked mainly by three features: Beowulf is destroying a marauder upon his people, whereas chivalric Fulk is saving a princess. Beowulf slays the dragon with Wiglaf's help, whereas Fulk kills his dragon with his friend Audolf present but relatively passive, having been assigned to protect the princess. Beowulf is slain along with his dragon, whereas Fulk survives, as the biographical plot of his romance and the need for a moral victory over King John require that he must. The most telling difference of all is one that marks epic from romance: in the former the hero tends to act on behalf of his people, in the latter for more personal motives, often including a maiden in distress. Robinson discusses the lack of 'romantic passion between the sexes' in *Beowulf* as the first of six major topics having 'markedly different cultural significance for the poet and his audience than it has for the modern student of the poem'.[51] Lest one consider these features as early and late, however, Perseus's rescue of Andromeda from the sea-dragon should be brought to mind.[52]

Stitt's record shows no Scandinavian analogues of the two troll fights followed by an actual dragon fight, but this similarity in the English stories of Beowulf and Fulk Fitzwarin may point to the relation of the stories to Indo-European myth rather than to each other, if it is not indeed simple coincidence. Yet Stitt offers evidence that argues against coincidence. In his chapter 'The Non-Märchen Tradition', he offers as a parallel to the northern Germanic tradition, including *Beowulf*, Indra's battle against Vṛtra in the *Rig-Veda* (perhaps ca 1000 B.C.). This story helps to bridge the gap between the Scandinavian Two-Troll tradition and the dragons fought by Beowulf and Fulk. Only two lines of the lengthy twelve-stanza passage that Stitt gives from the Indic story are quoted here:

> Indra with his own great and deadly thunder smote into
> pieces Vṛtra, worst of Vṛtras.
> As trunks of trees, what time the axe hath felled them, low
> on the earth so lies the prostrate Dragon.[53]

Stitt then interprets:

This passage, when supplemented with the various more fragmentary references to Indra's battle with Vṛtra, represents a tradition that parallels several aspects of our medieval tradition. The perpetrator of the villainy is Vṛtra, also known as Ahi, 'serpent', a demonic being conceived as a dragon. Vṛtra has imprisoned in his cave the life-giving waters, which are conceived as feminine entities in the anima of cows. Indra battles the dragon after drinking the Soma, a strength-giving liquid. After Vṛtra is slain Indra kills his mother. At this point Vṛtra's dismembered body is carried out of the cave by the newly freed torrents.[54]

In this story the monsters familiar to us in the Two-Troll tradition are expressed as the 'dragons' Vṛtra and his mother, along with the freeing of the waters reminiscent of Beowulf's cleansing of Grendel's mere. Stitt gives further analogues from later Iranian tradition,[55] and elsewhere in his book he calls attention to demonstrations by classicists Fontenrose[56] and Nagler[57] that themes in *Beowulf* and related works formerly thought specifically Germanic may be found also in earlier Indo-European epic tradition. Especially striking is the way the mythic power of the chthonic feminine seems to weaken and be lost as the story is reformulated through the centuries: The Formidable Female, Vṛtra's dragon-mother in the *Veda*, anticipates Grendel's more humanoid but still fearsome troll-mother, who in turn is finally replaced by a shaky old lady in Fulk's romance,[58] and the imprisoned life-giving waters (feminine entities) by an abducted maiden. In *Beowulf* the separate dragon theme is first introduced in a story about Sigemund, which from a narrative position between the two troll fights foreshadows Beowulf's own later exploit; this digression helps to weave the two troll fights together with the dragon fight separated from them by both time and space, the whole sequence of fights being integrated into traditional history. In the romance about Fulk the three fights are presented in close sequence; the troll fights are in a different country from the dragon fight, as in *Beowulf*, but no attempt is made to integrate them structurally or thematically either with each other or into the work as a whole. It seems that the storyteller, engaged with the formulaic quality of that sequence, is unconcerned with its potential as art.

A final point about the similarity of such monster fights is Stitt's, and true in general: 'It is clear that the *Beowulf* poet, and the saga redactors that came after him, created specific versions of a widely known tradition . . . a sequence of motifs related in structurally constant patterns'.[59] The meaning of this pattern 'is created (or recreated) anew each time the tradition is realized in some specific narrative and social context'.[60] Because of the flexible nature of such meaning our understanding of it has to be speculative, since we can retrieve from the literature of a culture so distant from ours only what our own culture allows or obliges us to see. Moreover, the relationship of these stories remains obscure. As R.M. Scowcroft has said, 'The lack of comparable analogues earlier than *Grettissaga* in any Germanic area other than Iceland, or at all commensurate to the full Grendel episode, leaves this axis between *Beowulf* and Iceland problematical. We cannot, in any case, reconstruct a Germanic prototype from only two constituent traditions, or a prototype of any kind from only two variants'[61]– or even from three. In fact, recent work by John Miles Foley[62] suggests that even the concept of 'a Germanic prototype' is misleading, just as today we might find it peculiar to assign a prototype 'rescuer of the maiden'. Though Perseus looms large as such a rescuer, this rescue has become, in the later medieval and modern hero stories, something that a dragon-slayer does. But when the way the story 'has to go' creates a need for the helpless captive within the northern tradition of strong women, this need in turn creates an interesting narrative tension; we see Fulk's princess discoursing upon dragon habits when she should be whimpering to be saved.

Aesthetic quality is a different matter from narrative tradition, however. We do not need a statement or manifesto from the alien culture to recognize that the artistry expressed in the monster fights in *Beowulf* far outshines that in *Fulk Fitzwarine*. But then, the monster fights are, as Tolkien taught us, central to the story of Beowulf, what *Beowulf* is 'about', whereas Fulk's monster fights constitute a digression from the true subject of the romance, his long disagreement with his king. Similarly, Grettir's monster fights seem a digression in the story of that outlaw's survival, though Glám's curse makes them more relevant to Grettir's story than Fulk's are to his. Grettir's fight with Glám may have been instigated by a tradition that he (like many outlaws) was afraid of the dark, in order to provide for that fear a supernatural cause that clears him of cowardice; and that fight with Grendel-like Glám could in turn have evoked the later fights with the two waterfall-trolls, which seem present chiefly to give Grettir some purpose to his time in Bardardale, where he may actually have spent the winter. Thorvald's troll-slaying provides a history for Droplaug, mother of notable men of Eastern Iceland. (There exists a related saga whose title itself commemorates her, *The Drop-laugarsons*, but this version lacks the shipwreck and troll-slaying, laconically telling us that Thorvald married Droplaug and died young.) Like Grettir's and Thorvald's fights, Fulk's Two-Troll plus Dragon fights are relatively brief, simplistically recounted, and perhaps added to the story to fill it out, in Fulk's case to make his romance conform to the exotic and chivalric (prin-cess-rescuing) adventure story demanded of the genre by the age, and also, much as in the case of Grettir's fights, to give the hero something to do in an unfilled story-space during a period when Fulk may actually have been at sea. It seems as though both storytellers added traditional monster fights to the historical or quasi-historical activities of their real-life outlaws,[63] whereas the *Beowulf* poet instead superimposed an imaginary hero with his monster fights upon 'real' (that is, mainly traditional) sixth-century history.

Modern criticism regarding *Beowulf* as a poem caught fire, as we all know, when Tolkien took umbrage at W.P. Ker's 1904 statement that 'the fault of *Beowulf* is that there is nothing much in the story ... The main story is simplicity itself, the merest commonplace of heroic legend ... The thing itself is cheap; the moral and the spirit of it can only be matched among the noblest authors.'[64] In re-establishing the value of the monsters at the centre, Tolkien slightly skews Ker's meaning, as becomes clear when we examine these analogues of *Beowulf*. The 'cheapness' of the story as commonplace heroic legend is clearly displayed by Fulk's three fights, which bear a cartoon resemblance to the Anglo-Saxon poem, and even the best of the other ana-logues does not approach *Beowulf* as serious art. The Anglo-Saxon poem is so serious partly because Beowulf dies at the end of his monster fights (as the more historical Fulk and Grettir do not), and the digressions that surround his fight to the death on his people's behalf doom them and the entire pagan world of the Wedergeats as well, in an amazing combination of sadness and exultation as they bury with their prince's ashes, to honour him, the dragon gold so fatally won – gold that he had hoped might help them survive (*Beowulf* 2799–801).[65] However enjoyable popular culture may be in its own right, one must be grateful to those great artists who know how to make even 'the irrelevances in the centre' (Ker) deeply significant to the condition of human beings 'caught in the chains of circumstance or of their own character, torn between duties equally sacred, dying with their backs to the wall' (Tolkien).[66]

Despite the weakness of execution of the *Fulk Fitzwarine* monster fights, readers of *Beowulf* should find interest in a generically similar sequence of events in a romance composed in rural England probably within a century and a half after the Conquest. Whatever date one chooses for *Beowulf*, the

Fulk story follows soon after, relative to the millenia-earlier Vedic tales of the dragon-slayer Indra. The very magnitude of the story's age can have the curious effect of implicating the modern reader with the two early English authors who use the threefold monster-fighting sequence as an archetypal confrontation for their heroes. But even more starkly than its Scandinavian-based analogues, Fulk's story demonstrates how the deeper significance of that confrontation with monsters is only available under the leadership of someone like the poet of *Beowulf*: refined, reflective, and sensitive to a host of religious and cultural implications that transcend the traditional story and inform its ancient meanings, or more precisely re-form them to suit the mood of his age and his own as yet mysterious purpose.[67]

NOTES

1 'Beowulf', in *The Cambridge Companion to Old English Literature*, ed. Malcolm Godden and Michael Lapidge (Cambridge 1991), 158.

2 Sidney Painter, 'The Sources of *Fouke Fitz Warin*', *Modern Language Notes* 50 (1935) 15.

3 The only modern popular retelling of Fulk's story is apparently that by Dorothy Margaret Stuart in *The Book of Chivalry and Romance* (London 1933), available only, so far as I know, in the Bodleian Library. I am grateful to Velma Bourgeois Richmond for this information and to Katherine McGuiness for obtaining a copy for me.

4 It has been edited as *Fouke le Fitz Waryn* for the Anglo-Norman Text Society by E.J. Hathaway, P.T. Ricketts, C.A. Robson, and A.D. Wilshere (Oxford 1975), cited hereinafter as *FFW*.

5 Susan Crane offers a sampling of negative critical responses to the 'insular romances', as she usefully labels these Anglo-Norman stories about native heroes, on pp. 3–4 of her study, *Insular Romance: Politics, Faith, and Culture in Anglo-Norman and Middle English Literature* (Berkeley 1986).

6 Ibid., 68.

7 Remarkably bloodthirsty vengeance upon large groups of people is taken, however, by such a respected romance hero as Bevis, whose brutal massacre of the citizens of London Crane reads as a sign of his ability to defy the king and maintain his autonomy (*Insular Romance*, 61).

8 Painter, 'Sources of *Fouke Fitz Warin*', 15.

9 Dates from W.R.J. Barron, *English Medieval Romance* (London 1987), 75.

10 New York 1992.

11 This 'digressive' monster-fighting recalls Tolkien's famous argument in his Gollancz Memorial Lecture ('*Beowulf*: The Monsters and the Critics', repr. from *Proceedings of the British Academy* 22 [1936]), about the centrality of Beowulf's monsters. He points out that W.P. Ker, against whom he takes up his position (8–10), must have been 'hampered by the almost inevitable weakness of his greatness: stories and plots must sometimes have seemed triter to him, the much read, than they did to the old poets and their audiences' (8). Yet the usual focus of these much-read monster-slayer stories may itself have led Ker to his judgment about *Beowulf*. In most of them, such as those of Grettir and Hrolf Kraki, the monster-slaying is presented as an incidental activity of a hero whose main concern is with

other matters.

12 R.W. Eyton, *The Antiquities of Shropshire*, 12 vols (London 1854–60), 6: 351.

13 Maurice Keen, *The Outlaws of Medieval England*, rev. ed. (London 1987), 40.

14 These companions include Baudwyn de Hodenet (*FFW*, 85), who may be the source of Robin Hood's companion Baldwin in legend (though there are many Baldwins). A Marian (Marion de la Bruere) also appears importantly in Fulk's romance; though she does not join the outlaws as a forest companion like Robin Hood's Maid Marian, she is a heroic fighter in the 'right' cause. Fulk's wife Matilda does join the band; n. 30 below explores her later association with Maid Marian.

15 Susan (Crane) Dannenbaum, 'Anglo-Norman Romances of English Heroes: "Ancestral Romance"?' *Romance Philology* 35 (1982) 604.

16 The editors of *FFW* suggest that Hawyse was a major source for the romance. Hawyse did not die in sorrow for her family's distress as the romance states; instead, 'she lived for well over twenty years, no doubt to pass on to the children of Fouke and Matilda [Fulk and Maud] the oft-told tale of the years of exile, which gained a fresh topicality with Fouke's renewed opposition [to the king] in the decade after Stamford and Magna Carta' (xxxii; see further xxxv and 86, n. on 25:31–32). In '"Bet . . . to . . . rede on holy seyntes lyves . . .": Romance and Hagiography Again', Jocelyn Wogan-Brown lists a number of noblewoman patrons of Anglo-Norman biographies, and more to the point here notes Guernes de Pont Ste Maxence's gratitude to Thomas Becket's sister Mary, the abbess of Barking, for her help in compiling Becket's vernacular biography (*Readings in Medieval English Romance*, ed. Carol M. Meale [Woodbridge 1994], 89). Hawyse herself is the subject of a verse romance composed centuries later by the famous medievalist W.W. Skeat, *A Tale of Ludlow Castle* (London 1866); at the time of this writing an autograph copy of this rare text is available in the open stacks of the UCLA library. Skeat explains that his tale 'is derived from a somewhat curious source', Leland's summaries of an alliterative Middle English verse romance about Fulk. With his focus on the blossoming of the love between Hawyse and Fulk le Brun recorded in the first part of the romance, Skeat does not mention the outlaw adventures of their son Fulk Fitzwarine, born later.

17 *FFW*, xxix–xxxii.

18 *The Chronicle of Peter Langtoft*, ed. Thomas Wright (London 1866, repr. 1964), 2: 373.

19 W.F. Bryan and Germaine Dempster, eds, *Sources and Analogues of Chaucer's Canterbury Tales* (New York 1958), 556–59.

20 *FFW*, xxxv.

21 Ibid., xxxiv; cf. xxxv, n. 31.

22 Ibid., xli. Their suggestions, which seem overly speculative when taken out of context, depend to a large extent upon the remarkably accurate toponyms betraying the author's local knowledge of terrain (ibid., xxx–xxxii). A similar attention to terrain in *Fergus of Galloway* has led the recent translator of that romance, D.D.R. Owen, to identify the self-proclaimed author, Guillaume le Clerc, as William Malveisin ([London 1991], 162–69). The author of the Middle English *Le Bone Florence of Rome*, ostensibly 'Pope Symonde' (line 2173), displays similarly knowledgeable interest in Italian terrain, as Carol Falvo Heffernan, the editor of that text, observes ([Manchester 1976], notes on ll. 140 and 382); what she does not observe is the accurate specificity of the Macedonian terrain where the convent in which Florence finds shelter is located (lines 1882–84), a detail missing in the French version of the romance. This apparently British fascination with terrain both native and foreign bears further examination.

23 Keen, *Outlaws*, 41.

24 *FFW*, 95–97. Two thirteenth-century didactic poets apparently refer to a verse-romance about Fulk. The earlier of them specifically praises the quality (*beaz*: *beaux*) of the verses, even though both urge against listening to such secular trivia, much as Alcuin admonishes the monks of Lindisfarne for listening to tales of Ingeld:

> Mais mįez vox vient oïr nostre petit sermon
> Ke les vers d'Apol[on]e u d'Aien d'Avinion;
> Laissiez altrui oïr les beaz vers de Fulcon
> Et ceaz qui ne sunt fait se de vaniteit non.

[But it is better for you to hear our little sermon than the verses about Apollonius or Aye d'Avignon; leave it to others to hear the lovely story [verses] of Fulk, and those which are merely made of vanity.] (*Poeme Moral*, lines 2309–12)

> Mais ja orrïez vos un conte
> Ou de Rollant ou d'Olyvier,
> D'Apoloine ou d'un chevalier
> Ou de Forcon ou d'Alexandre:
> Mout poez plus ici aprandre.
> Ce cist romanz ne vos delite,
> Si saichiez bien qu'il vos profite
> A celi qui entendre i vuet.

[But now you could listen to a story of Roland or Oliver or of Apollonius or a knight or of Fulk or of Alexander; but you could learn more from this [present text]. This text does not delight you, but you may be sure that it is profitable to the person who wants to understand.] (Adam de Suel's *Distichs of Cato*, prologue to book 4, lines 14–21)

The passages and translations are from Elizabeth Archibald's study *Apollonius of Tyre: Medieval and Renaissance Themes and Variations* (Cambridge 1991), 225 and 229. The first poet seems to know who Fulk is, but not, it would seem, the second (or his scribe), who, apparently drawing on the first in this passage, gets the name wrong. Then Archibald herself, her attention upon Apollonius, 'mislays' this forgotten hero in her commentary, as follows: 'The writer claims that this work is much more profitable to hear than romances such as those of Roland and Oliver, Apollonius and Alexander' (229).

25 *FFW*, xxxiii.

26 The earliest and perhaps most excessive of these, cited by Andreas Haarder, is the proposal of 'Pia' (an unidentified 1816 reviewer in German of Thorkelin's edition of the poem) that *Beowulf* should be translated into German with a commentary cutting away the intrusive monster stories from the more valuable ('echtes Gold') historical element (*Beowulf: The Appeal of a Poem* [Viborg 1975], 18–19).

27 *FFW*, 84.

28 The photograph is offered to attest to the natural-world setting of this tale incorporating elements of myth and legend, the castle also metonymically evoking the 'real' Fulk who lived there. The here and now reality of Whittington Castle may be said to function as a cognitive link between Fulk and his historical reality and the modern person who walks where he did – or who believes in the truth of a photograph. In fact, the castle in the photograph was built to replace the one Fulk knew, not long after his death.

29 The prophecy also mentions a vast treasure, including an image of the giants' god in the form of a golden bull, that Geomagog had kept in a secret house which he had built underground – a description that sounds strikingly Mithraic. The romance specifies that Payn did not discover this treasure; perhaps the prophecy incorporates the tradition of a real treasure that remains to be found. On the other hand, a closely similar treasure story may be found in the traditions of my own family, only in this case it includes a forty-foot-high crucifix statue of Christ, all of gold or covered in gold, buried 'somewhere' upon the huge ranch that my grandfather owned in Mexico. In 'Geoffrey of Monmouth, *Fouke le Fitz Waryn*, and National Mythology', *Studies in Philology* 91 (1994) 233–49, Timothy Jones shows how Payn's victory over the demonic giant both foreshadows Fulk's victory over the dragon later in the story and places both heroes in a paradigmatic relationship with monster-subduing saints. He offers evidence that the description of the dragon in the Mombritius tradition of the legend of St Margaret of Antioch 'has influenced the *Foulke*-author's depiction of Geomagog' [the giant] (Jones, 241–42).

30 *FFW*, 38–39. While the character Maid Marian is commonly thought indebted to, perhaps derived from, the folkloric Mayday Marian and the French play *Robin et Marion*, it seems probable that her actual role in the Robin Hood story comes indirectly from *FFW*. Fulk's first wife Matilda joins the outlaws for a time in the wilderness, in part so as to escape King John's lust, and she gives birth to her third child 'on a mountain in Wales'; the romance writer is uninhibited by the fact that, as the editors observe (arguing that the wilderness birth must therefore be a fiction), 'their marriage took place in 1207, after the outlawry' (xxvii, n. 17). The link to Robin Hood is provided by a play by Anthony Munday (1601) of which the full title is revealing in itself: 'The downfall of Robert, Earle of Huntington, afterward called Robin Hood of merrie Sherwodde: with his love to chaste Matilda, the Lord Fitzwaters daughter, afterwardes [called] his faire Maide Marian' (ed. John C. Meagher [Oxford 1964]). This play marks the rise of Robin Hood's status from a landless commoner in the earlier ballads to a dispossessed nobleman like Fulk, and links him forever to Maid Marian, Matilda in disguise, after whom King John lusts in the play as he does for Fulk's Matilda in the romance. It is of interest in this Fulk–Robin Hood connection that John Leland, half a century before, had access to a version of Fulk's romance in English alliterative verse; did Munday also know of this romance, or was he influenced by Leland's epitome of it? (See above, n. 16.)

31 *Chronicle of the Kings of England (Gesta regum Anglorum)*, trans. J.A. Giles (London 1847), 2: 4.

32 *FFW*, 41: lines 29–31.

33 Keen, *Outlaws*, 43.

34 From *FFW*, 43–48.

35 *The Reign of King John* (Baltimore 1949), 51.

36 Hermann Pálsson points out in 'Early Icelandic Imaginative Literature' that the Icelandic family sagas tend towards realism when set at home, towards romance when set abroad: 'There may be no lack of realism in episodes set in Iceland, but as soon as the hero leaves his native shore, the narrative mode tends to change and drift in the direction of the idealised landscape of romance, with its royal splendour and heroic exploits . . . The Icelandic hero abroad is a highly conventional figure' (*Sagas of the Icelanders: A Book of Essays*, ed. John Tucker [New York 1989], 29 and 31). The storyteller of *Fulk Fitzwarine* similarly gives attention so close to the real geography of Ludlow and its environs, apparently a landscape that he or his source knew well, as to elicit the suggestion that 'the eight pages containing the north Shropshire and Powys toponyms appear to have a distinct origin'

(*FFW*, xxxi). But the terrain of Fulk's adventures abroad is, like that of the sagas for events outside Iceland, the fantasy-landscape of romance. In 'Inside and Outside: Fact and Fiction in *Fouke le Fitz Waryn*', *Medium Ævum* 63 (1994) 53–60, Roger Pensom likewise emphasizes the relationship of genre to location as he reads the romance 'as an organized structure instead of a mixture of verifiable fact, garbled tradition and tall stories' (54). He sees that structure falling into 'three concentric shells' with factual history and topography at the centre, then the forest episodes incorporating folklore themes, then on the outside 'the fantastic exploits of Fouke and his band in exotic foreign places' (54), and he shows how these three 'shells' are related in 'a thematically ordered domain' (57).

37 *FFW*, xxviii.

38 Ibid., 104.

39 The saga defines this *hepti-sax* as a pike, though the first element is cognate with that of the *hæft-mece* wielded by Beowulf, and the second element of each word, *sax* and *mece*, means 'sword' (a *sax* is a special kind of short sword). Moreover each word is unique in its language. These similarities have caused much speculation among scholars concerning the relationship between the two stories in which they occur: 'We could have abandoned our search [for direct derivation], but for the truly wonderful coincidence: *hæftmece/heptisax*' (Anatoly Liberman, 'Beowulf–Grettir', in *Germanic Dialects: Linguistic and Philological Investigations*, ed. Bela Brogyanyi and Thomas Krömmelbein [Philadelphia 1986], 367). For a careful and thorough analysis of the implications of this similarity, see Liberman pp. 367–78. It may be worth observing that a 'sax' in each story, the *heptisax* in *Grettir's Saga* and a *seax* in *Beowulf* (line 1545), is wielded by the monster under the waterfall.

40 'Sources and Analogues [of *Beowulf*]', in *The Beowulf Handbook*, ed. Robert Bjork and John D. Niles (Lincoln 1997), 134.

41 *The Fljotsdale Saga and the Droplaugarsons*, trans. Eleanor Haworth and Jean I. Young (London 1990), 11.

42 Ibid., 12–13.

43 Ibid., 13.

44 *Beowulf and the Bear's Son*, 112.

45 Ibid., 57.

46 Ibid., 199.

47 Ibid., 57–58.

48 Ibid., 58.

49 Ibid., 36, 58.

50 Ibid.

51 *The Tomb of Beowulf and Other Essays on Old English* (Oxford 1993), 47–48.

52 The way that this myth as told by Ovid is rearranged in the film 'Clash of the Titans' (MGM 1981, with a cast including such luminaries as Lawrence Olivier and Maggie Smith) allows us to reflect upon analogue-theory in general. In the opening shots of the film, as in the myth, the infant Perseus is a castaway washed to shore, like Scyld Scefing. The sequence of monster-conflicts begins with Perseus fighting the enchanted former suitor of Andromeda, who bears the Browning-derived name Calibos and is now a monster; Perseus wins by chopping off his arm. The action that follows develops from the vengeful demand by Calibos's mother Thetis for the sacrifice of Andromeda, though her motivation is supposedly that of the original myth, to teach Andromeda's boastful mother a lesson. Perseus makes his way to the Medusa's island lair and conquers her, though her hot blood melts his shield just as Grendel's blood melts the swordblade in *Beowulf*. Finally, with that magical head, he confronts and petrifies the huge dragon from the sea. Then he

gets the girl. The cover notes on the video observe that the script fuses Greek and 'Nordic' legends. The structure of the Perseus story benefits enormously from the combination, as does the structure of the three-fight monster story imposed upon it; the second fight being a preparation for the third provides a coherence *Beowulf* lacks, and the Andromeda rescue provides the element that a romance-trained audience might miss most in *Beowulf*. The film of course *is* a romance, not a tragedy like *Beowulf*, Perseus and Andromeda having a happy married life after these adventures, then becoming constellations in the night sky.

53 Griffith translation, quoted by Stitt, *Beowulf and the Bear's Son*, 30.

54 *Beowulf and the Bear's Son*, 31.

55 Ibid., 31–36.

56 Ibid., 27.

57 Ibid., 204.

58 'This monstrous hag, the "Devil's Grandmother", seems originally to have been a feminine ruler of the land of the dead, yet it is clear that she has been associated with dragonslayer traditions since ancient times. Edvard Lehmann argues that this female's lessened role in tradition . . . reflects the masculine orientation of Indo-European cultures' (Stitt, *Beowulf and the Bear's Son*, 199). Jane Chance's recovery of the emphasis upon women at the centre of *Beowulf* (recovered from Tolkien's structuring of the poem into two parts and thereby erasing the fight with Grendel's mother) can be further reinforced at the mythic level by reference to this theme of 'formidible' females. (Chance's essay, 'The Structural Unity of *Beowulf*: The Problem of Grendel's Mother', is collected in *New Readings on Women in Old English Literature*, ed. Helen Damico and Alexandra Hennessey Olsen [Bloomington 1990], 248–61.)

59 *Beowulf and the Bear's Son*, 207–08.

60 Ibid., 208.

61 Quoted by Andersson, 'Sources and Analogues', 137.

62 Esp. *Immanent Art: From Structure to Meaning in Traditional Oral Epic* (Bloomington 1991).

63 A cautious reaction has been taking place to the canonized modern idea that the sagas are almost entirely fictional narratives. Most interesting among these in my view is Jesse Byock's recently published discovery in 'The Skull and Bones in *Egil's Saga*: A Viking, a Grave, and Paget's Disease' (*Viator: Medieval and Renaissance Studies* 24 [1993]: 23–50) that the symptoms of Paget's disease are clearly detailed in various passages throughout the saga, and the results of the disease are apparent in the deformities of Egil's skull specified in chapter 86 of the saga, where it is exhumed. The 'different and seemingly unrelated symptoms' (behavioural as well as physical) of the disease were not recognized as aspects of a single affliction until Sir James Paget described it in the late nineteenth century (34), so modern pathology can now interpret the evidence recorded in the saga in a manner unavailable to the medieval writer of the saga, thus authenticating that evidence.

64 *The Dark Ages* (Edinburgh 1904), 252–53.

65 Cf. Robinson, *The Tomb of Beowulf*, 3–4.

66 '*Beowulf*: The Monsters and the Critics', 17.

67 Robinson examines that purpose and puts forward his ideas concerning it in the first essay in *The Tomb of Beowulf*, 3–19. I am grateful to James Campbell, Nicholas Howe, Maurice Keen, Marc Couacaud, and Winfried Schleiner for valuable comments and suggestions concerning the subject of this essay.

Praise and Lament:
The Afterlife of Old English Poetry
in Auden, Hill, and Gunn

NICHOLAS HOWE

The idea of life and afterlife in works of art should be regarded with an entirely unmetaphorical objectivity.

Walter Benjamin[1]

The place of Old English in anthologies and histories of English literature rests more on an assumed continuity of culture and language, even of nationalist desire, than on the circulation of its texts during later periods. With a chronology that verges on the eschatological, these modern works create and record a tradition in which Shakespeare follows from Chaucer, Milton from Shakespeare, Blake from Milton, Yeats from Blake, and so on down to the current moment. A similarly unbroken line cannot, however, be traced back from Chaucer to the Old English poems that open these anthologies and histories. The move we make from *Beowulf* to *The Canterbury Tales* in teaching the Brit-lit survey raises more questions than we can answer easily, especially to students whose pleasure in these very different poems extends to asking how they might be related to each other. Similarly, even the most tentative assertion of an alliterative continuity between Old and Middle English, between *Beowulf* and *Piers Plowman*, rests on shaky evidence and theoretically suspect models of influence.

Deeply immersed in the words and works of pre-Conquest England, Anglo-Saxonists typically believe that the English literary tradition begins with their field. The tag '*Beowulf* to Virginia Woolf' asserts that whatever else may follow, wherever the canon may wander, it must always begin with Old English because nothing in the language comes before it. As literary studies shift their ground, however, '*Beowulf* to Virginia Woolf' seems an obsolete origin myth that, like others in circulation, obscures more than it clarifies. Indeed, as the number of students taking Old English declines, claims for cultural and textual continuity from Old to Middle and then to Modern English become harder to argue, because they rest typically on some knowledge of the language. In practice, one can follow a model of linguistic continuity from Old to Middle English, especially one complicated by a lively sense of historical contingency, without accepting a corresponding model of literary continuity. But that choice can have the unhappy consequence of distancing – even isolating – Old English texts from more recent works in English.

Old English may be better placed within the shifting field of literary studies if one holds to a disrupted or fragmented sense of tradition. Instead of assuming a majestic, unbroken sweep from *Beowulf* onwards, we might remember that Anglo-Saxon materials have had a habit of reappearing and becoming vital to the cultural and poetic life of later eras. As contemporary scholars have shown, these reappearances belong within a larger invention of tradition; readers from the early Renaissance to the present day have made extra-literary and often fiercely partisan uses of Anglo-Saxon texts in both the vernacular and Latin.[2] In a series of exemplary essays, Fred C. Robinson has argued for an 'afterlife of Old English poetry' that begins with poems written in this language after (often long after) the close of the Anglo-Saxon period but that also includes a more complex process of influence in which poets and translators of the last two centuries mastered and then transformed Old English poetics through their own practice.[3] The central figure in Robinson's vision of this afterlife is Ezra Pound, whose 'Seafarer' (1911) is undoubtedly the most famous Old English poem of its century.

I borrow with great pleasure Robinson's idea of an Old English poetic afterlife to read three poets who, like Pound, have enjoyed a transatlantic reputation: W.H. Auden (1907–73), Geoffrey Hill (b. 1932), and Thom Gunn (b. 1929). Their diverse work, spanning the last seventy years or so, offers a catalogue of the ways poets have drawn from the Old English language and poetics they learned as university students. Other poets of this century, such as Basil Bunting, David Jones, Seamus Heaney, and Ted Hughes, as well as some from the previous century, such as Tennyson, Hopkins, and Hardy, might also be read for their encounters with Old English.[4] The Anglo-Saxon and more generally medieval background of Hill and Hughes, as well as Philip Larkin, has been memorably sketched in an essay by the contemporary Irish poet Seamus Heaney, who has himself been shaped by a medieval Celtic past. As Heaney suggests through his title, 'Englands of the Mind', the Anglo-Saxonism of Larkin, Hill, and Hughes is for him largely a matter of cultural identity or ethos.[5] Yet it is poetic technique that assures the place of Old English in the literary tradition, that is, in a tradition which allows poets to transform the old into the new. Thom Gunn makes the point with disarming frankness: 'No writer passively inherits "the" tradition, you make your own choices, your own incongruous combinations of literary parents.'[6] For Gunn, as well as Auden and Hill, Old English has been one of these necessary choices.

The story of this poetic afterlife opens with Auden's first exposure to Old English as an undergraduate. In his Oxford Inaugural Lecture of 1956, Auden evoked the teaching of J.R.R. Tolkien from some thirty years earlier: 'I do not remember a single word he said but at a certain point he recited, and magnificently, a long passage of *Beowulf.* I was spellbound. This poetry, I knew, was going to be my dish.'[7] Auden went on to study Old English with C.L. Wrenn, whom he described (some would say unfairly) as 'so much a philologist that he couldn't read anything beyond the words', and Middle English with Nevill Coghill, who remained a friend throughout his life.[8] If Auden never became truly fluent in Old English, and he claimed only to have 'learned enough to read it, however sloppily', he did work his way through *The Dream of the Rood, The Wanderer, The Seafarer,* some of the Exeter Book Riddles, and parts of *Beowulf.*[9] For what Auden as a young poet most needed from Old English was what he could learn through his ears. His initial, revelatory encounter with the poetry was aural, and thus emphasized such acoustic features as alliteration, patterns of accentual stress, and use of the caesura.[10] The English Auden was, moreover, deeply rooted in the landscape and language of the Midlands, in that region once called Mercia. Even his name was an inheritance of place: St Wystan was a Mercian prince martyred in 849 after he protested the marriage of his widowed mother to his uncle. Auden called it a 'rather Hamlet-like story'.[11]

The encounter between the most charismatic and widely read (if only for his fiction) Anglo-Saxonist of this century, and the most English of the modernist poets who wrote in England has a certain glamour and thus exemplary value. In less dramatic but arguably more sustaining ways, this encounter has also marked our contemporaries Gunn and Hill.[12] Indeed Auden's story concerns what was until recently a not uncommon event in universities: an undergraduate taking Old English. Recent debates on Old English as a requirement in English universities have also reminded us that the language has for much of this century been taught throughout the English-speaking world.[13] The scholarly rediscovery of Old English that produced editorial treasures in the nineteenth century has borne unexpected pedagogical fruit in the twentieth as the language and its poetic technique entered the idiom of contemporary English poetry.

A few of the poets who learned or absorbed a bit of Old English are famous – most obviously, Ezra Pound – but many are known only to devotees of little magazines and chapbooks. For all his fame in the scholarly circle of Anglo-Saxonists, Pound is somewhat anomalous in this larger context. He knew the language quite well, but he opened himself to so many other poetries (Egyptian, Chinese, Provencal, Japanese, etc.) that he seems to occupy a momentary, if luminous, place in the afterlife of Old English poetry. Yet in making this claim, I am troubled by a shrewd remark Gunn has made about a poem by the contemporary American poet Donald Hall: 'It is written in a line based on the Old English accentual line as it was loosened and revised by Pound, one of the most useful and flexible technical innovations of the century.'[14] For Gunn, Pound's innovation did not require later poets to borrow the diction – that English neither Old nor Modern – which flaws Pound's 'Seafarer': 'mere-weary', 'nathless there knocketh now', 'a lasting life's blast', and the like. Rather, the loosening of the Old English line begun by Pound gained wider currency among later poets (such as Gunn), who learned to avoid nostalgic inflections like -th for -s, knocketh for knocks.

This blending of a long line with an idiomatic diction was achieved most decisively in the twentieth century by Auden. His importance to the afterlife of Old English poetry was to use it as a model of technique rather than as subject or, more accurately, merely as subject. One rarely feels about Auden, even at his most alliteratively clotted, that the medieval is simply a source of colour for him.[15] Nor does one feel a disjunction in his work between subject and form, as one can on reading Richard Wilbur's 'Beowulf' (1948); its intricately rhymed six-line stanzas (abbcac) suggest why Wilbur has been so inspired a translator of Molière but has never ventured a Beowulf.[16]

Through its repertory of metrical and alliterative techniques Old English poetry helped twentieth-century English poets break with or at least relax the seemingly inevitable English line of iambic pentameter. Auden acknowledged as much in remembering Tolkien's recital of Beowulf: 'Often some piece of technique thus learnt really unchains one's own Daimon quite suddenly'.[17] In the early 1930s, as Auden reshaped English poetry, his Anglo-Saxonism seemed so innovative that it frequently drew favourable comments from reviewers. These included such champions of High Modernism as F.R. Leavis, Edmund Wilson, and Geoffrey Grigson, who would have savaged any sentimental 'Ye Olde England' medievalism in a contemporary poet.[18]

These critics noticed most immediately Auden's unashamed use of alliteration. Grigson observed in 1932 that Auden had 'gone back beyond Middle to Old English for alliterative emphasis, a justified and excellent excursion'.[19] In the same year, Leavis explained Auden's use of alliteration by quoting from 'The Orators' to illustrate the poet's 'peculiar bent, as well as his gift for a kind of satire':

> Beethameer, Beethameer, bully of Britain,
> With your face as fat as a farmer's bum;
> Though you pose in private as a playful kitten
> Though the public you poison are pretty well dumb,
> They shall turn on their betrayer when the time is come.[20]

Leavis remarked that these lines 'exemplify also the technical habits that Mr. Auden has acquired from the study of Anglo-Saxon'.[21]

If lines like 'With your face as fat as a farmer's bum' were all that came from Auden's reading of Old English, we could move on to Hill and Gunn. But there are more subtle yieldings to consider. There is, for example, the shock of recognition that comes at the end of Auden's 1928 poem 'The Secret Agent' (known also as 'Control of the Passes'). The poem presents a characteristic Auden type of the period, an anonymous man described as 'the trained spy':

> Woken by water
> Running away in the dark, he often had
> Reproached the night for a companion
> Dreamed of already. They would shoot, of course,
> Parting easily two that were never joined. (*ACP*, 32)

This last line translates the close of *Wulf and Eadwacer*: 'Þæt mon eaþe tosliteð þætte næfre gesomnad wæs, / uncer giedd geador'.[22] This quotation comes from too obscure a source to work as an allusion of the type T.S. Eliot planted in *The Wasteland*. In its riddling obscurity, as a translation from perhaps the most baffling of all Old English poems, Auden's reference belongs to the discourse of the 'trained spy', who here represents the trained reader. To get the allusive clue at the poem's close one must know the code language of Old English.

Two years later, in 1930, Auden wrote perhaps the finest of his Anglo-Saxon poems, the meditative elegy that begins with a phrase from the *Sawles Warde*: 'Doom is dark and deeper than any sea-dingle.'[23] In early printings Auden called this poem 'The Wanderer' to acknowledge it was as much inspired by as translated from the Old English *Wanderer*. Anthony Hecht aptly calls it a 'brilliant lyric, with its Anglo-Saxon echoes and manner'.[24] The poem uses a relaxed alliterative line of varying length punctuated by a telling, because not quite predictable, placement of the caesura. To the reader who knows the Old English *Wanderer*, Auden's version gives pleasure through its clever allusions to favorite passages, its adaptive uses of the kenning, and an elegiac music that seems to elude most translators from the Old English:

> But ever that man goes
> Through place-keepers, through forest trees,
> A stranger to strangers over undried sea,
> Houses for fishes, suffocating water . . .

Later in the poem, Auden deftly turns the Old English tropes of exile to establish his voice in a later world:

> There head falls forward, fatigued at evening,
> And dreams of home,
> Waving from window, spread of welcome,
> Kissing of wife under single sheet;
> But waking sees
> Bird-flocks nameless to him, through doorway voices
> Of new men making another love. (*ACP*, 62–63)

Robert Lowell praised the innovation of 'Doom is dark' and other of Auden's poems from the period by speaking of 'the sad Anglo-Saxon alliteration of his beginnings'.[25] Lowell's phrase is persuasive, for its own sounds evoke the tone or valence of that Old English poetry we call conventionally, though very imprecisely, the elegiac: that measured, cadenced evocation of a past or passing world, of a time of camaraderie and generosity, of a time unlike Auden's famous label for the 1930s – a 'low dishonest decade' ('September 1, 1939').

Auden's accomplishment in 'Doom is dark' and similar poems was to pass that elegiac music from Old into Modern English. He does this perhaps most successfully in his signature poem of 1948, 'In Praise of Limestone'. Auden wrote this poem about an Italian landscape some nine years after he left England for the United States; he opens by alluding to the condition of those who, like the Old English Wanderer, are homeless and know only the *wræclast* or 'path of exile':

> If it form the one landscape that we, the inconstant ones,
>   Are consistently homesick for, this is chiefly
> Because it dissolves in water. (*ACP*, 540)

In Auden's poem, the land that has been left behind has no name or political identity; it endures as a geological or elemental territory that is not limited to any one historical period. It is the place the poet must evoke in exile: still contested, still so charged with the presence of the past that it forbids any nostalgic or consolatory sense of loss. Auden's speaker admits of this water-shaped landscape

> They were right, my dear, all those voices were right
> And still are; this land is not the sweet home that it looks,
>   Nor its peace the historical calm of a site
> Where something was settled once and for all. (*ACP*, 542)

The technical assurance of these lines belongs to the mature Auden. The alliteration is chastened, more elusive than insistent; the line flows beyond the frame of iambic pentameter. This style shows, as John Bayley notes, 'a cunning fusion of rhymeless classical measures with the stressed alliterations of Old English poetry'.[26]

Readers acquainted with Old English poetics are likely to feel quite comfortable with the stylistic habits of the early Auden.[27] Indeed as Anthony Hecht usefully reminds us, many of these traits were praised by Randall Jarrell in a list of Auden's linguistic habits that included (among others) 'the frequent omission' of such parts of speech as articles, demonstratives, pronouns when used as subjects, coordinating and subordinating conjunctions, and relative pronouns. Jarrell noted as well that Auden underpunctuated his poems, made use of a 'constant parataxis, often ungrammatical', and relied on 'portmanteau words'.[28] With a certain liberty, one might take Jarrell's description of the early Auden as a list of the characteristic linguistic features of Old English poetry: its heavy use of parataxis and compound forms, its lack of small function words, in short, its seeming ungrammaticality to a Modern English reader. This list of traits suggests the degree to which Auden internalized and made part of his own practice elements of the Old English poems he learned as an undergraduate.

This is, by way of conclusion, the crucial point to be made about Auden's Anglo-Saxonism: it contributes to a larger poetics in which alliteration can exist alongside rhyme, and in which the lingering persistence of a dissolving landscape becomes the great elegiac subject. There are other Anglo-Saxon elements in Auden's work but they deserve a separate study: the echoes in his verse play *Paid on Both Sides* (1928) of the Cynewulf and Cyneheard episode in the Anglo-Saxon *Chronicle* as well as its theme of peace-weaving; the collections of maxims, epigrams, and proverbs published under the title of 'Shorts' at various times in his career (*ACP*, 52, 296, 570, 716, 853, 883); the allusive quotation of Byrhtwold's great rallying speech at the end of *The Battle of Maldon* in 'Ode' (*ACP*, 72). If one also includes Auden's translations from Old Icelandic as well as his travel book about Iceland in the 1930s, one can see he had throughout his life a keen sense of belonging to a 'gothic North' with a 'potato, beer-or-whiskey / Guilt culture' (*ACP*, 642).[29]

The move from Auden with his Mercian patron-saint to Hill's *Mercian Hymns* (1971) seems inevitable, but it needs to be delayed, if only to acknowledge the remarkable work Hill has done across his career. Of the twenty-nine ferociously learned poems in his first book, *For the Unfallen* (1959), perhaps half are elegies, and many are elegies on history, often within an English setting. A few titles make the point: 'Requiem for the Plantagenet Kings', 'Two Formal Elegies (For the Jews in Europe)', 'Elegiac Stanzas (On a Visit to Dove Cottage)', 'The Death of Shelley', 'Ode on the Loss of the "Titanic"', 'In Piam Memoriam'. The opening of 'Merlin', another elegy in *For the Unfallen*, is typical of the early Hill in technique and subject: 'I will consider the outnumbering dead: / For they are the husks of what was rich seed'. At the other reach of Hill's career, the penultimate poem of his *New and Collected Poems, 1952–1992* is an elegy for William Arrowsmith called 'Cycles'; in lines of repeated free verse, it hammers out the imperative of his poetry: 'praise and lament / praise and lament' (*HNCP*, 212).

From Hill's fascination with the elegiac as historical discourse – 'History as Poetry' appears in his second book *King Log* – came the thirty prose poems or 'versets of rhythmical prose', as he calls them, that make up *Mercian Hymns*.[30] In his notes to the sequence, Hill acknowledges his debts to such scholars as Dorothy Whitelock, W.F. Bolton, J.J. North, Christopher Brooke, and A.H. Smith. He means to put us on notice that his evocation of Anglo-Saxon England will be demanding in technique and content precisely because it rejects any sentimentalizing vision of its hero: 'The Offa who figures in this sequence might perhaps most usefully be regarded as the presiding genius of the West Midlands, his dominion enduring from the middle of the eighth century until the middle of the twentieth (and possibly beyond)'.[31] This vision of Offa as embodying all English history yields a densely evocative interweaving of attributes and epithets, of rhythms and voices, that will be worked out through edgy juxtapositions across *Mercian Hymns*.

From its start, the sequence plays on our familiarity with such features of Old English poetics as variation and alliteration; yet it also, and very knowingly, denies us a purely distanced or historical response. The phrases and images that seem most anachronistic in *Mercian Hymns* are often the ones that most demand attention when we engage the sequence as a contemporary work. Its opening section, an encomium for Offa, introduces us to Hill's use of poetic variation much like that in Old English poetry; this technique of listing attributes is so pervasive that the syntax of these poems sometimes seems translated from Old into Modern English:

> King of the perennial holly-groves, the riven sand-
>   stone: overlord of the M5: architect of the his-
>   toric rampart and ditch, the citadel at Tamworth,
>   the summer hermitage in Holy Cross: guardian of
>   the Welsh Bridge and the Iron Bridge: contractor
>   to the desirable new estates: saltmaster: money-
>   changer: commissioner for oaths: martyrologist:
>   the friend of Charlemagne.

'I liked that', said Offa, 'sing it again.' (*HNCP*, 93)[32]

The occasion of these lines is the scop offering a praise poem to his king, who, like Beowulf, is *lofgeornost* – most eager for praise – so that he may live in the memories of those who follow. Yet those who follow Offa have lived and do live very different lives than he did, even if they dwell within the geographical and thus imaginative boundaries of what had been his king-dom. Their terms of praise must mingle holly-grove and M5 motorway, martyrologist and commissioner of oaths, because they all belong within the circumference of Hill's subject, that is, they belong within the boundaries of the Mercian landscape when read across time. The sly mix of items in this run of variation suggests that Hill is under no illusions about his central figure. Offa has all of his historical significance but he is also a suburban developer, a 'contractor to the desirable new estates', as the punning phrase puts it.

Hill's technique exemplifies in a modern vernacular the claim Arthur Brodeur made about the *Beowulf*-poet's use of variation, that it allowed him 'to exhibit the object of his thought in all its aspects'.[33] This pleasure in varia-tion is the most immediately Old English feature of *Mercian Hymns*; it ap-pears throughout the sequence but nowhere more wittily and yet more movingly than in Section XXVII:

> 'Now when King Offa was alive and dead', they were
>   all there, the funereal gleemen: papal legate and
>   rural dean; Merovingian car-dealers, Welsh mercen-
>   aries; a shuffle of house-carls. (*HNCP*, 119)

This is no random list of mourners. 'Papal legate' summons up Rome, Ca-
tholicism, and the foreign sources of Anglo-Saxon identity; 'rural dean' summons up England, Protestantism, and the native traditions of a post-Refor-
mation England. Merovingians and mercenaries from the past are intercut
with car-dealers and Welsh from the present. As for 'house-carls', they are
always with us. Read thus, the list proclaims the dominion of Offa's reign
across time and space. Past and present merge shockingly and yet accurately
in 'Merovingian car-dealers', for they were the great European traders of
Offa's time. Did they sell Citröen? Mercedes-Benz? What kind of car would
Charlemagne have sent Offa? We learn only, in Section xvii, that Offa in a
'maroon GT' drives 'at evening through the hushed Vosges' (*HNCP*, 109).

Elsewhere, Hill deepens the historical syncretism of *Mercian Hymns*, their
enforcing blend of past and present, by drawing on what seem to be memories from his own boyhood in Worcestershire. Section vii tells how a boy
named Ceolred drops his friend Offa's favorite toy – a biplane, 'two inches of
heavy snub silver' – through the floorboards of a schoolroom. To someone
born in 1932, like Hill, a toy biplane would be (as he says) 'already obsolete
and irreplaceable'. That his memory is no mere anecdote but rather an occasion to meditate on violence, authority, and the persistence of such themes
in Mercia becomes clear in the closing paragraph:

> After school he lured Ceolred, who was sniggering
>   with fright, down to the old quarries, and flayed
>   him. Then, leaving Ceolred, he journeyed for hours,
>   calm and alone, in his private derelict sandlorry
>   named *Albion*. (*HNCP*, 99)

Albion is a dazzling pun here: an old Latin name for England but also for a
now-defunct manufacturer of trucks. In that one word, Hill's themes collide:
the violent history of the kingdom, the boy's reveries of power, the fading of
English industry (the sandlorry is 'derelict'), the irreducible sense of place
conveyed by the Audenesque allusion to 'old quarries' – all of the immersion
in historical and temporal density that is Hill's abiding subject in *Mercian
Hymns*.

Hill might have cited his own use of *Albion* to prove his statement that 'in
handling the English language the poet makes an act of recognition that
etymology is history'.[34] The Latin origin of this English word as well as its
Gallic insinuations of 'perfidious' evoke other periods from Mercia's history.
Hill translates this idea of etymology, of original value that must be preserved through careful handling, to the historical evidence of coinage in Sec-

tion XI of *Mercian Hymns*:

> Coins handsome as Nero's; of good substance and
> weight. *Offa Rex* resonant in silver, and the
> names of his moneyers. They struck with account-
> able tact. They could alter the king's face.

> Exactness of design was to deter imitation; muti-
> lation if that failed. Exemplary metal, ripe for
> commerce. Value from a sparse people, scrapers of
> salt-pans and byres. (*HNCP*, 103)

The phrase 'exactness of design' refers to original form, to an authentic coin
that is forged at risk of mutilation, that is, mutilation of both original design
and detected forger.[35] The phrase also points to Hill's most audacious remod-
elling of Old English poetic technique.

Critics usually categorize the *Mercian Hymns* as prose poems, and they do
seem typical examples of that mixed genre: poems because of a visionary
intensity that Harold Bloom traces to Blake and the romantic sublime;[36] and
prose because of the justified right margin on the page. Yet there is another
way in which *Mercian Hymns* may be read more literally as prose-poems, a
way that any photographic facsimile of an Old English poem establishes;
they are written, like poems in Anglo-Saxon manuscripts, from margin to
margin across the page. The lineation of Old English poems, if it makes
sense to use that term, must be fixed by internal metrical features rather than
by layout on a page. Viewed in this way, Hill's poems establish their lineation
– their status as poetry in our typographical age – not through a fixed metre
such as iambic pentameter, or an alliterative pattern as could some of Auden's,
but through their use of the caesura. If one reads aloud the passage just quoted
about Offa's coinage and listens to it without obeying the tyranny of the
justified right margin, one can hear the echoing shape of an Old English
line, two phrases joined by a telling pause in the middle: 'Coins handsome as
Nero's; / of good substance and weight' or '*Offa Rex* resonant in silver, / and
the names of his moneyers'. In many of the *Mercian Hymns*, Hill marks the
caesura with a colon or semicolon, our conventional signs for punctuating a
significant, audible pause between two linked and balanced syntactical units
like the *a* and *b* halves of an Old English line.

If we read *Mercian Hymns* typographically as poems in an Anglo-Saxon
manuscript and, simultaneously, as prose pieces in a modern book, then we
may register Hill's use of form to contain his passionate historical syncre-

tism. If one asks whether these are Old or Modern English poems, the answer must be that they are both because the region they celebrate and the poetic language they play backwards and forwards is at once medieval and modern. In Seamus Heaney's elegant phrasing, 'Offa's story makes contemporary landscape and experience live in the rich shadows of a tradition'.[37] Hill's choice of title for the sequence, *Mercian Hymns*, derives from a section heading in *Sweet's Anglo-Saxon Reader* that prints Latin passages from the Bible (the Vespasian Psalter) with a running gloss in the Mercian dialect of Old English.[38] By analogy, Hill's poems combine a canonical text with a dialect gloss, and thus become elegies of place that summon up the voices of all who have lived there across the run of time. Exercises in historical reading, they remind us of an older elegiac poetry, such as the Old English *Wanderer*, that uses the personal as a device to depict the common experience of loss. At a time when the need for elegy seems to have grown all the more urgent, and yet when conventional forms of elegy in English poetry have come to seem strained or diluted, Hill has audaciously revived the oldest and yet freshest voice of elegy in the language, that of Old English poetry.

It is partly for their evocation of a common loss that I include in this afterlife of Anglo-Saxon poetry Thom Gunn's poems prompted by the presence of AIDS and published in 1992 as *The Man with Night Sweats*. To understand these poems, which seem at first glance untouched by Old English poetry, it helps to begin with some of Gunn's early poems published in the late 1950s and early 60s. One of these poems, 'The Byrnies', came originally with two scholarly glosses: '*byrnie* – chain mail' and '*nicker* – water monster'.[39] Even a brief quotation of two stanzas establishes the poem's Old English provenance:

> Byrnie on byrnie! as they turned
> They saw light trapped between the man-made joints,
>   Central in every link it burned,
> Reduced and steadied to a thousand points.
>
> Thus for each blunt-faced ignorant one
> The great grey rigid uniform combined
>   Safety with virtue of the sun.
> Thus concepts linked like chainmail in the mind. (*GCP*, 106–07)

That this kind of Anglo-Saxonism had for Gunn a contemporary reference is established by another poem from a few years earlier, his famous celebration of motorcyclists titled 'On the Move' and subtitled in early printings '*Man, you gotta Go*':

On motorcycles, up the road, they come:
Small, black, as flies hanging in heat, the Boys,
Until the distance throws them forth, their hum
Bulges to thunder held by calf and thigh.
In goggles, donned impersonality,
In gleaming jackets trophied with the dust,
They strap in doubt – by hiding it, robust –
And almost hear a meaning in their noise. (*GCP*, 39)

Byrnie-clad warrior in 'the great grey rigid uniform' and leather-jacketed biker 'in goggles, donned impersonality' become types of the same male performance. The distance between them seems more technological than cultural, more sartorial than personal.[40]

Throughout his career Gunn has been, in the words of Charles Berger, a 'demotic formalist [who uses] all the resources of the nonvisionary English lyric'.[41] These early poems suggest that Gunn has always been finely attuned to the vernacular and demotic resonances that Old English poetry can still have in our world. In *The Man with Night Sweats*, these resonances have changed from the evocation of mail-clad warriors to the haunting laments of a gay man who has lost lover and friends 'In Time of Plague' (to cite a poem from the book). Reading these laments, one hears in their line the truth of Gunn's observation that Pound, as he loosened and revised Old English poetics, accomplished 'one of the most useful and flexible technical innovations of the century'. To illustrate Gunn's claim, I would turn to his own poem called simply 'Lament'. Beneath its quite regular meter and fixed rhyme scheme, one hears its deftly shaped alliteration:

Your dying was a difficult enterprise.
First, petty things took up your energies,
The small but clustering duties of the sick,
Irritant as the cough's dry rhetoric.
Those hours of waiting for pills, shot, X-ray
Or test (while you read novels two a day)
Already with a kind of clumsy stealth
Distanced you from the habits of your health. (*GCP*, 465)

The recurring *d*-sound as it weaves through this stanza – difficult, duties, dry, day, distanced – reminds us of its subject, of the word that cannot yet be articulated: death. The subtlety of Gunn's technique here proves that alliteration can still have its sad music in a culture that typically squanders it on advertising jingles.

In another poem from *The Man with Night Sweats*, the heart-rending 'Words for Some Ash', Gunn plays out his sad alliterative music again; but here he breaks his line typographically into two short halves that, when read as if with a caesura rather than a line-break between them, recombine to form the long line of the Old English elegy:

> Death has wiped away each sense;
> Fire took muscle, bone, and brains;
> Next may rain leach discontents
> From your dust, wash what remains
>
> Deeper into damper ground
> Till the granules work their way
> Down to unseen streams, and bound
> Briskly in the water's play (*GCP*, 472)

The echoes of Old English poetics are faint here, as seems only right in a poem written so late in this century of loss and death and plague, but they are unmistakably present for the listener who remembers Gunn's earlier poems like 'The Byrnies'. One might even argue that the revival of Gunn's poetic accomplishment that many critics saw in *The Man with Night Sweats* owes more than a little to this return to an Old English poetic. His earlier celebration of physical energy, of men in the glory of their strength, has given way with the passing of time to an evocation of the dead. What remains is a memory of those Old English poetic patterns that can shape an elegiac voice.

That Auden, Hill, and Gunn, having been required at Oxford or Cambridge to learn Old English, never forgot its alliterative line and dramatic caesura should be clear to anyone who listens to their poetry. Yet what, to use Emerson's phrase from 'The Poet', is the 'meter-making argument' that explains why they should draw on Old English metre, taken in the large, inclusive sense of the term? I would not look for any answer in a sentimental love for a fabled past, or in a reactionary rejection of all that is modern and difficult in this century. I would argue instead that in a century which has offered occasion after occasion for lamentation and grieving, the resources of the elegiac English lyric (as written in this century by, for example, Hardy, Yeats, or Larkin) have come to seem, if not overused, then certainly overfamiliar. One response, at least for these poets, has been to draw on the alliterative cadences, the line balanced around its caesura, they learned from hearing Old English.

That the line came with associations of exile and loss, death and grieving, made it all the more resonant to these poets as they turned to set these themes into the history of their own time.

Walter Benjamin's remark, offered as epigraph for this study, that the afterlife of art should be 'regarded with an entirely unmetaphorical objectivity' finds its uncanny fulfilment in the return of Old English poetry during this century. Benjamin proceeds in this essay on translating Baudelaire to make a yet more unsettling claim: 'For in its afterlife – which could not be called that if it were not a transformation and a renewal of something living – the original undergoes a change'.[42] How then does placing Auden, Hill, and Gunn within the afterlife of Old English poetry force the original to undergo change? It might mean reading and teaching *The Wanderer* through the music of Auden's 'sad Anglo-Saxon alliteration'. It might mean adapting Hill's dense variation to translate *Beowulf* into an idiom that contemporary readers could recognize as vital. It might mean, most crucially, rejecting the claim that Old English begins a literary tradition that marches unbroken to the current moment, and instead arguing that the language emerged at various moments to reshape that tradition long after speakers ceased using it as a vernacular. Seen in that way, the afterlife of Old English poetry does not represent the inheritance of privilege, the accent of class or nationality, but instead the struggle of later poets to fulfil the laconic promise of *The Seafarer*: 'Mæg ic be me sylfum soðgied wrecan . . .'[43]

NOTES

1 Walter Benjamin, *Illuminations: Essays and Reflections*, ed. Hannah Arendt, trans. Harry Zohn (New York 1969), 71.
2 Among such scholars are the contributors to *Anglo-Saxon Scholarship: The First Three Centuries*, ed. Carl T. Berkhout and Milton McC. Gatch (Boston 1982), as well as Allen J. Frantzen, *Desire for Origins: New Language, Old English, and Teaching the Tradition* (New Brunswick 1990); Claire A. Simmons, '"Iron-worded Proof": Victorian Identity and the Old English Language', *Studies in Medievalism* 4 (1992) 202–14; and Roberta Frank, 'The Search for the Anglo-Saxon Oral Poet', *Bulletin of the John Rylands Library* 75 (1993) 11–36.
3 These essays, including '"The Might of the North": Pound's Anglo-Saxon Studies and *The Seafarer*', 'Ezra Pound and the Old English Translational Tradition', and 'The Afterlife of Old English', appear in Fred C. Robinson, *The Tomb of Beowulf and Other Essays on Old English* (Oxford 1993), 239–303. For the afterlife of Old English among Spanish and French writers, see Fernando Gálvan, 'Rewriting Anglo-Saxon: Notes on the Presence of Old English in Contemporary Literature', *SELIM: Journal of the Spanish Society for Mediaeval English Language and Literature* 2 (1992) 70–90.
4 James Joyce drew on, in his words, 'the earliest English alliterative and monosyllabic and Anglo-Saxon' as well as 'the double-thudding Anglo-Saxon motive' for writing *Ulysses*; see Richard Ellmann, *James Joyce* (New York 1976), 489–90.

5 Seamus Heaney, *Preoccupations: Selected Prose, 1968–1978* (London 1980), 150–69. See also John Mathias, 'Such a Kingdom: The Poetry of Geoffrey Hill, 1952–1971', in his *Reading Old Friends: Essays, Reviews, and Poems on Poetics, 1975–1990* (Albany, N.Y., 1992), 151–60.
6 Thom Gunn, *Shelf Life: Essays, Memoirs, and an Interview* (Ann Arbor 1993), 45.
7 W.H. Auden, *The Dyer's Hand* (New York 1968), 41–42. The fundamental work on Auden's Anglo-Saxonism appears in John Fuller's invaluable *A Reader's Guide to W.H. Auden* (New York 1970).
8 Humphrey Carpenter, *W.H. Auden: A Biography* (Boston 1981), 55. If Auden's remark seems unfair, he did make it before Wrenn did his important work in literary studies. Auden dedicated *The Dyer's Hand* (1968) to Coghill and also wrote a 'Eulogy' on his retirement in 1966; see W.H. Auden, *Collected Poems*, ed. Edward Mendelson (New York 1991), 762. All further references to this work are cited as *ACP*.
9 *The Dyer's Hand*, 42.
10 Malcolm Godden and Michael Lapidge introduce *The Cambridge Companion to Old English Literature* (Cambridge 1991) by quoting Auden's testimony as well as Gerald Manley Hopkins's remark of 1882 that 'I am learning Anglo-Saxon and it is a vastly superior thing to what we have now' (ix). The old poets in their dead language can still speak to us as students and scholars, these passages suggest, because they spoke to poets who followed them across that long interval when Old English was silent, that is, when it was largely unread because not yet widely taught.
11 Carpenter, *W.H. Auden*, 4.
12 Hill graduated from Keble College, Oxford with a degree in English; Gunn graduated from Trinity College, Cambridge, with a degree in English and then did graduate work at Stanford with Yvor Winters. See Gunn's memoir, 'Cambridge in the Fifties', in Thom Gunn, *The Occasions of Poetry: Essays in Criticism and Autobiography*, rev. ed. by Clive Wilmer (San Francisco 1985), 167–78.
13 See, e.g., the polemic by Valentine Cunningham in the *Times Literary Supplement* for 30 August 1991, p. 11, and responses in subsequent issues.
14 Gunn, *Shelf Life*, 98.
15 As in line 2 of 'The Exiles': 'Up frozen fjord forging from freedom' (*ACP*, 65).
16 See Richard Wilbur, *New and Collected Poems* (San Diego 1988), 316–17. For other examples of Wilbur's Anglo-Saxonism, as subject and technique, see 'Gnomons' (6), 'Two Riddles from Aldhelm' (91), 'The Lilacs' (118–19), 'Junk' (185–86), and 'Speech for the Repeal of the McCarran Act' (268).
17 Quoted in Carpenter, *W.H. Auden*, 55. Tolkien returned the compliment in metrical form when he wrote a poem in Old English for Auden's sixtieth birthday; see 'For W.H.A.', *Shenandoah* 18 (Winter 1967) 96–97. Auden expressed his admiration for Tolkien in the rather flat 'A Short Ode to a Philologist' (1962): 'a lot of us are grateful for / What J.R.R. Tolkien has done / As bard to Anglo-Saxon' (*ACP* 754). For photographs by Cecil Beaton showing Auden wearing a Tolkien sweatshirt, see *W.H. Auden: A Tribute*, ed. Stephen Spender (London 1974).
18 That their equivalents today would not be as quick to detect the influence of Old English on a contemporary poet is suggested by the reception of Hill's *Mercian Hymns*; these poems were celebrated and attacked for many reasons, but their very knowing use of Anglo-Saxonism as technique (that is, as distinct from explicit subject) has gone largely unnoticed.
19 Repr. in *W.H. Auden: The Critical Heritage*, ed. John Haffenden (London 1983), 107. In 1933, the more hostile Henry Bamford Parkes remarked that Auden 'has a fondness, not

obviously justifiable, for imitating Anglo-Saxon, chiefly by making excessive use of alliteration' (Haffenden, 124).

20 Edward Mendelson, ed., *The English Auden: Poems, Essays, and Dramatic Writings, 1927–39* (London 1977), 86.

21 *W.H. Auden: The Critical Heritage*, ed. Haffenden, 101. As several readers have suggested to me, these lines sound less like Old English than Middle English, especially the satirical 'Winner and Waster'.

22 G.P. Krapp and E.V.K. Dobbie, eds, *The Exeter Book*, ASPR 3 (New York 1936), 180.

23 If most modern scholars would treat *Sawles Warde* as early Middle rather than late Old English, it is worth remembering that Auden most likely read this work in R. Morris's 1868 edition titled *Old English Homilies* (EETS 34). See Morton W. Bloomfield, '"Doom is dark and deeper than any sea-dingle": W.H. Auden and *Sawles Warde*', *Modern Language Notes* 58 (1948) 548–52.

24 Anthony Hecht, *The Hidden Law: The Poetry of W.H. Auden* (Cambridge, Mass., 1993), 68.

25 See *Shenandoah* 18 (Winter 1967) 45.

26 *W.H. Auden: The Critical Heritage*, ed. Haffenden, 458.

27 For an introduction to Old English poetics, see Donald G. Scragg, 'The Nature of Old English Verse', in *The Cambridge Companion*, ed. Godden and Lapidge, 55–70.

28 Jarrell's list is quoted most accessibly in Hecht, *The Hidden Law*, 10. Hecht also responds in very interesting ways to Jarrell's polemical aim in creating this list.

29 W.H. Auden and Louis MacNeice, *Letters from Iceland* (London 1937). His translations are gathered in W.H. Auden and Paul B. Taylor, *Norse Poems* (London 1981). On Auden's affinity for the North, see John Hollander, 'Auden at Sixty', in *W.H. Auden: Modern Critical Views*, ed. H. Bloom (New York 1986), 13–20, esp. 18.

30 Quoted from an interview with Hill in John Haffenden, *Viewpoints: Poets in Conversation* (London 1981), 93. In earlier printings, *Mercian Hymns* was followed by a brief essay, 'Funeral Music', in which Hill explains: 'In this sequence I was attempting a florid grim music broken by grunts and shrieks'; see Hill, *Somewhere Is Such a Kingdom: Poems, 1952–71*, with introduction by H. Bloom (Boston 1975), 125. This essay as well as Hill's valuable notes to *Mercian Hymns* do *not* appear in Hill, *New and Collected Poems, 1952–1992* (Boston 1994). This work is hereinafter cited as *HNCP*. For general studies of *Mercian Hymns*, see Heather Glen, 'Geoffrey Hill's "England of the Mind"', *Critical Review* 27 (1985) 98–109; Michael Edward's 'Hill's Imitations' in *Geoffrey Hill: Essays on His Work*, ed. Peter Robinson (Milton Keynes 1985), 159–71; and Vincent Sherry, *The Uncommon Tongue: The Poetry and Criticism of Geoffrey Hill* (Ann Arbor 1987), ch. 4.

31 Hill, *Somewhere Is Such a Kingdom*, 127.

32 According to Charles Tomlinson, Hill has been known to sing the first of the *Mercian Hymns* at poetry readings; see David Lloyd, 'The Public and Private Realms of Hill's *Mercian Hymns*', *Twentieth Century Literature* 34 (1988) 407–15, n. 7.

33 Arthur Brodeur, *The Art of Beowulf* (Berkeley 1959), 39.

34 See Haffenden, *Viewpoints: Poets in Conversation*, 88.

35 Michael North, 'The Word as Bond: Money and Performative Language in Hill's *Mercian Hymns*', *ELH* 54 (1987) 463–81.

36 Bloom, 'Introduction' to *Somewhere Is Such a Kingdom*, xiii. See also Martin Dodsworth, '*Mercian Hymns*: Offa, Charlemagne, and Geoffrey Hill', in *Geoffrey Hill: Essays on His Work*, 49–61.

37 Heaney, *Preoccupations*, 160.

310   Nicholas Howe

38 *Sweet's Anglo-Saxon Reader in Prose and Verse*, 15th ed. by D. Whitelock (Oxford 1967), 184–96.
39 Thom Gunn, *Collected Poems* (New York 1994), 490. This work is hereinafter cited as *GCP*.
40 For this aspect of Gunn's work, see Robert K. Martin, 'Fetishizing America: David Hockney and Thom Gunn', *The Continuing Presence of Walt Whitman: The Life after the Life*, ed. Martin (Iowa City 1992), 114–26.
41 Charles Berger, 'Review of *The Man with Night Sweats*', *Raritan Review* (1993), 141–55, at 141.
42 Benjamin, *Illuminations*, 73.
43 I read an early version of this paper at the Conference on Anglo-Saxonism held in March 1994 by the Berkeley Old English Colloquium. I owe many thanks to John D. Niles for inviting me to participate, and to Robert Bjork, Dolores W. Frese, Seth Lerer, and Marijane Osborn for their comments during the conference. I must also thank Peter Baker, Charles Berger, Roberta Frank, Georgina Kleege, John Mathias, and Jeredith Merrin for reading drafts of this essay.